FRAMES OF PROTEST

FRAMES OF PROTEST

Social Movements and the Framing Perspective

Edited by HANK JOHNSTON and
JOHN A. NOAKES

ROWMAN & LITTLEFIELD PUBLISHERS, INC.
Lanham • Boulder • New York • Toronto • Oxford

ROWMAN & LITTLEFIELD PUBLISHERS, INC.

Published in the United States of America
by Rowman & Littlefield Publishers, Inc.
A wholly owned subsidiary of The Rowman & Littlefield Publishing Group, Inc.
4501 Forbes Boulevard, Suite 200, Lanham, Maryland 20706
www.rowmanlittlefield.com

P.O. Box 317, Oxford OX2 9RU, UK

British Library Cataloguing in Publication Information Available

Library of Congress Cataloging-in-Publication Data Available

ISBN 0-7425-3806-0 (cloth : alk. paper)
ISBN 0-7425-3807-9 (pbk. : alk. paper)

Printed in the United States of America

♾™ The paper used in this publication meets the minimum requirements of American
National Standard for Information Sciences—Permanence of Paper for Printed Library
Materials, ANSI/NISO Z39.48-1992.

CONTENTS

Part III. Framing and Political Opportunities

Part IV. Refining the Perspective

Chapter 1

FRAMES OF PROTEST:
A ROAD MAP TO A PERSPECTIVE

John A. Noakes and Hank Johnston

One of the earliest and most important lessons a student of social movements must learn is that there is no simple relationship between injustice and mobilization. Injustice is much more common and much more persistent than collective efforts to oppose it. "There are many political movements," William Gamson (1992a: 6) reminds us, "that try in vain to activate people who, in terms of some allegedly objective interests, ought to be up in arms." Social movement scholars have identified several factors affecting the rise of social movements. At the macro level, movements are considered more likely to occur when broad forces of social change (e.g., industrialization, war, and cultural contact) upset existing power relations. Under these circumstances, a faction of elites may break from the ruling consensus and sponsor challenging groups, or state policies may open political opportunities and facilitate challenges to the ruling group (Jenkins and Perrow 1977; McAdam 1982; Skocpol 1979). At the meso or organizational level, there is broad agreement that mobilization is more likely when challenging groups have more resources at their disposal. Also, studies have shown that the likelihood of mobilization increases as social networks among potential participants and social movement activists become denser (Gould 1991; McAdam and Paulsen 1993; Mueller 1994).

In contrast, this chapter and the others in this book focus mostly on the micro level of social construction processes and their relation to social movement participation. This is because the other levels cannot explain—either by themselves or in combination with each other—the occurrence of protests or the rise of social movements. Within movements there are often debates over both what constitutes an

1

opportunity and whether a particular moment is ripe for action (Gamson and Meyer 1996). If a movement fails to recognize an opportunity as such, it is lost (Barker and Lavalette 2002). The flip side of this is that social movement organizers regularly exaggerate the opportunities present in a particular situation in an effort to mobilize people to act (Gamson and Meyer 1996). On more than one occasion, a strongly held belief that change is possible has inspired collective action, even when objective evidence suggests only a slim chance of success (Kenney, this volume; Kurzman 1996; Casquette 1996). In short, mobilizing people to action always has a subjective component, and in recent years this subjective component—the element of perception or consciousness—has been conceptualized as a social-psychological process called framing. Understanding social movement mobilization requires attention to how "collective processes of interpretation, attribution, and social construction . . . mediate between opportunity and action" (McAdam, McCarthy, and Zald 1996b: 2). Before anyone leaves the house to go protest in the streets, there are processes of cognition and interpretation that invariably occur. These intervene between the objective pressures and opportunities that are shaped by social-structural relations and the decision to protest or to join a social movement.

In the simplest of terms, framing functions in much the same way as a frame around a picture: attention gets focused on what is relevant and important and away from extraneous items in the field of view. Even when oppression is intense or when leaders' tactics open up clear opportunities for action, individuals must be convinced that an injustice has occurred, persuaded that collective action is called for, and motivated to act if a social movement is to occur (see Walgrave and Manssens's chapter and Valocchi's chapter, both in this volume). Moreover, collective action frames not only must indicate what is going on and why it's important, but must do it in a convincing way. Successful frames must not only analyze events and identify who is responsible but also ring true with an audience—or *resonate*. This imparts a strategic, rational quality to social movement framing activities that have been widely researched (see Oliver and Johnston's chapter and Westby's chapter in this volume for full discussions of strategic framing).[1]

The process of defining what is going on in a situation in order to encourage protest is referred to as the forging of *collective action frames*—or *framing processes*. Over the last two decades it has been one of the three broad focus areas dominating social movement research, along with the study of political opportunities and organizational resources. This introductory chapter reviews the core concepts of frames and framing processes. It is intended as an introduction and broad overview of the perspective for nonspecialists and students. Our goal is to provide a road map of the framing perspective by bringing together and synthesizing the research and theoretical work on frames and framing of the past twenty years. To date, this material remains widely dispersed among journal articles, monographs, and edited volumes. We will review the most important empirical research on how frames are constructed and communicated, how they shape and are shaped by other aspects of social movements, how they resonate, and how different frames are promoted by different parties vying for the people's hearts and minds—including social movement entrepreneurs, countermovements, the state, and the media.

THE HISTORY OF THE CONCEPT

Gregory Bateson first used the concept of the *frame* in 1954 in an essay about epistemology and animal behavior. Today scholars use the term in several areas of social inquiry, including linguistics, social psychology, media studies, and policy studies, and it is also used by sociologists and political scientists who study social movements (Benford 1997; Oliver and Johnston, this volume). A frame is an "interpretative schema that simplifies and condenses the 'world out there' by selectively punctuating and encoding objects, situations, events, experiences, and sequences of action" (Snow and Benford 1988: 137), thus organizing experience and guiding action by "rendering events or occurrences meaningful" (Snow et al. 1986: 464). Erving Goffman (1974, 1981) first imported the concept into sociology in order to help explain the microsociology of everyday interactions and communicative acts (for more on Goffman's work, see Johnston in this volume). Social movement scholars were drawn to the concept because of its potential to provide insight into the various forms of interpretation that are part of the dynamics of social movements.

Frames were quietly introduced into the lexicon of social movement research by Todd Gitlin (1980). His study of the media's treatment of the Students for a Democratic Society (SDS) showed how the vested interests of corporate media and the social-change interests of protest movements are often in conflict. Among other things, Gitlin's research demonstrated how the *New York Times* negatively portrayed the SDS in news stories by applying several different negative frames. Gitlin did not look at the other side of the coin, namely how SDS framed its messages, although he did look at SDS's efforts to gain media attention for its cause. Two years later, William Gamson, Bruce Fireman, and Steven Rytina's *Encounters with Unjust Authority* (1982) switched the emphasis from media to the political actor by examining the social-psychological processes by which people in controlled settings rejected authoritative explanations of events and constructed alternative understandings of what was occurring. Subjects had to "break the frame" that was officially provided as part of a contrived market research project that was shown to misrepresent its intentions. Once the old frame was broken, participants constructed new frames to explain events. Gamson and his colleagues identified these "reframing acts" as the first steps in calling attention to injustice and as a prelude to collective action.

In the early 1980s, the dominant theories of social movements were rooted in organizational theory and decision-making models that stressed participants' cost-benefit calculations (Gamson 1992b). By demonstrating how interpretative processes lie at the heart of spontaneous collective action, Gamson, Fireman, and Rytina's research (1982) made possible a return to a social psychology of collective action that, in other theoretical forms and manifestations, had fallen into disfavor. Over the next several years, a variety of social movement scholars followed Gamson's lead and articulated a full-fledged critique of social movement theories as overly structural and failing to account for the various forms of "meaning work" involved in social movement processes (cf. Klandermans 1984, 1992; Cohen 1985; Tarrow 1992). During this period, David Snow and his collaborators pushed the study of framing processes forward by elaborating the concepts that would become foundational to the framing perspective: *frame alignment, frame resonance,* and *master frames* (Snow and Benford 1988, 1992; Snow et al. 1986). By the mid-1990s, the study of framing processes was widely recognized as one of the central approaches to understanding social movements (McAdam, McCarthy, and Zald, 1996b; Benford and Snow 2000; Oliver and Johnston, this volume).

The rise of framing studies in the 1980s and 1990s established a new perspective on the role of social-psychological processes. During the 1950s and 1960s, social-psychological variables had a central role in what are now referred to as "classical" social movement theories (Gamson 1992b; McAdam 1982). At that time, collective behavior and social movements were generally attributed to the disruptive social-psychological effects of structural strain in society. Mass society theorists, for example, postulated that social isolation produced alienation and anxiety and, consequently, a rise in the number of people with a "disposition to engage in extreme behavior to escape from these tensions" (Kornhauser 1959: 32). Other collective behavior theorists attributed the rise of social movements to social-psychological phenomena such as perceptions of relative deprivation, cognitive dissonance, normative ambiguity, and emergent norms (cf. Lenski 1954; Smelser 1962; Turner and Killian 1957).

The social movement cycle of the 1960s—the civil rights movement, women's movement, antiwar movement, Chicano movement, Native American movement, and others—exposed the weaknesses of such explanations. The clear political, social, and economic grievances of these groups suggested that participation in social change efforts were hardly irrational. Moreover, research demonstrated that participants were not alienated and disconnected, but rather strongly linked with their communities, and that this was an important element in recruiting friends and acquaintances to the movement. New models of social movement mobilization stressed the rationality of collective action and stressed organizational and structural variables such as the control of resources, the capacity for strategic planning, and the changing political context. These models have contributed a great deal to our understanding of social movement dynamics, but in the move away from old social-psychological variables such as relative deprivation and emergent norms, researchers—as the old saying goes—threw the baby out with the bath water. In their effort to demonstrate that social movement activity was not rooted in irrational psychological impulses, they overemphasized the rational calculations made by social movement activists, "gloss[ed] over questions concerning the interpretation of events and experiences" (Snow et al. 1986: 465), and minimized the role of human agency in the rise of social movements (Westby, this volume).

The study of framing processes pushes these questions back into the forefront of social movement research. Starting in the 1980s, framing scholars began to study and map what Tarrow (1998) has called "the struggle for cultural supremacy." This refers to efforts by the state, media, and social movements to influence the interpretative processes by which individuals negotiate the meaning of political events (see also Melucci 1989; Benford and Hunt 1992). Among the questions addressed in this literature are:

- How do people understand and interpret political and social problems? (cf. Gamson 1992a; Scheufele 1999)
- How do media interpret and present political issues and events? (cf. Gitlin 1980; Ryan 1991; Scheufele 1999)
- How do social movement entrepreneurs produce and reproduce cultural codes in an effort to sway target audiences to their interpretation of events? (cf. Berbrier 1998; Kubal 1998; Zald 1996)
- How do countermovements present competing interpretations of similar events? (cf. Staggenborg 1991; Meyer and Staggenborg 1996);

- How do state officials promote demobilizing frames and interpret political dissent? (cf. Noakes, this volume; della Porta 2002; Zuo and Benford 1995).

Two social movement scholars stand out as particularly important to the laying of the conceptual groundwork for the study of framing processes. Working separately, both William A. Gamson and David A. Snow, each with a variety of collaborators, developed typologies of the core framing concepts. Because they worked at different levels of analysis, these typologies differ on important points. Gamson and his colleagues described the social-psychological processes whereby individuals are transformed from bystanders to participants in collective action. His work helps us understand the meaning systems available to people when interpreting political issues and the symbolic resources used by people to negotiate meaning in political contexts (Gamson 1988, 1992a; Gamson and Stuart 1992; Gamson and Modigliani 1989; Gamson and Wolsfeld 1993).

Snow and his collaborators (most notably Robert Benford) focus the bulk of their attention on the relationship between social movement entrepreneurs and their potential constituents. They describe (1) how social movement entrepreneurs align movement frames with those of potential participants, (2) variations in a frame's mobilizing potency, and (3) the clustering of social movements according to general frames, or *master collective action frames* in their terminology (Benford 1993a, 1993b, 1997; Benford and Hunt 1992; Snow et al. 1986; Snow and Benford 1988, 1992; see also Snow 2004 for a review). The practical effect of this influential research was to shift the focus of framing research away from how frames affect the negotiation of meaning by potential movement participants and toward the strategic activities of social movement entrepreneurs (Oliver and Johnston, this volume; Tarrow 1998). It is fair to say that Snow and his colleagues' work has proven more influential in subsequent research than Gamson's, but—as we hope to demonstrate—much of it is more complementary than competitive. Taken together, they allow us a more complete understanding of frames and framing processes than one or the other offers by itself.

CORE CONCEPTS

At its most basic, a frame identifies a problem that is social or political in nature, the parties responsible for causing the problem, and a solution (Ryan 1981). Most studies of framing processes, however, begin not with this basic conceptualization of a frame, but rather with Snow and Benford's identification of the core functions of a *collective action frame*—namely, what frames must do. Collective action frames offer strategic interpretations of issues with the intention of mobilizing people to act. Snow and Benford (1988) identify the three basic framing tasks as *diagnostic, prognostic,* and *motivational:*

- *Diagnostic framing* presents to potential recruits a new interpretation of issues or events; like a medical diagnosis, it tells what is wrong and why.
- *Prognostic framing* presents a solution to the problem suggested in the diagnosis.

- *Motivational framing* attempts to give people a reason to join collective action—the problem defined in the diagnosis and the solution in the prognosis are usually not sufficient to get people to act.

Focusing on how people negotiate meaning, Gamson offers an alternative list of basic components of a collective action frame—*identity, agency,* and *injustice:*

- The *identity component* specifies an aggrieved group with shared interests and values. It identifies the "we" and the "them."
- The *agency component* recognizes that the grievous conditions defining the "we" and the "them" can be changed, which encourages those in the "we" to become agents of their own history.
- The *injustice component* places the blame for grievances on the individuals or institutions that compose the "them" and sparks members of the "we" to respond.

The major difference between these alternative conceptions of collective action frames concerns the role of injustice in mobilization. Gamson argues that collective action frames necessarily contain an injustice component—a "hot cognition" that something is wrong and should be changed. While acknowledging that injustice frames are ubiquitous in political and economic movements, Benford and Snow (2000) have recently observed that injustice frames are not found in all collective action frames, pointing to religious and self-help movements as examples. Otherwise, the overlap between these two approaches is substantial enough that we consider them two sides of the same mobilization coin. Snow and Benford explain the work of frames in the mobilization process from the perspective of the social movement, Gamson from the perspective of the potential participants. Moreover, there is considerable overlap between Gamson's conception of a frame and Snow and Benford's conception of a collective action frame—if the identification of responsible parties in Gamson's schema is collapsed into the diagnosis of the problem and a requirement that the schema motivate people to action is added, they are almost identical.

It may be that the similarity of the two models has led many social movement scholars to simply focus on Snow and Benford's rather than Gamson's. Also, Snow and Benford's emphasis on framing tactics, as planned and implemented by social movement organizations, synchronized more easily with the organizational focus that dominated the field in the 1980s. This is unfortunate, because Gamson's approach helps us understand the less strategic aspects of framing, including the construction of meaning by those on the receiving end of framing strategies—whether they are implemented by movements, media, or the state. For example, target audiences may not accept a movement's motivational frame and never join a protest although they understand the diagnosis and prognosis. Moreover, as Goffman (1974) suggested, individuals need not even be able to articulate a frame or recognize all of its components to apply it as an interpretive schema.

In addition, the frames advanced by media rarely include an explicit motivational component (see Walgrave and Manssens in this volume for an exception). Social movement entrepreneurs act strategically, but as Tarrow (1998: 23) reminds us, "not all framing takes place under their auspices." Most of the cognitive frames individuals use to navigate daily events, and most frames promoted by mass media and the state, interpret situations in ways that are in synchrony with the status quo, thus working to discourage collective action. If nothing else, this reminds us why social movements are necessary and why they are so relatively infrequent. All social movements must "break the frames" of quiescence and acceptance of the status quo that characterizes everyday life.

THE CONSTRUCTION OF COLLECTIVE ACTION FRAMES

The question of how collective action frames are constructed can be answered in two ways. First, if we acknowledge that framing can be purposive action, it can be answered by examining who builds frames (Tarrow 1998). Although framing processes are "active, ongoing, and continuously evolving" (Snow and Oliver 1995: 587) and no person or organization can fully control this process, the role of social movement entrepreneurs in the construction of collective action frames is crucial. Second, if we acknowledge that frames are constructed from a cultural fabric and that they have a specific content, we can describe the "materials" that make them up—that is, the components of an interpretive schema (Johnston, this volume). To explain their actions and to motivate participants, movements must produce interpretive packages that explain a range of problems in relatively narrow terms, highlight some issues, and ignore others. The process of assembling these packages is historically specific, but there are patterns across movements in the kinds of materials assembled.

The Strategic Construction of Collective Action Frames

Frames occasionally develop in the streets as protesters mobilize—especially, it seems, in nondemocratic nations where there is little free space for movements to construct alternative interpretations of events. Oberschall (1996: 97), for example, argues that "the people themselves framed the issues in mass demonstrations in East Germany" during 1989. Notably, their rally cry became: "*We* are the people!" In that same year in China, the demands of the Democracy Movement evolved as the original protesters interacted with Beijing residents (Calhoun 1994; Zuo and Benford 1995). Observers in Western nations have noted that framing processes are generally less conscious at the beginning of a movement, becoming more strategic as the battle is waged (McAdam, McCarthy, and Zald 1996a). Others have suggested that frames evolve over time as they confront alternative interpretations of events, sometimes being co-opted and used for purposes unintended by their originators (della Porta 2002; Naples 2002). Granting all of this, many collective action frames are still primarily the product of social movement entrepreneurs making practical decisions in response to the styles, forms, and normative codes of the target audience (Kubal 1998). The construction of most collective action frames requires the conscious action of social movement entrepreneurs interested in mobilizing people to engage in collective action.

The term "social movement entrepreneur" is an imperfect one. Many movement leaders and organizers are strongly committed to their cause—something not reflected by the common understanding of the term *entrepreneurship*—and would reject comparisons of their motives to those of someone driven, at least in part, by personal gain. But when sociologists use the term "entrepreneur," they are referring not to venture capitalists or owners of small businesses, but rather to people who exhibit strategic initiative in spreading the word about their cause and promoting its message—like the moral entrepreneurs who produce social problems and rules to address them in Becker's (1963) classic description of how rule enforcement agencies acquire more resources and expand their domain.

The primary role of the social movement entrepreneur is to communicate the movement's frames to current and potential constituents. According to Snow and Benford, this is done through two processes, *articulation* and *amplification*. Social movement entrepreneurs articulate frames by connecting and aligning events "so they hang together in a relatively unified and compelling fashion," thus offering a new perspective on events or situations (Benford and Snow 2000: 614). The "cultural tool kits" of the potential recruits may already contain the symbols constituting a particular collective action frame (Swidler 1986), but these symbols are "are not automatically available as mobilizing symbols" and "require concrete agency to turn them into collective action frames" (Tarrow 1998: 133). Moreover, because a cultural stock contains diverse and often contradictory symbols, social movement entrepreneurs must choose which symbols to emphasize and how they will be packaged. It is this selective "punctuating and encoding of objects, situations, events, experiences, and sequences of action" that renders events meaningful to potential recruits (Snow and Benford 1988: 137). In other words, social movement entrepreneurs often must navigate their organizations through cultural fields awash with alternative interpretative schemata in order to label some acts or events as unjust, define the opposition, and make the case for action (Gamson 1988).

Collective action frames must also be *amplified*, which requires another set of strategic choices. Frame amplification involves the highlighting or accenting of various issues, events, or beliefs from the broader interpretive sweep of the movement. The development of a poignant set of symbols allows a movement's frame to be carried quickly and efficiently. Perhaps the most obvious, but by no means the only, form of frame amplification is the bumper sticker. Framing debates between the pro-choice and pro-life movements, for example, are amplified on the car bumpers of their respective supporters:

- "I'm Pro-Choice and I Vote"
- "It's a Child Not a Choice"
- "Keep Your Hands off My Body"
- "Abortion Is Murder"

Catchphrases such as these crystallize the essential components of the frame in an easily recalled clip. They are one example of condensing symbols that facilitate the communication of frames. Other powerful symbols that can amplify a frame include historical examples, metaphors, and visual images (Ryan 1991). How, for example, the nineteenth-century Swiss democracy movement interpreted the role of business interests in society is clearly and forcefully articulated in the short statement of one of its leaders: "The system, just like cholera, can not be touched with your hand, but you can feel it in your limbs" (Kriesi and Wisler 2002: 49).

As the processes of amplification and articulation make clear, strategic framing is not so much about the creation of new ideas or the presentation of the greatest truth, but the splicing together of old and existing ideas and the strategic punctuating of certain issues, events, or beliefs. Though Benford and Snow (2000) identify frame amplification and frame articulation as discursive processes, both involve more than the packaging and repackaging of language. Frames can also be communicated through nonverbal devices, such as presentation of self, tactics, and organizational forms. The costumes worn by rebel leaders, for example, including "the simple khadi of Indian nationalists and the scruffy beards of Latin American *guerrilleros*" are both a symbol of revolt and a means of communicating their differences from ruling parties and their ideas (Tarrow 1998: 118).

Tactical choices can also serve to amplify a frame. During the 1989 Chinese Democracy Movement, for example, student leaders staged a hunger strike in Tiananmen Square to emphasize their claim that China's political leadership had betrayed its people (Calhoun 1994; Zuo and Benford 1995). On a smaller scale, the Asamblea de Barrios, a poor people's movement organization in Mexico City, used street theater productions featuring the mythic wrestling figure Superbarrio to amplify a similar claim. By pitting Superbarrio, the fair and clean fighter, against tricky and corrupt opponents who represented, variously, landlords, their lawyers, and government officials, the Asamblea de Barrios used the popular arc of the wrestling narrative to highlight the corruption of Mexican government officials (Cadena-Roa, this volume). The form of a social movement organization communicates a group's preferred way of acting and its analysis of the type of action most likely to affect a particular problem. The rise of anarchist environmental movement groups at the end of the twentieth century, for example, indicates not only a distaste among some activists for large, professional movement organizations but also an argument that grassroots, disruptive direct action protests are necessary to achieve environmental goals (Rootes 1999).

The Content of Collective Action Frames

We turn now from those who construct frames, and the means by which they do so, to the materials from which frames are built. Collective action frames are rarely, if ever, fashioned from whole cloth. Instead, in an effort to increase the frames' intelligibility to potential constituents, movement entrepreneurs assemble them by drawing on the symbols and themes found in the cultural stock of the target audience (Naples 2002; Snow and Benford 1988). As Swidler (1986) suggests, we can think of culture as a "tool kit" that an individual carries around. A person's social experiences are made meaningful by shared components contained in the tool kit. People use these cultural components to assemble "strategies of action" that guide their decision making and practices.

Social movement entrepreneurs use this tool kit, too. They seek ways to align their collective action frames with various aspects of their target audiences' cultural stock or to link new or unpopular ideas with existing themes or values in the cultural stock (d'Anjou and Van Male 1998; Snow et al. 1986). Framing processes, however, are not simply fishing expeditions in which social movement entrepreneurs seek to hook potential participants with whatever frame will mobilize the most people. Although the popular media often portray political activists as professional troublemakers who will protest anything and everything, most social movements seek to redress specific grievances or reach policy goals, not just engage in collective action as an end in itself. Social movement entrepreneurs must balance their appeals to popular culture and their awareness of regional variation in norms and values against the goals and values of the movement organization. Failure to do so risks losing existing members in an effort to attract new ones. Moreover, while collective action frames must have a familiar ring to them (or *resonance*—to use a framing term), they also must mobilize people to take collective action. Since popular culture mostly contains interpretations of situations synchronized to support the status quo, if a frame includes too much from the popular tool kit, it loses its oppositional edge and does not encourage collective action (Tarrow 1998).

With these provisions in mind, social movement entrepreneurs frequently draw on two general sources for framing devices: prior or concurrent social movements and the cultural symbols of the dominant group. Social movement entrepreneurs often borrow pretested frames from one or more ongoing or past movements, which, over time, they then transform to fit their own particular social and historical situation (Mooney and Hunt 1996; Swart 1995). During the late 1960s and early 1970s, for example, several movement organizations in the United States—including those struggling to advance the causes of women, Hispanics, and gays and lesbians—borrowed the "rights frame" successfully advanced by the black civil rights movement beginning in the 1950s (Evans 1979; Tarrow 1998; Valocchi, this volume). As a result, these movements were able to cast their claims of discrimination and their demand for equality in terms of familiar prognoses and diagnoses, namely the denial of constitutionally guaranteed rights and a combination of public protest and legislative initiatives. The familiarity of these increased the likelihood they would resonate with both potential constituencies and the general public.

When numerous movements share aspects of their collective action frames, researchers ask whether there is a *master frame* that is operating (Snow and Benford 1992; Kubal 1998). A master frame is a more general, but especially powerful—in that it evokes powerful cultural symbols—interpretative package. Master frames are linked to *cycles of protest*—periods of intense social movement activity in which the mobilization of various movements overlap in time and are often linked to one another. An innovative master frame, for example, can spark derivative collective action frames and tactical innovations at the initiation of a cycle. As the cycle continues, however, the framing and tactical choices of late-rising movements are limited by the parameters of the master frame. The adoption of the "rights frame" by all the major national civil rights organizations in the early 1960s restricted the political space available to later groups, including radical groups that adopted liberation frames (Valocchi, this volume). Generally speaking, organizations advancing these alternative frames did not fare as well, at least in part because they were unable to counter criticism that they had departed from the more legitimate rights frame (Haines 1984, 1988).

Paradoxically, symbols of the dominant group are sometimes used as tools for constructing collective action frames. Williams (2002: 247) argues, "Movements must produce rhetorical packages that explain their claims within extant, culturally legitimate, boundaries." To achieve this, many social movement entrepreneurs draw upon the cultural legitimacy of dominant groups by appropriating their symbols and narratives to construct collective action frames. This practice is so widespread that Noonan (1995: 83) observes that opposition movements do not always use oppositional frames. In Chile during the 1970s, for example, one key source of opposition to the Pinochet regime was mothers of the "disappeared" and other female activists who, in order to avoid immediate repression at the hands of Pinochet's forces, adopted the mantle of traditional womanhood. Presenting themselves as mothers and protectors of the family, a revered role in the regime's official pronouncements, these women created the ideological space necessary to raise questions about the regime's actions from a privileged position in society (Noonan 1995). Evidence to support Noonan's claim that such framing tactics are necessary in nondemocratic regimes can be found in China, where student protesters sang the "Internationale" as they marched to occupy Tiananmen Square (Calhoun 1994; Zuo and Benford 1995), and Poland, where antiregime activists drew on familiar themes of the Communist regime, such as nationalism (Kenney, this volume). But the success of this framing tactic is not limited to nondemocratic regimes. Martin Luther King, Jr., frequently framed his appeals for racial integration within the interpretative schema of the status quo, drawing potent mobilizing symbols from the Bible and the United States Constitution to develop the civil rights movement's oppositional frame (Washington 1986; Williams 2002).

FRAME RESONANCE

"The key to framing," Valocchi (this volume) argues, "is finding evocative cultural symbols that resonate with potential constituents and are capable of motivating them to collective action." In general terms, *frame resonance* describes the relationship between a collective action frame, the aggrieved community that is the target of mobilizing efforts, and the broader culture. A collective action frame is said to be resonant if potential constituents find its interpretation and expression of grievances compelling. They are more likely to do so if the frame is articulated by cultural symbols that "appear natural and familiar" to them (Gamson 1992a: 135). However, repackaging the existing political culture to express the grievances of potential constituents is fraught with potential missteps—"Some metaphors soar, others fall flat; some visual images linger in the mind, others are quickly forgotten" (Gamson 1992a:135).

As with the other important aspects of framing processes, Gamson and Snow develop distinct perspectives on frame resonance and emphasize different features. Gamson (1992a) focuses on the political consciousness of the audience, detailing how individual and groups use personal experiences, the popular wisdom of their communities, and media discourse to make sense of the various frames they encounter. Frames that resonate with all three of these resources, he argues, have the greatest chance to mobilize potential constituencies. Snow and Benford (1992), alternatively, focus on the strategic choices made by movement entrepreneurs, identifying various characteristics of the frame and various actions by movement entrepreneurs as central to the question of frame resonance. They identify six factors that affect frame resonance:

- *frame consistency*—resonant frames are logically complementary in their different aspects: tactics, diagnosis, prognosis, core values and beliefs, etc.
- *empirical credibility*—whether a movement's frames make sense with the way the target audience sees the world
- *credibility of the frame's promoters*—it certainly makes sense that credible and persuasive speakers would help the resonance of a frame that they describe
- *experiential commensurability*—the congruency of a frame with the target's everyday experience (more on the similarity with empirical credibility shortly)
- *centrality*—how essential the core values and beliefs, as articulated by movement frames, are to the lives of the targets

- *narrative fidelity*—resonant frames tend to mesh, draw upon, and synchronize with the dominant culture of the target, its narratives, myths, and basic assumptions

In addition, Snow and colleagues (1986) identified four frame alignment strategies that movements use to increase the resonance of their frames:

- *frame bridging*—linking two or more frames that have an affinity but were previously unconnected; for example, Marxism + ecology = ecological-Marxist frames; or feminism + ecology = ecological-feminist frames
- *frame amplification*—akin to coming up with a catchy phrase or slogan to market a product, in this case the essence of the movement
- *frame extension*—extending aspects of a frame to new areas that are presumed to be important to the target audience
- *frame transformation*—"changing old understandings and meanings [the content of the frame] and/or generating new ones" (Benford and Snow 2000: 625)

For the new student, this lexicon of "resonant framing" is daunting indeed. In our experience, however, mastering the whole host of distinctions is not necessary for understanding the concept of frame resonance.[2] Close examination of research shows considerable overlap in how these terms are used and little empirical support for some of the conceptual distinctions (McAdam, McCarthy, and Zald 1996b). There appears, for example, to be is little difference in practice between empirical credibility—"the apparent fit between the framings and events in the world" (Benford and Snow 2000: 620)—and experiential commensurability—the congruency between "movement framings . . . [and] the personal, everyday experiences of the target of mobilization" (Benford and Snow 2000: 621).[3] In case studies of framing processes that apply these concepts, authors either suggest these "two dimensions of frame resonance tend to work hand in hand" (Zuo and Benford 1995: 140) or simply collapse the two categories without comment (cf. Babb 1996). The same can be said about frame bridging, frame amplification, and frame transformation. Even Benford and Snow (2000), in their recent comprehensive review of the framing perspective, could identify only limited empirical support for many of these concepts.

In this chapter, therefore, we suggest a more straightforward way of organizing the terms—one that focuses on the most significant aspects of frame resonance. Specifically, we suggest that it is both parsimonious and practical to categorize the processes of frame resonance according to three sources of frame resonance:

- *the frame makers*—social movement entrepreneurs
- *the frame receivers*—potential constituents
- *the frame itself*—a snapshot of the various components of a collective action frame: values, beliefs, goals, rhetoric, ideological elements, and other resources from the cultural tool kit such as slogans, tactics, motivations, portraits of "us" and "them," prognoses, and diagnoses

Table 1.1 shows how the terms line up with our simplified categories. In addition to simplifying the discussion of frame resonance and de-emphasizing finer distinctions that have not proven empirically fruitful, our frame resonance schema allows for consideration of *frames* as well as *framing*. In other words, it allows for the isolation of various qualities of the frame itself. Most discussions of meaning work in social movements focus on the verb form of the term, *framing,* in order to indicate the on-going processes of articulating resonant frames. But frames also have content, and our conception of their component parts allows for the isolation of various qualities of frames themselves, thus facilitating the comparison of the frame resonance across frames and social movements.[4]

Table 1.1 Variables Affecting a Frame's Resonance

Makers of a frame—movement entrepreneurs	Receivers of a frame—the target audience	Frame qualities—a frame schema's contents[a]
• **Credibility of the promoters**—their organizational and professional credentials and expertise • **Charismatic authority**—rare and unique personal qualities of a movement leader • Stategic/marketing orientation (or cynicism) [b]	• Ideological orientations (the target of **frame bridging**) • Demographic, attitudinal, moral orientations (the intent of **frame extension** and **frame transformation**)	• Cultural compatibility—the frame's valuational **centrality**, its **narrative fidelity**, and slogans **(amplification)** • **Frame consistency,** do its components synchronize? • Relevance—including **empirical credibility** and **experiential commensurability**

[a] As social constructs, frames are emergent phenomena. To speak of a frame's qualities presumes specifying a point in time, which is usually determined by the availability of data sources (see note 4).

[b] Not in Snow and Benford's original scheme.

Qualities of the Frame's Promoters

Because collective action frames are constructed by movement activists and promoted by movement organizations, how the target population perceives frame promoters affects frame resonance. Snow and Benford (1988) stress that the credibility accorded the frame's promoters is a key variable. Social movements often make claims of expertise about their speakers or supporters in an effort to amplify their frame and increase its resonance (Benford 1987; Coy and Woehrle 1996). Moreover, as Shemtov (1999) shows, activists often become experts on the issues they are struggling over. In contrast, concerns about being perceived as acting outside their area of expertise may inhibit some actors from promoting their frames as aggressively as they would like (Noakes, this volume).

Other attributes beyond expertise and credentials are important as well. Charismatic leaders, for example, can amplify frames and attract followers by the force of their commitment and personality (Jamison and Eyerman 1994). Other leadership

qualities may be projected more strategically. Civil rights activists in the South during the 1960s, for example, self-consciously presented themselves as cool-headed
and reasonable in an effort to remain legitimate in the eyes of federal officials (Robnett 1998).[5] Similarly, several white supremacist groups in the United States during
the late 1980s and early 1990s transformed their self-presentation in order to change
the emotional response of moderate and mainstream conservative whites to their
claims. They did this by co-opting the cultural pluralist frame to assert claims of
"white pride," and by altering the appearance of their spokespersons. David Duke,
for example, a former Klan leader, presented himself as a mainstream politician advancing a mainstream political position after assuming the helm of the newly created
National Association for the Advancement of White People (Berbrier 1998).

In a mass-consumption society where marketing is king, the cynicism of movement entrepreneurs is a crucial factor affecting frame resonance. Johnston (1980)
described the marketing of the transcendental meditation (TM) movement whereby
its leaders consciously strategized different marketing pitches to different audiences—students, businessmen, women, and religious seekers—and actively sought
to recruit famous personalities to exploit their newsworthiness. The cynical marketing of the TM movement is not typical of most movements, where leaders are often
principled advocates of their cause, but the choice between means and ends is an
ever-present dilemma for leaders—and this makes their orientation about strategic
promotion of the movement an important variable in how a frame might resonate.
The marketing machine of Greenpeace in the 1990s was a good example—a highly
strategized and resonant collective action frame promoted by professionalized social
movement entrepreneurs.

Qualities of the Potential Constituents

By "qualities of the potential constituents," we refer to the beliefs and values of
the group targeted for mobilization. These beliefs and values affect how targeted
groups perceive a frame's claims and symbols and, consequently, whether they are
likely to be mobilized by it. Potential constituents are more likely to embrace a frame
that draws on beliefs and values that make up part of the target group's cultural tool
kit. "In the absence of references to one's own history and to the particular nature of
one's roots," della Porta and Diani (1999: 77) point out, "an appeal to something
new risks seeming inconsistent and, in the end, lacking in legitimacy." In his
explanation of how individuals make sense of the frames they encounter, Gamson
(1992) argues that people rely on personal experiences, the popular wisdom of their
community, and media discourse to negotiate meaning. To the extent that these three
cultural resources differ in some patterned way across groups, regions, or nations, we
would expect frame resonance to do so as well.

Cadena-Roa (in this volume) shows how the dramatic portrayal of good and evil
in the popular political theater staged by the Asamblea de Barrios discussed earlier
resonated with the lived experience and community values of working-class
Mexicans who were being victimized by exploitative landlords and corrupt
politicians. He also points out how the wrestling narrative has a different resonance
in Mexico than in the United States, where the narrative is understood to be about the
"American Dream." (Cadena-Roa, this volume; Lincoln 1989). In the United States,
different narratives have seemingly universal qualities. Many American movements,
for example, feature religious symbols or are framed in terms of rights (Tarrow
1998).

Qualities of the Frame

In table 1.1 we listed three qualities of a frame that are particularly important to its resonance:

- *cultural compatibility*: whether the collective action frame and the symbols used to carry it synchronize with society's cultural stock—and especially the "cultural tool kit" of the target audience; most studies of frame resonance focus on this
- *consistency*: the internal consistency of the movement's beliefs, ideology, claims, and actions and whether these "hang together"
- *relevance*: its capacity to make sense of what is happening in the lives of its target audience.

The concept of relevance collapses Snow and Benford's concepts of empirical credibility and experiential commensurability and covers ground similar to Gamson's discussion of how individuals negotiate and interpret meaning. Seen in this way, relevance is both an individual, or micro-level, and group, or meso-level, phenomenon. Berbrier (1998), for example, locates frame resonance in the correspondence between a frame and the "fundamental sentiments people hold about self and others that are evoked by the definition of the situation." Most discussions of frame relevance, however, refer to group-level experiences. Babb (1996), for example, argues that disgruntled industrial workers withdrew their allegiance from the Knights of Labor when the "class conflict" frame of the incipient American Federation of Labor (AFL) made better sense of what was happening in their lives than did the Knights' "labor-greenbackism" frame.

Consistency between frame elements can increase a frame's resonance. Czech democracy protesters in 1989 chose to simply withdraw their support from the Communist government rather than seize government ministries or in any other way suggest they were interested in staging a coup (Oberschall 1996). Their apparent disinterest in power increased the resonance of their prodemocracy frame and helped mobilize mass protests. On the other hand, inconsistency between elements can undermine a frame. Antiabolitionists in nineteenth-century Cincinnati, for example, had successfully stymied the abolitionist cause in that city by claiming that it threatened national security and the vitality of the city's trade with the South. This argument quickly lost favor with city residents, however, when antiabolitionists participated in riots and attempted to burn down the abolitionist press, thus threatening the same values they claimed to represent (Ellingson 1995).

When there is considerable overlap between a frame and the cultural stock of the potential constituents, the frame can be considered culturally potent. As such, cultural compatibility is different from relevance because of its focus on broader cultural themes, rather than daily, lived experiences. When we discussed the resonance of the Superbarrio street theater to the Mexican poor earlier, we noted that it was consistent with their lived experience and community values. But the wrestling narrative of also had deep cultural synchrony. All Mexicans, Cadena-Roa argues, are literate in the symbolism of wrestling, the nation's most popular form of entertainment.

As we noted earlier, social movement entrepreneurs often construct frames from the inside out by incorporating symbols borrowed from the common cultural tool kit. The cultural synchrony of these symbols increases the resonance of the collective action frames they help constitute. The Solidarity movement in Poland, for example, borrowed so heavily from Catholic symbolism in framing its appeals that Tarrow (1998: 132) concludes, "Never in the history of revolt did the practice of revolt appear to draw so heavily on the inherited symbols of consensus!" The revolt had little to do with religion and the group's claims were not overtly religious, but the repackaged Catholic imagery—such as the veneration of striking workers who had been killed by repressive state forces as martyrs—resonated with the deeply Catholic population (Johnston 1989; Laba 1990; Tarrow 1998).

Frame Resonance as a Dependent Variable?

There is little doubt that the concept of resonance captures an important aspect of framing processes, but the question remains whether frame resonance, per se, can be operationalized and measured in ways that impart confidence—and some degree of precision—about its effects on mobilization processes. Snow and Benford (1988) define frame resonance as related to mobilizing potency. Most studies of frame resonance, including the influential scholarship cited above, are after-the-fact reconstructions of a frame's mobilizing potency that impute the influence of a resonant frame. At best, they present arguments to demonstrate elements of a frame's cultural conduciveness, but they never provide concrete measures of a frame's resonance that can be associated with other measures of mobilization or social movement growth (or decline). Simply stated, frame resonance and mobilizing potency are distinct phenomena. The latter is, at best, a proxy for the former that is useful in preliminary steps of theory building, but equating the two assumes that all people who mobilized did so in response to the (resonant) frame in question—an assumption that is usually never tested. Moreover, as we noted earlier, there are multiple reasons why people with whom a frame resonates don't join in collective action.

As compelling as the concept of frame resonance is, it represents an extremely difficult phenomenon to measure. Two reasons for this stand out. First, researchers cannot freeze social movement mobilization in order to measure frame resonance when it matters most. In practice, frames are constantly evolving, and so are the responses of target audiences to them. Most social movement studies are done retrospectively, after a movement has already mobilized. At that point it is easy to justify collapsing movement mobilization and frame resonance. Second, there are very few studies of frames that do not resonate. It is probably impossible to define the target universe of any particular collective action frame. A constituency that finds a frame compelling usually becomes apparent to researchers by its mobilization, but those social actors for whom the frame is not compelling are generally lost to history. It is notable that Gamson's pathbreaking study of how individuals negotiate meaning in political situations—perhaps the closest we have come to a direct study of frame resonance—utilizes focus groups to delimit the population exposed to various frames and controlled the frames to which they were exposed (Gamson 1992a).

THE STRUGGLE FOR CULTURAL SUPREMACY

The framing of problems, events, and issues by social movement entrepreneurs does not go uncontested in the political arena. Quite the contrary—the most compelling public issues are usually awash with competing frames promoted by social movements, countermovements, elite opponents, mass media, and the state (Noakes, this volume; Tarrow 1998; Whittier 2002). These frames are interpreted by potential constituents, who assemble packages of meaning from those aspects of competing frames that have personal resonance—with the effect that some choose to participate, but most don't. On this crowded political field the contestants respond to one another's frames, more likely than not confronting and challenging them, but also sometimes absorbing them, sometimes co-opting aspects, and sometimes shaping their own frames to avoid explicit conflict, especially with more powerful players. It is this contest between competing frames that Tarrow refers to as the struggle for cultural supremacy. Social movement entrepreneurs generally enter this contest at a distinct disadvantage. At least two of its usual opponents—the state and the media—control more cultural resources than your typical social movement (Tarrow 1998; Whittier 2002).

Countermovements

The fairest fight, at least in the abstract, is between a social movement for change and a countermovement that opposes its goals and interests. Countermovements alter typical movement dynamics and may reorient framing decisions. In the absence of an effective countermovement, victories increase political opportunities for the movement, its constituency, and related movement organizations. But countermovements may use opponents' victories as a mobilizing tool, inspiring efforts to roll back enemy gains, qualifying the political opportunities created by victories, and shaping the efforts of the movement for years to come (Staggenborg 1991; Meyer and Staggenborg 1996). The 1973 *Roe v. Wade* Supreme Court decision, for example, was simultaneously a major gain for the incipient pro-choice movement and the primary spark of a pro-life countermovement (Staggenborg 1991; Luker 1984). Over the next two decades, the intersection between these two movements drove the major pro-choice movement organizations to formalize their organizational structures, shift their tactics to emphasize lobbying over direct-action protests, and limit the range of issues they pursued (Staggenborg 1991).

Struggles between movements and countermovements also affect framing processes directly. Again, the struggles between the pro-choice and pro-life movements provide a good example. Facing a strong countermovement, mainstream pro-choice movement organizations increasingly adopted a single-issue focus, limiting their diagnosis of events and narrowing the range of solutions they offered. They did this to avoid losing their soft supporters who might be offended by a collective action frame that "bridged" to other feminist causes. In other cases, movement victories may cause a countermovement to shift the arena of conflict in an attempt to force its opponent to respond to issues in which the movement's frame may have less cultural resonance. For example, after the pro-choice movement gained several legal victories in the early 1980s, the pro-life movement regained its footing by introducing a documentary film purporting to show a fetus experiencing pain during a standard abortion procedure, thereby shifting the debate from the legal to the ethical realm. Pro-choice organizations were forced both to respond to the new cultural debate over the medical ethics of abortion and to develop tactics to shift the debate to issues on which their framing was likely to be more resonant. They did this by organizing a series of public speak-outs during which women spoke of their experiences with illegal abortions, in an effort to shift the focus of the debate from the fetus to the woman (Staggenborg 1991).

When elite opponents launch countermovements, the extensive resources they control commonly have significant effects on framing dynamics. U.S. employers, for example, have twice engaged in coordinated campaigns to discredit labor unions and promote the principles of capitalism. In the late nineteenth century, employers, drawing on themes prominent in the civic reform movement, constructed unions as "mob-like, incompatible with managerial rights, and un-American" (Haydu 1999: 325). Several decades later, in the aftermath of World War II, the U.S. business community once again launched a campaign to delegitimate organized labor and New Deal liberalism after unions had gained significant power under prewar New Deal policies (Fones-Wolf 1994). In both cases, elite countermovements had considerable success defining progressive movement frames as illegitimate, thus limiting the field of interpretation available to later movements.

State Agencies and Institutions

The state has always been recognized as a significant player in shaping social movement dynamics through its decisions about which groups to tolerate and which to repress (McAdam 1982; McAdam, Tarrow, and Tilly 2001). But the state also engages in the struggle for cultural supremacy—albeit at a considerable advantage— by promoting frames that, if accepted, increase its legitimacy and expand its domain (Becker 1963). A state's legitimacy provides it with a unique advantage in the struggle for cultural supremacy. As Edelman (1971: 7) argued a decade before framing became fashionable:

> Government affects behavior chiefly by shaping the cognitions of large numbers of people in ambiguous situations. It helps to create their beliefs about what is proper; their perceptions about what is fact; and their expectations about what is to come.

Media producers, for example, rely on government officials "both for definitions of problems and for information" (Olien, Tichenor, and Donahue 1989: 198). Journalists have multiple incentives to use them as sources, including the prestige they add to a story, their assumed objectivity, and their ready availability in the time-sensitive cycle of news production (McLeod and Hertog 1998; Paletz and Entman 1981; Soley 1992). This access to media enjoyed by government officials provides them with frequent opportunities to articulate their interpretations of events and issues. Given the ubiquity of official frames in media discourse, the frames advanced by state officials generally have considerable resonance with members of the public as they receive and process the din of information produced by the various players in the struggle for cultural supremacy (McCarthy, Smith, and Zald 1996; Ryan 1991; Tarrow 1998). State explanations of events, therefore, form part of the external culture which movements must consider when devising their strategies and constructing their frames (Whittier 2002).

Despite its vast resources, the state does not always win the struggle for cultural supremacy—especially when its legitimacy is questioned. In Eastern Europe in 1989, for example, the very act of protesting helped undermine the state's authority and the demand for democracy placed the state in an awkward rhetorical position. When Communist regimes proved unable to take action to control the protests or counter the protester's claims, the erosion of state authority hastened the overthrow of the government (Oberschall 1996; Zdravomyslova 1996; Tarrow 1998). In contrast, during the American civil rights movement, Martin Luther King and the Southern

Christian Leadership Conference (SCLC) were able to induce the state to act in ways beneficial to the civil rights cause. When selecting the locations of major protest campaigns, King and the SCLC chose cities where the police were likely to respond to nonviolent protest with force. When this masterful use of strategic dramaturgy induced a violent response, as it did in Birmingham and Selma, the images produced during the clash made the civil rights activists appear "good" in comparison to the "evil" state officials. Moreover, by courting crisis, they forced the Kennedy administration to abandon its neutral frame and support the movement (McAdam 1996).

Communications Media

Tarrow (1998: 119) argues that media actors "do as much if not more to control the construction of meaning than state or social actors." Media frames, which are advanced via the printed word through descriptions of groups and protests or visually presented by means of photographs, cartoons, or maps, "select some aspects of a perceived reality and make them more salient in a communicating text," thus defining problems, causes, and resolutions (Entman 1993: 52). While media outlets are one of the primary means by which information by and about a movement is communicated, they are more than mere conduits of information for social movements or the state (Barker-Plummer 1996; Gitlin 1980). Journalistic norms and practices shape media framing of issues and events. Once articulated, media frames interact with and influence the construction of social movement, official, and individual frames.

The relationship between media and social movements is a complicated one. As Gamson and Meyer (1996: 287) point out: "On one hand, the media play a central role in the construction of meaning and the reproduction of culture. . . . On the other hand, the media are also a site . . . in which symbolic contests are carried out." Media exposure is an external resource for social movement mobilization, and media outlets tend to be more open to some aspects of collective action frames, such as charges of injustice. Newspaper and television stories about a movement can raise the public's consciousness of particular problems, as it did about the dangers of nuclear energy in the 1980s (Gamson and Modigliani 1989). They can also serve as a vehicle for recruitment and maintenance of support, even when the story's overall frame is negative (Gitlin 1980). When media discourse is positive, a movement's collective action frame is more likely to resonate with a broader array of people (Walgrave and Manssens, this volume).

But media producers are also generally inhospitable to key aspects of the collective action frame, such as the structural analysis implicit in many injustice claims. News coverage tends to be more episodic than thematic, focusing on specific events, such as individual acts of violence, and tends to attribute responsibility to individuals (Wallack et al. 1993). Thematic frames, in contrast, include the social and historical conditions that gave rise to events, ideological discussion and analysis, and detailed articulation of grievances (Gamson, Fireman, and Rytina 1982). Moreover, because social movements have a hard time achieving consistent access to media outlets, they are often forced to stage dramatic events to capture media attention. The unusual nature of these events all but guarantees that they will be framed episodically, obscuring the broader issues underlying the collective action the movement hopes to promote. This sequence of events has contributed to the development of what communication scholars have called the "protest paradigm," a ready-made frame template that the media apply to social movement activity that, among other things, trivializes and demonizes social movement activities and beliefs (Ashley and Olson 1998; Chan and Lee 1984).

POLITICAL OPPORTUNITIES

We conclude this chapter by providing an overview of how framing processes intersect with a key concept in social movement analysis—that of political opportunities. Political opportunities are structural factors that affect the actions and outcomes of social movements but are external to them. Tarrow (1992) identifies channels of access to political decision making, the availability of political allies to challenging groups, the stability of political alignments and institutions, and division among political elites as common political opportunities. When any of these factors are available, they create openings that enable challengers' demands to be heard. When these factors are absent, mobilization is constrained and opponents may be forced underground into "submerged networks" or "abeyance structures" where innovative frames are often elaborated (Kriesi and Wisler 2002; Johnston and Snow 1998; Melucci 1989; Swidler 1986; Taylor 1989).

Political opportunities can be thought of as variables that shape how challenging groups perceive the likelihood of success. In practice, political opportunities are looked at differently depending on the research question's scope. In analyses of contentious politics in a single nation-state, for example, political opportunities are dynamic, referring to "changes in the institutional structure or informal power relations" (McAdam, McCarthy, and Zald 1996b: 3). If the goal is to compare social movements in different nations, however, political opportunities are more static, referring to "differences in the political characteristics of the nation states" in which the movements occur (McAdam, McCarthy, and Zald 1996b: 3). Variation, in this latter conception, occurs across space rather than time. Most discussions of the relationship between political opportunity and framing processes take the former perspective, attending to the relationship between changes in institutional structures and informal power relations in state and society as movements develop over time.

To begin our discussion, it is useful to conceive the relationship between political opportunities and framing dichotomously: namely, (1) that changes in political opportunities shape movement framing, and (2) that movement framing can cause openings or closings of political opportunities. We think it is fair to a say that, like most things, a middle course—one that recognizes joint influences of both—is not only safer but also more accurate and that the predominance of either political openings or framing as determining influences will vary according the cases being studied. However, it is also fair to say that this middle road is not as theoretically interesting as research that shows the strong causal effect of one or the other; as a result, many framing studies focus on cases that give evidence for the extremes. We begin our review, therefore, by exploring the two poles of framing and political opportunities and end with a walk down the middle path.

Regarding the first approach, there is good evidence that political structure can shape movement framing significantly (Koopmans and Duyvendak 1995; Diani 1996). For example, Diani's 1996 analysis of the Italian Northern League's success stresses the primary role of political context. He holds that different configurations of political structure are conducive to different master frames. Implied in his analysis is that these frames are present in varying degrees in the polity and are carried by different political groups. Diani presents evidence that the Northern League's populist frame fortuitously intersected with changes in Italian political structure. The weakening of traditional political alignments based on religion and working-class identity meant that Italy's main parties, the Christian Democrats and the Communists, were not able to offer persuasive alternatives to the Northern League's populism. Moreover, the league's hostility toward political elites, its xenophobia, and its general suspicion of political activity found fertile soil at a time when limited opportunities for interest representation were offered by the political structure. In a sense, Diani argues that that many movements are successful because "their time has come" in terms of political opportunity. Although tactics surely enter the equation of success, the Northern League's antisystem rhetoric gave it significant advantages over other movements, making it a case where changes in political structure privilege one movement's frame above others.

A somewhat different approach lays greater emphasis on movement agency by recognizing that changes in political structure can shape movement framing choices. For example, Zdravomyslova's 1996 analysis of contentious politics in the waning days of the Soviet Union shows that when constraints existed on political activity during the ascendant phase of the opposition, motivational framing focused primarily on collective identity. Later, when constraints on political activity had declined and mass protests were common, movement organizations began to develop issue-oriented diagnostic and motivational frames. Similarly, Rothman and Oliver (2002) have shown that changes in political opportunities influence a movement's frame-bridging and frame-extension activities. They trace how a rural movement against a huge hydroelectric project in Brazil originally framed its struggle in terms of class-based land claims and Catholic liberation theology. Later, as Brazil's political structure liberalized—moving toward free democratic elections—the movement shifted its mobilizing frame from a poor people's land struggle to environmentalism in order to take advantage of resources from transnational environmental NGOs. This is a poignant case of how shifting political opportunities can influence a movement's definition of itself.

Political opportunities can also shape frames across movements. In this volume, Schneider compares the framing strategies of three Puerto Rican community movements in New York City, arguing that differences in local political opportunity structures shaped the framing strategies chosen by movement entrepreneurs. Local political opportunities were determined by the distribution of power between ethnic groups in the neighborhood, opportunities for political coalition building, and the framing and trajectories of past community movements. AIDS activists, for example, confronting the role intravenous drug use has played in the transmission of the disease, "needed to frame drug abuse in ways that resonated with the frame of previous neighborhood movements." As a result, in three separate neighborhoods, drug users were framed respectively as antisystem revolutionaries, victims of colonialism and oppression, or victims of class oppression, in response to variations in the political culture of past movements in those neighborhoods.

The second approach stresses how movement framing can trump political structure, or in some instances generate its own political opportunities. One way this can occur is that a movement can either unintentionally misread or strategically ignore the political context and mobilize in the absence of objective opportunities such as state weakness or shifts in power relations. Under these circumstances, movements can adopt framing strategies to attack the state and mobilize mass resistance, thereby generating their own political opportunities if their mobilization is successful

(Kurzman 1996). It is important to note, however, that the framing-political structure relationship is dependent on the intermediate variable of mobilization success:

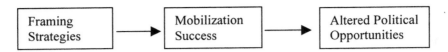

In fact, we suggest that cases where framing activities by themselves alter institutional political structures directly are relatively rare.

However, this may be less true regarding *discursive* opportunity structures (Gamson and Meyer 1996; Koopmans and Statham 2002).[6] Gamson and Meyer distinguish between institutional and cultural opportunities and then classify them according to their volatility. For example, popular ideas ("ideas in good currency") may offer political opportunities to movements by opening "policy windows" (Kingdon 1984) among politicians. Public outrage from pictures of slain women and children during wartime may cause fissures in elite alliances and open opportunities for antiwar movements. Although these discursive opportunities are fleeting, it makes sense that movement framing can be especially potent—during the limited opportunity window—in articulating, defining, and congealing the opportunity. Framing may have less effect with less-volatile discursive opportunities, such as strongly embedded cultural templates—a social belief system or a national myth, for example. Gamson and Meyer (1996) also posit a middle-range category of discursive political opportunities, such as changes in national mood or climate of public opinion, where one might expect relatively more vulnerability to movement framing practices. Finally, Gamson and Meyer suggest a category of volatile *institutional* structures, such as elections or using the army to repress large demonstrations. These would seem to be more prone to framing influence than established state structures such as the judiciary or legislature.

Kenney's analysis (in this volume) of the success of Poland's Freedom and Peace (WiP) movement in 1989 offers a good example of how framing can open political opportunities. Central to WiP's victory was the ability of movement entre-preneurs to reframe state repression as evidence of the illegitimacy of the Commu-nist state. The success of this strategy was facilitated by WiP's choice of issues, which exposed the contradictions between the government's ideological rhetoric and its governing style. If, for example, nationalism was a central tenet of the Polish state, then how could Poland's army be used to repress its citizens? This was a framing strategy that took advantage of volatile institutional opportunities, namely, incomplete social control. There was a parallel argument that was made later by the Solidarity movement: if the Communist party was the vanguard of the working class, why was it necessary to have an independent trade union to defend workers' inter-ests? In Solidarity's early years, this framing tactic opened institutional opportunities for the nascent trade union.

The third perspective takes a middle road, affirming that most movements mo-bilize within a political context that exerts strong determining influence, but also in which movement framing plays an important role—recursively feeding back to affect political opportunities. Several of the chapters in this volume navigate the middle course—Valocchi's treatment of the gay movement's development, Cadena-Roa's analysis of Mexican neighborhood mobilization, Walgrave and Manssens's research on Belgium's white march. The overriding theoretical question is not posed in terms of either/or but rather in terms of the relative weight of political opportunities versus movement framing practices. Moreover, research does not always support the analyst's intuition or first impressions. Regarding European new social movements, for which one might expect framing influences to predominate because of strong emphasis on culture and identity issues, Koopmans and Duyvendak (1995) have found that political structures are the best predictors of movement success. On the other hand, Oberschall (1996) describes the significance of framing elements in the Eastern European opposition movements that brought about the fall of Communist regimes in 1989. These are movements where the division of elites, erosion of social control, and erratic liberalization policies—all of which are elements of political structure—would be expected to play an instrumental role. Although no research to date has offered accurate measures of structural versus framing inputs, moral indignation, democracy, the people's will, and the people's determination all were significant motivating frames in the mass protests that brought down the Communist regimes (Oberschall 1996).

It is axiomatic that the mix of structural constraints and framing actions will vary according to the movement being analyzed. It is also axiomatic that a longer view of movement development will reveal processes of mutual influence between frames and political structures. We are suggesting that the middle path is best examined in the long term to capture the mutual and recursive influences of political context and framing. In this model, either a compelling political opening or an especially effective framing of an issue might get the movement off the ground, and subsequent movement successes (or failures) will affect openings (or closings) of political structure and/or further adjustments in the movement's frame. Social movement actors may take advantage of the most conducive frames in a given period and adjust movement framing as political contexts change. This is the process traced in Suh's recent analysis of Korean union mobilization (2004). Based on close examination of documents and participants' interviews, he shows that government repression made the union movement's initial economic well-being frame useless, which gave rise to new frames of political struggle for democratic opening. These eventually were successful in bringing about a democratic transition, which in turn led to yet new frames emphasizing union solidarity.

Most research in the political opportunity perspective considers framing processes as an intermediate variable in explaining movement development (Tarrow 1998). However, when political structures change, adaptations in framing can open new opportunities for movement development. Moreover, evidence is accumulating that it is common that opportunities are not easily read and must therefore be interpreted by movement participants (Barker and Lavalette 2002). As Gamson and Meyer (1996) point out, whether political opportunities are favorable is often the subject of debates between competing social movement factions, some arguing the moment is ripe for action and others advising patience. While the character of an event surely constrains how much opportunity may be imputed to it, the student of social movements must also recognize that *political opportunities cam be framed in different ways* and that this is a necessary part of the agency component of a collective action frame. It is the agency component of a collective action frame, you will recall, that encourages aggrieved parties to become agents of their own history (Gamson and Meyer 1996).

CONCLUSION

To successfully mobilize adherents and potential followers, a social movement entrepreneur must be attuned to the cultural stock of his or her target audience and to the social and political context in which the movement is operating. Otherwise, the collective action frame promoted by the movement will fall short in comparison to the competing or negating frames promoted by the state, countermovements, or the media. To understand why some movements are successful while others fail, students of social movements must be similarly attuned to the systems of meaning and interpretation operating in every moment of contentious politics. Social movements are not reducible to "meaning work," but it is impossible to understand the arc of a social movement's life course—mobilization, engagement, and decline—without understanding how the various players interpret what the problem is, what must be done, who the opponents are, and what opportunities are present.

NOTES

1. While social movement framing is often strategic, it can also be an emergent social process that evolves "automatically" as a result of complex interaction among groups, leaders, opponents, and other parties such as the state and media—much more on this later.

2. But a word of caution is necessary. Framing research employs the entire gamut of terms, although some much more than others. When relevant, critical evaluation of these studies' logic and methods requires knowledge of the finer distinctions.

3. Both categories refer to the knowledge and experience of target group members. The distinction seems to refer to knowledge that is independent of everyday experiences, say from reading versus that which comes from your job. If our interpretation is correct, this is a very fine distinction.

4. All researchers speak of both framing processes and frames, yet the analysis of frame qualities presumes "freezing the frame" at a point in time to describe it and compare it with frames at other intervals. This is a necessary methodological tactic to answer some research questions, such as how qualities of frames may affect mobilization trajectories. Nevertheless, a frame's "snapshot" is but a shadow of an emergent phenomenon, and its "real" existence is merely (mostly) operational. See Oliver and Johnston's and Johnston's chapters in this volume for discussions of these issues.

5. Claims makers' demeanor can affect frame resonance in indirect ways was well. Police are more tolerant of "contained" as opposed to "transgressive" protest, a distinction based on the police's familiarity with the protesters and the means by which they make their claims (della Porta 1998; Tilly 2000). Police repression hampers frame articulation, diverts claimsmakers' attention away from their primary cause, and may create an unfavorable impression of the movement in the eyes of some potential constituents.

6. Koopmans and Statham (2002: 228) suggest that these impose limits on "which ideas are considered 'sensible,' which constructions are seen as 'realistic,' and which claims are held as 'legitimate' in a certain polity at a certain time." The concept suggests cultural compatibility aspects of frame resonance discussed earlier.

REFERENCES

Ashley, Laura, and Beth Olson. 1998. "Constructing Reality: Print Media's Framing of the Women's Movement, 1966-1986." *Journalism and Mass Communication Quarterly* 75: 263-277.

Babb, Sarah. 1996. "'A True American System of Finance': Frame Resonance in the U.S. Labor Movement, 1866 to 1886." *American Sociological Review* 61: 1033-1052.

Barker, Colin, and Michael Lavalette. 2002. "Strategizing and the Sense of Context: Reflections on the First Two Weeks of the Liverpool Docks Lockout, September-October 1995." Pp. 140-156 in *Social Movements: Identity, Culture, and the State,* David S. Meyer, Nancy Whittier, and Belinda Robnett, eds. New York: Oxford University Press.

Barker-Plummer, B. 1996. "The Dialogic of Media and Social Movements." *Peace Review* 8: 27-34.

Becker, Howard. 1963. *The Outsiders.* New York: The Free Press.

Benford, Robert D. 1987. *Framing Activity, Meaning, and Social Movement Participation: The Disarmament Movement.* Ph.D. diss., University of Texas.

———. 1993a. "Frame Disputes within the Nuclear Disarmament Movement." *Social Forces* 71: 677-701.

———. 1993b. "'You Could Be the Hundredth Monkey': Collective Action Frames and Vocabularies of Motive within the Nuclear Disarmament Movement." *Sociological Quarterly* 34: 195-216.

———. 1997. "An Insider's Critique of the Social Movement Framing Perspective." *Sociological Inquiry* 67: 409-430.

Benford, Robert, and Scott A. Hunt. 1992. "Dramaturgy and Social Movements: The Social Construction and Communication of Power." *Sociological Inquiry* 62: 36-55.

Benford, Robert, and David Snow. 2000. "Framing Processes and Social Movements: An Overview and Assessment." *Annual Review of Sociology* 26: 611-639.

Berbrier, Mitch. 1998. "'Half the Battle': Cultural Resonance, Framing Processes, and Ethnic Affectations in Contemporary White Supremacists' Rhetoric." *Social Problems* 45: 431-450.

Calhoun, Craig. 1994. *Neither Gods nor Emperors.* Berkeley: University of California Press.

Casquette, Jesús. 1996. "The Sociopolitical Context of Mobilization: The Case of the Antimilitary Movement in the Basque Country." *Mobilization* 1: 203-217.

Chan, Janet B. L., and C. Lee. 1984. "The Journalistic Paradigm on Civil Protests: A Case Study of Hong Kong." Pp. 183-202 in *The News Media in National and International Conflict,* Arno Andrew and Wimal Dissanayake, eds. Boulder, CO: Westview.

Cohen, Jean. 1985. "Strategy or Identity: New Theoretical Paradigms and Contemporary Social Movements." *Social Research* 52: 663-716.

Coy, Patrick G., and Lynne M. Woehrle. 1996. "Constructing Identity and Oppositional Knowledge: The Framing Perspective of Peace Organizations during the Persian Gulf War." *Sociological Spectrum* 16: 287-327.

D'Anjou, Leo, and John Van Male. 1998. "Between Old and New: Social Movements and Cultural Change." *Mobilization* 3: 207-226.

della Porta, Donatella. 1998. "Police Knowledge and Protest Policing: Some Reflections on the Italian Case." Pp. 228-252 in *Policing Protest,* Donatella della Porta and Herbert Reiter, eds. Minneapolis: University of Minnesota Press.

———. 2002. "Protests, Protesters, and Protest Policing: Public Discourse in Italy and Germany from the 1960s to the 1980s." Pp. 66-96 in *How Social Movements Matter,* Marco Giugni, Doug McAdam, and Charles Tilly, eds. Minneapolis: University of Minnesota Press.

Diani, Mario. 1996. "Linking Mobilization Frames and Political Opportunities: Insights from Regional Populism in Italy." *American Sociological Review* 61: 1053-1069.

Edelman, Murray. 1971. *Politics as Symbolic Action.* Chicago: Markham.

Ellingson, Stephen. 1995. "Understanding the Dialectic of Discourse and Collective Action: Public Debate and Rioting in Antebellum Cincinnati." *American Journal of Sociology* 101: 100-144

Entman, Robert M. 1993 "Framing: Toward Clarification of a Fractured Paradigm." *Journal of Communication* 43: 51-58.

Evans, Sara. 1979. *Personal Politics: The Roots of Women's Liberation in the Civil Rights Movement and the New Left.* New York: Alfred Knopf.

Fones-Wolf, Elizabeth A. 1994. *Selling Free Enterprise: The Business Assault on Labor and Liberalism, 1945-1960*. Chicago: University of Illinois Press.

Gamson, William A. 1988. "Political Discourse and Collective Action." *International Journal of Social Movements, Conflicts, and Change* 1: 219-244.

———. 1992a. *Talking Politics*. New York: Cambridge University Press.

———. 1992b. "The Social Psychology of Collective Action." Pp. 53-76 in *Frontiers of Social Movement Theory*, Aldon Morris and Carol McClurg Mueller, eds. New Haven, CT: Yale University Press.

Gamson, William A., Bruce Fireman, and Steven Rytina. 1982. *Encounters with Unjust Authority*. Homewood, IL: Dorsey Press.

Gamson, William A., and David S. Meyer. 1996. "Framing Political Opportunity." Pp. 275-290 in *Comparative Perspectives on Social Movements: Political Opportunities, Mobilizing Structures, and Cultural Framings*, Doug McAdam, John D. McCarthy, and Mayer N. Zald, eds. Cambridge: Cambridge University Press.

Gamson, William A., and Andre Modigliani. 1989. "Media Discourse and Public Opinion on Nuclear Power: A Constructionist Approach." *American Journal of Sociology* 95:1-37.

Gamson, William A., and David Stuart. 1992. "Media Discourse as a Symbolic Contest: The Bomb in Political Cartoons." *Sociological Forum* 7: 55-86.

Gamson, William A., and Gadi Wolsfeld. 1993. "Movements and Media as Interacting Systems." *Annals of the American Academy of Political and Social Science* 528: 114-125.

Gitlin, Todd. 1980. *The Whole World Is Watching: Mass Media in the Making and Unmaking of the New Left*. Berkeley: University of California Press.

Giugni, Marco, Doug McAdam, and Charles Tilly, eds. *How Social Movements Matter*. Minneapolis: University of Minnesota Press.

Goffman, Erving. 1974. *Frame Analysis: An Essay on the Organization of the Experience*. New York: Harper Colophon.

———. 1981. *Forms of Talk*. Philadelphia: University of Pennsylvania Press.

Gould, Roger. 1991. "Multiple Networks and Mobilization in the Paris Commune, 1871." *American Sociological Review* 56: 716-729.

Haines, Herbert. 1984. "Black Radicalization and the Funding of Civil Rights, 1957-1970." *Social Problems* 32: 31-43.

———. 1988. *Black Radicals and the Civil Rights Mainstream, 1954-1970*. Knoxville: University of Tennessee Press.

———. 1996. *Against Capital Punishment*. New York: Oxford University Press.

Haydu, Jeffrey. 1999. "Counter Action Frames: Employer Frames and the Union Menace in the Late Nineteenth Century." *Social Problems* 46: 313-331.

Jamison, Andrew, and Ron Eyerman. 1994. *Seeds of the Sixties*. Berkeley: University of California Press.

Jenkins, J. Craig, and Charles Perrow. 1997. "Insurgency of the Powerless: Farm Workers' Movements, 1946-1972." *American Sociological Review* 42: 249-268.

Johnston, Hank. 1980. "The Marketed Social Movement: A Case Study Rapid Growth of TM." *Pacific Sociological Review* 23: 333-354.

———. 1989. "Toward an Explanation of Church Opposition to Authoritarian Regimes." *Journal for the Scientific Study of Religion* 28: 493-508.

Johnston, Hank, and David Snow. 1998. "Subcultures of Opposition and the Estonian Nationalist Movement, 1945-1990." *Sociological Perspectives*: 41: 473-497.

Kingdon, John. 1984. *Agendas, Alternatives, and Public Policies*. Boston: Little, Brown.

Klandermans, Bert. 1984. "Social-psychological Expansion of Resource Mobilization Theory." *American Sociological Review* 49: 583-600.

———. 1992. "The Social Construction of Protest and Multiorganizational Fields." Pp. 77-103 in *Frontiers of Social Movement Theory*, Aldon Morris and Carol McClurg Mueller, eds. New Haven, CT: Yale University Press.

Koopmans, Ruud, and Jan Willem Duyvendak. 1995. "The Political Construction of the Nuclear Energy Issue and Its Impact on the Mobilization of Antinuclear Movements in Western Europe." *Social Problems* 42: 235-251.

Koopmans, Ruud, and Paul Statham. 2002. "Ethnic and Civic Conceptions of Nationhood and the Differential Success of the Extreme Right in Germany and Italy." Pp. 225-252 in *How Social Movements Matter,* Marco Giugni, Doug McAdam, and Charles Tilly, eds. Minneapolis: University of Minnesota Press.

Kornhauser, William. 1959. *The Politics of Mass Society.* Glencoe, IL: The Free Press.

Kriesi, Hanspeter, and Dominique Wisler. 2002. "The Impact of Social Movements on Political Institutions: A Comparison of the Introduction of Direct Legislation in Switzerland and the United States." Pp. 42-65 in *How Social Movements Matter,* Marco Giugni, Doug McAdam, and Charles Tilly, eds. Minneapolis: University of Minnesota Press.

Kubal, Timothy. 1998. "The Presentation of Political Self: Cultural Resonance and the Construction of Collective Action Frames." *Sociological Quarterly* 39: 539-554.

Kurzman, Charles. 1996. "Structural Opportunity and Perceived Opportunity in Social Movement Theory: The Iranian Revolution of 1979." *American Sociological Review* 61: 153-170.

Laba, Roman. 1990. *The Roots of Solidarity: A Political Sociology of Poland's Working Class Democratization.* Princeton, NJ: Princeton University Press.

Laraña, Enrique, Hank Johnston, and Joseph Gusfield, eds. 1994. *New Social Movements: From Ideology to Identity.* Philadelphia: Temple University Press.

Lenski, Gerhard. 1954. "Status Crystallization: A Non-vertical Dimension of Social Status." *American Sociological Review* 19: 5-13.

Lincoln, Bruce. 1989. *Discourse and the Construction of Society.* New York: Oxford University Press.

Luker, Kristin. 1984. *Abortion and the Politics of Motherhood.* Berkeley: University of California Press.

Marullo, Samuel, Ronald Pagnucco, and Jackie Smith. 1996. "Frame Changes and Social Movement Contraction: U.S. Peace Movement Framing after the Cold War." *Sociological Inquiry* 66: 1-28.

McAdam, Doug. 1982. *Political Process and the Development of the Black Insurgency, 1930-1970.* Chicago: University of Chicago Press.

———. 1996. "The Framing Function of Movement Tactics: Strategic Dramaturgy in the American Civil Rights Movement." Pp. 338-355 in *Comparative Perspectives on Social Movements: Political Opportunities, Mobilizing Structures, and Cultural Framings,* Doug McAdam, John D. McCarthy, and Mayer N. Zald, eds. Cambridge: Cambridge University Press.

McAdam Doug, John D. McCarthy, and Mayer N. Zald, eds. 1996a. *Comparative Perspectives on Social Movements: Political Opportunities, Mobilizing Structures, and Cultural Framings.* Cambridge: Cambridge University Press.

———. 1996b. "Introduction: Opportunities, Mobilizing Structures, and Framing Processes— Toward a Synthetic, Comparative Perspective on Social Movements." Pp. 1-20 in *Comparative Perspectives on Social Movements: Political Opportunities, Mobilizing Structures, and Cultural Framings.* Doug McAdam, John D. McCarthy, and Mayer N. Zald, eds. Cambridge: Cambridge University Press.

McAdam, Doug, and Ronelle Paulsen. 1993. "Specifying the Relationship between Social Ties and Activism." *American Journal of Sociology* 99: 640-677.

McAdam, Doug, Sidney Tarrow, and Charles Tilly. 2001. *Dynamics of Contention,* New York: Cambridge University Press.

McCarthy, John D., Jackie Smith, and Mayer Zald. 1996. "Assessing Public Media, Electoral, and Governmental Agendas." Pp. 291-311 in *Comparative Perspectives on Social Movements: Political Opportunities, Mobilizing Structures, and Cultural Framings,* Doug McAdam, John D. McCarthy, and Mayer N. Zald, eds. Cambridge: Cambridge University Press.

McLeod, Douglas, and James K. Hertog. 1998. "Social Control and the Mass Media's Role in the Regulation of Protest Groups: The Communicative Acts Perspective." Pp. 305-330 in *Mass Media, Social Control, and Social Change,* David Demers and K. Viswanath, eds. Ames: Iowa State University Press.

Melucci, Alberto. 1989. *Nomads of the Present.* Philadelphia: Temple University Press.

Meyer, David, and Suzanne Staggenborg. 1996. "Movements, Countermovements, and the Structure of Political Opportunity." *American Journal of Sociology* 101: 1628-1660.

Meyer, David S., Nancy Whittier, and Belinda Robnett, eds. 2002. *Social Movements: Identity, Culture, and the State.* New York: Oxford University Press.

Mooney, Patrick, and Scott Hunt. 1996. "A Repertoire of Interpretations: Master Frames and Ideological Continuity in U.S. Agrarian Mobilization." *Sociological Quarterly* 37: 177-197.

Mueller, Carol. 1994. "Conflict Networks and the Origins of the Women's Movement." Pp. 234-263 in *New Social Movements: From Ideology to Identity,* Enrique Laraña, Hank Johnston and Joseph Gusfield, eds. Philadelphia: Temple University Press.

Naples, Nancy A. 2002. "Materialist Feminist Discourse Analysis and Social Movement Research: Mapping the Changing Context for 'Community Control.'" Pp. 226-246 in *Social Movements: Identity, Culture, and the State,* David S. Meyer, Nancy Whittier, and Belinda Robnett, eds. New York: Oxford University Press.

Noonan, Rita K. 1995. "Women against the State: Political Opportunities and Collective Action Frames in Chile's Transition to Democracy." *Sociological Forum* 10: 81-111.

Oberschall, Anthony. 1996. "Opportunities and Framing in the Eastern European Revolts of 1989." Pp. 93-121 in *Comparative Perspectives on Social Movements: Political Opportunities, Mobilizing Structures, and Cultural Framings,* Doug McAdam, John McCarthy, and Mayer N. Zald, eds. Cambridge: Cambridge University Press.

Olien, Clarice N., Philip J. Tichenor, and George Donahue. 1989. "Media Coverage and Social Movements." Pp. 139-163 in *Information Campaigns,* Charles T. Salmon, ed. Newbury Park, CA: Sage.

Paletz, David L., and Robert M. Entman. 1981. *Media Power and Politics.* New York: Free Press.

Robnett, Belinda. 1998. "African American Women in the Civil Rights Movement: Spontaneity and Emotion in Social Movement Theory." Pp. 65-95 in *No Middle Ground: Women and Social Protest,* Kathleen Blee, ed. New York: New York University Press.

Rootes, Christopher. 1999. *Environmental Movements: Local National and Global.* London: Frank Cass.

Rothman, Franklin Daniel, and Pamela Oliver. 2002. "From Local to Global: The Antidam Movement in Southern Brazil, 1979-1992." Pp. 115-132 in *Globalization and Resistance: Transnational Dimension of Social Movements,* Jackie Smith and Hank Johnston, eds. New York: Rowman and Littlefield.

Ryan, Charlotte. 1991. *Prime Time Activism.* Boston: South End.

Scheufele, Dietram. 1999. "Framing as a Theory of Media Effects." *Journal of Communication* 49: 103-122.

Shemtov, Ronit. 1999. "Taking Ownership of Environmental Problems: How Local NIMBY Groups Expand Their Goals." *Mobilization* 4(1): 91-106.

Shoemaker, Pamela J. 1984. "Media Treatment of Deviant Political Groups." *Journalism Quarterly* 61: 66-75.

Skocpol, Theda. 1979. *States and Social Revolutions.* Cambridge: Cambridge University Press.

Smelser, Neil. 1962. *Theories of Collective Behavior.* New York: Free Press.

Smith, Jackie, and Hank Johnston, eds. *Globalization and Resistance: Transnational Dimensions of Social Movements.* New York: Rowman and Littlefield.

Snow, David A. 2004. "Framing Processes, Ideology, and Discursive Fields." Pp. 380-412 in *The Blackwell Companion to Social Movements.* New York: Blackwell.

Snow, David A., and Robert D. Benford. 1988. "Ideology, Frame Resonance, and Participant Mobilization." *International Social Movement Research* 1:197-218.

————. 1992. "Master Frames and Cycles of Protest." Pp. 133-155 in *Frontiers of Social Movement Theory*, Aldon Morris and Carol McClurg Mueller, eds. New Haven, CT: Yale University Press.

Snow, David, and Pamela Oliver. 1995. "Social Movements and Collective Behavior: Social-psychological Dimensions and Considerations." Pp. 571-599 in *Sociological Perspectives on Social Psychology*, Karen Cook, Gary Fine, and James House, eds. Boston: Allyn and Bacon.

Snow, David A., E. Burke Rochford, Jr., Steven K. Worden, and Robert D. Benford. 1986. "Frame Alignment Processes, Micromobilization, and Movement Participation." *American Sociological Review* 51: 464-481.

Soley, Lawrence C. 1992. *The News Shapers*. New York: Praeger.

Staggenborg, Suzanne. 1991. *The Pro-Choice Movement*. New York: Oxford University Press.

Suh, Doowon. 2004. "Outcome Framing and Movement Dynamics: Korean White-Collar Union's Political Mobilization and Interunion Solidarity, 1987-1995." *Mobilization* 9: 17-37.

Swart, William J. 1995. "The League of Nations and the Irish Question: Master Frames, Cycles of Protest, and 'Master Frame Alignment.'" *Sociological Quarterly* 36: 465-481.

Swidler, Ann. 1986. "Culture in Action: Symbols and Strategies." *American Sociological Review* 51: 273-286.

Tarrow, Sidney. 1992. "Mentalities, Political Cultures, and Collective Action Frames: Constructing Meaning through Action." Pp. 174-202 in *Frontiers of Social Movement Theory*, Aldon Morris and Carol McClurg Mueller, eds. New Haven, CT: Yale University Press.

————. 1998. *Power in Movement: Social Movements and Contentious Politics.* 2nd ed. New York: Cambridge University Press.

Taylor, Verta. 1989. "Social Movement Continuity: The Women's Movement in Abeyance." *American Sociological Review* 54: 761-775.

Tilly, Charles. 2000. "Spaces of Contention." *Mobilization* 5: 135-159.

Tuchman, Gaye. 1978. *Making News*. New York: Free Press.

Turner, Ralph, and Lewis Killian. 1957. *Collective Behavior*. Englewood Cliffs, NJ: Prentice-Hall.

Wallack, Lawrence, Lori Dorfman, David Jernigan, and Makani Themba. 1993. *Media Advocacy and Public Health.* Newbury Park, CA: Sage.

Washington, James M., ed. 1986. *A Testament of Hope: The Essential Writings and Speeches of Martin Luther King, Jr.* San Francisco: HarperCollins.

Whittier, Nancy. 2002. "Meaning and Structure in Social Movements." Pp. 289-308 in *Social Movements: Identity, Culture, and the State*, David S. Meyer, Nancy Whittier, and Belinda Robnett, eds. New York: Oxford University Press.

Wilson, John. 1973. *Introduction to Social Movements*. New York: Basic Books.

Zald, Mayer. 1996. "Culture, Ideology, and Strategic Framing." Pp. 261-274 in *Comparative Perspectives on Social Movements: Political Opportunities, Mobilizing Structures, and Cultural Framings*, Doug McAdam, John D. McCarthy, and Mayer N. Zald, eds. Cambridge: Cambridge University Press.

Zdravomyslova, Elena. 1996. "Opportunities and Framing in the Transition to Democracy: The Case of Russia." Pp. 122-137 in *Comparative Perspectives on Social Movements: Political Opportunities, Mobilizing Structures, and Cultural Framings*, Doug McAdam, John D. McCarthy, and Mayer N. Zald, eds. Cambridge: Cambridge University Press.

Zuo, Jiping, and Robert Benford. 1995. "Mobilization Processes and the 1989 Chinese Democracy Movement." *Sociological Quarterly* 36: 131-135.

Part I

Framing and Mobilization Processes

Chapter 2

EXPLAINING SUFFRAGE MOBILIZATION: BALANCE, NEUTRALIZATION, AND RANGE IN COLLECTIVE ACTION FRAMES

Lyndi Hewitt and Holly J. McCammon

Recruitment is a crucial task for social movements. However, only a few studies demonstrate how framing activities influence a movement's capacity to draw participants (Diani 1996; Jasper and Poulsen 1995; Johnston 1991; Koopmans and Duyvendak 1995; McCammon 2001; Noonan 1995; Zuo and Benford 1995). Moreover, existing studies focus primarily on the role of frame resonance, while neglecting other frame characteristics that may influence recruitment. Existing work also tends to analyze a single mobilization attempt, rather than investigating positive and negative mobilization outcomes within the same movement over time. Thus, it has been difficult to discern what kinds of frames contribute to successful or failed attempts at organizing, and, importantly, *why* they do so.

Our study focuses on the impact of framing activity on a movement's capacity to organize new members. We draw on data from the U.S. state woman suffrage movements to provide a comparison of the mobilizing capacities of different collective action frames. Rather than assuming that all frames utilized in a successful mobilization outcome contribute equally to success, we attempt to distinguish between effective and ineffective frames used by a movement. Our explanations as to the differential mobilizing capacities of these frames help illuminate the specific qualities of frames that do and do not lead to successful recruitment.

We utilize cross-sectional time series data on the state woman suffrage movements from 1892 to 1919 to investigate the complex set of factors influencing the recruitment of movement participants. Our dependent variable is annual membership in the state suffrage organizations. Because we analyze data from the U.S. states over twenty-eight years rather than a single successful campaign, we can examine the predictors of both positive and negative mobilization outcomes, making our analysis a more systematic assessment of a frame's mobilizing capacity. As we theorize the impact of framing efforts on organizing, we consider the role of cultural resonance (Snow and Benford 1988) in attracting participants to the movement.

Unlike most of the existing research on framing, we also move beyond a focus simply on cultural resonance. We recognize that the great challenge for movement actors is to construct frames so that they simultaneously resonate with *and contest* elements of the broader cultural and political environment. For collective action frames to succeed in organizing potential recruits, they must strike the appropriate *balance* between resonating with the existing cultural repertoire and challenging the status quo. By balance, we suggest that if a frame either fails to draw adequately on dominant belief systems or mounts too great a challenge to them, it runs the risk of alienating potential recruits. Therefore, we test the hypothesis that when movements deploy frames that both draw effectively on "existing ideational materials in their societies" (Tarrow 1992: 175) and articulate a reconfiguration of prevailing relations, more favorable mobilization outcomes will be achieved.

Furthermore, we examine two additional characteristics of collective action frames that have been theorized but rarely studied empirically. The first is the capacity of a frame to neutralize the frames of rival groups. When movements deploy frames, they must consider the arguments of their opposition and attempt to respond in ways that undermine them (Benford 1987; Benford and Hunt 2003). Frames that effectively rebut or neutralize the claims of countermovements will be more likely to attract participants. The second feature is the breadth of issues addressed by a frame. Gerhards and Rucht (1992: 580) hypothesize that "the larger the range of problems covered by a frame, the larger the range of social groups that can be addressed with the frame and the greater the mobilization capacity of the frame." Our study will therefore also compare the mobilizing capacity of frames based on the range of issues addressed.

In the sections that follow, we first provide a discussion of three dominant collective action frames used by the suffragists and then review the extant literature on mobilization processes. We consider three theoretical models—framing, resource mobilization, and structural and cultural opportunity—and discuss how their insights help us understand the dynamics of participant mobilization in the state suffrage movements. We demonstrate that although resources and broader opportunities contribute to fluctuations in organizational membership, the use of collective action frames plays a critical role in a movement's ability to organize new members, independent of these factors. Furthermore, we show that the frames with the greatest mobilizing capacity are those which maintain a balance between resonance with and opposition to existing cultural values, respond effectively to frames of the countermovement, and address a broad range of related problems. We then conclude by discussing the implications of our findings for future research on the efficacy of collective action frames and their influence on movement organizing.

SUFFRAGE MOVEMENT FRAMES

Our study focuses on the differential impact of three collective frames used by suffragists as they worked at the turn of the twentieth century to win voting rights for women. We include the following frames in our analysis: justice, societal reform, and home protection.[1] By far, these were the frames most commonly used by suffrage activists[2] (Kraditor [1965] 1981; McCammon, Hewitt, and Smith 2004); therefore, we limit our discussion to these dominant frames. Here, we simply introduce the content of the frames. Below, as we discuss framing theory, we develop our hypotheses about which of these frames should have had the most potent influence on recruiting new members.

The justice frame used by the suffragists consisted of rhetoric emphasizing natural rights and women's equality with men. Suffragists argued that women deserved the right to vote because they were men's equals and, therefore, had an equal right to representation. Often, these frames drew on language from the American Revolution, the Declaration of Independence, and other sources of democratic ideals. In these ways, the justice frame tapped into deeply resonant American values; but in other ways, it represented a radical challenge to prevailing beliefs about the role of women in society (DuBois 1998). The justice frame held that women should be equal players in politics, with voting rights and thus a formal voice in political affairs. This contradicted contemporary beliefs that women's place was not in politics but in the home. Various examples of the justice frame can be found in table 2.1.

Both the societal reform and home protection frames, in contrast, encompassed a set of arguments that were much more conservative with respect to gender roles. The rhetoric focused not on women's sameness with men, as justice arguments did, but rather on their differences from men. Emphasis was placed on women's special qualities, such as their domestic sense, their nurturing abilities, and their moral superiority over men. With the reform and home protection frames, the suffragists argued that women should have a role in politics because they knew how to care for people, including the poor, the troubled, and (especially) children.

The reform and home protection frames differed in one important respect. While the home protection frame firmly maintained women's place in the private domestic sphere, the reform frame invited women to use their unique attributes to enter the public sphere. In particular, the narrow language of the home protection frame focused on how enfranchisement would help women be better wives and mothers and protect their homes and children. The reform frame, on the other hand, highlighted women's ability to initiate necessary societal reforms and to "purify politics" with the vote. And in this way, the reform frame addressed a much broader array of problems in society—such as drunkenness, poverty, urban ills, and political corruption—than did the home protection frame. To use Williams's (1995) language, the home protection frame did not "construct the public good" in the same way that the reform frame did. However, neither of these frames contested traditional gender ideology to the same extent as did the justice argument. Instead, they relied on deeply held beliefs about gender, that women were different from men, possessing distinct nurturing and purifying qualities. But at the same time, both the reform and home protection frames still challenged conventional wisdom simply by asserting that women should have the vote. We provide examples of the reform and home protection frames in table 2.1 as well.

FRAMING, RESOURCE MOBILIZATION, AND OPPORTUNITIES

Explanations of social movement emergence and development have consistently been dominated by resource mobilization approaches (Gamson 1990; McCarthy and

Table 2.1 Selective Suffrage Activists' Quotations Illustrating Justice, Societal Reform, and Home Protection Frames, from Various States

Justice Frames

Louisiana (1913) "[Suffrage is a] birth right of an American citizen" (Lindig 1982).

Iowa (1886) "[We] demand the ballot for women, not as a privilege, or as an experiment, but as the inalienable right of every citizen irrespective of sex, in a government based on the consent of the governed . . ." (NAWSA 1886).

Arkansas (1892) ". . . women should be allowed to vote because they [are] subject to the laws of the land and should have a voice in their making" (Taylor 1956).

Connecticut (1911) "The disenfranchisement of any human being because of sex is an absolute injustice" (NAWSA 1911).

Societal Reform Frames

Minnesota (1914) "[Woman suffrage is] a tool for bringing about social betterment" (Stuhler 1995).

New York (1909) "There is a great deal of municipal housekeeping to be done which women can do far better than men" (NAWSA 1909).

Tennessee (1912) "Give us the ballot. We deserve it. We are capable of using it for the good of the country" (Taylor 1943).

Colorado (1882) ". . . if woman had the ballot in her hands it would not be many years before the mighty power of the liquor interest would tremble . . ." (Marilley 1996).

Home Protection Frames

Arizona (1912) ". . . the ballot for women is desired not as a means of diversion but as a weapon by which they can obtain . . . greater opportunities for the home" (Tisdale 1965).

Illinois (1906) "The women who do the housekeeping and manage the homes of the community should have some voice as to the conditions under which they must manage those homes" (NAWSA 1906).

Mississippi (1895) ". . . women needed the ballot for protection of the home" (Taylor 1992).

Texas (1914) "It is no more than right that the mother should have a voice in stating what should be done to protect her home, her family's food, and her family's surrounding" (McArthur 1992).

Wolfson 1996) and political process perspectives (Amenta, Carruthers, and Zylan 1992; McAdam 1982; Tarrow 1989). More recently, however, research emphasizing the cultural aspects of social movements has gained considerable momentum (Johnston and Klandermans 1995; McAdam 1994; Morris and Mueller 1992). Specifically, frame alignment processes lie at the forefront of this shift. Benford and Snow (2000: 612) state that "framing processes have come to be regarded, alongside resource mobilization and political opportunity processes, as a central dynamic in understanding the character and course of social movements." It is with this in mind that we present our primary theoretical argument.

Framing Activity: Resonance/Opposition/Balance, Neutralization, and Range

Snow and colleagues (1986, 1988) define framing as the process through which movement actors engage in interpretive work to produce and maintain meaning for movement participants and potential supporters, as well as antagonists. Collective action frames, then, are "action-oriented sets of beliefs and meanings that inspire and legitimate the activities and campaigns of a social movement organization" (Benford and Snow 2000: 614). Using the innovative conceptual tools provided by Snow, Benford, and others (for example, Gerhards and Rucht 1992), a number of scholars have undertaken research addressing a range of important questions regarding the relationship between framing and social movements. Unfortunately, a large portion of existing empirical research remains at the level of description, leaving numerous key issues unresolved. As Benford and Snow (2000) tell us, much time has been spent identifying and discussing the various types of frames and their characteristics, as well as the political and cultural constraints faced by movement actors who seek to deploy effective frames. Far less attention has been devoted to analysis of the consequences of framing activity, including its effects on movement participation.

Prior to the popularization of the framing perspective, Klandermans (1984: 584) noted that "the efficacy of a mobilization campaign in persuading the individual is a key determinant of participation." Furthermore, McAdam, McCarthy and Zald (1988) acknowledge that participants in collective action are ultimately motivated at the cognitive level. Framing processes serve as the primary means of persuasion and cognitive communication with potential recruits. As such, it is surprising that more research has not critically examined the mobilizing capacity of collective action frames. Important questions regarding the characteristics of persuasive, effective frames remain unanswered.

Despite the paucity of attention devoted to this topic, a few noteworthy studies suggest that *frame resonance* is closely linked to successful organizing, and in so doing these studies have broken important new ground. Snow and Benford (1988) tell us that frames must be central (i.e., salient), be credible (i.e., verifiable), and have "narrative fidelity" in order to achieve resonance with their intended targets. Additionally, Williams (1995) and Williams and Kubal (1999) note the importance of a frame's consistency with the available cultural resources (see Tarrow 1992 and Gamson 1988 for similar claims). Their discussions speak to the fact that not all frames are equal; frames with particular qualities are more likely to "strike a responsive chord" with the masses (Snow and Benford 1988: 207) and therefore to mobilize more participants. Jasper and Poulsen (1995) distinguish between the processes necessary to mobilize friends and those necessary to mobilize strangers. In their examination of recruitment in the animal rights and antinuclear movements, they argue that framing is a crucial mechanism in recruiting strangers because the movement must tap into beliefs the potential recruit already holds. Their evidence ultimately suggests that the cultural resonance of frames is a major explanatory factor of recruitment. Diani (1996) provides further insight in his research on the populist movement in Italy. He highlights the necessity of frames demonstrating congruence with existing master frames, and thus the prevailing political context, in order to mobilize participants effectively. Other research on the importance of consistency between frames and the broader cultural and political themes include

Noonan's (1995) account of the Chilean women's movement, Johnston's (1991) analysis of Catalan national opposition, and Zuo and Benford's (1995) study of the Chinese democracy movement. All of these suggest that a frame's success or failure lies in its resonance.

Because researchers have focused so intensely on the resonance factor, the oppositional nature of frames has been underemphasized. But we know that in order to persuade potential recruits to join a movement, collective action frames must not simply resonate with existing belief systems, but also mount a meaningful challenge to prevailing ideology. For instance, Zuo and Benford (1995: 139) describe the dilemma of student activists in the Chinese democracy movement as a "dangerous tightrope"; they faced the task of constructing frames that resonated with Chinese citizens through a challenge to the government, but that also were firmly grounded in familiar cultural narratives so as to avoid the risk of state repression. McAdam (1994: 38) notes that the efficacy of Martin Luther King, Jr.'s, civil rights framing lay in his ability to tap into both the "culture of the oppressed" and the "culture of the oppressor." It is reasonable to assume that there are two instances when a frame's mobilizing capacity will be decreased: (1) when it resonates well with existing values but fails to pose a cogent oppositional argument or (2) when it voices a meaningful challenge to dominant structures but fails to tap into widely held beliefs. The overriding point here is that persuasive frames are neither solely resonant nor solely radical. *Balance* between resonant and oppositional elements must be achieved in order for movements to attract supporters effectively through framing. This principle of balance, rather than resonance alone, guides our expectations regarding the impact of the justice, societal reform, and home protection frames on membership in the state suffrage associations.

We noted earlier that the reform and home protection frames, in spite of their resonance with traditional gender beliefs, still constituted a challenge to the political system by asserting that women should have political rights. At the turn of the twentieth century, women possessed limited political agency. Arguing that they deserved a formal political voice, at the time, was an argument that challenged existing beliefs, regardless of the reasoning behind the argument. Thus the reform and home protection frames simultaneously resonated with and contested existing gender ideology. This balance, we argue, increased their mobilizing potential. We do emphasize, though, that the reform frame embodied a stronger opposition to dominant beliefs about gender than did the home protection frame. While the reform frame rejected the public/private dichotomy, the home protection frame maintained the notion of separate public and private spheres, as well as the proper place of men and women in those spheres. We expect that the more challenging message of the reform frame provided an even more favorable balance than that of the home protection frame, which may not have been challenging enough.

The justice frame, on the other hand, put forward a radical and more oppositional argument, because it rejected prevailing gender roles entirely. Although it did contain elements of salient American ideals in that it emphasized freedom, democracy, and rights, we argue that the justice argument was not balanced in the same way in which the reform and home protection frames were. The justice frame consisted of too much opposition (in short, it was tilted in that direction) when it did not acknowledge and reinforce the widely held belief that women's place was in the home and in the role of caring for others. Moreover, although the justice frame relied on democratic themes, we speculate that these ideals were, for many individuals, somewhat abstract and removed from daily living, while traditional gender beliefs about women's and men's appropriate roles were experienced routinely on a day-to-day basis by most citizens (see Snow and Benford's 1988 discussion of centrality and experiential commensurability). The ideological source of the justice frame's resonance (democratic beliefs), may have been less salient to potential activists than that of the reform and home protection frames (women's nurturing roles). For these reasons, then, we believe the mobilizing potential of the justice frame is hindered compared to that of the reform and home protection frames.

We propose that other dimensions of frames must be considered to understand fully their potential to aid organizing efforts. In addition to the balance between resonant and oppositional elements of frames, we examine two other qualities of frames and framing that have been theorized but not yet empirically demonstrated to influence the mobilization of movement recruits. These are (1) the degree to which a movement utilizes arguments that will *neutralize* the frames deployed by an opposition movement and (2) the degree to which a frame encompasses a variety or *range* of issues that may appeal to individuals and groups (Benford and Hunt 2003; Gerhards and Rucht 1992). Both of these characteristics, we argue, enhance the mobilizing capacity of frames.

Benford (1987), Benford and Hunt (2003), and Klandermans (1992) note that the arguments of a countermovement constrain movement framing. The movement and countermovement become part of a cultural struggle in which each is forced to address the claims of the other. In such a struggle, movement actors cannot simply ignore the arguments of their opposition, but rather must find ways to counter, combat, and/or reframe the claims of their opponents (Benford and Hunt 2003).

Building on this logic, we argue that the reform and home protection frames will demonstrate greater capacity to organize participants than the justice frame for another reason: they more effectively neutralized a prominent frame used by the anti-suffragists, the groups that organized explicitly in opposition to the suffragists' attempts to win the ballot. Marshall (1986) demonstrates that an ideology of separate spheres underlay the vast majority of antisuffragist rhetoric. That is, the anti-suffragists held that a gendered division of labor and a distinct delineation between public and private spheres were the result of natural, immutable law. They argued that women should remain in the home, and should be content to do so, while men belonged in the public (including political) sphere. The justice frame did not successfully address these claims of the antisuffragists, given that it failed to acknowledge women's traditional roles at all, but simply asserted that women belonged as well in the public sphere.

Conversely, the reform and home protection frames were antidotes to voices of the countermovement in that they provided a plausible alternative view of women's roles. A woman could fruitfully participate in politics, the suffragists argued with the reform and home protection frames. She did not have to remain isolated in the domestic sphere. By bringing her unique womanly abilities and knowledge into politics, she could improve both home life and society. This logic, inherent in the suffragists' reform and home protection frames, provided a potent counterargument to the antisuffragists' separate-spheres rhetoric in that it highlighted the utility of women's traditional contributions in the public sphere. The use of this logic, we argue, is likely to have augmented the suffragists' ability to organize participants.

Finally, we consider a third aspect of the suffragist frames that influenced their ability to recruit new members. Gerhards and Rucht (1992) suggest that frames addressing a wide (but interrelated) range of issues will have greater mobilizing capacity than those addressing a narrow set of issues, simply because the chances are increased that those on the receiving end of the frame will find a place to "latch on" to the frame. Potential activists may find more compelling impetus to action in frames that cover a diverse set of social problems, assuming the problems are conceptually linked to one another (e.g., the problems are all consequences of the same flawed social system). Generally speaking, then, the range or breadth of a collective action frame will aid organizing efforts.

We believe that the reform frame may have had a stronger effect on mobilizing new members than the home protection frame due to the wide range of issues the reform frame addressed. While the home protection frame concentrated on how women could protect the home and their children with the vote, the reform frame encompassed a wide range of social issues when it argued that women would improve society with the vote. Women would, the frame held, reduce corruption in government; bring about temperance; improve schools, workplaces, and prisons; lessen poverty; improve sanitation in cities; reduce infant mortality; end wars; and cure a variety of sexual vices. A greater number of individuals were likely to find their beliefs and goals included in this broad frame, more so than they were in the narrower home protection frame, which focused only on women's ability to influence the private sphere. Thus, we found that more individuals were persuaded to join the suffrage cause by the reform frame than by the home protection frame. In short, more people could find their niche in the movement by way of the reform frame.

In sum, then, we propose a hierarchy of effectiveness for the justice, societal reform, and home protection frames, with the reform frame most capable of mobilizing suffrage recruits, the justice frame least capable, and the home protection frame residing between the other two in terms of its mobilizing capacity.

Resource Mobilization and Political Opportunities

Social movement researchers have repeatedly documented the role of resources in facilitating mobilization (Jenkins and Perrow 1977; Jenkins 1983; McAdam, McCarthy, and Zald 1988; McCarthy and Zald 1977; Tilly 1978). Monetary resources, labor power, organization, and communication are all vital factors in determining not only movement emergence but also development and levels of future mobilization. Movements that possess higher resource levels are better equipped to recruit new participants and sustain their organizations than movements that are resource-poor.

McCarthy and Wolfson (1996) and McCammon (2001) find that agency (i.e., amount of effort), strategy, and organizational structure are key predictors of membership growth. Following their example, we consider whether or not suffragists were engaged in organizing and fundraising activities. We expect that when suffrage activists exerted more effort to organize and raise funds, membership increased. Additionally, we examine the possibility that different public speaking strategies may have differentially appealed to potential supporters by assessing the impact of both formal and informal speaking events on membership. Sometimes the suffragists gave formal speeches in public halls, which were announced in advance and usually required an entrance fee. On other occasions, particularly in the later years of the movement, the suffragists relied on less-formal means of interacting with the public. They gave street speeches, sometimes from the backseats of roofless automobiles and sometimes simply on soapboxes. These were, from the public's point of view, impromptu actions. They were designed to appeal to people going about their daily activities in the public sphere. These informal activities may have been more effective in recruiting new members because they brought suffragists into contact more with the general public—many of whom, no doubt, had not thought about women's voting rights. In contrast, formal speaking engagements may have simply exposed suffragists to the already converted.

Finally, we take into account two other factors, resource allocation from the National American Woman Suffrage Association (NAWSA) and the age of the state organization. It is likely that an influx of financial and other resources from NAWSA would have contributed to organizations' ability to recruit new members. The same should be true for organizational age; older organizations should be more experienced and capable in recruiting new members.

Scholars have also been careful to consider the broader political and cultural context in which movement actors must function (Kriesi et al. 1992; McAdam, McCarthy, and Zald 1996; Tarrow 1994). For example, support by political elites can signal to potential participants an increased likelihood of movement success. By decreasing the perceived costs of joining a movement, elite endorsement can function to increase membership or facilitate mobilization. We therefore investigate whether public endorsement by elites in state political parties had a positive impact on participant mobilization. Additionally, we examine the possibility that passage of suffrage legislation in neighboring states may have increased membership. Political successes for nearby movements would likely have sent a hopeful and positive message to potential recruits.

McCammon, Campbell, Granberg, and Mowery (2001) also alert us to the influences that gendered opportunity structures have on movement success. As women entered the labor force in increasing rates, the strict delineation between public and private spheres softened somewhat, removing a barrier to women's participation in the movement.[3] World War I also catalyzed a major cultural shift and pushed women into new roles in the public sphere, as women filled in for the many men who left public service and employment to fight the war (Flexner 1975). This, too, may have resulted in a greater pool of women willing to join suffrage organizations. Thus, we consider the impact of both women's labor force participation and World War I in our model of suffrage mobilization.

An additional structural opportunity is what Staggenborg terms a "critical event" (1993). Her analysis of mobilization in the pro-choice movement suggests that policy outcomes can serve as critical events that catalyze or depress participation. Her data reveal that favorable policy outcomes for the pro-choice movement tended to boost mobilization in the pro-life movement; conversely, favorable policy outcomes for the pro-life movement tended to boost mobilization in the pro-choice movement. Thus, we examine the influence of failed suffrage legislation on suffrage organizational membership. Finally, we assess the degree to which levels of antisuffrage mobilization affected the suffrage movement. It may be the case that when anti-suffrage activists were more organized, membership in state suffrage organizations declined.

DATA AND METHODS

Because we are interested in explaining variation in the success of movement organizing both over time and across states, we utilize cross-sectional time series analysis. Our unit of analysis is thus the state-year. We estimate our model using ordinary least squares (OLS) regression with panel-corrected standard errors (Beck and Katz 1995).[4] This method enables us to produce more efficient estimates of the standard errors and thus more accurate statistical tests. We include a lagged endogenous variable in the model in order to reduce the possibility of serial correlation and also to account for what Ostrom (1990) refers to as "bureaucratic momentum," that is, that organizational membership from the previous year is likely to impact membership in the current year. In other models not shown here, we used a Cochrane-Orcutt transformation to correct for possible first-order autocorrelation; however, because no autocorrelation appears to be present in our model, and standard errors were nearly identical, we present only the simpler OLS model here. Additionally, we tested for multicollinearity among the explanatory variables, but found no such problem.

Membership in State Suffrage Organizations

Our analysis of movement organizing spans the years 1892 to 1919. The earlier year is the first for which data on state suffrage association membership are available from the National American Woman Suffrage Association annual proceedings (NAWSA 1893-1920). The final year is when the U.S. Congress passed the Nineteenth Amendment on women's voting rights.

Our dependent variable is a measure of the number of members in the state suffrage association divided by the size of the state's population (NAWSA 1893-1920, U.S. Bureau of the Census 1975). Suffragists across the United States organized in state-level suffrage associations with names like the "Pennsylvania Woman Suffrage Association." In every case except Wyoming (which had no state association and thus is not included in our analysis), the state organization formally affiliated with the National American Woman Suffrage Association, and in almost all cases the affiliation was for most of the life span of the state suffrage association. The state organizations paid dues to NAWSA, ten cents per year per member, and NAWSA published, beginning in 1892, the total amount of dues paid by the states to the national headquarters. We use this information to construct a measure of membership in the state-level suffrage movements. Table 2.2 provides the membership data aggregated for the whole United States, both absolute membership and membership per 10,000 in the general population (the latter measure, at the state level, we use in our analysis). While, as Banaszak (1996) points out, these measures are not a perfect representation of the state memberships, they are the best available measures,[5] in that their fluctuations over time fit well with the overall historical record that traces the vicissitudes of strength in the state suffrage movements (e.g., Buechler 1986; Gullet 2000; McBride 1993; Wheeler 1993). Because the NAWSA data do not begin until 1892, the earliest years of the state suffrage movements, from just after the Civil War until 1891, cannot be examined with these data. However, the period for which data are available represents the critical era of suffrage movement growth and ultimately political success (Graham 1996). Study of this period helps us understand how the suffragists mobilized new members and particularly how suffrage framing efforts worked to increase membership.

Explanatory Variables

Most of our independent variables, which are also measures of various aspects of the state suffrage movements are drawn from a larger data set on the U.S. state woman suffrage movements compiled by McCammon, Campbell, Granberg, and Mowery (2001) and McCammon, Hewitt, and Smith (2004). For the details of how

Table 2.2 Membership in state suffrage associations, 1892-1919*

Year	Absolute Membership	Members per 10,000 in population
1892	5,576	58.9
1893	7,240	78.1
1894	8,195	93.8
1895	7,732	77.1
1896	10,501	106.8
1897	19,871	229.6
1898	8,846	68.3
1899	9,148	54.9
1900	9,910	60.4
1901	10,314	67.7
1902	12,402	88.4
1903	12,584	80.2
1904	15,499	95.4
1905	16,003	95.8
1906	16,544	91.5
1907	16,723	86.4
1908	17,608	93.9
1909	15,895	79.5
1910	19,013	87.5
1911	26,878	133.6
1912	34,742	177.7
1913	45,558	291.7
1914	65,947	442.4
1915	53,320	275.5
1916	59,765	281.0
1917	56,016	260.7
1918	46,665	230.5
1919	68,985	337.1

* Membership figures are high in 1897 due to a concerted effort by NAWSA officials to collect dues from delinquent members. Our membership figures are based on dues paid by the states. The absence of mention of such an effort in years just after 1897 suggests that they did not continue this policy in following years (NAWSA 1899-1905).

these state-level movement measures were collected, see McCammon et al. 2001 and McCammon and Campbell 2001. Suffice it here to say that an exhaustive content analysis of over 650 secondary sources on the state movements was combined with archival research for a number of states in order to construct a myriad of measures of the various state movements. Unless stated otherwise below, all of our independent variables, including our framing measures, come from this larger suffrage data set.

We include in our analysis three measures of suffrage framing. Each is a count of the number of times the particular frame (justice, reform, or home protection) was used in the particular state and year. We measured the use of these suffrage frames from secondary and primary historical accounts of suffrage speech acts. We define a speech act as a written or verbal argument publicly offered by a suffragist for why women should have voting rights. These speech acts included formal and informal public speeches, newspaper columns, banners carried in parades, and leaflets or handbills distributed to the public. Because our data could include every speech act in which a suffrage activist utilized one of these frames, we also used dichotomous measures of the presence or absence of each frame in a given state-year in models not shown here. Differences in the model results, however, were negligible. To reiterate, justice frames emphasize women's equality with men, their inalienable right to the vote, or other rationales for the vote deriving from democratic principles. Reform and home protection frames emphasize differences between men and women, with reform frames focusing on the ways women would improve society as a whole with the vote, while home protection frames emphasizing how women would use the vote to protect their homes and families. Each measure is lagged one year in the analysis in order to exclude reverse causality from the analysis—namely that changes in membership influenced suffragist frame construction. We are confident that the variety of data sources used to construct these framing measures ensures that the various arguments of suffragists are well represented in the data sources. More than one researcher participated in the content analysis to create these frame measures (McCammon, Hewitt, and Smith 2004), and Krippendorff's (1980) alpha for interrater reliability equals .82.[6]

We measure the suffrage movements' resource mobilization with six variables. First, we construct a measure of whether the suffragists in a state engaged in organizing activities in a given year. Organizing activities include attempts by organizers to recruit new members, social events (e.g., banquets, teas, and picnics) designed to attract potential recruits, and suffrage conventions to which the general public was invited. The variable is a count of whether one, two, or all three of these practices were employed. Second, we include a measure of whether the state movement engaged in fundraising in a given year—more funds could be used to recruit new members. This measure equals one if fundraising took place and zero otherwise. Third, we include an additional dichotomous measure indicating whether NAWSA sent resources (typically financial resources, but sometimes pamphlets and other written materials for distribution) to the state movement. Our fourth and fifth resource mobilization measures allow us to gauge the impact of two broad types of suffrage strategies on membership levels: formal and informal speech giving. Each of the measures is a dichotomous indicator equal to one if the type of strategy was used and zero otherwise. Our final indicator of resource mobilization is a measure of the age (in years) of the state suffrage organization. It is a countermeasure beginning with the year after the state organization was formed.

We measure structural opportunities in the broader movement environment with six variables. A political opportunity for movement mobilization is indicated with a measure of endorsements of woman suffrage by the political parties, including the Democratic, Republican, and various third parties. The variable is a count of the number of such endorsements received by the suffragists. A gendered opportunity for movement mobilization is measured with the proportion of the labor force that is female (Lee et al. 1957). Staggenborg's (1993) notion of a critical event is captured with a measure of whether suffrage (full or partial suffrage, such as presidential or primary suffrage) was defeated in the previous year by a legislative vote or referendum. The variable equals one if such a defeat occurred and zero otherwise. The opportunity for boosting membership brought about by the passage of suffrage in a neighboring state (and thus the concomitant promise of success in the particular state) is indicated with a measure of the proportion of neighboring states having passed full or partial suffrage by the previous year. World War I is measured with a dichotomous variable equal to one for years the nation was at war (1917-1919). The variable equals zero otherwise. The presence of antisuffragists is measured at the state level. The measure equals one if out-of-state antisuffragists were present, two if a few of them were active, and three if an antisuffragist organization existed. The measure equals zero otherwise.

We also include a dichotomous variable that is equal to one if the year is 1897, and zero otherwise. We use this variable to gauge whether NAWSA's policy actions concerning dues in that year affect our measure of membership.

RESULTS

The results of OLS regression analyses examining the influence of framing, resource mobilization, and political opportunity factors on membership in state suffrage organizations are shown in table 2.3. The R-squared value of .57 indicates that we were able to explain a reasonable portion of the variation in membership over time. Generally, our results suggest that framing activity, resources, and political opportunities all play an important role in determining the mobilization of participants. Below, we discuss each of these influences in detail.

We turn first to the impact of framing on organizational membership. The use of the reform frame significantly increased membership in the state suffrage associations, net of other factors. When the suffragists argued that if women had the vote, they could reform society, membership in their organizations rose. However, we found no such effect for either the justice or the home protection frame. When the suffragists argued that women were men's political equals and thus should have the right to vote, or when they argued that women could take better care of their homes with the vote, membership did not increase. Thus, our hypothesis is supported about the reform frame's potency. However, our results for the justice and home protection frames do not show a difference in their mobilizing capacities; neither augmented membership. Rather than finding a hierarchy of mobilizing capacity, where the reform framed outperformed the home protection frame, which outperformed the justice frame, we found that only the reform frame helped the suffragists build their organizations. We discuss the implications of these findings in the conclusion.

As expected, several of the resource measures positively influenced organizational membership. Our results indicate that suffragists' engagement in either organizing or fundraising activities contributed to increases in membership. Our findings are therefore consistent with those of McCarthy and Wolfson (1996) and McCammon (2001)—that amount of effort is positively related to membership recruitment. Strategy was also an important factor in determining membership levels. While formal speech making had no effect, we found that informal speech making was an effective form of communicating and drawing participants into the movement. These informal strategies may have been more effective for the suffragists because they allowed the suffragists to go where the people were (in city streets, parks, and the like). The suffragists did not have to wait for the people to come to them (as occurred when the suffragists gave a formal lecture in a lecture hall). Although the formal strategies may have invited the already converted, the informal strategies allowed the suffragists opportunities to appeal to those less familiar with the suffrage cause. The final two measures of resource mobilization, the receipt of resources from NAWSA and the longevity of an organization, had no influence on participant mobilization. That is, membership levels were not affected one way or the other when the state organizations received funds or other resources from the national organization nor were they affected by the age of the organization.

Table 2.3 OLS Regression Coefficients for Factors Influencing Membership in State Suffrage Organizations, 1892-1919.

Independent Variables	Unstandardized Coefficients	Standard Errors (Panel-Corrected)
Collective Action Frames		
Justice (lagged)	- .17	.16
Societal reform (lagged)	.75**	.27
Home protection (lagged)	- .22	.27
Resource Mobilization		
Organizing	.59**	.17
Fundraising	.91**	.34
Formal speeches	- .15	.27
Informal speeches	1.46**	.51
Resources from national	.17	.26
Age of organization	- .02	.01
Opportunities		
Political endorsement (lagged)	.71**	.22
Women's labor force participation	5.86*	2.51
Suffrage defeat (lagged)	- .51	.29
Proportion of neighboring states that passed suffrage	5.40**	1.91
World War I	.74	.64
Presence of antisuffrage organizations	- .07	.13
Controls		
Membership (lagged)	.81**	.09
1897	2.26*	1.10
Constant	-1.67	.72
Wald chi-square	377.69**	
R-squared	.57	
N	1,134	

*p < .05   **p < .01   (two-tailed tests)

We next consider the influence of political opportunities on membership in state suffrage organizations. The results show that when political elites came out in public support of suffrage, membership increased. Likewise, a higher proportion of neighboring states having passed presidential, primary, or full suffrage also had a positive effect on membership. It is likely that each of these events in the broader political environment removed barriers to participation by convincing potential recruits that the time was right for change, thus positively influencing overall membership. As we expected, gendered opportunity also played a key role in boosting membership. As the number of women participating in the labor force increased, so too did membership in state suffrage organizations. We also examined three other variables measuring opportunities. Neither recent legislative defeats, World War I, nor the activity of antisuffragist organizations had a significant impact, either positive or negative, on organizational membership.[7]

Finally, both our control measures, the lagged endogenous variable and the dichotomous variable for 1897, were significant. Membership in state suffrage organizations during a given year was thus influenced by membership during the previous year. Additionally, NAWSA policies designed to enforce dues payments in 1897 increased the reported membership levels for that particular year.

DISCUSSION AND CONCLUSION

We set out to assess the impact of collective action frames on movement organizing and to identify characteristics of frames that result in differential levels of efficacy for the purposes of recruiting. In the end, our investigation reveals two important and related findings. First, the deployment of effective collective action frames can and does exert an independent and direct effect on movement organizing. We find that even with various measures of movement resources and structural and cultural opportunities in our model, framing activity plays a crucial and independent role in recruitment. Thus, movement actors striving to organize supporters should carefully and strategically consider the collective action frames they choose to deploy.

Second, and more importantly, our results show that the efficacy of collective action frames is dependent on particular qualities or characteristics of the frames. The degree to which frames (1) provide a balanced (i.e., culturally resonant and oppositional) message, (2) neutralize the frames of opponents, and (3) encompass a broad array of issues increases their capacity for organizing support. The reform frame fulfills each of these criteria, while the justice and home protection frames do not, and thus, as our results show, only the reform frame helped the suffragists increase their organizational membership.

The fact that the reform frame significantly increased membership in state suffrage organizations, while neither the justice nor the home protection frames had any effect, suggests an important point about cultural resonance. Again, movement actors must strive to construct frames that contain both resonant and oppositional elements. We propose that the reform frame represented the ideal balance between cultural resonance and contestation. While the justice frame may have gone too far in contesting gender belief systems, and the home protection frame not far enough, the reform frame achieved equilibrium. Implicit in the reform frame was the pervasive idea that women were different from men, that they possessed distinctive womanly qualities. And though the frame argued that women should have a formal voice in politics and improving society, it added that they would do so armed with their female qualities. Thus, the reform frame resonated with the widely held belief that women and men were inherently different and that women had distinct nurturing abilities, while its opposition lay in the fact that it advocated women coming out of the home and into the public sphere to reform society. This oppositional stance to existing gender relations was not as clearly stated in the home protection frame. This is a critical difference between the reform and home protection frames and may, at least in part, explain the greater appeal of the reform frame. That is, women who were willing to join the suffrage movement would likely have been drawn to the idea that women could play important roles in the public sphere; likewise, it is possible they could have been frustrated by the more conservative nature of the home protection frame, which limited women's roles to the private sphere. We believe our findings indicate that the balanced combination of culturally resonant and oppositional ideas accounts for the mobilizing capacity of the reform frame and the lack thereof for the justice and home protection frames.

In her recent discussion of feminist framing, Ferree (2003) suggests that collective action frames are *either* resonant *or* radical, but not both. The results of our analysis indicate that this may be a false and unnecessary dichotomy. The reform frame provides just such an illustration. The use of the reform frame was not simply an effort on the part of the suffragists to affirm existing beliefs. Considering the strict patriarchal belief systems of the time, any assertion of women's political rights was quite controversial indeed. Furthermore, our results suggest that a frame that is too radical (e.g., the justice frame), or perhaps not challenging enough (e.g., the home protection frame), will be unsuccessful in organizing participants. Frames that provide a balanced message, one that is simultaneously resonant *and* oppositional, we find, have the greatest mobilizing capacity.

Our findings also suggest that we must look to other factors besides resonance/ opposition to determine the mobilizing capacity of frames. That the reform frame, and not the justice frame, aided the suffragists in organizing supporters demonstrates that when frames rebut the arguments of their opponents, they will be more likely to attract participants. Suffragists used the reform frame to neutralize the antisuffragist claim that women should remain in the private sphere. The suffragists argued convincingly that women could use their unique nurturing qualities to make a whole host of societal improvements, assuring potential supporters of the differences between men and women. However, the reform frame also provided an alternative way to view women's traditional responsibilities. While affirming women's roles as wives, mothers, and caretakers, the suffragists expanded the roles to include care taking in society at large. And while the home protection frame could have also effectively neutralized the separate-spheres frames of the antisuffragists, it did not successfully attract movement participants. We argue that its lack of appeal resided not only in its lack of balance but also in its limited range of arguments.

The final dimension of the reform frame that contributed to its organizing success is the range of issues it addressed. Unlike the justice or the home protection frame, the reform frame covered a variety of problems deemed important in society. From political corruption to poverty to sexual vices, suffragists asserted that women could cure a myriad of social ills if only they had the vote. Also, the strength of this range lies not just in the sheer number of issues addressed but also in the fact that all of the issues fall under the rubric of the public good (see Williams 1995 for an extended discussion of constructions of the public good). The reform frame was difficult to reject because it held the promise of a society that would be improved in so many ways. This finding is particularly important because few empirical studies consider frame potency as a function of the range of issues addressed.

Our results also suggest that range may be as important a characteristic of collective action frames as balance. The fact that the reform frame had the capacity to mobilize new members, while the home protection frame did not, tells us that both balance and range in a frame are important. The reform and home protection frames differed on these two dimensions. The reform frame was both more balanced *and* had a broader range. Both balance and range appear to have played critical roles in enabling the suffragists to organize recruits.

We believe that future research on organizing must focus on comparing characteristics of collective action frames and discerning which characteristics matter for which types of consequences (e.g., recruitment, collective identity, political outcomes, changes in dominant discourse). A few studies have taken us in this direction already (Cress and Snow 2000; McCammon et al. 2001), but we have only begun to consider the numerous dimensions of framing activity that may influence social movement dynamics. More specifically, future work must go beyond the concept of cultural resonance to unpack other differential features of frames, for instance, the balance between resonance and opposition, the range of frames, and the ability of frames to neutralize the claims of opponents. Then we can examine the ways in which these aspects of frames affect social movement development.

NOTES

1. We borrow the term "home protection" from Frances Willard (Bordin 1990). Willard, a leader of the late nineteenth-century temperance movement, argued that women should be allowed to vote to protect their families and homes from intemperance.

2. Though there is evidence that the suffragists used other types of frames, none came close in prevalence to the justice, reform, and home protection frames. Our data indicate that the justice frame accounted for 30.0 percent, the societal reform frame 16.6 percent, and the home protection frame 15.3 percent of the total frames deployed between 1892 and 1919. Each was widely used throughout the period of study.

3. We should point out here that although men occasionally participated in the suffrage movements, membership in state suffrage organizations was overwhelmingly female.

4. Beck and Katz provide convincing evidence that, except in cases where T is substantially larger than N, OLS regression with panel-corrected standard errors performs better than feasible generalized least squares regression (commonly known as the Parks method). Panel-corrected standard errors are more conservative estimates and thus reduce the possibility of overconfidence.

5. The membership data are not perfect because they are influenced by the dynamics of dues paying. NAWSA, of course, wanted the state associations to pay their dues and at times instituted new policies to foster payment (see, e.g., NAWSA 1898). Such policy actions could, however, affect the membership levels reported in the annual NAWSA proceedings. We introduce a control in the analysis to assess the impact of an 1897 change in policy.

6. Our reliability measure indicates agreement in identifying frames in our textual sources. We did not compute reliability measures for identifying types of frames (i.e., for example, justice vs. reform arguments), because the coders collectively determined which type of argument(s) a speech act contained.

7. Koopmans and Duyvendak (1995) question whether framing is likely to have an independent effect on recruitment or whether the effect is mediated by political opportunity. We tested for possible interactions between framing and political opportunities, but found no evidence of such a relationship.

REFERENCES

Amenta, Edwin, Bruce G. Carruthers, and Yvonne Zylan. 1992. "A Hero for the Aged? The Townsend Movement, the Political Mediation Model, and U.S. Old-Age Policy, 1934-1950." *American Journal of Sociology* 98: 308-309.

Banaszak, Lee Ann. 1996. *Why Movements Succeed or Fail: Opportunity, Culture, and the Struggle for Woman Suffrage*. Princeton, NJ: Princeton University Press.

Beck, Nathaniel, and Jonathan N. Katz. 1995. "What to Do (and Not to Do) with Time-Series Cross-Section Data." *American Political Science Review* 89: 634-647.

Benford, Robert D. 1987. *Framing Activity, Meaning, and Social Movement Participation: The Nuclear Disarmament Movement.* Ph.D. diss., University of Texas.

Benford, Robert D., and Scott A. Hunt. 2003. "Interactional Dynamics in Public Problems Marketplaces: Movements and the Counterframing and Reframing of Public Problems." Pp. 153-186 in *Challenges and Choices: Constructionist Perspectives on Social Problems,* edited by James A. Holstein and Gale Miller. New York: Aldine de Gruyter.

Benford, Robert D., and David A. Snow. 2000. "Framing Processes and Social Movements: An Overview and Assessment." *Annual Review of Sociology* 26: 611-639.

Bordin, Ruth. 1990. *Woman and Temperance: Quest for Power and Liberty, 1873-1900.* New Brunswick, NJ: Rutgers University Press.

Buechler, Steven M. 1986. *The Transformation of the Women Suffrage Movement: The Case of Illinois, 1850-1920.* New Brunswick, NJ: Rutgers University Press.

Cress, Daniel M., and David A. Snow. 2000. "The Outcomes of Homeless Mobilization: The Influence of Organization, Disruption, Political Mediation, and Framing." *American Journal of Sociology* 105: 1063-1104.

Diani, Mario. 1996. "Linking Mobilization Frames and Political Opportunities: Insights from Regional Populism in Italy." *American Sociological Review* 61: 1053-1069.

DuBois, Ellen Carol. 1998. *Woman Suffrage and Women's Rights.* New York: New York University Press.

Ferree, Myra Marx. 2003. "Resonance and Radicalism: Feminist Framing in the Abortion Debates of the United States and Germany." *American Journal of Sociology* 109: 304-344.

Flexner, Eleanor. 1975. *Century of Struggle: The Women's Rights Movement in the United States.* Cambridge, MA: Belknap Press of Harvard University Press.

Gamson, William. 1988. "Political Discourse and Collective Action." *International Social Movement Research* 1: 219-244.

———. 1990. *The Strategy of Social Protest.* 2nd ed. Belmont, CA: Wadsworth.

Gerhards, Jurgen, and Dieter Rucht. 1992. "Mesomobilization: Organizing and Framing in Two Protest Campaigns in West Germany." *American Journal of Sociology* 98: 555-595.

Graham, Sara Hunter. 1996. *Woman Suffrage and the New Democracy.* New Haven, CT: Yale University Press.

Gullet, Gayle. 2000. *Becoming Citizens: The Emergence and Development of the California Women's Movement, 1880-1911.* Urbana: University of Illinois Press.

Jasper, James M., and Jane D. Poulsen. 1995. "Recruiting Strangers and Friends: Moral Shocks and Social Networks in Animal Rights and Anti-Nuclear Protests." *Social Problems* 32: 493-512.

Jenkins, J. Craig. 1983. "Resource Mobilization Theory and the Study of Social Movements." *Annual Review of Sociology* 9: 527-553.

Jenkins, J. Craig, and Charles Perrow. 1977. "Insurgency of the Powerless: Farm Worker Movements, 1964-1972." *American Sociological Review* 42: 249-268.

Johnston, Hank. 1991. "Antecedents of Coalition: Frame Alignment and Utilitarian Unity in the Catalan Anti-Francoist Opposition." *Research in Social Movements, Conflicts, and Change* 13: 241-259.

Johnston, Hank, and Bert Klandermans. 1995. *Social Movements and Culture.* Minneapolis: University of Minnesota Press.

Klandermans, Bert. 1984. "Mobilization and Participation: Social-Psychological Expansions of Resource Mobilization Theory." *American Sociological Review* 49: 583-600.

———. 1992. "The Social Construction of Protest and Multiorganizational Fields." Pp. 77-103 in *Frontiers in Social Movement Theory,* Aldon D. Morris and Carol McClurg Mueller, eds. New Haven, CT: Yale University Press.

Koopmans, Ruud, and Jan Willem Duyvendak. 1995. "The Political Construction of the Nuclear Energy Issue and Its Impact on the Mobilization of Anti-Nuclear Movements in Western Europe." *Social Problems* 42: 235-251.

Kraditor, Aileen. [1965] 1981. *The Ideas of the Woman Suffrage Movement*. New York: Columbia University Press.

Kriesi, Hanspeter, Ruud Koopmans, Jan Willem Duyvendak, and Marco Giugni. 1992. "New Social Movements and Political Opportunities in Western Europe." *European Journal of Political Research* 22: 219-244.

Krippendorff, Klaus. 1980. *Content Analysis: An Introduction to Its Methodology*. Beverly Hills, CA: Sage.

Lee, Everett S., Ann Rather Miller, Carol P. Brainerd, and Richard A. Easterlin. 1957. *Population Redistribution and Economic Growth in the United States, 1870-1950*. Philadelphia: American Philosophical Society.

Lindig, Carmen Meriwether. 1982. "The Woman's Movement in Louisiana, 1879-1920." Ph.D. diss., North Texas State University.

Marilley, Suzanne M. 1996. *Woman Suffrage and the Origins of Liberal Feminism in the United States, 1820-1920*. Cambridge, MA: Harvard University Press.

Marshall, Susan E. 1986. "In Defense of Separate Spheres: Class and Status Politics in the Antisuffrage Movement." *Social Forces* 65: 327-351.

McAdam, Doug. 1982. *Political Process and the Development of Black Insurgency*. Chicago: University of Chicago Press.

———. 1994. "Culture and Social Movements." Pp. 36-57 in *New Social Movements*, Enrique Laraña, Hank Johnston, and Joseph R. Gusfield, eds. Philadelphia: Temple University Press.

McAdam, Doug, John D. McCarthy, and Mayer N. Zald. 1988. "Social Movements." Pp. 695-737 in *The Handbook of Sociology*, Neil J. Smelser, ed. Newbury Park, CA: Sage.

———. 1996. *Comparative Perspectives on Social Movements: Opportunities, Mobilizing Structures, and Framing*. Cambridge: Cambridge University Press.

McArthur, Judith Nichols. 1992. "Motherhood and Reform in the New South." Ph.D. diss. University of Texas, Austin.

McBride, Genevieve G. 1993. *On Wisconsin Women: Working for Their Rights from Settlement to Suffrage*. Madison: University of Wisconsin Press.

McCammon, Holly J. 2001. "Stirring Up Suffrage Sentiment: The Formation of the State Woman Suffrage Organizations, 1866-1914." *Social Forces* 80: 449-480.

McCammon, Holly J., and Karen E. Campbell. 2001. "Winning the Vote in the West: The Political Successes of the Women's Suffrage Movements, 1866-1919." *Gender & Society* 15: 55-82.

McCammon, Holly J., Karen E. Campbell, Ellen M. Granberg, and Christine Mowery. 2001. "How Movements Win: Gendered Opportunity Structures and U.S. Women's Suffrage Movements, 1866-1919." *American Sociological Review* 66: 49-70.

McCammon, Holly J., Lyndi Hewitt, and Sandy Smith. 2004. "No Weapon Save Argument: Strategic Frame Amplification in the U.S. Woman Suffrage Movements." Manuscript.

McCarthy, John D., and Mark Wolfson. 1996. "Resource Mobilization by Local Social Movement Organizations: Agency, Strategy, and Organization in the Movement against Drinking and Driving." *American Sociological Review* 61: 1070-1088.

McCarthy, John D., and Mayer N. Zald. 1977. "Resource Mobilization and Social Movements: A Partial Theory." *American Journal of Sociology* 82: 1212-1241.

Morris, Aldon D., and Carol McClurg Mueller. 1992. *Frontiers in Social Movement Theory*. New Haven, CT: Yale University Press.

National American Women Suffrage Association (NAWSA). 1893-1920. *Proceedings of the National American Woman Suffrage Association*.

———. 1886, 1906, 1909, 1911. *The Woman's Journal*.

Noonan, Rita K. 1995. "Women against the State: Political Opportunities and Collective Action Frames in Chile's Transition to Democracy." *Sociological Forum* 10: 81-111.

Ostrom, Charles W. 1990. *Time Series Analysis: Regression Techniques*. 2nd ed. Newbury Park, CA: Sage.

Snow, David A., and Robert D. Benford. 1988. "Ideology, Frame Resonance, and Participant Mobilization." *International Social Movement Research* 1: 197-217.

Snow, David A., E. Burke Rochford, Jr., Steven K. Worden, and Robert D. Benford. 1986. "Frame Alignment Processes, Micromobilization, and Movement Participation." *American Sociological Review* 51: 464-481.

Staggenborg, Suzanne. 1993. "Critical Events and the Mobilization of the Pro-Choice Movement." *Research in Political Sociology* 6: 319-345.

Stuhler, Barbara. 1995. *Gentle Warriors: Clara Ueland and the Minnesota Struggle for Woman Suffrage*. St. Paul: Minnesota Historical Society.

Tarrow, Sidney. 1989. *Democracy and Disorder: Protest and Politics in Italy, 1965-1975.* Oxford: Clarendon Press.

———. 1992. "Mentalities, Political Cultures, and Collective Action Frames: Constructing Meanings through Action." Pp. 174-202 in *Frontiers in Social Movement Theory*, Aldon D. Morris and Carol McClurg Mueller, eds. New Haven, CT: Yale University Press.

———. 1994. *Power in Movement: Social Movement, Collective Action, and Politics.* Cambridge: Cambridge University Press.

Taylor, A. Elizabeth. 1943. "A Short History of the Woman Suffrage Movement in Tennessee." *Tennessee Historical Quarterly* 2: 195-215.

———. 1956. "The Woman Suffrage Movement in Arkansas." *Arkansas Historical Quarterly* 15: 17-52.

———. 1992. "The Woman Suffrage Movement in Mississippi, 1890-1920." Pp. 192-225 in *History of Women in the United States: Historical Articles on Women's Lives and Activities*, Nancy F. Cott, ed. New York: K. G. Saur.

Tilly, Charles. 1978. *From Mobilization to Revolution.* Reading, MA: Addison-Wesley.

Tisdale, Nancy K. 1965. "The Prohibition Crusade in Arizona." Master's thesis, University of Arizona.

U.S. Bureau of the Census. 1975. *Historical Statistics of the United States: Colonial Times to 1970.* Bicentennial ed. Pt. 1. Washington, DC: Government Printing Office.

Wheeler, Marjorie Spruill. 1993. *New Women of the New South: The Leaders of the Woman Suffrage Movement in the Southern States.* New York: Oxford University Press.

Williams, Rhys H. 1995. "Constructing the Public Good: Social Movements and Cultural Resources." *Social Problems* 42: 124-144.

Williams, Rhys H., and Timothy J. Kubal. 1999. "Movement Frames and the Cultural Environment: Resonance, Failure, and the Boundaries of the Legitimate." *Research in Social Movements, Conflicts, and Change* 21: 225-248.

Zuo, Jiping, and Robert D. Benford. 1995. "Mobilization Processes and the 1989 Chinese Democracy Movement." *Sociological Quarterly* 36: 131-156.

Chapter 3

COLLECTIVE ACTION FRAMES IN
THE GAY LIBERATION MOVEMENT, 1969-1973

Stephen Valocchi

We are the Stonewall girls.
We wear our hair in curls . . .
We wear our dungarees
Above our nelly knees.

Gay power to gay people!

Tourists to New York City who happened upon the Stonewall Inn in Greenwich Village in the early morning hours of June 28, 1969, would have heard these two very different protest chants during the police disturbance that has come to signal the beginning of the gay liberation movement (Duberman 1993: 194-211). Embedded in these chants and in "the Stonewall Rebellion" lie many questions of interest to social movement scholars. Was "Stonewall" simply another example of a previously quiescent group politicized by the sixties protest wave? Did that protest wave set the tone for the subsequent gay liberation movement? Did the activism around civil rights, black power, feminism, and in the New Left contribute to the major gay liberation collective action frames that helped "market and sell" this new social movement? Did homosexual collective action prior to the sixties contribute to the framing efforts of the post-Stonewall movement? The events outside the Stonewall Inn suggest that the answers to these questions are neither straightforward nor simple. On the one hand, the camp sensibility of "the Stonewall girls" indicates that there was something unique about these riots. On the other, the rapid diffusion of sixties "power" rhetoric suggests a commonality with the struggles of many other groups during this time.

Most scholars assert that the imbeddedness of the early gay liberation movement in the sixties protest cycle helps explain the dynamics of its rise. While historians and sociologists acknowledge that the earlier organizations of gay men and lesbians—the Mattachine Society and the Daughters of Bilitis—built the groundwork for the post-Stonewall movement (Adam 1987; D'Emilio 1983; Duberman 1993), these same scholars suggest that most of this groundwork was rapidly transcended in favor of a more militant, self-assertive, sixties-style political movement. None of this work systematically isolates key features of the early gay liberation movement and analyzes their origins, however.

This chapter begins that process. It describes and documents the major collective action frames developed by the movement and traces their origins either to some aspect of the sixties protest wave or to the older homophile movement of lesbian and gay collective action of the fifties and sixties. It accomplishes this task through a critical reading of the many documents, newspapers, memoirs, and historical accounts of homophile, homosexual, gay, and lesbian activism from the 1950s to the 1970s. Some of this material is organized into several volumes of already published gay liberation documents. Other material is from archival sources. Based on these data, I inductively organize the major frame fragments of the gay liberation movement into internally consistent larger frames. Following Meyer and Whittier (1994), I trace these frames and fragments back in time to when they appear in either sixties-movement or homophile-movement discourse. Although no research has systematically periodized the modern lesbian and gay movement, most historical and journalistic accounts bracket 1969 to 1973 as the period of gay liberation (Adam 1987; Vaid 1995). This period is the focus of analysis. Beginning in 1973, the language of liberation gave way to the language of rights, and the grassroots nature of the movement gave way to national efforts to coordinate and organize the local activism (Marcus 1992). This period of approximately four years generated the major and minor frames that exist in the movement today.

FRAMING THE GAY LIBERATION MOVEMENT

The current culturalist turn in social movement research explores, among other things, the meaning systems created by movement actors that move people to act in non-normative ways (Taylor and Whittier 1995). One useful concept developed out of this body of research is framing.

Framing "refers to an interpretive schema that simplifies and condenses the 'world out there' by selectively punctuating and encoding objects, situations, events, experiences, and sequences of action within one's present or past environment" (Snow and Benford 1992: 137). It calls attention to the grievance, names it as unjust and intolerable, attributes blame and responsibility, and suggests how to best ameliorate the situation (Snow et al. 1986). The key to framing is finding evocative cultural symbols that resonate with potential constituents and are capable of motivating to collective action (Tarrow 1994).

The gay liberation movement embraced four collective action frames. First was the idea that "gay is good." This message was an appeal to homosexuals themselves to transform their own self-concept as a necessary prelude to changing the culture's concept of gay people. Second was the idea of sexual liberation. The early organizations of gay liberation criticized American culture as sexually repressive. In this light, gay people were the vanguard of a new, sexualized society. Third was heterosexism, the idea that male dominance and normative heterosexuality were fused to deny gay people, and lesbians in particular, their full humanity. Fourth was the idea that the external source of oppression was not located solely in the state—an extension of the heterosexism frame. Instead, the movement targeted the dominant culture as a location of sexual repression, discrimination, hostility, and invisibility.

Based on the analysis presented below, I contend that these gay liberation frames were constructed in dialectical fashion with the ideological material from other movements of the period on the one hand, and the ideological material of the homophile movement on the other. It was through the creative "coming together" of these two ideological streams that gay liberationist frames were constructed. This coming together, moreover, did not produce a unitary ideology or master frame from which the movement drew its strategy, goals, and collective identity. Instead, it produced a tension between the notion of gay people as a quasi-ethnic minority group and the notion of gay people as cultural critics, a tension that has persisted within the movement ever since.

SOCIAL MOVEMENT FRAMES, CONTINUITY, AND PROTEST CYCLES

Two related bodies of scholarship explore the origins of collective action frames during the emergence phase of a movement. One deals with the continuities of collective action across historical periods. Another deals with the ways collective action is unique when occurring within a cycle of protest.

Reacting against the "immaculate conception" theory of movement emergence, the first body of scholarship traces connections between different phases of activity in a single movement sector. Taylor (1989) uses the concept of social movement abeyance to capture the ways in which the modern women's movement was connected to an earlier, more quiescent phase of the movement from 1945 to the mid-1960s. Taylor demonstrates that the National Women's Party (NWP) promoted ideas about equal rights and the primacy of the public sector for achieving those rights during the earlier phase, and that these ideas became core elements of the sixties feminist collective action frame (Rupp and Taylor 1990). Beyond this, however, little is said about how these ideas interacted with "newer" ideas not derived from the NWP and how this interaction affected framing efforts.

A second strand of research focuses not so much on connections between phases of the same movement but on the dynamics of different movements during the same period—a cycle of protest. According to Tarrow (1994: 153), a cycle of protest is a temporal phase of heightened conflict and contention across the social system caused by a shift in the structure of political opportunities for the initiator movement. The cycle is characterized by diffusion from one social movement sector to another, innovation in the forms of contention, new collective action frames that bring new people to participate in collective action, and heightened contact and conflict between challengers and authorities. The initiator movement creates a master frame—a generic interpretive scheme that helps these other groups understand their grievances and that serves as a spur to mobilization.[1] In the course of the protest cycle, moreover, this frame is interpreted and changed by the subsequent movements (McAdam 1995: 229; Tarrow 1994: 157).

Although highlighting cultural innovation in the rise of "spin-off movements," the protest-cycle perspective never specifies the innovations spin-off movements make on master frames, nor does it explore the consequences of these innovations for other features of the movement. We will see below, for example, that gay liberation took the master frame of minority group from earlier movements in the cycle and combined it with notions of both personal and cultural transformation. The literature on protest cycles provides few clues as to where these notions came from and what their consequences were for movement development.

THE MOVEMENT ON THE EVE OF STONEWALL

The first organizations seeking to reform America's views, laws, and institutions about homosexuality were formed in the early 1950s (D'Emilio 1983; Faderman 1991; Timmons 1990). Despite an extremely hostile climate, the organization for men—the Mattachine Society—and the organization for women—the Daughters of Bilitis—experienced steady but slow growth in membership and newly chartered chapters in the two decades prior to the Stonewall riots (D'Emilio 1983).

These organizations have often been characterized as timid, conservative, and assimilationist. Much of the work of Mattachine and the Daughters of Bilitis was support-group focused, offering counseling and safe haven for men and women (D'Emilio 1983: chap. 9; Marotta 1981: chaps. 2 and 3). Inspired by the civil rights militancy of the early sixties, however, the New York and Washington, DC, chapters of Mattachine moved beyond their earlier support-group focus and "actively and publicly worked for equal rights and an end to government discrimination" (Marcus 1992: 90). Still, on the eve of the Stonewall riots, the activities of the Mattachine Society and the Daughters of Bilitis had not spurred mass mobilization.

When mass mobilization did occur in the latter half of 1969, the civil rights movement was no longer the ideological touchstone for homosexual political activity. The spirit of militancy in the service of political and social integration of the civil rights movement had been replaced by the more aggressive assertion of group identity and by an ambivalent attitude toward integration as expressed by the black power and women's liberation movements. The ways in which these themes and others from the sixties protest cycle manifested themselves in the gay movement can be understood only in interaction with the longstanding concerns of the homophile movement.

GAY IS GOOD

One only needs to read the proceedings of the 1964 Eastern Regional Conference of Homophile Organizations (ERCHO) to first hear the sentiment that "gay is good" (Mattachine Society NY 1964). The keynote speech given by a lawyer, officially titled "Civil Liberties and Social Rights," documented the existence of prejudice and discrimination toward homosexuals and counseled that "education and understanding" were necessary to convince people of the "basic goodness of the homosexual" (King 1964). This message was repeated throughout the ERCHO 1965 as doctors, sociologists, clergy, and lawyers took the podium to present evidence of or lay claim to the nondeviant, nonsinful nature of homosexuals (ERCHO 1965).

This message that gay is good emerged out of a dilemma of the pre-Stonewall movement: how to counter the constant claims of the dominant culture—that homosexuals were mentally ill and sinful—with a more positive, self-affirming message. The homophile organizations of the sixties helped to build self-esteem by supporting straight professionals who spoke on behalf of homosexuals or by proving the goodness of their members by sponsoring blood drives or charity events (D'Emilio 1983). In addition, these organizations held discussion groups for men and women that would focus on the prevailing psychiatric views of "their condition": The Daughters of Bilitis, for example, urged lesbians to accept themselves "without guilt or anxiety" (quoted in Gorman 1985: 46). These activities did not challenge dominant cultural views but sought to demonstrate that homosexuals were solid citizens in spite of these views (Marcus 1992: 97-98; Seidman 1991: 163).

This approach changed in the mid-1960s as Frank Kameny, head of the newly formed Washington, DC, chapter of Mattachine, rejected the organization's old line. Speaking at ERCHO 1965, he insisted that "homosexuality is not a sickness, disturbance, or other pathology in any sense, but is merely a preference, orientation, or propensity, on par with, and not different in kind from, heterosexuality" (Kameny 1965). As the civil rights movement captured the public's attention in the first half of the sixties, Kameny framed his critique of the homophile organizations and his rejection of the medical model of homosexuality with the language of the civil rights movement. Speaking in 1964, Kameny made this connection explicit: "I do not see the NAACP and CORE worrying about which chromosome and gene produced a black skin, or about the possibility of bleaching the Negro" (Marotta 1981: 62).

The position that gay is good was adopted by the National American Conference of Homophile Organizations in 1968. It was essentially an appeal to the homophile movement to redirect its energies away from a discussion of the causes of homosexuality and toward a discussion of prejudice and discrimination (Teal 1971: 59). In adopting this rhetoric, the coalition of homophile organizations did not depart from its essentially assimilationist position regarding the relationship between homosexuals and the larger society. As Kameny stated at the 1968 conference, "Minorities could be, should be like members of the majority" (Marotta 1981: 66).

The formation of this initial frame—an interpretive scheme that stressed the essential goodness of a culturally vilified group—had implications for other aspects of collective action. As Kameny's comments indicate, it suggested a movement for civil rights based on integration and focused on changing laws. At ERCHO 1965, Kameny cited "the example of the Negro" to argue that "our major efforts should be directed at changes of law, regulation, and procedure, whether brought about through legislative means or judicial ones" (Kameny 1965). This strategy changed as the gay-is-good frame was refashioned into gay power. This also was accomplished in interaction between the unique concerns of the movement and the rapidly changing protest environment of the sixties.

As the Black Panther party asserted "black is beautiful" along with its calls for "black power," a space opened for the refashioning the gay-is-good rhetoric with an emphasis on gay pride as a prelude to gay power—a move away from rationales of "prejudice and discrimination." The emphasis was no longer on identifying discrimination and prejudice and educating the public; it was now about gaining access to social institutions in order to change laws and practices and, by so doing, gain power.

While not exactly what Frank Kameny and others had in mind when introducing the gay-is-good rhetoric, the concerns of the homophile movement had met and been shaped by the social movement context within which gay liberation unfolded. Writing in November 1969, Bob Martin, one of the militant homophile activists, helped to fashion the gay-is-good rhetoric into "gay power":

> [Gay power] is demanding to be recognized as a powerful minority with just rights
> which have not been acknowledged; it is an insistence that homosexuality has made
> its own unique contribution to civilization and will continue to do so; and it is the
> realization that homosexuality, while morally and psychologically on a par with
> heterosexuality, does nonetheless have unique aspects which demand their own
> standards of evaluation and their own subculture. (Teal 1971: 60)

Still, this frame of gay power was rooted in the notion of self-image. In one of the
feature articles in the premier issue of *Come Out!*, the first newspaper of gay liberation, Dr. Leo Louis Martello describes the importance of gay pride in terms of
positive image: "Homosexuality is not the problem in itself. The problem is society's
attitude toward it" (Martello 1969). He then describes "five steps to a positive self
image," but unlike suggestions that would have appeared in the pages of *Mattachine
Review*, these suggestions were not individual-level coping strategies but action
strategies: "participate in a zap," "come out to your friends."

Thus, the rhetoric associated with the struggle for self-determination and cultural integrity for African Americans provided the vehicle through which the gay
liberation movement turned a struggle for acceptance of a preference, orientation, or
a propensity into a struggle for acceptance of a group. It was the perfect solution to
the homophile dilemma of building self-image in a hostile culture.

The newly reconstituted frame of gay power, an interpretive scheme that combined symbols of personal and political efficacy, also had implications for the goals
of the gay liberation movement. If integration was not the goal, then what was? The
answer to this question was far from clear. As the gay liberation movement developed its unique elements and combined them with elements from the protest cycle,
goals such as sexual liberation and cultural resistance developed. They stood, however, uneasily and oftentimes contradictorily, beside the goals of equal access and
nondiscrimination.

Perhaps the most significant aspect of the gay-power frame was its use of a
minority-group model of collective identity, which became a dominant model of gay
people by the late 1970s.[2] This model competed with other models of group identity.

SEXUAL LIBERATION

Resonating throughout the pages of one of the major newspapers of gay liberation
was the frame of sexual liberation: "Gay liberation is committed to replacing the
American Empire with the sexually liberated community we know is the only one in
which all people can be free" (Sagarin 1970). The message of sexual liberation echoed throughout the discourse of the first gay liberation organization after Stonewall,
the Gay Liberation Front (GLF). As stated in its "Notes for a Political Platform and
Program for Gay Liberation" (1970) the GLF is a "vehicle primarily for the liberation of homosexuals and ultimately for the liberation of the homosexual in everyone." As Allen Young, an active participant in both the New Left and the Gay
Liberation Front, states: "Gay . . . means not homosexual but sexually free" (Jay and
Young [1972] 1992: 11).

This frame emerged from the New Left-informed counterculture and gained
additional strength from the sex-phobic nature of the older homophile organizations.
In addition, as this frame developed and interacted with the other frame of gay is
good, it created a dilemma about the movement's collective identity and strategy.

By the late sixties, elements of the New Left counterculture conceived the body as a source of personal pleasure and political consciousness, whether arrived at through sex or with psychedelics (Dickstein 1977). Despite this celebration of the erotic, the taboo of homosexuality within the new left prevented gays and lesbians from extending this analysis to homosexual eroticism (Calvert 1991).

The popularity of the sexual liberation frame had as much to do with the relationship of the early homophile movement to sex as it did with the sexual liberalism of the New Left counterculture. The sixties counterculture was the positive impulse in the creation of this collective action frame; the homophile organizations of the fifties and sixties were the negative impulses. As mentioned above, the homophile organizations of the fifties searched for respectability and in the sixties pursued civil rights. At no point did they talk about the integrity or aesthetics of gay sex or gay culture. Indeed, the very name "homophile" was chosen to divert attention away from the sexual acts and impulses that define gay people as different. As the secretary of the National American Homophile Conference explained in 1967, the term homophile "takes the sex out of homosexuality" (Gunnison 1967).

As a lesbian and gay subculture emerged in the decades after World War II, a main portion of that subculture revolved around sex, sexual styles, and sexual desire (Kennedy and Davis 1993; Nestle 1987; Sadownick 1996). For the most part, homophile organizations did not recruit from nor address the issues of that subculture (D'Emilio 1983; Faderman 1991). It is not surprising then that, once sex became infused with political meaning for the counterculture, it would also ignite longstanding and unaddressed issues around sex in the post-Stonewall movement.

Gay liberation, according to a member of the GLF, was "as much about sexual or erotic liberation as about freedom from discrimination and prejudice" (Altman [1971]1993: 80). It was an understanding of sexuality not narrowly focused on a specific object or activity. In one of the early manifestos of the GLF from December 1969, Carl Wittman declares, "Nature leaves undefined the object of sexual desire. The gender of that object is imposed socially. . . . The reason so few of us are bisexual is because society made such a big stink about homosexuality that we got forced into seeing ourselves as either straight or non-straight" (Wittman [1972] 1992: 331). Comparing "good sex" with "making music," Wittman argues that "what we have called sexual 'orientation' probably just means that we have not yet learned to turn on the total range of musical expression" (336-337). Thus, in seeking to apply to their own situation the ideas and practices of sexual liberalism weaving its way around the culture of the New Left, gay men pushed those ideas and practices to their logical limits and, in the process, developed a critique of a society that forces people to adopt narrow and confining sexual scripts.

Not surprisingly, this frame of sexual liberation existed uneasily beside the minority-group model of collective identity derived from the gay-is-good frame: for if they were all capable of a polymorphous sexuality, shouldn't the movement have developed a strategy and a collective identity that dissolved the categories of gay and straight, not one that reinforced them?

This question animated the meetings, newspapers, and position papers of the Gay Liberation Front during this time (Altman [1971] 1993). One of the founding members of GLF, Jim Fouratt, expressed his reservations about the term "gay":

> I find the word hard to relate to because it puts me in a category which limits my potential. It prescribes a whole system of behavior to which I'm supposed to conform, which has nothing to do with the reality of my day-to-day living. What I do with my cock

should not determine who or what I am. (Fouratt 1970)

Another gay liberationist captured the tension between this idea of fluid sexual categories and the more fixed notion of a newly emerging minority group:

> Staying in the ghettoes, wearing the labels, and limiting our demands to "gay power" (as opposed to "people power"), we're perhaps supporting the Homosexual Revolution, but we're sure as hell copping out of the Sexual Revolution. (Teal 1971: 61)

Implicit in these debates were dilemmas about the nature of collective identity and the type of strategy pursued by a social movement using the sexual liberation frame. This frame resonated so forcefully for many because it was part of a larger utopian and revolutionary ideology. It envisioned a world where oppressive institutions would be smashed and people would no longer be confined by them. The sexual liberation frame suggested a social movement goal, but not a viable way to reach it. The gay-is-good frame with its minority-group discourse suggested a strategy as well as a collective identity that had boundaries and techniques to enforce those boundaries. These frames existed in tension with one another until around 1973 when the minority-group discourse became dominant not only in gay liberation but in many of the other sixties movements.

HETEROSEXISM

As the movement was developing its critique of "confining sexual scripts," lesbian feminists challenged the gay liberation movement to incorporate notions of male chauvinism and heterosexism.[3] The language of these challenges came directly from the feminist movement. In a widely circulated tract on gay liberation, "The Women-Identified Women," a group called Radicalesbians exhorted gay women to appreciate the links between sexism, male supremacy, and "the plight of lesbians."

> It should first be understood that lesbianism, like male homosexuality, is a category of behavior possible only in a sexist society characterized by rigid sex roles and dominated by male supremacy. Those sex roles dehumanize women by defining us as a supportive/serving caste in relation to the master caste of men, and emotionally cripple men by demanding that they be alienated from their own bodies and emotions in order to perform their economic/political/military functions effectively. (Jay and Young [1972] 1992: 172-173)

This tract, which was widely used to teach women about the gay movement, extended the feminist critique of sex roles by asserting that the rigid standards of masculinity and femininity were enforced not just by sexism but also by heterosexism.

As these ideas came together, a new frame evolved, one which called into question the cultural standard of heterosexuality. The opening statement for the 1971 Chicago Gay Pride Celebration develops this frame of heterosexism:

> Most of homosexual oppression . . . grows from the assumption that people are inborn heterosexual. . . . To maintain sex roles heterosexual standards had to manufacture artificial definitions of male and female. A "real man" and "real women" are not so by their chromosomes and genitals, but by their respective degrees of "masculinity"

and "femininity," and by how closely they follow the sex role script in their relationships with individuals and society. (Jay and Young [1972] 1992: 252)

This frame of heterosexism resonated loudly, especially for women already active in the feminist movement, and served as a primary vehicle for the mobilization of feminist women into the gay liberation movement. These links between the feminist movement and gay liberation are evident in the emergence of the group Radicalesbians and in its assertion that "a lesbian is the rage of all women condensed to the point of explosion" (Jay and Young [1972] 1992: 172).

Although this frame emerged from the feminist movement, it did so dialectically. The feminist movement was initially resistant to this reformulation of sexism into heterosexism. Two of the people within the feminist movement who pushed the movement to see the connections between feminism and lesbianism were Phyliss Lyon and Del Martin, founders of the homophile organization Daughters of Bilitis. Frustrated with the organization's reluctance to pursue actively the connections between lesbianism and feminism, Lyon and Martin joined the newly formed National Organization for Women (NOW) soon after its formation in 1966 and pushed NOW to see these connections (Gorman 1985; Tobin and Wicker 1975: 54-58). Thus, this heterosexism frame derived from a dialectical relationship between earlier homophile activism and feminist activism of the sixties protest wave. Women activists moved back and forth between the two movements and mixed the ideas from each.

This frame had consequences for the gay liberation movement's collective identity. Not surprisingly, this frame resonated more strongly for women than for men. Indeed, much of the early period of gay liberation was spent in conflict between women and men over issues of sexism and chauvinism.[4] In a much-quoted article by GLF member Steve Dansky (1971), Dansky took his gay "brothers" to task for having either avoided or attacked the most important movement in the world today: the struggle for the liberation of women. While some men in the movement did the difficult work of consciousness raising necessary to recognize that even gay men enjoyed male privilege, these nods to feminism were for the most part too little too late.

In this collective action frame, in the conflicts surrounding its implementation, and in its interaction with other movement frames are implications for gay liberation collective identity. This frame existed uneasily besides the sexual liberation frame: while many men were talking about sex as a tool of liberation, many women were talking about it as a source of oppression. Thus, the heterosexism frame contested the gay-is-good notion of a unitary group. Were gay men *and* lesbians members of one minority group? Partly as a consequence of these struggles, many lesbians did not define themselves as members of a unitary gay minority (Cruikshank 1992: chap. 6).[5]

OPPRESSION IS EVERYWHERE

The oppression-is-everywhere frame emphasized the multisited nature of homosexual oppression and the connection of gay people to similarly oppressed groups. This frame emerged out of the New Left's revolutionary rhetoric of restructuring all social institutions and the ongoing concerns of the pre-Stonewall movement about how gay people were viewed by the dominant culture (e.g., in the media, in religion, in medicine).

Perhaps the best way to observe the emergence of this frame is to highlight several points from a document produced by the Youth Committee of the National Coalition of Homophile Organizations in August 1969. This committee was composed of several people who had been active in the homophile movement of the late sixties but had, since Stonewall, gotten involved in the Gay Liberation Front. This "radical manifesto" provides a unique opportunity to see the coming together of the old concerns of culture and new concerns of multiple oppressions.

This frame was constructed, in the first instance, with the rhetoric of the late-sixties New Left. The opening salvo in *A Radical Manifesto: The Homophile Movement Must Be Radicalized* states:

> We see the persecution of homosexuality as part of a general attempt to oppress all minorities and keep them powerless. Our fate is linked with these minorities; if the detention camps are filled tomorrow with blacks, hippies and other radicals, we will not escape that fate, all our attempts to dissociate ourselves from them notwithstanding. A common struggle, however, will bring common triumph. (Teal 1971: 38)

This frame of multiple oppressions resonated with many gay men and women from the New Left; the technique, established in the New Left, of analyzing the ways in which various institutions as well as the dominant culture stigmatized, marginalized, or discriminated against different groups was naturally extended to gay people.

Relevant in this regard are several other points in the twelve-point manifesto. Points number four, five, and eight, for example, state:

> 4) Our enemies, an implacable, repressive governmental system, much of organized religion, business and medicine, will not be moved by appeasement or appeals to reason and justice, but only by power and force.
>
> 5) We regard established heterosexual standards of morality as immoral and refuse to condone them by demanding an equality which is merely the common yoke of sexual repression.
>
> 8) We call upon the churches to sanction homosexual liaisons when called upon to do so by the parties concerned. (Teal 1971: 38)

Implicit in each of these points are the concerns of the old homophile organizations about the perception and treatment of homosexuals by government, religion, medicine, and the church. Repackaged and reframed with the rhetoric of the New Left, these concerns became unaddressed demands.

The best example of the origins, operation, and consequences of this collective action frame is the gay liberation movement's assault on the psychiatric establishment. A longstanding issue of the homophile movement had been the prevailing medical model of homosexuality. The oppression-is-everywhere frame brought a new analysis to bear on this old problem: to get the psychiatric profession to eliminate homosexuality from its list of mental illnesses.

Prior to Stonewall, the psychiatric community was approached quite gingerly, usually by enlisting the support of sympathetic doctors to talk to groups of gay people or to quietly lobby the medical profession. Now, post-Stonewall activists confronted the psychiatric community by taking over their meetings with "zaps," "challenging" the doctors to rap sessions, and serving on panels at conferences to actively contest the "sickness" label (Marcus 1992: 222-225). The concern with the sickness image was an old one; how the movement chose to confront it was new. Thus, this new frame had implications for social movement strategy as it turned former allies into current adversaries.

Another feature of this framing strategy was the explicit interconnectedness of the sites of oppression. When pre-Stonewall activists spoke of the need to change the psychiatric profession's understanding of homosexuality, they did so as part of an appeal for acceptance by the broader society. The post-Stonewall assault was very different. It called into question the values and principles of the broader society and connected the psychiatrists' oppressivness to that of other powerful institutions.

As part of the zap at the national convention of the American Psychiatric Association, for example, the San Francisco Gay Liberation Front linked the "establishment school of psychiatry" to the repressive forces of the state:

> You are the pigs who make it possible for the cops to beat homosexuals; they call us queer; you so politely call us sick. But it's the same thing. You make possible the beatings and rapes in prisons. You are implicated in the tortuous cures perpetuated on desperate homosexuals. (quoted in Teal 1971: 274-275)

This language of interconnectedness of oppression came directly from the revolutionary rhetoric of the New Left during the period:

> We refuse to accept our oppression and believe that the key to the mental health of all oppressed peoples in a racist, sexist, capitalist society, is a radical change in the structure and accompanying attitudes of the entire social system. (quoted in Jay and Young [1972] 1992: 146)

Clearly, these statements indicate that the old concerns of sickness had been revived and broadened as the New Left influenced the agenda of sexual minorities. The concern with the culture's perceptions of gay people was forged by the pre-Stonewall movement; but New Left ideology forged the notion that the purveyors of culture were connected and that they needed to be directly confronted.

These examples also have implications for the strategies of the gay liberation movement. If oppression *was* everywhere then the movement had no choice but to confront it in its multiple guises or to withdraw from it as much as possible by constructing separate institutions. This frame contributed to the overall sense of the gay liberation movement as one of cultural and social transformation. This stood in dynamic tension with the idea derived from the gay-is-good frame that gay people are a minority group and, like other minority groups, should use the government and the courts to gain equal rights.

DISCUSSION AND CONCLUSION

Understanding the diverse and creative ways in which the collective action frames of the gay liberation movement were constructed points to the utility of a joint focus on social movement continuity and social movement protest waves in analyzing the ideological framework of various social movements. The origins of the content of these frames must be seen as both a function of the position of the gay liberation movement in the protest wave and a function of an autonomous history of homophile organizing prior to and during that protest wave. It is through an interaction of the two that the gay liberation ideology was constructed.

Consistent with the theoretical expectations in work on protest cycles, gay liberation activists did indeed "interpret the cultural lessons of the early risers [in the protest wave]" and did indeed "fashion ideologies and specific cultural practices distinct from the movement(s) that set them in motion" (McAdam 1995: 229). Consistent with the work on social movement continuity, one of the major factors affecting the nature of the collective action frames constructed by the gay liberationists was the "extent to which the movement has access to a latent activist tradition or history of struggle that can serve as another 'tool kit' into which the new generation of activists can dip for inspiration" (McAdam 1995: 230; Rupp and Taylor 1987: chap. 8).

In addition, this research adds some nuance to these twin concepts. Although most analyses of the interaction among movements in a protest cycle describe a one-way process of cultural diffusion from initiators to spin-offs, the gay liberation movement suggests that this interaction can be reciprocal. One only needs to appreciate the influence that lesbians had on the women's movement and, in turn, lesbian feminists had on the gay liberation movement to see this reciprocity. Thus, the appropriate image may be not of one wave crashing forward but of a series of waves ebbing and flowing. Similarly, the gay liberation movement did not adopt or adapt a master frame from the earlier movements in the protest wave. Again, the image is of multiple frames being created in multiple ways.

This image of interaction also applies to the concept of social movement continuity. Several frames were held in abeyance by Mattachine and Daughters of Bilitis, for example, the gay-is-good frame by Mattachine and an incipient feminism by Daughters of Bilitis. These frames, however, were radically transformed as they interacted with the "rallying cries" of the sixties protest movements. In this instance, Mattachine and Daughters of Bilitis were abeyance structures in the dual sense of the term: they functioned so that the group could continue "to mount some type of challenge even in a nonreceptive environment" (Taylor 1989: 772), but they also served as organizational constraints on new ideas. Individuals reacted to the changing social context but found their initiatives thwarted by existing social movement organizations.

Given the diverse traditions upon which the gay liberation movement was constructed it should not be surprising that the collective action frames constructed by the movement were also diverse and that they coexisted uneasily and even contradictorily with one another. The gay-is-good frame suggested a quasi-ethnic group collective identity; the sexual liberation frame suggested a more fluid collective identity defined in terms of cultural transformation. The oppression-is-everywhere frame also emphasized the importance of cultural transformation while the gay-is-good frame suggested a more polity-oriented strategy. The heterosexism frame implied a separatist collective identity while other frames asserted the importance of a unitary gay and lesbian identity engaged in changing some features of society.

After 1973, the minority-group discourse, derived from the gay-is-good frame, became the dominant discourse in the movement. Future research would do well to investigate why that discourse became dominant and how and why these dominant discourses vary over time. We know from other movements what the possible answers are: factors such as shifts in political opportunities and changes in organizational resources from research on the civil rights movement (McAdam 1983; Morris 1984); and factors such as organizational stasis and political repression from research on the labor movement (Moody 1988; Piven and Cloward 1979). In addition, recent research has also pointed to the role of countermovements in influencing the framing strategies of social movements (Meyer and Staggenborg 1996). The rise of the religious right and the symbolism of "the homosexual menace" in framing strategies of the religious right suggest that this dynamic would be a fruitful one to pursue.

Regardless of which frame is dominant, this research suggests that social movements rely on a broad range of collective action frames in order to encourage as many people as possible to participate. This research also suggests that these attempts are fraught with tensions and contradictions. We have seen some of them above in the emergence phase of the gay liberation movement from 1969 to 1973. Of course, these tensions and contradictions exist today as well. We continue to debate whether the goal of the movement is political inclusion on their terms or cultural transformation on ours (Sullivan 1995; Vaid 1995) and whether it is possible to construct a collective identity fluid enough to incorporate other groups but bounded enough to pursue a concrete politics (Gamson 1995). Indeed, the specific debates within the movement today about gay marriage and the family, gays in the military, the position of transsexuals and bisexuals in the movement, the sexual practices of gay men, and the divisions between men and women are understandable only in the context of these historical debates. The Stonewall tension between cultural dissent and political engagement continues to animate the movement today.

NOTES

1. Snow and Benford (1992: 139) state, "Master frames . . . provide the interpretive medium through which collective actors associated with different movements within a cycle assign blame for the problem they are attempting to ameliorate."

2. It proposes that gay people, like other minorities, experience denial of civil liberties, discrimination, inferior social position, and exclusion from mainstream culture. It assumes relatively clear boundaries between the minority group and everyone else. The pursuit of civil rights and equal treatment are built upon these assumptions (Epstein 1987; Seidman 1993).

3. The identification of heterosexism as an explanation for gay oppression is somewhat different from the more generalized oppression identified by other segments of the gay liberation movement. The oppression-is-everywhere frame captures this more generalized sense derived from the New Left, especially the idea that gay oppression, while unique, connects gay people to other groups. The heterosexism frame builds on the New Left-inspired frame of systematic oppression by asserting that sexism and heterosexism need to be added to the list of oppressions.

4. Many writers and activists of the gay liberation movement have noted its male-dominated nature and the splits and factions that existed between men and women in the movement. Homosexual organizing has always been divided by gender, and the gay liberation phase was the first in which the issue was directly confronted.

5. The move to lesbian separatism in the 1970s derives, in part, from the ambivalence over a unitary gay identity. The tension reemerges in the late eighties as other groups of people with same sex desire find themselves outside the boundaries of the minority-group model. These groups included African American, Latino, and other ethnic minorities as well as bisexuals and transgendered people.

REFERENCES

Adam, Barry D. 1987. *The Rise of a Gay and Lesbian Movement.* Boston: Twayne.
Altman, Dennis. [1971] 1993. *Homosexual: Oppression and Liberation.* New York: New York University Press.
Calvert, Gregory Nevala. 1991. *Democracy from the Heart.* Eugene, OR: Communitas Press.
Cruikshank, Margaret. 1992. *The Gay and Lesbian Liberation Movement.* New York: Routledge,

Chapman, and Hall.

Dansky, Steve. 1971. "Hey Man. Come Together." London. Reprint from GLF NY. Periodicals Box 17. International Gay Information Collection. New York Public Library.

D'Emilio, John. 1983. *Sexual Politics, Sexual Communities: The Making of a Homosexual Minority in the United States, 1940-1970*. Chicago: University of Chicago Press.

Dickstein, Morris. 1977. *Gates of Eden: American Culture in the Sixties*. New York: Basic Books.

Duberman, Martin. 1993. *Stonewall*. New York: Penguin Books.

Epstein, Steven. 1987. "Gay Politics, Ethnic Identity: The Limits of Social Constructionism." *Socialist Review* 93/94: 9-54.

ERCHO. 1965. "Statement of ERCHO Conference," 1965 Proceedings, Miscellany, Box 3, file 124. International Gay Information Collection. New York Public Library.

Faderman, Lillian. 1991. *Odd Girls and Twilight Lovers: A History of Lesbian Life in Twentieth-Century America*. New York: Penguin Books.

Fouratt, Jim. 1970. "Word Thoughts." *Come Out!* 1, no. 2. Periodicals Box 17. International Gay Information Collection. New York Public Library.

Gamson, Joshua. 1995. "Must Identity Movements Self-Destruct? A Queer Dilemma." *Social Problems* 42: 390-407.

GLF. 1970. "Notes for a Political Platform and Program for Gay Liberation." Pamphlet. Ephemera/Organizations Box 7, GLF NYC. International Gay Information Collection. New York Public Library.

Gorman, Phyllis. 1985. "The Daughters of Bilitis: A Description and Analysis of a Female Homophile Social Movement Organization, 1955-1963." M.A. thesis, Ohio State University.

Gunnison, Foster. 1967. "Letter from Foster Gunnison to Barbara Gittings and Kay Tobin, February 7, 1967." Mattachine Society NY, Series 2, Box 5, File 1. International Gay Information Collection. New York Public Library.

Jay, Karla, and Allen Young, eds. [1972] 1992. *Out of the Closets: Voices of Gay Liberation*. New York: New York University Press.

Kameny, Frank. 1965. "The Example of the Negro . . ." Proceedings, Miscellany, ERCHO Conference 1965, Box 3, file 24. International Gay Information Collection. New York Public Library.

Kennedy, Elizabeth Lapovsky, and Madeline D. Davis. 1993. *Boots of Leather, Slippers of Gold: The History of a Lesbian Community*. New York: Penguin Books.

King, Robert. 1964. "Civil Liberties and Social Rights." Proceedings, Miscellany, ERCHO Conference 1964, Box 3, file 23. International Gay Information Collection. New York Public Library.

Marcus, Eric. 1992. *Making History: The Struggle for Gay and Lesbian Equal Rights, 1945-1990*. New York: HarperCollins.

Marotta, Toby. 1981. *The Politics of Homosexuality*. Boston: Houghton-Mifflin.

Martello, Leo Lewis. 1969. "A Positive Self Image." *Come Out!* 1, no. 1. Periodicals Box 17. International Gay Information Collection. New York Public Library.

Mattachine Society NY. 1964. Series 2. Topical Files: ERCHO Conference 1964. International Gay Information Collection. New York Public Library.

McAdam, Doug. 1983. *Political Process and the Development of Black Insurgency, 1930-1970*. Chicago: University of Chicago Press.

———. 1995. "'Initiator' and 'Spin-off' Movements: Diffusion Processes in Protest Cycles." Pp. 217-239 in *Repertoires and Cycles of Collective Action*, Mark Traugott, ed. Durham, NC: Duke University Press.

Meyer, David, and Suzanne Staggenborg. 1996. "Movements, Countermovements, and the Structure of Political Opportunity." *American Journal of Sociology* 101: 1628-1660.

Meyer, David, and Nancy Whittier. 1994. "Social Movement Spillover." *Social Problems* 41: 277-298.

Moody, Kim. 1988. *An Injury to All*. London: Verso.

Morris, Aldon D. 1984. *The Origins of the Civil Rights Movement*. New York: The Free Press.

Nestle, Joan. 1987. *A Restricted Country*. Ithaca, NY: Firebrand Books.

Piven, Frances Fox, and Richard Cloward. 1979. *Poor People's Movements: How They Succeed, Why They Fail.* New York: Random House.

Rupp, Leila J., and Verta Taylor. 1987. *Survival in the Doldrums: The American Women's Rights Movement, 1945 to the 1960s.* New York: Oxford University Press.

Sadownick, Douglas. 1996. *Sex between Men: An Intimate History of the Sex Lives of Gay Men Postwar to the Present.* San Francisco: Harper and Row.

Sagarin, Edward. 1970. "Beyond the GLF." *Come Out!* 1, no. 1. Periodicals Box 17. International Gay Information Collection. New York Public Library.

Seidman, Steven. 1991. *Romantic Longings: Love in America, 1830-1980.* New York: Routledge.

———. 1993. "Identity Politics in a 'Postmodern' Gay Culture: Some Historical and Conceptual Notes." Pp. 105-142 in *Fear of a Queer Planet,* Michael Warner, ed. Minneapolis: University of Minnesota Press.

Snow, David, and Robert D. Benford. 1992. "Master Frames and Cycles of Protest." Pp. 133-155 in *Frontiers in Social Movement Theory,* Aldon D. Morris and Carol McClurg Mueller, eds. New Haven, CT: Yale University Press.

Snow, David A., E. Burke Rochford, Jr., Steven K. Worden, and Robert D. Benford. 1986. "Frame Alignment Processes, Micro-mobilization, and Movement Participation." *American Sociological Review* 51: 464-481.

Sullivan, Andrew. 1995. *Virtually Normal: An Argument about Homosexuality.* New York: Alfred A. Knopf.

Tarrow, Sidney. 1994. *Power in Movement: Social Movements, Collective Action, and Politics.* Cambridge: Cambridge University Press.

Taylor, Verta. 1989. "Social Movement Continuity: The Women's Movement in Abeyance." *American Sociological Review* 54: 761-775.

Taylor, Verta, and Nancy Whittier. 1995. "Analytical Approaches to Social Movement Culture: The Culture of the Women's Movement." Pp. 163-187 in *Social Movements and Culture,* Hank Johnston and Bert Klandermans, eds. Minneapolis: University of Minnesota Press.

Teal, Donn. 1971. *The Gay Militants.* New York: St. Martin's.

Timmons, Stuart. 1990. *The Trouble with Harry Hay, Founder of the Modern Gay Movement.* Boston: Alyson.

Tobin, Kay, and Randy Wicker. 1975. *The Gay Crusaders.* New York: Arno Press.

Vaid, Urvashi. 1995. *Virtual Equality: The Mainstreaming of Gay and Lesbian Liberation.* New York: Doubleday

Wittman, Carl. [1972] 1992. "A Gay Manifesto." Pp. 330-341 in *Out of the Closets,* Karla Jay and Allen Young, eds. New York: New York University Press.

Chapter 4

STRATEGIC FRAMING, EMOTIONS, AND SUPERBARRIO— MEXICO CITY'S MASKED CRUSADER

Jorge Cadena-Roa

On March 7, 1993, the Mexican newspaper *La Jornada* reported a wrestling match held the day before in Mexico City's Zócalo, the capital's main square, between Superbarrio and Senator No. Superbarrio was dressed in a red and yellow mask, red tights, a shirt emblazoned with the letters "SB," yellow briefs, and matching boots and cape; Senator No was also masked and dressed all in black, with the word "NO" across his chest. The match promoted a plebiscite to be held in a few days to decide whether people wanted to elect the mayor of the Federal District (Superbarrio was for the "Yes") or to continue being ruled by presidential appointees (Senator No's position). The newspaper published a quarter-page picture of Superbarrio holding Senator No on the front page, as well as three more pictures of the match and a chronicle of the event. According to the daily, a cheering crowd welcomed Superbarrio to the ring. Senator No arrived soon after amidst jeers and thumbs down, to which he responded with insults and corresponding gestures, further inciting the crowd. Superbarrio was technically superior to his opponent and won the first pin. Then, while the referee was distracted, Senator No threw some lime-like powder at Superbarrio's face. As soon as Superbarrio was blinded and defenseless, Senator No walloped him while the crowd angrily protested and demanded fair play to no avail; the second pin was awarded to Senator No. As the match continued, Senator No used more dirty tricks. One picture shows the moment when, according to the caption, the "Yes," i.e., Superbarrio, was boycotted by both the referee and Senator No's manager. Nonetheless, Superbarrio managed to overcome the cheating and won the third pin and the match.

I will use the role of Superbarrio in Mexico City's urban movements to illustrate the importance of performance and emotion in certain kinds of collective action frames. There is a growing consensus among social movement scholars that structural models cannot fully explain social movements and social change. A much-needed corrective to structural theories has been the concept of strategic framing of grievances (Snow and Benford 1988, 1992; Snow et al. 1986) that stresses the importance of social-construction processes and illuminates how a given structural situation is defined and experienced. Nonetheless, it is fair to say that there is an ideational or cognitive bias (McAdam 1996) in our understanding of framing processes—an almost exclusive concern with formal pronouncement of ideas by movement actors. Using the Asamblea de Barrios in Mexico City as a case study, I argue that the public's response to framing and a movement's capacity to provoke reactions in different target publics are *mediated by the emotions that dramatic representations of conflict can arouse.* Movements stage dramatic representations, not to convince target publics with impeccable and irrefutable arguments but to invoke values and basic moral principles and redefine situations, events, and relations in ways that would legitimate action, sanction inaction, arouse bystanders' sympathy, reduce governments' ability to use social control resources, and attract media attention to reach distant publics. That is, movement actors try to appeal not only to audiences' reason or self-interest but also to their values and normative judgments, and they do so by tapping an audience's emotions. This chapter analyzes the Asamblea de Barrios's efforts at strategic framing and the mediating role played by the emotions in various publics' responses to those efforts.

STRATEGIC FRAMING OF GRIEVANCES

Since the mid-1980s, there has been a growing consensus among social movement scholars that structural models cannot fully explain social movements and social change. From the perspective of social psychology, several social movement scholars called for attention to cognitive and ideational factors such as interpretation, symbolization, and meaning (Cohen 1985; Ferree and Miller 1985; Gamson, Fireman, and Rytina 1982; Klandermans 1984; McAdam 1982; Turner 1983). Particularly influential has been the concept of strategic framing of grievances (Snow and Benford 1988, 1992; Snow et al. 1986), which redirected attention to subjective dimensions in the analysis of social movements. The framing perspective sees grievances as interpreted in different ways by individuals and social movement organizations. The link between intensely felt grievances and susceptibility to movement participation is not immediate, but rather mediated by interpretation.

Framing concepts enable us to examine empirically the process through which a given objective situation *is defined and experienced.* Adopting a new injustice frame, for example, may lead people to redefine situations that were previously seen as an unfortunate but tolerable as inexcusable, unjust, or immoral. For action to occur, injustice frames should be accompanied by shifts in attributional orientation that shift blame or responsibility from self to system. Framing denotes "an active, process-derived phenomenon that implies agency and contention at the level of reality construction" (Snow and Benford 1992: 136). Thus, mobilization depends not only on the availability and deployment of tangible resources, the opening or closing of political opportunities, or a favorable cost-benefit calculus, but also on the way these variables are *framed* and the degree to which they *resonate* with targets of mobilization (Snow and Benford 1988: 213).

McAdam (1996) makes a convincing case for giving more attention to the framing function of movement *tactics*—the way tactics are consciously designed to frame action, attract media attention, shape public opinion in favorable ways to the movement, and signify the degree of threat embodied in the movement and its ability to disrupt public order. McAdam (1996: 348) uses the term *strategic dramaturgy* to denote these kinds of framing efforts that are mindful of the messages and symbols encoded in movement actions and demands. One strategy is to stage actions with the purpose of framing situations in ways that appeal to publics' values and moral convictions, trying to provoke predictable reactions. Because movements have moral and cultural dimensions that involve insurgents' and publics' consciousness, beliefs, and practices, the concept of strategic dramaturgy enables the analyst to move away from the cognitive bias of framing and recognize that movements often dramatically invoke values and basic moral principles to frame grievances and legitimate action. Emotions are especially relevant to these dimensions of strategic framing. Yet as Benford (1997) points out, frame analysts have ignored emotions, thus failing to elaborate the mediating role that emotions have in the communication and interpretation that goes on among movements and their publics.

EMOTIONS AND SOCIAL MOVEMENTS

The argument that emotions mediate people's reactions to strategic dramaturgy raises the question: What is an emotion? Research on emotion has been complex and controversial. There has been disagreement about what counts as an emotion because emotions are not a set of homogenous phenomena amenable to parsimonious classification. All taxonomies of emotion have problems because emotions refer to a disparate set of mental and physiological states.[1] Following recent work on emotions (Calhoun and Solomon 1984; Hansberg 1996; Jaggar 1989; Smith-Lovin 1995; Solomon 1984; Thoits 1989), we can nevertheless identify several relevant characteristics.

1. *Emotions are not simple inner feelings.* They differ from other mental and physiological states. Emotions are referential; they are always directed toward some real (or perceived-as-real) object.[2] Moods, which are much like emotions, do not have an object, however—in other words, they are diffuse, all-embracing, and long-lasting states of mind or dispositions (anxiety, depression, melancholy). In contrast, feelings are the physical sensations associated with emotions and frequently have a definite location in the body (upset stomach, tears, sweating). Only in pathological or abnormal states are emotions independent of experience. Emotions are not merely somatic reactions to the world nor reflexes or irrational responses to external stimuli without intermediary interpretation of emotional context.

2. *Emotions have two sides, physiological and cognitive.* The physiological reactions to emotions (increase in heartbeat, trembling, blushing) are conditioned by biology. The physiological disturbance is necessary to emotion, but emotion cannot be reduced to bodily changes—if emotions were just somatic sensations, it would make no sense to talk about them as rational-irrational or adequate-inadequate (Calhoun and

Solomon 1984; Hansberg 1996). The cognitive side of emotions involves values, beliefs, and social expectations. The behavioral expression of emotion may be learned and depends on the *meaning* a certain object has for us. Emotions are conditioned by prevailing forms of social life, particularly by culture and religion.[3]

3. *People interpret their emotions.* Physiological reactions to and/or identifications of emotional states can be thought of as value judgments about emotional objects. When we feel our stomach turning in disgust, we tend to disapprove the object of that feeling. In this way, emotions provide us with information about their objects through the way we feel about them. Emotions are, in part, ways of making sense of the empirical world because they provide information (sometimes partial and distorted) about what is going on—even when we experience contradictory emotions and ambivalence—and in this sense accompany or parallel other cognitive activities.

4. *Emotions may conflict with other cognitions.* Sometimes what emotions tell us about an object differ from what other cognitions suggest. Emotions may be inappropriate to the actual situation because we hold mistaken beliefs about the situation. Thus, emotions are not reliable cognitions and may have or may lack evidence—just as reason can. Sometimes emotion provides information that is more insightful than the information retrieved by our senses or by reason and logic.

5. *Emotions are not blind, irrational reactions.* They do not prevent us of seeing the world objectively, nor are they necessarily in conflict with cool reason and logic. Some emotions, such as indignation, guilt, remorse, shame, empathy, and sympathy, are *moral emotions,*[4] which depend on values, beliefs, and social expectations. Moral emotions are not just something we feel inside us but are also associated with evaluations about the empirical world. Emotions signal how we feel about their objects and what should be done about them. Emotions are thus epistemologically important mental phenomena that complement reason's insight by leading to the world of moral and aesthetic values (Calhoun and Solomon 1984).

6. *Emotions mediate between cognition and action in a two-step process.* First, we experience emotions and thereby learn something about the object of that emotion. Then we develop the ability to reflect on our emotions and ask ourselves if, as in the Aristolean model of moral virtue, our emotions are appropriate to the situation—that is, whether the emotion we are experiencing is the right emotion, directed toward the right object, in the right intensity—and then fine-tune our emotions accordingly to our values, normative commitments, social expectations, *and* goals. Thus, emotions neither overcome us nor are they beyond our control.

These observations have rarely found their way into social movement theory—a situation that derives from the field's origins in collective behavior research.[5] In the mid-1970s, social movement theories reacted against the "madding crowd" by stressing the rationality of movement goals and actions. Resource mobilization theory assumed rational actors weighing costs and benefits of participation vis-à-vis nonparticipation, and goal-oriented action constrained and enabled by the availability of resources at their disposal (Jenkins 1983; McCarthy and Zald 1973, 1977). Subsequently, political-process models focused on the relations between movements and the state, particularly the circumstances under which the state is more vulnerable or receptive to challengers' action (Kitschelt 1986; McAdam 1982; Perrow 1979; Tilly 1978, 1984). McAdam (1982) considered "cognitive liberation" along with external opportunities, but further developments of the political opportunity model emphasized strategy, organization, and external opportunities at the cost of social constructionist dimensions. The abandonment of psychological, social-psychological, and normative perspectives was perceived as a necessary step to place due attention on "objective" variables leading to a false dichotomy between rationality and emotions, planning and spontaneity, the subjective and the objective.[6]

Recently, it has been pointed out that this dichotomy between rationality and emotion is strongly related to gender issues. Feminist scholars contend that the separation of passion and reason serves not only to dichotomize thought and feeling but also to elevate what has come to be called *abstract masculinity* over women's standpoint. Feminist scholars have been among the most vocal critics of the rationalist bias in Western thinking that privileges rational, independent, self-interested action over action that is driven by emotion, undertaken collectively, and motivated by altruism or the desire to affirm the group (Taylor 1995). Feminist groups try to channel emotions tied to women's subordination (fear, shame, resignation) into emotions conducive to protest (anger). For example, Groves's (1995) research on animal rights activists shows how movements perceived as emotional are not considered respectable. To gain respectability, activists developed a "vocabulary of emotions" to rationalize their participation to others and to themselves. Animal rights activists reproduced organizationally the dominant gender division of emotion: recruiting men was considered a strategic device to bring credibility to the movement because men were believed to be less emotional and more rational than women. As a consequence, male activists were often chosen for spokesperson and leadership positions while women tended to be overlooked for those positions.

In sum, emotions are pervasive in social movements and play an important role in different points of a movement's life course (Aminzade and McAdam 2001). Sometimes, for instrumental reasons, emotions are hidden from the public and only displayed backstage. Robnett (1998) makes the case that civil rights movement leaders strategically displayed a calm rationality in order to maintain their legitimacy with the state, while emotions clearly prevailed behind the scenes. At other times, emotion and passion happen before our eyes, but we rarely analyze them or even discuss them because they are considered irrelevant to our theories (Goodwin, Jasper, and Polletta 2000). Yet through the lens of strategic dramaturgy, the case of Superbarrio and the Asamblea de Barrios helps clarify how emotions are instrumental in a movement's strategic framing processes.

EMOTIONS IN THE ASAMBLEA DE BARRIOS

The death toll and destruction left by the 1985 earthquakes in Mexico City attracted national and international aid and attention. Pre-existing and emergent social networks provided vehicles to challenge the state when it was most vulnerable to popular demands, at a time when recourse to authoritarian social control measures would be condemned. Under the rising pressure of popular mobilization and international attention (both because of the disaster and because Mexico was hosting the 1986 soccer World Cup), the government decreed the expropriation of several thousand properties in downtown Mexico City to launch a federal program to restore, reconstruct, and build houses in the expropriated plots. In addition, the state extended credit that enabled the earthquake victims to buy the plots. It also recognized the *Coordinadora Unica de Damnificados* (Single Coordinating Committee of Earthquake Victims, CUD) as an independent umbrella organization representing the earthquake victims.

CUD's success in winning concessions to the earthquake victims' demands meant that it faced dissolution. Foreseeing movement decline, several CUD leaders sought to continue mobilizing housing applicants other than the earthquake victims and founded the *Asamblea de Barrios* (Neighborhood Assembly) to challenge unfair economic policies. The mobilizations after the earthquake made obvious the housing shortage for low-income families. Moreover, the unavailability of soft credit condemned the poor to live in ruinous *vecindades*, stacked in small rooms with relatives, or to squat the city's periphery. Left-wing groups (dominant among independent urban movements) had been organizing the homeless and renters in the downtown areas to squat in the outskirts of the cities. Contrary to this practice, the Asamblea leaders wanted to stay in the downtown area of Mexico City. For them, moving out could only mean renouncing their rights, livelihood, and *barrio* culture, in exchange for land in the middle of nowhere, without legal tenure, drinking water, paved streets or any other urban services. CUD's success and the reconstructed housing units owned by their former renters provided the hope housing applicants needed to join the Asamblea. The Asamblea leaders, distancing themselves from old-left discourse, tried to combine street protests with actions designed to attract sympathizers and media attention. In this ambiance, an unofficial contest to see who had the most amusing proposal to attract public attention to the Asamblea's mobilizations began.

> In the *Asamblea* [*de Barrios*] the idea of generating a more festive movement, less solemn, was developing. Several buddies tried to recover characters from the culture, the defenders, the champions of justice, these mysterious guys who adopt just causes, noble causes, and started showing up as paladins. But it was more an idea with which we fooled around, with which we tried to give the *Asamblea* a festive atmosphere, than something we would carry out for real. (Superbarrio, quoted in Schwarz 1994: 24)

In one of these moments of festive collective effervescence, Superbarrio was born. The outrage caused by the cry for help from an old lady who had had property stolen by her landlord was the catalyst. The following narrative describes how Superbarrio was born:

> One of the persons who lived in a small subleased area in a warehouse in *La Merced* was fifteen days late with the rent. Then, the landlord showed up and stole some gas tanks to pay himself. This lady went to the *Asamblea* to complain about it. We were in a gathering of more than one thousand people. She denounced it, [and said] she had been robbed. The *Asamblea* decided to go to the La Merced warehouse to detain that person and bring him before the authorities. When all these people arrived at the warehouse, this fellow [the landlord] had already gone taking away everything he got at hand. There was the feeling that these kinds of injustice should end, somehow. . . . And the question was raised louder: "When these abuses happen, why doesn't *El Santo* show up, or some champion of justice show up, someone who could stop abuses like this? I wish Superman, or I don't know who, would come." (Superbarrio, quoted in Schwarz 1994: 24-25)

People felt frustrated and angry about what happened that day and kept talking and thinking about it for several days.

> Even though I had never been a direct victim of precisely this kind of situation I know that feeling of impotence, of fury. My concern was how to stop it, how to put

an end to this problem—no one in the city should be left out in the street just because a landlord wants to squeeze a tenant even more. How to make justice, how to put these people in their place? I went round with this, how to do it, how to do it—how to release this uneasiness? Those were nights without sleep, going to work but thinking about other things. (Superbarrio, quoted in Brooks 1989: 87)

Then, "the idea emerged that if the landlords have their protectors—the court officials, the judges, the police, and the government as a whole—then the poor, the tenants, should also have someone to defend them" (Superbarrio, quoted in Cuéllar 1990). At some point, they decided to put this idea into practice and, on the way to a rally, bought a mask from a street vendor.

The red and yellow uniform was because we found the mask in Moneda Street, behind the National Palace. And in fact he dressed up right there, asking someone to get the tights and a T-shirt, and someone else to make the red and yellow emblem. And he remained that way. At that time he was wearing a pair of tennis shoes [instead of the wrestling boots he wore later]. (Rascón, quoted in Schwarz 1994: 70)

The design of Superbarrio was the result of strategic dramaturgy catalyzed by the emotions derived from an episode of injustice and abuse. The emotions involved were frustration and outrage caused by injustice in the context of a festive movement. But clearly, not everything that happened was planned. There were spontaneous reactions that catapulted Superbarrio into popularity.

Originally, Superbarrio was conceived of as someone who would head demonstrations and serve as silent witness in meetings with authorities. Events took an unforeseen twist and pulled Superbarrio rapidly in a different direction: The character's persona resonated among the people. Bystanders were curious and started asking questions: Who are you really? Why in the world do you decide to dress up like that? What is the meaning of the red and yellow in the costume? But perhaps more importantly, Superbarrio appealed to journalists and photographers who thought that government officials' reactions to the masked crusader merited being in print. Unexpectedly, both bystanders and journalists started looking for him more than for any of the Asamblea's leaders or spokespersons.

The first person who played the character was good at interpreting a silent Superbarrio, but was not very articulate and would get nervous whenever bystanders and journalists questioned him. The masked character attracted much more attention than he could handle, and eventually he gave up the Superbarrio role. The Asamblea's leaders wanted to keep Superbarrio in action to take advantage of the unpaid media attention and his sudden popularity, but no one was willing to surrender his personality and wear those funny lycra tights and mask (personal interviews with Superbarrio).

A militant from one of the cadre organizations to which some of the Asamblea's leaders belonged came to Mexico City for a vacation. Having nothing better to do and known to only a few people in the metropolis, one day he agreed to wear the mask—"just for a while," he said, until he returned to his home state. After leading a couple of demonstrations as Superbarrio, he discovered that he enjoyed portraying the character. In fact, he was so good at it that his comrades in Mexico City and his home state demanded that he keep doing it. After considering it for a while, he moved to Mexico City and performed Superbarrio for almost ten years, until 1997. Of course, he tells a different story about his origins.

Suddenly a red-and-yellow light came, it was so big that it blinded me. I looked at the mirror and there I was, as you see me now [dressed as a masked professional wrestler]. Then I asked myself, what's the point of this? A stereophonic voice told me: "You are Superbarrio, defender of poor tenants, scourge of [greedy] landlords!" And I said: "That's fine, let's start." (*La Jornada*, August 9, 1987)

Superbarrio's popularity and the emotional response he elicits from the public come from the cultural resonance of wrestling and the memory of the most popular professional wrestler ever in Mexico, El Santo.

WRESTLING SYMBOLISM

According to Barthes's semiotic analysis, wrestling displays the great spectacle of suffering, defeat, and justice. The first is represented by the wrestler who suffers in a hold which is reputedly cruel and "offers an excessive portrayal of suffering; like a primitive Pieta, he exhibits for all to see his face, exaggeratedly contorted by intolerable affliction. . . . Suffering appears as inflicted with emphasis and conviction, for everyone must not only see that the man suffers, but also and above all understand why he suffers" (Barthes [1957] 1990: 90-91). In wrestling, "defeat is not a conventional sign, abandoned as soon as it is understood; it is not an outcome, but quite the contrary, it is a duration, a display, it takes up the ancient myths of public suffering and humiliation: the cross and the pillory. It is as if the wrestler is crucified in broad daylight and in the sight of all" (Barthes [1957] 1990: 92). It is fairly common in Mexico that important wrestling matches (when a championship is at stake or when wrestlers are long-standing rivals) are settled "mask versus mask," "mask versus hair," or "hair versus hair." That is, wrestlers bet their mask or hair on two out of three pins. Removing his mask or having his head shaved right on the spot marks the loser. In wrestling, defeat comes along with public humiliation. The victor keeps his hair or mask, which thus become markers of superiority.

Wrestling is a dramatic representation of the endless struggle between good and evil and, depending on who wins the bout, justice and injustice. There are many ways of representing this struggle, with varying degrees of success in eliciting an audience's emotional response. In Shakespeare's *Romeo and Juliet*, for example, our interest is held by the emotional response to the tragic standard story—love against grave adversity. Similarly, wrestling stages a well-known dramatic structure—the never-ending fight between good and evil. As in any other representation, the story per se is important. The enjoyment of the representation is not weakened by the audience's familiarity with the story—on the contrary, recognizing familiar themes increases its enjoyment. The emotional response that a given performance elicits depends on their familiarity with the story, the empathy raised by some of the characters, and how it is staged. Also, given the familiarity of wrestling's drama, who wins a match is less important than how that outcome is reached. What wrestling aficionados enjoy is not necessarily the representation of a known story but the mise-en-scène.

Wrestlers are actors representing established and clear-cut characters. In one corner of the ring is the *hero* who fights clean and fair—the *babyface*, in the jargon of the trade. Across the ring is the *villain*, the cruel and cowardly bastard—the *heel*.

Each wrestler expresses his ultimate goodness or badness through their name, appearance, and behavior. But what makes wrestling even more shocking to the public is that the referee always sides with the heel, allowing him to abuse the babyface. The heel commits sadistic acts (like gouging eyes or kicking in the groin) when the referee pretends he is not looking. But if the babyface commits a minor infraction, the referee yells at him out of proportion. The wrestlers and the referee perform their obvious roles with studied gestures and exaggerated mimicry to an aroused crowd that participates in the bout by enthusiastically approving or condemning what happens in the ring. This dramatic structure underscores wrestling's intention to portray a purely moral concept: that of justice.

> The idea of "paying" is essential to wrestling, and the crowd's "Give it to him" means above all else "Make him pay." . . . The baser the action of the "bastard," the more delighted the public is by the blow which he justly receives in return. If the villain—who is of course a coward—takes refuge behind the ropes, claiming unfairly to have right to do so by a brazen mimicry, he is inexorably pursued there and caught, and the crowd is jubilant at seeing the rules broken for the sake of a deserved punishment. (Barthes [1957] 1990: 92)

Wrestling fans know that not everything that takes place in the ring is real. They are aware that it is a representation, that the gestures and most of the blows and cruel holds are vastly exaggerated. But this conventional dramatic structure has plenty of room for surprises, drama, accidents, and tension. This dramatic structure is not peculiar to wrestling in Mexico. But the corrupted and authoritarian features of Mexican government give a different resonance to wrestling in Mexico than in the United States,[7] where wrestling resonates with the "American Dream" (Lincoln 1989: 158).

WRESTLING IN MEXICO

In Mexico, wrestling is more popular than bullfights or baseball. There are dozens of professional wrestlers who travel all over the country to wrestle opponents for the amusement and catharsis of a mostly working-class audience. In sports such as boxing, soccer, football or hockey, precise rules demarcate what is allowed from what is forbidden. All these sports require a referee (or referees) whose job is to enforce the rules and guarantee a fair and clean match to the best of their ability. Sports fans expect that the rules will be observed and that the best athlete or team will prevail. Wrestling matches have no limits on time or number of contenders, which might be uneven. Sometimes team members unexpectedly change sides in the middle of a bout and wrestle each other or all against one single wrestler. There is nothing to prevent a wrestling match ending up in a savage attack on one wrestler or in a general free-for-all in which even the referee receives and gives blows. Obviously, wrestling is not a sport in the usual sense, and it is certainly not an elite sport associated with an aristocratic worldview and ethics (fair play, will to win, etc., see Bourdieu 1984: 209). It is a spectacle that reproduces the real world's unfair competition, as opposed to the ideal of fair competition. It encodes a subliminal message that says that there are hurdles built into competition that do not affect everybody in the same way, that is, there's no fair play. Wrestling is a spectacle where courtesy and chivalry are replaced by unleashed competition and violation of the rules—even by those whose job it is to enforce the rules.

In Mexico, wrestling happens to be a well-suited metaphor of class relations and the corrupt Mexican authoritarian regime.[8] Superbarrio is the fair and clean athlete (representing the popular movement) wrestling a tricky and cruel opponent (the landlord and his lawyers), who usually is helped by a corrupt and partial referee that fails to enforce the rules (the judges, state officials, riot police). It is expected that good guys have to fight bad guys. What defies expectations is that the referee would favor the bad guys.

> Just as there are bad guys inside the ring, there are also bad guys on the streets. And just as the referees inside the ring are always partial to the rude ones and allow them to do their tricks and prohibited things, in the streets it is the same. In the barrio the government wants to be the referee and it supports the landlords and lends them riot police to assist in evictions of families. (Superbarrio, quoted in Brooks 1989: 88)

This drama resonates with the daily lives and lived experience of the vast majority of working-class Mexicans. In wrestling they empathize with the babyface, who needs support from the audience to keep both the referee and the heel in check. The heel pretends to shield his illegal maneuvers and concealed weapons from the audience who can't help but angrily condemn his wrongdoing and the referee's partiality that allows abuse. The heel responds to the audience with insults, further infuriating the crowd. In Mexican politics, the wrestling metaphor is played out in Superbarrio's symbolic field.

SUPERBARRIO IN THE SYMBOLIC FIELD

Based on wrestling symbolism, the presence of Superbarrio at a collective event transforms it into a symbolic field, to use Bourdieu's (1984) term, in which the crowd applies the dramatic structure of wrestling to its own struggle: the powerless must fight not only to improve their condition or have their demands met but even to have their rights observed. Moreover, the authorities are partial and will not concede anything just because people are entitled to it. In wrestling, as in real life, good people follow the rules and wicked people use illegal methods and dirty tricks. Popular movements that ignore this basic fact will inevitably be crushed. Superbarrio's presence further suggests that some suffering will be inflicted on the people, that it's immoral to remain aloof in the presence of abuse and injustice, and that the audience should help to correct the unfair situation.

Superbarrio devalues the symbolic power of suits, ties, titles, and other symbols of distinction that bureaucrats, politicians, and the upper class use, with the symbolic power of popular superheroes. He also devalues superheroes with his paunchy figure and curved legs of a regular working-class body in lycra tights. The rituals of politics and bureaucratic decision making are opposed with humor and popular culture by a superhero whose powers come from organized people. The myth of state power and bureaucratic structures is opposed with the popular mythology of struggle and self-organization. At least for a short while, people stop seeing themselves through the eyes of the masters (Gramsci [1918] 1985). They refuse to "look at the situation of the dominated through the social eyes of the dominant" (Bourdieu 1990: 130). The symbolic power of the desk is opposed with the symbolic power of the mask. Superbarrio breaks the norms, rituals, and routines of politics, challenging the terms of the relationship between state and local authorities and the popular movement. Officials, who are used to talking solemnly and pompously about laws, regulations, and technical and budgetary constraints become disadvantaged when they face a popular organization posing heartfelt demands through a masked and caped crusader for justice.

In performances designed after popular theater, Superbarrio stages mock wrestling matches against popular movement foes. The authorities have sometimes repressed these performances because they seriously challenge the dominant symbolic order. The police confiscated the ring the night before Superbarrio was to hold his first wrestling match in a public square. The Asamblea denounced the event as the first ring abduction for political reasons in Mexico's history and demanded its immediate release. The old slogan "Freedom to political prisoners!" was modified accordingly to demand "Freedom to political rings!" (*La Jornada*, July 19, 1987). The city regent admitted that the municipal authorities took away the ring because the bout would be "a disrespect to the Constitution Square" (*La Jornada*, July 24, 1987).

The response of government officials when they faced Superbarrio for the first time was a mix of emotions; sometimes they took offense and responded in anger. These reactions indicate that authorities perceive Superbarrio as a threat to the dominant symbolic order, which usually works to the movement's disadvantage. Once, Superbarrio was addressing a meeting in front of the governor's house in Guadalajara, Jalisco. The furious governor approached Superbarrio and asked him, "Who are you? What are you doing here? Why are you manipulating these people?" Then the governor took the microphone from Superbarrio and tried to unmask him. The people in the meeting protected Superbarrio and impeded his unmasking. The disgruntled governor said, "I show my face. I want to know who I'm talking with" (*Proceso*, December 7, 1987).

Superbarrio's resonance is derived from the memories of popular wrestling heroes. In the 1960s and 1970s, the Mexican culture industry transformed several professional wrestlers into comic book and film heroes, the most popular of which was *El Santo*, who dressed in a silver mask, with immaculate white boots, tights, briefs, and cape over his naked torso. He wrestled approximately fifteen thousand matches in forty-five years and never had been unmasked by any of his opponents. Nobody ever knew his real name or what his face looked like until he died in 1984—the year before the deadly earthquakes hit Mexico City (Carro 1984; Sánchez 1989). El Santo enjoyed immensely popular status and was the top star of weekly comics, photo novels, and wrestling films where he tirelessly fought the forces of evil. From 1952 to 1983, around 150 wrestling films were made, in which at least fifty featured El Santo in the leading role. During the 1960s, El Santo alone filmed twenty-one movies (Carro 1984: 31).

Still in the late 1980s, most of the Mexican mass media represented and promoted conservative business interests closely related to political elites in the government and the ruling party. With few exceptions, there was virtually no media representation of the voices of other social groups. Having unpaid access to the media became a major goal for the Asamblea, and Superbarrio turned out to be its main instrument. Photographers were Superbarrio's best allies. When they knew that a top official was going to be in some public event or ceremony, they called Superbarrio and snuck him in when the officials showed up. Superbarrio describes his relationship with photographers as a game of mischief. Some photographers used to tell him: "Hey, Superbarrio, give us the picture!" Then, he was expected to perform some audacious move. The more audacious, the more pictures they would take, and the more likely at least one of them would be published (personal interview with Superbarrio).

Superbarrio's presence in the media was double-edged, though. The television networks reported his activities only when they could hurt his public image, framing him as a vandal, a radical agitator who should be in jail. He did not worry about this. He even liked bad press: "I like a lot of headlines like: 'Superbarrio vandalizes.' 'Superbarrio damaged national property.'" He admits that some people reading those headlines would like to have him in jail, but also realizes that some people would applaud his actions and even say, "Do it again! Give it to them! Make them pay!" For the Asamblea, the worst media is no media. Being in the media is a way to make the public consider the popular movement's point of view and not only that of the government or the powerholders (personal interview with Superbarrio).

Reflecting Superbarrio's influence, several organizations all over the country have adopted wrestling symbolism as part of their repertoire of protest. Wearing flashy professional wrestling outfits, a cohort of masked heroes have appeared leading protests and voicing the demands of the organizations they represent. Most of them did not last long. They did not handle the stress well nor have the devotion that is required to maintain a masked character representing a popular movement. A case that merits separate study is Subcommander Marcos, spokesperson and most visible leader of the Ejército Zapatista de Liberación Nacional. He and most of the Indian guerrilla fighters wear ski masks or bandannas over their faces. For Superbarrio, "The mask is not a disguise but a symbol. [It] represents the idea that our struggle is a collective one, which doesn't belong to one individual" (*Los Angeles Times*, February 25, 1989). Similarly, Marcos explains why the Zapatistas cover their faces: They don't act as individuals; they represent the community. "If someone wants to see my face he should look to the mirror and will discover who's behind the mask," Marcos once declared.

CONCLUSION

The creation of Superbarrio was prompted by strong moral emotions. The outrage caused by the cry for help from an old lady and the frustration resulting from their inability to help her were the catalysts for conceiving Superbarrio. At the time, the Asamblea was trying to create an aura of a festive movement that combined serious problem-solving mobilizations with actions designed to attract sympathizers and capture media attention. Struggling with these collective emotions, "the idea emerged that if the landlords have their protectors . . . then the poor . . . should also have someone to defend them" (Superbarrio, quoted in Cuéllar 1990).

Superbarrio's performances provoked emotions both in the man who played him and in his audiences. The first person who played the character was good at interpreting a silent Superbarrio, but the public wanted him to speak up. The second Superbarrio enjoyed it so much, and was so good making up outlandish stories about his origins and mission, that he moved to Mexico City to perform the role on a permanent basis.

Wrestling symbolism accounts for Superbarrio's emotional resonance on the audiences. The reason? Wrestling portrays an unfair situation so that the audience cannot help but empathize with the babyface and react against injustice and abuse. The everyday experience of poor and dominated people is that hard work seldom provides enough to live decent lives. Wrestling symbolism provides a key to understand the "systemic" hurdles that work to their disadvantage. The referee costume is a disguise that hides his complicity with the heels. Idealized assumptions of fairness and equality before the law hide class, gender, and race distinctions that produce different sets of constraints and opportunities for different groups. In practice, women are not equal to men, straights to gays, blacks to whites, Indians to *mestizos*, rich to poor, and so on. Paraphrasing Orwell (1954), all citizens are equal but some citizens are more equal than others. The mechanisms that create a gap between reality and principle are transparent but rule like iron law. Everyday experience in the context of economic inequality in a corrupt authoritarian state granted resonance to wrestling symbolism. The people, the good movement, was represented as being martyred by an evil and corrupted system.

Mexico City's urban poor experienced a mixture of different emotions—with indignation as the dominant one—when they saw Superbarrio wrestling popular movement foes. Indignation is a moral emotion that involves a set of concepts, beliefs, and social expectations. The *Merriam-Webster Dictionary* defines indignation as anger aroused by something unjust, unworthy, or mean. To be indignant it is necessary to recognize a given situation as unjust. It is an emotion that results from empathy with the one who suffers and evaluation of the reasons why he suffers. In this emotion, the interest or dignity of the person who has the emotion does not intervene until she pictures herself in the same situation: victimized by people breaking the law with authorities' indifference or complicity. Indignation is provoked by the belief that some moral norm has been deliberately broken and that harm and suffering are being inflicted upon undeserving people. Indignation requires that the indignant person believe that there is a responsible party whose action or lack thereof shows hostility, ill will, or indifference toward another individual or group. The quotidian experience of invisible hurdles that poor and dominated people have to overcome transforms indignation into resentment, and resentment into anger. Indignation, resentment, and anger can then be mobilized against political targets.

When government officials, undoubtedly literate in wrestling symbolism, faced Superbarrio, they could see the role assigned to them. Journalists and photographers tried to register government officials' reaction to being defined as villains in front of an audience that expected Superbarrio to make them pay. Authorities frequently perceived the challenges to the dominant symbolic order as disrespectful, took offense, and made efforts to restore it. Had the authorities not reacted the way they usually did to strategic dramaturgy, Superbarrio would not have received the media coverage the Asamblea was looking for.

The success of the Asamblea de Barrios in meeting their demands cannot be explained by its use of compelling strategic dramaturgy alone. But its use made the organization well known nationally and internationally, primarily because of its symbol of struggle and newsworthy protest events rather than for its formal pronouncements. The attention Superbarrio attracted severely limited the possibilities of ignoring, neglecting, or silencing him or the organization he represented, as well as constraining authoritarian social control options. Through its linkages with other social movement organizations, with the Party of the Democratic Revolution (PRD), with the local and federal legislatures and with national and international organizations, the Asamblea rapidly acquired conventional political resources. Thus, through street protests, strategic dramaturgy, lobbying, and skillful negotiations, the Asamblea achieved substantive housing victories.

What attracted media attention was not the issues the Asamblea was fighting for—housing issues in Mexico City were hardly news! Strategic dramaturgy accounts for it. Many organizations promoting housing demands made the news only when life and property were threatened. Dressed up as a wrestler, Superbarrio suggested struggle and the threat of violence. But he was not calling for violent struggle. Superbarrio invited people to organize themselves and struggle for their rights and clearly, and repeatedly, declared himself against the use of violence.

The earthquake victims organized in the CUD had to overcome their grief over the loss of relatives, friends, and possessions and transform it into anger against the authorities (who delayed adequate response to the emergency) and the landlords (who tried to take advantage of the situation by tossing out poor people from the downtown *barrios*). After several months of struggle the CUD succeeded in attaining several important demands. Some movement leaders decided to continue exploiting the perceived vulnerability of the government instead of letting the CUD die of success and return to a quiet home life—after all, they were full-time activists with a long record of movement participation.

The formation of the Asamblea and the creation of Superbarrio benefited from, and contributed to, a happy succession of events. The Asamblea leaders were known and trusted, and they were familiar with the intricacies of housing policy in the Federal District. They knew how to pressure and negotiate with the authorities without compromising the movement's political independence. Simultaneously, an elite group that opposed the government's neoliberal policies split from the PRI (Partido Revolucionario Insitutional). The splinter group had basically the same demands as the popular movements that resisted the International Monetary Fund's austerity programs followed by the government. This coincidence coalesced in an electoral front that ran Cuauhtémoc Cárdenas for president in 1988, the Frente Democrático Nacional (FDN). Superbarrio's action was initially limited to housing demands and tenant issues. After a couple of months on the street and in the printed media, he became known nationally and internationally, thus extending his struggle beyond the barrio limits. The Asamblea endorsed Cárdenas's bid for the presidency and several of its leaders ran tickets under the FDN. After the election, they became very influential in the transition from the anti-PRI coalition, the FDN, to the center to left-wing PRD. As result, several of the Asamblea's leaders became party officials, siphoning off leaders and cadres from the movement sector into the institutional politics sector. This situation created tension between movement and party politics. Disagreements within the PRD on party or national politics were brought into the movement organization, which until then had had a remarkable consensus on movement and local matters. This tension caused a split in the Asamblea. Each splinter kept its own Superbarrio.

In 1997 the PRD won the first election for chief of government of the Federal District. As a result, the Asamblea was confronted with a stark dilemma: stage protests against Cárdenas and the PRD or adopt less confrontational and more accommodating tactics. Eventually, institutionalization and lobbying became more salient than street protests and strategic dramaturgy aimed to challenge the symbolic order. The Asamblea continues representing housing applicants but all of the founding leaders followed political careers in the PRD, in the federal and local legislature, and after 1997, in the government of the Federal District. Among those who did was the man who performed as Superbarrio.

NOTES

1. The diversity of what we call emotion is considerable. Some emotions are related to feelings and physiological changes (blush), others to cognitive activities (pride in an accomplishment), and still others to wishful attitudes (hope). Some have typical behavioral expressions (nervousness), while others have a variety of behavioral expressions (regret). Some are amenable to change through changes in beliefs and attitudes (shame). Some seem to be beyond our control (depression), while others may be manipulated (empathy). Some are closely related to pleasure (joy) or pain (sorrow), while others are not so closely related (boredom). Some are related to immediate circumstances (embarrassment), while others are possible in different situations (anxiety). Some provide us with reasons for action (anger), while other emotions are not connected to action in an obvious way (wonder). Some emotions are violent and short lived (rage), while some are mild and long lasting (affection). Some are only human (pride), while others are common to humans and nonhumans (fear). Some seem to depend on the level of arousal (anger, rage, frenzy, ire, fury, wrath), while still others do not (resignation) (Hansberg 1996; Rorty 1980).

2. I use "object" here as shorthand for things, symbols, people, relations, situations, and events.

3. Note the gendered quality of most cultural rules about emotion, and how the Bible condemns emotions such as wrath and praises other emotions such as love and hope.

4. The idea that emotions have a cognitive dimension and that they are a sort of value judgment has its own tradition. In the eighteenth century, the moral philosophers David Hume, Francis Hutcheson, and Adam Smith argued that emotions such as sympathy play an important function in sociability.

5. Collective behavior theories define ordinary behavior as rational and collective behavior as irrational and even pathological. Following Turner (1964), there are two types of such theories: contagion and convergence theories. Contagion theories set themselves to explain the discontinuity between individual and collective behavior on the basis of psychological processes whereby moods, attitudes, and behavior are communicated rapidly and accepted uncritically. These theories (Blumer 1939; Lang and Lang 1961; Le Bon [1895] 1969; Park and Burgess 1921; Smelser 1963; Tarde [1890] 1903) take as their focal point some form of imitation and emotional contagiousness that lead to unanimous, intense feeling and behavior at variance with usual predispositions. Mechanisms such as anonymity, restriction of attention, and isolation are believed to neutralize normal inhibitions and social pressures against types of behavior that occur in the crowd.

Convergence theories assume continuity between individual and crowd behavior, which thereby results from the simultaneous presence of people with the same predispositions. These predispositions are activated by the event or object toward which their common attention is directed. Convergence theories identify authoritarianism, anomie, alienation, and relative deprivation as the main causes that predispose individuals to uniformity of response and in some cases equate crowd behavior with some form of psychopathy (Adorno et al. 1959; Arendt [1948] 1973; Freud 1921; Horkheimer and Adorno [1944] 1995; Kornhauser 1959).

6. The assumption of the false dichotomy between rationality and emotion has been far from unanimous. The emergent norm theory (Turner 1964; Turner and Killian 1987) stresses the continuity between normal group behavior and crowd behavior, questioning the "illusion of unanimity" in crowds. Just as ordinary groups give rise to, and are governed by, norms, so crowds generate and are governed by a norm that arises in a special situation. In a related vein, Lofland (1981, 1985) argues that collective behavior requires the suspension of the "attitude of

everyday life" by a relatively large number of people and that such suspension is accompanied by increased levels of emotional arousal in participants. He contends that the "dominant emotion" in collective behavior episodes has the same logical status as the emergent norm; the shift is from the cognitive (the norm) to the affective (the emotion).

7. Lincoln (1989: 152) examined an individual episode, chosen at random, of the syndicated TV show "All-Star Wrestling." He describes the show as follows: "In the four matches that followed the opener, the villains consistently triumphed, and triumphed easily, using illegal and sadistic means in every case. They strangled their victims and bit them, hit them with chairs and concealed weapons. They gouged eyes and kicked them, threw their hapless opponents from the ring and smashed them to the mat. They sneered at referees, abused fallen heroes, taunted the crowd, and made mockery of the rules. Truly, these four matches constituted a chamber of horrors: an abandonment of all normative morality, without a hint of retribution."

8. The PRI ruled the country for a world-record seventy-one years behind a democratic façade that veiled an electoral system that was not free, impartial, or fair (Cadena-Roa 2003).

REFERENCES

Adorno, Theodor W., E. Frenkel-Brunswik, D. J. Levinson, and R. N. Sanford. 1959. *The Authoritarian Personality*. New York: Harper.

Aminzade, Ron, and Doug McAdam. 2001. "Emotions and Contentious Politics." Pp. 14-50 in *Silence and Voice in Contentious Politics*. New York: Cambridge University Press.

Arendt, Hannah. [1948] 1973. *The Origins of Totalitarism*. New York: The Free Press.

Barthes, Roland. [1957] 1990. "The World of Wrestling." Pp. 87-93 in *Culture and Society: Contemporary Debates*, Jeffery Alexander and Steven Seidman, eds. Cambridge: Cambridge University Press.

Benford, Robert D. 1997. "An Insider's Critique of the Social Movement Framing Perspective." *Sociological Inquiry* 67: 409-430.

Blumer, Herbert. 1939. "Collective Behavior." Pp. 219-288 in *Principles of Sociology*, Robert E. Parks, ed. New York: Barnes and Noble.

Bourdieu, Pierre. 1984. *Distinction*. Cambridge: Harvard University Press.

———. 1990. "Social Space and Symbolic Power." Pp. 122-139 in *In Other Words*, Pierre Bourdieu, ed. Stanford, CA: Stanford University Press.

Brooks, David. 1989. "We Are All Superbarrio." *Zeta Magazine*, April, 85-90.

Cadena-Roa, Jorge. 2003. "State Pacts, Elites, and Social Movements in Mexico's Transition to Democracy." Pp. 107-143 in *States, Parties, and Social Movements*, J. A. Goldstone, ed. New York: Cambridge University Press.

Calhoun, Cheshire, and Robert C. Solomon, eds. 1984. *What Is an Emotion? Classic Readings in Philosophical Psychology*. New York: Oxford University Press.

Carro, Nelson. 1984. *El cine de luchadores*. Mexico City: UNAM.

Cohen, Jean L. 1985. "Strategy or Identity: New Theoretical Paradigms and Contemporary Social Movements." *Social Research* 52: 663-716.

Cuéllar, Angélica. 1990. "Con ánimo de triunfo: Entrevista a Superbarrio Gómez." *Acta Sociológica* 3: 107-116.

Ferree, Myra Marx, and Frederick D. Miller. 1985. "Mobilization and Meaning: Toward an Integration of Social Psychological and Resource Perspectives on Social Movements." *Sociological Inquiry* 55: 38-61.

Freud, Sigmund. 1921. *Group Psychology and the Analysis of the Ego*. London: IPP.

Gamson, William A., Bruce Fireman, and Steven Rytina. 1982. *Encounters with Unjust Authorities*. Homewood, IL: Dorsey Press.

Goodwin, Jeff, James Jasper, and Francesca Polletta. 2000. "Return of the Repressed: The Fall and Rise of Emotions in Social Movement Theory." *Mobilization* 5: 65-84.

Gramsci, Antonio. [1918] 1985. "Culture and Class Struggle." Pp. 31-34 in *Antonio Gramsci:*

Selections from Cultural Writings, D. Forgacs and G. Nowell-Smith, eds. Cambridge: Harvard University Press.

Groves, Julian McAllister. 1995. "Learning to Feel: The Neglected Sociology of Social Movements." *Sociological Review* 43: 435-461.

Hansberg, Olbeth. 1996. *La diversidad de las emociones*. Mexico City: FCE.

Horkheimer, Max, and Theodor W. Adorno. [1944] 1995. *Dialectic of Enlightenment*. New York: Continuum.

Jaggar, Alison. 1989. "Love and Knowledge: Emotion in Feminist Epistemology." *Inquiry* 32:161-176.

Jenkins, Craig. 1983. "Resource Mobilization Theory and the Study of Social Movements." *Annual Review of Sociology* 9: 527-553.

Kitschelt, Herbert. 1986. "Political Opportunity Structures and Political Protest: Anti-Nuclear Movements in Four Democracies." *British Journal of Political Science* 16: 57-95.

Klandermans, Bert. 1984. "Mobilization and Participation: Social-Psychological Expansions of Resource Mobilization Theory." *American Sociological Review* 49: 583-600.

Kornhauser, William. 1959. *The Politics of Mass Society*. New York: Free Press.

Lang, Kurt, and Gladys Engel Lang. 1961. *Collective Dynamics*. New York: Crowell.

Le Bon, Gustave. [1895] 1969. *The Crowd: A Study of the Popular Mind*. New York: Ballantine Books.

Lincoln, Bruce. 1989. *Discourse and the Construction of Society*. New York: Oxford University Press.

Lofland, John. 1981. "Collective Behavior: The Elementary Forms." Pp. 378-446 in *Social Psychology: Sociological Perspectives*, M. Rosemberg and R. H. Turner, eds. New York: Basic Books.

———. 1985. "Crowd Joys." Pp. 71-88 in *Protest: Studies of Collective Behavior and Social Movements*, John Lofland, ed. New Brunswick, NJ: Transaction Books.

McAdam, Doug. 1982. *Political Process and the Development of Black Insurgency, 1930-1970*. Chicago: University of Chicago Press.

———. 1996. "The Framing Function of Movement Tactics: Strategic Dramaturgy in the American Civil Rights Movement." Pp. 338-355 in *Comparative Perspectives on Social Movements: Political Opportunities, Mobilizing Structures, and Cultural Framings*, Doug McAdam, John D. McCarthy, and Mayer N. Zald, eds. Cambridge: Cambridge University Press.

McCarthy, John D., and Mayer N. Zald. 1973. *The Trend of Social Movements in America*. Morristown, NJ: General Learning Press.

———. 1977. "Resource Mobilization and Social Movements: A Partial Theory." *American Journal of Sociology* 82: 1212-1242.

Orwell, George. 1954. *Animal Farm*. New York: Harcourt, Brace & World.

Park, Robert E., and Ernest E. Burgess. 1921. *Introduction to the Science of Sociology*. Chicago: University of Chicago Press.

Perrow, Charles. 1979. "The Sixties Observed." Pp. 192-211 in *The Dynamics of Social Movements*, M. N. Zald and J. D. McCarthy, eds. Cambridge, MA: Winthrop.

Robnett, Belinda. 1998. "African American Women in the Civil Rights Movement: Spontaneity and Emotion in Social Movement Theory." Pp. 65-95 in *No Middle Ground: Women and Radical Protest*, K. M. Blee, ed. New York: New York University Press.

Rorty, Amelie Oksenberg. 1980. "Explaining Emotions." Pp. 103-126 in *Explaining Emotions*, A. O. Rorty, ed. Berkeley, CA: University of California Press.

Sánchez, Francisco. 1989. *Crónica antisolemne del cine Mexicano*. Mexico City: UV.

Schwarz, Mauricio-José. 1994. *Todos somos Superbarrio*. Mexico City: Planeta.

Smelser, Neil J. 1963. *Theory of Collective Behavior*. New York: Free Press.

Smith-Lovin, Lynn. 1995. "The Sociology of Affect and Emotion." Pp. 118-148 in *Sociological Perspectives on Social Psychology*, K. S. Cook, G. A. Fine, and J. S. House, eds. Boston: Allyn and Bacon.

Snow, David A., and Robert Benford. 1988. "Ideology, Frame Resonance, and Participant

Mobilization." Pp. 197-217 in *From Structure to Action: Comparing Social Movement Research across Cultures*, vol. 1, *International Social Movements Research*, B. Klandermans, H. Kriesi, and S. Tarrow, eds. Greenwich, CT: JAI Press.

————. 1992. "Master Frames and Cycles of Protest." Pp. 133-155 in *Frontiers in Social Movement Theory*, A. D. Morris and C. M. Mueller, eds. New Haven, CT: Yale University Press.

Snow, David A., E. Burke Rochford, Jr., Steven K. Worden, and Robert D. Benford. 1986. "Frame Alignment Processes, Micromobilization, and Movement Participation." *American Sociological Review* 51: 464-481.

Solomon, Robert C. 1984. "Emotions and Choice." Pp. 305-326 in *What Is an Emotion? Classic Readings in Philosophical Psychology*, C. Calhoun and R. C. Solomon, eds. New York: Oxford University Press.

Tarde, Gabriel. [1890] 1903. *The Laws of Imitation*. New York: Henry Holt.

Taylor, Verta. 1995. "Watching for Vibes: Bringing Emotions into the Study of Feminist Organizations." Pp. 223-233 in *Feminist Organizations: Harvest of the New Women's Movement*, M. M. Ferree and P. Y. Martin, eds. Philadelphia: Temple University Press.

Thoits, Peggy A. 1989. "The Sociology of Emotions." *Annual Review of Sociology* 15: 317-342.

Tilly, Charles. 1978. *From Mobilization to Revolution*. Reading, MA: Addison-Wesley.

————. 1984. "Social Movements and National Politics." Pp. 297-317 in *Statemaking and Social Movements*, C. Bright and S. Harding, eds. Ann Arbor: University of Michigan Press.

Turner, Ralph H. 1964. "Collective Behavior." Pp. 382-425 in *Handbook of Modern Sociology*, R. E. L. Faris, ed. Chicago: Rand-McNally.

————. 1983. "Figure and Ground in the Analysis of Social Movements." *Symbolic Interaction* 6: 175-181.

Turner, Ralph H., and Lewis M. Killian. 1972. *Collective Behavior*. 3rd ed. Englewood Cliffs, NJ: Prentice Hall.

Part II

Non-Movement Framing: The State and Media

Chapter 5

OFFICIAL FRAMES IN SOCIAL MOVEMENT THEORY: THE FBI, HUAC, AND THE COMMUNIST THREAT IN HOLLYWOOD

John A. Noakes

With increased interest in the cultural aspects of political activity, frame analysis became one of the dominant approaches to studying social movements in the 1990s (Benford 1997; Goodwin and Jasper 1999; Johnston 2002). A *frame* is an "interpretative schema that simplifies and condenses the 'world out there,'" thus giving organization to experience and guiding action by "rendering events or occurrences meaningful" (Snow and Benford 1992:137). Imported into sociology from the study of the psychology of communication by Erving Goffman (1972, 1981) as a means of analyzing how culture is reflected in social interactions, frame analysis has become, in the hands of social movement researchers, a means of conceptualizing how people understand and interpret political and social problems (Gamson 1992). Of particular interest to social movement researchers are the cultural and cognitive processes necessary to mobilize people to engage in extra-institutional political action (Gamson, Fireman, and Rytina 1982; Snow et al. 1986).

Most frames support existing versions of reality by reiterating dominant expressions or reinforcing elite interpretations of events and, therefore, discourage collective action by aggrieved populations. Thus, social movement researchers have distinguished what they call collective action frames—interpretive schemata developed by movement entrepreneurs to encourage and facilitate social movement activity by reframing a problem in such a way as to highlight or reveal the injustice inherent in the status quo (Gamson 1992; Snow and Benford 1992).

Frame analysis deepens our understanding of the micromobilization processes that convert potential recruits into active members of social movement organizations by carefully dissecting how activists work to develop frames that resonate with the broadest range of potential recruits (Snow et al. 1986; Swart 1995). They have also contributed to our understanding of the historical trajectory of movements by explaining, on the one hand, the persistence of certain interpretive schemata over time (Mooney and Hunt 1996; Swart 1995), and on the other, the clustering of social movements at particular points in history (Snow and Benford 1992; Tarrow 1994).

Impressive as it is, this list of accomplishments reveals the limited focus of most work pursued by proponents of frame analysis. Researchers have carefully examined processes within social movements and interactions between social movement organizations and their members and potential recruits. But collective action frames developed and diffused by social movement activists do not succeed or fail merely on their substantive merit. As Doug McAdam, John McCarthy, and Mayer Zald (1996b: 17) and others (Tarrow 1994; Zald 1996) have argued, the frames advanced by social movement organizations are subject to an "intense contestation between collective actors representing the movement, the state, and any existing counter movements." More provocatively, Sidney Tarrow (1994: 123) calls these framing contests "struggles for cultural supremacy."

Social movement researchers have addressed framing contests between countermovements (Jasper 1997; Jasper and Poulsen 1993; Meyer and Staggenborg 1996) and the relationship between media frames and social movements (Gamson 1988; Gitlin 1980; Tarrow 1994). Moreover, some have researched the construction and promotion of countermobilizing elite frames (Haydu 1999; Roy and Parker-Gwin 1999). But, with few exceptions (Zuo and Benford 1995), frame analysts continue to ignore or gloss over the mobilization of *official frames* by state agencies. Researchers have long recognized that states frame issues (Anderson 1991; Gusfield 1981) and that governments manipulate the perceptions of constituents (Edelman 1971). But social movement research has long slighted the relationship between social movements and the state (Jenkins 1995), despite the celebrated bringing of the state "back in" to political analysis in the 1980s (Evans, Rueschemeyer, and Skocpol 1985; Skocpol 1979) and the centrality of the political opportunity structure in recent social movement research. Political opportunity *structures* are too often conceived of as relatively static factors in the social movement equation (that is, they are either opened or closed), and too little attention is paid to the interaction between state actors and social movement actors (Goodwin and Jasper 1999).

One conclusion that can be drawn from this gap in the social movement literature is that the processes by which officials construct frames are considered too universal, too constant, or too derivative to be an interesting factor in the movement equation (Gamson 1975; McAdam 1996b). Thus, McAdam (1996b: 338) can declare that he has illustrated how civil rights activists used specific tactics to frame actions and shape public opinion "in ways that led to a decisive victory in the movement's 'frame contest' *with federal officials and Southern segregationist*" (emphasis added), without identifying, much less analyzing, the frames advanced by either set of state actors. Likewise, Tarrow (1994: 122) can refer to the need for movement entrepreneurs to select cultural symbols "that they hope will mediate among the cultural underpinnings" of potential recruits, movement militants, and "*the sources of official culture*" (emphasis added), without specifying what those sources of official culture are, how they are mobilized, or how they affect the success or failure of collective action frames mobilized by social movements.

The discounting of official frames is reminiscent of the assumptions about the nature of the grievances that mobilized collective action among aggrieved populations made by resource mobilization theorists and challenged by early proponents of frame analysis (Snow et al. 1986). "What is at issue," David Snow, E. Burke Rochford, Steven Worden, and Robert Benford (1986: 466) argued, "is not merely the presence or absence of grievances, but the manner in which grievances are interpreted and the generation and diffusion of those interpretations." I extend this insight to the question of official frames. What is at issue in this chapter is not merely the presence of official interpretations, but the processes by which these interpretations are constructed and promoted. To the extent that frame analysts have insisted that movement-centered structural explanations of social movements recognize the cultural aspects of movement mobilization, I insist that state-centered structural explanations of social movements recognize the cultural aspects of the political opportunity structure.

In particular, I examine how the Federal Bureau of Investigation (FBI) framed the Communist threat in Hollywood during the 1940s. A full analysis of framing processes involving all the relevant collective actors—including the American Communist party, various popular front groups, anticommunist organizations, motion picture companies, and several key state agencies—is beyond the scope of this chapter. I focus on the framing processes engaged in by one state agency in order to reveal what frame analysts have ignored: the construction and promotion of official frames. Two areas in which analysts of framing processes have not always been clear (Zald 1996) are addressed: the "cultural resources" utilized by the FBI to forge its official interpretation of the Communist threat in Hollywood and the FBI's "strategic decision making" concerning the promotion of this frame. This case is then used as a jumping-off point for a comparison of the construction and promotion of official frames and collective action frames.

Two other underexamined aspects of frames are relevant to this case, and I will touch on each briefly. The FBI chose not to promote the countersubversive frame itself, deciding instead to launder its surveillance information through the House Un-American Activities Committee (HUAC) and self-consciously withdraw from the public debate over the interpretation of Communists in Hollywood. Frame analysts have recognized that some frames are more successful than others (Gamson 1992; Snow and Benford 1992), but they have not expended much analytical effort on frames that fail (Babb 1996; Benford 1997). HUAC proved very successful, at least in the short term, at mobilizing the countersubversive interpretation of the Communist threat in Hollywood (Ceplair and Englund 1980; Schatz 1997). But in terms of the FBI, the countersubversive frame must be considered a failed frame. In addition, the fact that a frame fails for one organization and succeeds for another suggests that the success of a frame depends on more than just its ideational content (McAdam 1996b). A comparison of the institutional functions of the FBI and HUAC reveals the material basis of frame resonance.

To identify how the FBI framed the Communist threat in Hollywood and to understand their decision not to promote this frame, I have reviewed files from the FBI's investigation of "Communist activity in the motion picture industry" between 1942 and 1958, documents that were released several years ago under the Freedom of Information Act and are now available in a microfilm collection entitled "Communist Activity in the Entertainment Industry: FBI Surveillance Files on Hollywood, 1942-1958" (Leab 1991). Though caution must be used when interpreting FBI documents (Keen 1999), they are particularly useful in this case because I am interested in the FBI's own interpretation of events and how this interpretation affected the agency's decision making. Therefore, I paid particular attention to two types of documents. First, I analyzed reports, memoranda, and letters discussing the nature of the Communist threat in Hollywood and the FBI's efforts to uncover and expose it. These include correspondence between FBI Director J. Edgar Hoover and Richard Hood, the special agent in charge of the FBI's Los Angeles field office; memoranda between Hoover and other high-ranking FBI officials discussing various aspects of the operation; and periodic reports written in Los Angeles or Washington summarizing the investigation. Second, I looked at reports filed by the special agents in Los Angeles assigned to investigate Hollywood. Among other things, these reports included reviews of over two hundred movies. These documents reveal the FBI's actions, a frequently neglected aspect of frame construction (McAdam 1996b; Zuo and Benford 1995), and the interpretive schemata through which the FBI rendered the Communist threat in Hollywood meaningful.

FRAMING THE COMMUNIST THREAT IN HOLLYWOOD

To be successful, frame entrepreneurs must be attuned both to the systems of meaning that make sense of the world for their adherents and potential recruits and to the social and political context in which the frame is being constructed (Kubal 1998; Mooney and Hunt 1996; Tarrow 1994). When movements first arise, they often borrow ideological themes from existing master frames enjoying a cyclical period of success to provide a new diagnosis of the target population's situation and to motivate them to act (Snow and Benford 1992). Master frames function similarly to movement-specific collective action frames but on a larger scale (Snow and Benford 1992). That is, master frames are more abstract or generic interpretive schemata that render events or occurrences meaningful for a variety of movements, either during one specific period (e.g., the rights frame during the 1960s) or over time, as cultural values and dominant ideologies go in and out of style (Mooney and Hunt 1996; Swart 1995; Tarrow 1994). These themes are then modified to meet the particular needs of the movement and its members.

When a movement has had a long life punctuated by periods of engagement and dormancy, repertoires of interpretation persist over time in *structures of abeyance* (Mooney and Hunt 1996; Swidler 1995). Structures of abeyance, which can be formal or informal institutions, function as "halfway houses," sustaining master frames and providing entrepreneurs with knowledge of past movement frames until a new period of mobilization makes them relevant once more (Morris 1984; Mooney and Hunt 1996; Swart 1995). Movement entrepreneurs can, when political opportunities ripen, draw on these ideological themes to "reinterpret and reconstruct systems of meaning already present in their life worlds" (Mooney and Hunt 1996: 179).

To frame the Communist threat in Hollywood, the FBI drew on a master frame that had been in abeyance since the end of the post-World War I Red Scare. Several anticommunist frames had been constructed and promoted during this earlier period. Among the most successful was the countersubversive frame constructed by, among others, J. Edgar Hoover, then head of the Radical Division of the Bureau of Investigation (later renamed the Federal Bureau of Investigation). Hoover wrote several legal briefs arguing that particular aliens or alien members of particular groups should be deported. These briefs, in which Hoover outlined the basic points of the countersubversive master frame, were released to the general public as part of a drive to pass a federal sedition law and to place the Radical Division at the center of an emerging national anticommunist movement. In them, Hoover portrays the Communist threat as primarily a domestic issue, arguing that a well-organized domestic Communist movement beholden to puppet masters in Moscow was engaged in a struggle for the hearts and minds of vulnerable working-class and immigrant Americans. While portrayed as generally content, these unsophisticated populations were said to have only a fragile commitment to American values and traditions and, therefore, to be vulnerable to the seductive, if false, promises of radicals (Powers 1995).

To stave off this threat, the U.S. Department of Justice executed a series of raids aimed at capturing alien radicals who were poisoning the American working class, and the "brains" who guided the movement in the United States (Murray 1964; Powers 1995; Preston 1963). The countersubversive frame constructed in these briefs served both as a rallying point for anticommunists during the first Red Scare and as "essential blueprints" for the FBI's response to Communism for the remainder of Hoover's long tenure at the agency (Powers 1987: 97) Moreover, given the extraordinary fealty that Hoover demanded and received from his agents, the countersubversive master frame became the exclusive interpretation of Communist activity throughout the Bureau (Powers 1987; Theoharis and Cox 1988).

Though initially quite popular, the countersubversive frame lost media, elite, and public support in 1920 as disconfirming evidence mounted (Babb 1996). The credibility of countersubversive entrepreneurs, including Hoover and Attorney General A. Mitchell Palmer, for example, was weakened when several predicted radical uprisings failed to materialize (Coben 1963; Powers 1987; Preston 1963). As a result, fears of a Communist revolution deflated as quickly in 1920 as they had risen in 1919, and the countersubversive master frame was discredited. Hoover's promotion to director in 1924, however, provided one of the primary architects of the master frame with a secure institutional foothold. In the years between the postwar Red Scares, the Bureau served as a structure of abeyance for the countersubversive interpretation of the Communist movement.

During early ears of the Cold War, the FBI once again mobilized the countersubversive master frame to diagnose the Communist threat in Hollywood. In their initial report, special agents in the FBI's Los Angeles field office attributed the spread of Communist ideas in the motion picture industry to the false teachings of Hollywood intellectuals, particularly those in the "cultural field." FBI special agents had investigated the "immense program of infiltration" to which the studio unions had been subject, citing reports from industry informants that nearly half of the studio unions in Hollywood, representing twenty thousand workers, were controlled by Communists or were following the Communist line for "business reasons."[1] But the FBI concluded that it was among the writers, directors, and actors that "most of progress has been made and . . . Communist sympathy and influence is the strongest and most far-reaching."[2] FBI sources in Hollywood, for example, indicated that for several years writers had been using meetings such as the Western Writers Conference to search for ways to "utilize Hollywood and the motion picture industry for the Communist cause."[3] To the FBI, the intellectual pedigree of the Communist movement in Hollywood was further evidence of its fundamental mendacity:

> While the Communist Party pretends to be a worker's movement, it is not. . . . The Communists, and all workers movements, in fact are movements led by frustrated and satiated [*sic*] intellectuals. . . . The makers of the Russian Revolution . . . were all intellectuals—they never worked a day in their lives at manual labor.[4]

The reference to Moscow was not random. "Communist activity in the motion picture industry," the Bureau argued, was part of a "gigantic world-wide conspiracy of control which has its origins and codirection in the Communist Party of the Soviet Union."[5] The FBI traced the lineage of this particular part of the global Communist conspiracy to a 1925 edition of the *Daily Worker* in which Gregory Zinoviev, chairman of the executive committee of the Communist International, and other prominent Communists proposed that the motion picture "can and must become a mighty weapon of Communist propaganda for the enlightenment of the widest working masses."[6]

But the FBI's framing of the Communist threat in Hollywood was not complete. As Richard Hood, special agent in charge of the FBI's Los Angeles office, argued as early as April 1945, the FBI's usual procedures in political investigations, namely, the investigation of political affiliations and associations, was not sufficient in this case. Should Hoover be called on to state whether Communist propaganda had in fact been inserted into Hollywood movies, Hood argued, "it will not be sufficient to state that a certain known Communist wrote, directed or produced a particular motion picture. . . . On the contrary it would be necessary under these circumstances to be able to state specifically what there is in a script or picture that is believed to be Communist propaganda."[7] The Bureau, Hood feared, could report reasoned conclusions about the cause of the Communist activity in Hollywood, but not its effect.

In July 1947, however, the Bureau completed the framing process by adopting guidelines published in a report written by Ayn Rand for the Motion Picture Alliance for the Preservation of American Ideals (MPAPAI), an ad hoc group of anticommunist Hollywood writers, producers, and directors who, "alerted to a common menace within the industry," had compiled a list of eleven "common devices used to turn non-political pictures into carriers of political propaganda" (Ross 1948).[8] The FBI's investigation of the subversive content of motion pictures provided the final piece of the countersubversive frame. Now the FBI could identify evidence to support a key contention in the master frame, that Communists spread their ideas by manipulating the unsophisticated masses. In this case, it was Communist writers, directors, and actors slyly inserting Communist propaganda into their movies in order to subvert American mores and values.

I have grouped these common devices into two broad categories (table 5.1). Category one, smearing American values or institutions, includes negative presentations of, or references to, the free enterprise system, described in the MPAPAI report as inseparable from Americanism "by body and soul," and associated phenomena such as industrialists, wealth, and the "independent man."[9] According to the MPAPAI report, Communists inserted subtle propaganda into movies suggesting that villainous industrialists and wealthy men were evil because of their success or class positions, not because of individual character flaws. Category-two propaganda includes the glorification of values and institutions considered by the MPAPAI to be anti-American or procommunist, such as failure and depravity. "It is the Communist intention," Rand wrote, "to make men accept misery, depravity, and degradation as their natural lot in life." Celebration of "the common man" was also identified as procommunist: "It is not an American idea," she argued, "to be either 'common' or 'little.'"[10]

In four reports submitted between August 7 and November 17, 1947, the Los Angeles office sent FBI headquarters reviews of seventeen movies released between 1943 and 1948 that it determined were subversive based on the MPAPAI criteria (see table 5.2). The FBI found category-one problems with all but two of these films.

Table 5.1 FBI's Criteria for Determining If a Motion Picture Contained Communist Propaganda

Category	*Criteria*	*Examples*
1	Values or institutions judged to be particularly American are smeared or represented as evil in the movie, either explicitly or through casual references to current political events	the free enterprise system; industrialists; wealth; the profit motive; success; the independent man
2	Values or institutions judged to be particularly anti-American or pro-Communist are glorified in the movie, either explicitly or through casual references to current politics	failure; depravity; the "common man"; the collective

Source: Leab 1991, Reel 3, Frames 134-147.
Note: The FBI determined that a motion picture contained Communist propaganda if its themes, images, or dialogue fit into either of these categories (borrowed from the Motion Picture Alliance for the Preservation of American Ideals).

The American values or institutions smeared or presented as evil in them included the congressional form of government, Catholicism, law enforcement, and the military. But by far the most frequent category-one problem involved the smearing of the economic system and/or its principal figures. The FBI reported negative portrayals of the wealthy, bankers, big business, or industrialists in nine of the seventeen movies. For example, according to the FBI, *All My Sons*, Arthur Miller's story of a man who discovers that his father sold defective airplanes to the government during World War II, implied that all industrialists were "criminal monsters."[11]

The two most well-known films on the FBI's list, *It's a Wonderful Life* and *The Best Years of Our Lives*, both include negative portrayals of bankers. The agents found the former "a rather obvious attempt to discredit bankers by casting Lionel Barrymore as a 'scrooge-type' so that he would be the most hated man in the movie,"[12] conveniently ignoring the central narrative of the film, Jimmy Stewart's portrayal of a banker as the town's hero (Noakes 1998). *The Best Years of Our Lives*, the FBI concluded, went even further, advocating "an irresponsible economy in the name of moral responsibility" when it represented a bank president who refuses a loan to a GI who could not put up collateral "as a smugly inhuman reactionary."[13]

To FBI agents and industry informants viewing Hollywood movies through the countersubversive frame, other category-one problems included a portrayal of law and order as "almost as a case history in depravity" (*Brute Force*),[14] the belittling of the American form of government (*The Farmer's Daughter; So Well Remembered*),[15] the depiction of the Catholic religion as "revoltingly cruel" (*In Place of Splendor*),[16] and an attempt to discredit the American military (*Crossfire*).[17]

Category-two problems were more diffuse. The values or institutions judged to be particularly anti-American or procommunist included obvious ones such as collectivism and socialism. In their review of *North Star*, for example, the story of a Russian village under Nazi attack, the FBI incorporated excerpts from a letter sent to the Bureau by a private citizen complaining that Russian life had been unduly celebrated in the film. "Even the cows and pigs were glorified," the letter writer

Table 5.2 Movies Determined by the FBI to Contain Communist Propaganda in 1947

All My Sons	*In Place of Splendor*
Another Part of the Forest	*It's a Wonderful Life*
The Best Years of Our Lives	*Keeper of the Flame*
Body and Soul	*Monsieur Verdoux*
Brute Force	*North Star*
Crossfire	*Pride of the Marines*
The Farmer's Daughter	*So Well Remembered*
Gentleman's Agreement	*Song to Remember*
Hazard	

Source: Leab 1991.

complained. "They moo'ed and squealed in soft dulcet tones."[18] Other concerns were less obvious. For example, the FBI cited as evidence of Communist propaganda the positive portrayal of black characters in two films (*Body and Soul*; *Hazard*)[19] and the undue emphasis on the country's racial antagonisms in another (*Crossfire*).[20] Other films were condemned for glorifying lawbreakers (*Brute Force*),[21] depravity (*The Best Years of Our Lives*),[22] the poor and common men (*In Place of Splendor*; *It's a Wonderful Life*);[23] and various forms of economic morality (*The Best Years of Our Lives*; *The Farmer's Daughter*).[24]

From the FBI's perspective, these movies could no longer be considered merely entertainment vehicles—particularly with the American public buying movie tickets at a weekly rate of eighty-five million. "We'll have a Communist government to-morrow," argued a movie reviewer from the conservative periodical *Plain Talk*, from which the FBI quoted extensively in its review of the 1948 Academy Award winner for best picture, "if the propaganda in *The Best Years of Our Lives* fools enough people."[25] Like the unsophisticated workingman of the post–World War I era, the average moviegoer could not be trusted to notice Communist propaganda and, thus, avoid being duped. After all, Communists were not openly advocating communism but rather were employing the means and techniques that they had been taught by the party to corrupt nonpolitical movies. "Few people would take Communism straight," the MPAPAI had argued in the report that the FBI had adopted as its own,

> but a constant stream of hints, lies, touches, and suggestions battering the public from the screen will act like drops of water that split a rock if continued long enough. The rock that they are trying to split is Americanism.[26]

Armed with its intimate knowledge of communism and intelligence information from within the motion picture industry, the FBI initially envisioned itself as the force necessary to hold together that rock of Americanism.

THE LIMITS OF OFFICIAL FRAMES

The FBI, however, never advanced its interpretation of Communists in Hollywood publicly. Though HUAC would advance a version of the frame in its infamous hearings on Communism in Hollywood, in terms of the FBI, the countersubversive frame remained in the "back region" of intra- and interagency reports. This does not mean, however, that the adoption of this particular frame was inconsequential to the FBI (Haydu 1999). On the contrary, I argue that the FBI's interpretation of the Communist threat severely limited the agency's options in this case. This was not because of any inherent weakness in the frame itself. In fact, by either of the two most prominent criteria, the FBI's framing of the Communist threat in Hollywood qualifies as a collective action frame (Gamson 1992; Snow and Benford 1992). A quick review of William Gamson's (1992) specification of the characteristics of collective action frames, with the corresponding aspects of the FBI's frame in this case in parentheses, should suffice to illustrate this point. Collective action frames identify previously undetected threats (Communist propaganda in motion pictures), identify who is responsible for the threat (Communist-trained writers, directors, and actors and who is at risk (the unsuspecting and unsophisticated American public), and offer a solution to the problem (FBI decoding of the movies).

Moreover, for the FBI the countersubversive frame also solved the "double problem" first identified by Howard Becker (1963). To maintain or increase their control over allocative and authoritative resources, law enforcement agencies such as the FBI must simultaneously convince people of the existence of a severe threat to the public order that they are responsible for maintaining and, nonetheless, present themselves as the only reasonable solution to the crisis. Throughout its history the FBI has excelled at this political game. Between its founding in 1908 and 1947, for example, the FBI's expansion was driven by a series of socially constructed law-and-order crises, not unlike the Communist threat in Hollywood, including the white slavery scare, the threat of internal subversion during World War I, the postwar Red Scare, the gangster era, and the twin threats of Communism and Nazism in the 1930s (Noakes 1994; Potter 1998; Powers 1987). In each case the FBI framed the threat in such a way that its solution increased the agency's funding and jurisdiction.

But the FBI chose not only *not* to present itself as a solution to the Communist threat in Hollywood but also to withdraw from the public debate altogether and launder its surveillance information through HUAC on the condition that the source of the information not be revealed. Having scrambled unsuccessfully for several months to acquire the kind of intelligence information the FBI had collected, HUAC had faced the prospect of embarrassing itself when the Hollywood hearings they had promised several months earlier commenced. The FBI saved them from this fate by providing the following: background information on the first nine witnesses who had been subpoenaed by the committee; a list of names and affiliations of alleged Communists or "fellow travelers" in the motion picture and radio industry; a list of thirty-two potential friendly or cooperative witnesses (including Ronald Reagan); and a memo summarizing the FBI's information on "Communist Activities in Hollywood."[27]

The FBI's decision to forgo promoting the anticommunist frame in this case was influenced by two related factors. First, the public nature of much of the evidence supporting the FBI's claim made it impossible for Hoover to ignore the possible reaction of the public. In most FBI investigations of subversiveness, especially those featuring extensive surveillance, the information collected by the Bureau was, by its very nature, virtually unverifiable and, therefore, incontestable. But the targets in this case were not obscure to the general public, and much of the evidence that the FBI used to reach its conclusions could be viewed at the local movie house.

Second, evidence from Hoover's correspondence suggests that he was worried that the FBI would have difficulty successfully promoting its diagnosis. Frames have a greater chance of success if they resonate with the general public. A frame's resonance is affected by several factors, including its empirical credibility, or the degree to which a target population believes or accepts the empirical claims made by frame entrepreneurs in support of their diagnosis and prognosis, and its experiential commensurability, or the degree to which the frame's interpretations are consistent with the target population's interpretations gained from firsthand experience of similar events (Snow et al. 1986; Snow and Benford 1992).

Hoover's concerns about the potential resonance of the FBI's frame are outlined in a letter he sent to Hood on April 14, 1945. In an earlier letter, Hood had asked Hoover for permission to launch an extensive investigation of the content of Hollywood movies in search of examples of Communist propaganda and had provided a sample analysis of the movie *The Master Race.* Hood argued that, should Hoover be asked to testify about the Communist infiltration of Hollywood, simply noting the radical affiliations of various writers, directors, and actors would not be enough; Hoover needed to be able to state which movies contained Communist propaganda and specify what exactly was subversive about them. Concerned about the public's reaction to the FBI's analysis of motion pictures, Hoover instructed Hood only to investigate the content of a movie if it was "obviously of a Communist propaganda nature" and to include in his reports only information obtained from confidential industry informants whom the FBI could claim were experts.[28]

"One of the main reasons" for this decision, Hoover explained to Hood, was that "while the opinions of Agents well versed in Communist activities are of value, they still do not constitute opinions of persons who could be classified as expert witnesses."[29] Though he believed that most people accepted FBI special agents as experts on Communism, Hoover feared that if the FBI made public its analysis of particular films, "there undoubtedly would result an immediate challenge since it could be stated . . . that non-expert opinions are involved."[30]

Anticipating one of the central arguments of the then-only-incipient field of communications, Hoover also worried that, even if Communist propaganda had been inserted into a film, the FBI special agent had no way of knowing what effect the propaganda had on viewers. Unsophisticated moviegoers might miss the subtle propaganda that the expert special agent uncovered, thus providing disconfirming evidence to the target population that could discredit the frame and its bearer.

The countersubversive frame is based on the assumption that experts on Communism had a better capacity to decipher subversive propaganda than average Americans. This aspect of the frame had served the FBI well in the past when the targets of the FBI's investigations of subversives were foreign born or otherwise marginal members of American society and when the evidence against them was found in obscure political tracts and largely unheard speeches. But in applying the countersubversive frame to Hollywood, the FBI suggested not only that it understood Communism better than the American public but also that the FBI knew how to interpret movies better than the average American moviegoer. Any American who could afford a movie ticket could, however, judge for themselves whether a movie was subversive. If the public did not find the FBI's analyses of Communist propaganda in motion pictures produced by Hollywood credible, or if viewers' experience of watching a motion picture (e.g., it was entertaining) was not commensurate with the FBI special agent's experience (e.g., it was a vehicle for Communist propaganda), then the Bureau's capacity to successfully establish the countersubversive master frame in this case would be undermined and the legitimacy of its bearer brought into question.

In other words, Hoover was unwilling to risk the translation of the Bureau's

Nonetheless, the assumption made by frame analysts that the advantages enjoyed by state managers render the mobilization of official frames uninteresting must be challenged. Despite the apparent advantages enjoyed by state agencies, the struggle for cultural supremacy remains a dynamic process and, as this research illustrates, the construction of an official frame does not guarantee its successful promotion. We need further examination of official frames to understand under what conditions they can be successfully mobilized and to specify the limits of these frames. As with the processes by which official frames are constructed, we can learn something about their limits by examining the limits of collective action frames. Social movement theorists, for example, recognize that repertoires of interpretation not only facilitate action but also restrain it (Babb 1996; Sewell 1992; Tarrow 1994). The evidence in this case suggests that this holds true for official as well as collective action frames. The FBI's fears that the countersubversive framing of the Communist threat in Hollywood created potential experiential and empirical resonance problems limited the options available to the agency. In an interesting variation on this point, Jiping Zuo and Robert Benford (1995: 136) argue that the Chinese government was hesitant to repress early manifestations of the student uprising in 1989 because its official propaganda had promoted the students as "young, innocent, brave, and promising."

Social movement researchers also recognize that collective action frames often compete with collective action frames mobilized by competing movements or countermovements, providing one of the primary sources of dynamism in the struggle for cultural supremacy (Jasper 1997; McAdam, McCarthy, and Zald 1996b; Meyer and Staggenborg 1996). Though frame analysts often assume unity and stasis among state actors, the evidence in this case suggests that the frames advanced by state managers have to compete with frames advanced by other state managers, further fueling the struggle for cultural supremacy.

During the periods immediately following both World Wars, deep divisions existed between Hoover and the respective White Houses over the framing of the Communist threat. Specifically, the countersubversive anticommunist frame competed with the liberal anticommunist frame advanced by Woodrow Wilson and Harry Truman. Though both are anticommunist frames, the countersubversive and liberal frames contain irreconcilable contradictions, most notably concerning the primary target of Communist propaganda. Countersubversives argued that Communists sought to undermine America and foster revolution in this country. Liberal anticommunists, however, argued that the primary threat was in the extension of Communist support to developing Third World countries and dismissed the domestic threat as a distracting irrelevancy. From the perspective of the countersubversives, liberal anticommunists not only misunderstood the Communist psyche but were dangerously derelict in their duty. At one point, in fact, Hoover suggested that the FBI found it difficult to prove that someone had purposefully injected Communist propaganda into a motion picture when "the present Communist 'line' is, at least on its surface, most harmonious with the [Truman administration's] policies."[32] Further research on cases in which there is competition between official frames promises to deepen our understanding not only of official frames and the struggle for cultural supremacy but also of divisions among elites and their relationship to social movement mobilization.

Finally, I turn to a point of dissimilarity between efforts to mobilize collective action frames and official frames. My discussion, however, begins with a point of similarity. The evidence above suggests that state managers, like social movement entrepreneurs (Einwohner 1999), must be concerned about frame resonance. Collective action frames are more likely to be successful if they resonate with the cultural values, beliefs, and practices extant in the target community at the time they are promoted (Snow and Benford 1992; Swart 1995). They are also more likely to be successful the more the diagnosis, prognosis, and rationale they provide are commensurate with recruits' personal experiences and supported by empirical evidence deemed credible by the target population (Gamson 1992). The evidence reviewed above suggests that the FBI decided to withdraw from the public contest over the meaning of the Communist threat in Hollywood at least in part because of concerns about negotiating the journey between the "back regions" of the Bureau's bureaucracy, where the countersubversive frame was readily accepted and actively constructed, and the moviegoing public in the "front region" (Kubal 1998). Specifically, Hoover feared that the diagnosis, prognosis, and rationale for action contained within the countersubversive frame would, when applied to the Communist threat in Hollywood, not be commensurate with the public's experiences of the movies and, therefore, that the public would not deem the empirical evidence put forward by the FBI as credible.

The state managers' concern with the resonance of official frames, however, includes an issue not faced by social movement entrepreneurs—the need to maintain political legitimacy in order to protect its claim to the legitimate exercise of repressive actionse Zuo and Benford (1995: 143), for example, argue that the Chinese government's official framing of the Tiananmen Square uprising as a "turmoil" and a "plotted conspiracy" did not resonate with the experience and knowledge of Beijing citizens, thus undermining the government's legitimacy and broadening the protests despite threats, later realized, of official repression. Moreover, Anthony Oberschall's 1996 discussion of the East European revolutions of 1989 points out that the relevance of political structures depends upon the maintenance of legitimacy by the political organizations in which these structures manifest themselves. According to Oberschall, the loss of the moral authority to rule by East European Communist governments created political opportunities not only by weakening the loyalty to the state on the part of agents of repression but also by placing the regimes at a distinct disadvantage in framing contests. In other words, their inability to promote a version of reality that served their interests created political opportunities for insurgent groups.

This point is relevant even in the absence of severe crises such as in China and Eastern Europe in 1989. Contemporary analyses of legitimacy have challenged Max Weber's conception of legitimacy as the moral authority to rule (Gerth and Mills 1958). Scharr (1984), for example, argues that force of habit, expediency, and necessity have replaced deep convictions as the mandate to rule in the second half of the twentieth century. Moreover, Giddens (1987) proposed that the modern state's monopoly over the means of violence need not be invested with moral authority but merely recognized and observed. The legitimacy of law enforcement, then, often manifests itself in an absence of active opposition, in indifference, or in contingent approval of the actions of law enforcement agencies, instead of in deep beliefs about their moral authority. This might at first seem to relieve social control agencies from the burden of maintaining legitimacy, but I would argue just the opposite. In the absence of deep sentiments attaching citizens to the state's activities, state managers must constantly engage in framing contests to reproduce the more tenuous attachments of the contemporary era. The relationship between official framing processes and the building and maintenance of these tenuous attachments deserves further study.

CONCLUSION

My primary goal in this chapter was to demonstrate that state agencies are active signifying agents engaged in the construction and maintenance of official frames and that these frames have consequences. Official frames have had somewhat of a subterranean existence in the frame analysis literature. Social movement researchers acknowledge that a struggle for cultural supremacy takes place and that the state is among the contestants. But few analyses have addressed the processes by which official frames are constructed and promoted or the consequences of their mobilization. As a result, our understanding of the political and cultural terrain upon which social movements rise, flourish, and decline is incomplete.

Though more research is needed, this analysis of the FBI's framing of the Communist threat in Hollywood suggests several points about the construction and promotion of official frames that can serve as the basis for a more complete integration of the state's signifying practices into the social movement literature. I argue, for example, that state managers draw on a familiar repertoire of interpretation when constructing official frames and that state agencies have an exceptional capacity to serve as structures of abeyance. Moreover, I argue that, in terms of both material and cultural resources, state managers enjoy significant advantages over social movement entrepreneurs and that the official frames they construct have a greater chance of triumphing in the struggle for cultural supremacy than do collective action frames mobilized by social movement entrepreneurs. But I also argue that there are limits to official frames. As this case illustrates, official frames may also limit state activity, and the frames advanced by one state agency may have to compete with those advanced by other state agencies, as well as with collective action frames promoted by social movement entrepreneurs. In addition, state managers, despite the significant advantages they maintain, must be concerned with the resonance of official frames, in large part because they must be wary of undermining their political legitimacy.

Including official frames in analyses of political contention should also yield results in areas well beyond the limits of my study. Such inclusion produces a much more dynamic model of the struggles between states and social movements over the meaning of cultural phenomena and political power. If, for example, the state's construction and promotion of official frames is recognized, then one can argue that the struggle for cultural supremacy is an important and potentially volatile aspect of the political opportunity structure. State-centered theorists have argued that state organizational structures "indirectly influence the meaning and methods of politics for all groups in society" (Orloff and Skocpol 1985). With the inclusion of official frames in both frame analysis and the broader social movement literature, a similar argument can be fashioned about official frames.

This raises the possibility of more fully incorporating frame analysis into the political process model by providing a way of reconceptualizing the cultural aspects of the political opportunity structure. Proponents of the political process model have been criticized for ignoring the cultural aspects of social movements (Goodwin and Jasper 1999; Kurzman 1996; Polletta 1997). One response to this criticism has been to incorporate frame analysis, and its attention to "the central importance of ideas and cultural elements" in the micro processes of social movement mobilization (Zald 1996: 261), into the political process model. But because frame analysts have defined their interests relatively narrowly, analyzing only the frames constructed and promoted by social movements and neglecting official frames, proponents of the political process model have been able to relegate the question of cultural opportunities to the discussion of participant mobilization (McAdam 1994). Most notably, with only a few exceptions (Zdravomyslova 1996; Oberschall 1996), proponents of the political process model have continued to insist on drawing strict analytical distinctions between the political opportunity structure and the making of political meaning (Polletta 1997). As McAdam (1996a: 25-26) puts it: "Political opportunities should not be confused with the collective process by which these changes are interpreted and framed."

Recently several researchers have argued that there are cultural dimensions of political structures and political opportunity (Gamson and Meyer 1996; Goodwin and Jasper 1999; Kurzman 1996; Polletta 1997; Zdravomyslova 1996). Elena Zdravomyslova (1996), for example, argues that, as a result of the opening of political opportunities in Russia during the 1980s (*perestroika*), interpretive master frames were generated that, by encouraging electoral participation, influenced the further expansion of political opportunities. The promotion of official frames that fail to resonate may undermine the legitimacy of the state and, as a result, open political opportunities for those who can promote more resonant frames. This suggests that if the mobilization of official frames is incorporated into the analysis of contentious politics, then the framing contests among state agencies and between state agencies and social movements may be rightly considered an aspect of the political opportunity structure.

My analysis of the FBI's framing of the Communist threat in Hollywood also suggests that social movement researchers need to move beyond the social movement literature and into the broader political sociology literature, particularly the literature on the state. My goal in this chapter has been to reveal the relevance of analyzing official frames from within, so to speak, by operating on terrain well trod by frame analysts. Several questions remain. Why, for example, is the countersubversive master frame so resilient? It is not difficult to identify other instances in which Hoover's FBI mobilized this master frame. Recent research on the FBI's surveillance of sociologists, for example, reveals that criteria similar to those used to assess films were used to interpret sociological analyses during the 1940s and 1950s. Research interest in the Soviet Union, for example, generated suspicion, as did any criticism of U.S. social institutions (Keen 1999). Also, the FBI's discounting of racism as the source of black discontent in the United States during the 1940s and 1950s, and its subsequent identification of civil rights leaders as dupes of an international Communist conspiracy, can be attributed in part to the FBI's continued allegiance to the countersubversive anticommunist frame (Branch 1988, 1998; O'Reilly 1989).

Clearly the countersubversive aspects of the master frame served the FBI's institutional interests as rule enforcers. But what should we make of its procapitalist aspects? The collapsing of capitalism and Americanism in the FBI's framing of the Communist threat, for example, is consistent with the interpretation of social and economic conditions in the United States aggressively promoted by the business community in the early years of the Cold War (Fones-Wolf 1994).

Drawing from the literature on the determinants of social policy, we might ask whether official frames reflect some underlying logic of industrialism, the state's contribution to reproducing the social requirements of advanced capitalism, or autonomous actions by state managers. None of these possibilities are necessarily excluded by the evidence in this case. It is only with further examination of the construction and promotion of official frames that we can identify the most prominent official master frames and how they shaped political discourse, social movement activity, and public policy.

NOTES

1. Special Agent Report, Los Angeles, "Communist Infiltration into the Motion Picture Industry," February 16, 1943, Leab 1991, Reel 1, Frame 8.

2. *Ibid.*, Frames 105-106.

3. *Ibid.*, Frames 11-12.

4. *Ibid.*, Frames 105-106.

5. *Ibid.*, Frame 10.

6. "Running Memorandum on Communist Infiltration into the Motion Picture Industry." December 31, 1955, Leab 1991, Reel 14, Frame 589.

7. Hood to Hoover, April 2, 1945, Leab 1991, Reel 2, Frame 20.

8. Special Agent Report, Los Angeles, "Communist Infiltration into the Motion Picture Industry," August 7, 1947, Leab 1991, Reel 3, Frame 134.

9. *Ibid.*, Frames 135-136; see also Ross 1948.

10. *Ibid.*, Frames 136-138.

11. Special Agent Report, Los Angeles, "Communist Infiltration into the Motion Picture Industry," October 20, 1947, Leab 1991, Reel 3, Frames 349-357.

12. Special Agent Report, Los Angeles, "Communist Infiltration into the Motion Picture Industry," August 7, 1947, Leab 1991, Reel 3, Frame 163.

13. *Ibid.*, Frame 158.

14. *Ibid.*, Frames 168-169.

15. *The Farmer's Daughter*: *Ibid.*, Frames 164-166; *So Well Remembered*: "Summary of the Communist Infiltration into the Motion Picture Industry," July 15, 1949, Leab 1991, Reel 13, Frames 928-929.

16. Leab 1991, Reel 13, Frames 918-928.

17. Leab 1991, Reel 3, Frames 168-169.

18. *Ibid.,* Frames 151-152.

19. *Body and Soul:* Special Agent Report, Los Angeles, "Communist Infiltration into the Motion Picture Industry," September 12, 1947, Leab 1991, Reel 3, Frames 223-224; *Hazard:* "Summary of the Communist Infiltration into the Motion Picture Industry," July 15, 1949, Leab 1991, Reel 13, Frame 929.

20. Special Agent Report, Los Angeles, "Communist Infiltration into the Motion Picture Industry," August 7, 1947, Leab 1991, Reel 3, Frames 166-168.

21. *Ibid.*, Frames 168-169.

22. *Ibid.*, Frames 156-162

23. *In Place of Splendor:* "Summary of the Communist Infiltration into the Motion Picture Industry," July 15, 1949, Leab 1991, Reel 13, Frames 918-928; *It's a Wonderful Life:* Special Agent Report, Los Angeles, "Communist Infiltration into the Motion Picture Industry." August 7, 1947, Leab 1991, Reel 3, Frame 163.

24. *The Best Years of Our Lives:* Leab 1991, Reel 3, Frames 156-162; *The Farmer's Daughter:* Leab 1991, Reel 3, Frames 164-166.

25. Leab 1991, Reel 3, Frame 160.

26. *Ibid.*, Frame 134.

27. This act, coupled with Hoover's testimony before HUAC earlier in 1947, marked the suspension of the long feud between the FBI and HUAC, which shared the Bureau's interpretation of Communism. The FBI/HUAC feud had been brewing since the latter's inception in 1937. Hoover viewed HUAC as a group of incompetent amateurs unnecessarily infringing on the FBI's turf and refused to cooperate with the committee on several cases (Schrecker 1998; Powers 1987). In 1940, HUAC Chairman Martin Dies stoked the feud by labeling the FBI "a bunch of Boy Scouts" and implying that it was too hamstrung by legal

niceties to uncover and expose subversive activities (O'Reilly 1983). As he did with most critics, Hoover responded by ordering an investigation of Dies. But the FBI's decision to cooperate with HUAC in 1947 made it possible for the committee to present itself as the standard bearer of the countersubversive anticommunist master frame and as the solution to the Communist threat in Hollywood from the late 1940s through the mid-1950s.

28. Hoover to Hood, April 14, 1945, Leab 1991, Reel 2, Frame 22.
29. *Ibid.*
30. *Ibid.*
31. Hoover to Olson, Tam, Ladd, and Nichols, June 24, 1947, Leab 1991, Reel 2, Frames 641-642.
32. Hoover to Hood, April 14, 1945, Leab 1991, Reel 2, Frame 22.

REFERENCES

Anderson, Benedict. 1991. *Imagined Communities*. London: Verso.
Babb, Sarah. 1996. "'A True American System of Finance': Frame Resonance in the U.S. Labor Movement, 1866 to 1886." *American Sociological Review* 61: 1033-1052.
Becker, Howard. 1963. *Outsiders: Studies in the Sociology of Deviance*. London: Free Press of Glencoe.
Benford, Robert. 1997. "An Insider's Critique of the Social Movement Framing Perspective," *Sociological Inquiry* 67 (4): 409-430.
Branch, Taylor. 1988. *Parting the Waters: America in the King Years, 1954-1963*. New York: Simon and Schuster.
———. 1998. *Pillar of Fire: America in the King Years, 1963-1965*. New York: Simon and Schuster.
Ceplair, Larry, and Steven Englund. 1980. *Inquisition in Hollywood: Politics in the Film Community, 1930-1960*. Garden City, NJ: Anchor Press.
Churchill, Ward, and Jim Vander Wal. 1990. *The COINTELPRO Papers: Documents from the FBI's Secret Wars against Dissent in the United States*. Boston: South End Press.
Coben, Stanley. 1963. *A. Mitchell Palmer: Politician*. New York: Columbia University Press.
Edelman, Murray. 1971. *Politics as Symbolic Action*. Chicago: Markham.
Einwohner, Rachel. 1999. "Practices, Opportunity, and Protest Effectiveness: Illustrations from Four Animal Rights Campaigns." *Social Problems* 46 (2): 169-186.
Evans, Peter, Dietrich Rueschemeyer, and Theda Skocpol. 1985. *Bringing the State Back In*. New York: Cambridge University Press.
Fones-Wolf, Elizabeth. 1994. *Selling Free Enterprise: The Business Assault on Labor and Liberalism, 1945-1960*. Urbana: University of Illinois Press.
Gamson, William. 1975. *The Strategy of Social Protest*. Chicago: Dorsey Press.
———. 1988. "Political Discourse and Collective Action." Pp. 219-244 in *From Structure to Action: Comparing Social Movement Research across Cultures*, Bert Klandermans, Hanspeter Kriesi, and Sidney Tarrow, eds. Vol. 1 of *International Social Movement Research*. Greenwich, CT: JAI Press.
———. 1992. *Talking Politics*. New York: Cambridge University Press.
Gamson, William, Bruce Fireman, and Steven Rytina. 1982. *Encounters with Unjust Authority*. Homewood, IL: Dorsey Press.
Gamson, William, and David Meyer. 1996. "Framing Political Opportunity." Pp. 275-290 in *Comparative Perspectives on Social Movements: Political Opportunities, Mobilizing Structures, and Cultural Framings*, Doug McAdam, John D. McCarthy, and Mayer N. Zald, eds. New York: Cambridge University Press.
Gerth, Hans, and C. Wright Mills. 1958. *From Max Weber*. Oxford: Oxford University Press.
Giddens, Anthony. 1987. *The Nation State and Violence*. Vol. 2 of *A Contemporary Critique of Historical Materialism*. Berkeley: University of California Press.
Gitlin, Todd. 1980. *The Whole World Is Watching*. Berkeley: University of California Press.
Goffman, Erving. 1972. *Frame Analysis*. New York: Harper and Row.

————. 1981. *Forms of Talk*. Philadelphia: University of Pennsylvania Press.

Goodwin, Jeff, and James Jasper. 1999. "Caught in a Winding, Snarling Vine: The Structural Bias of Political Process Theory." *Sociological Forum* 14: 27-54.

Gusfield, Joseph. 1981. *The Culture of Public Problems: Drinking-Driving and the Symbolic Order*. Chicago: University of Chicago Press.

Haydu, Jeffrey. 1999. "Counter Action Frames: Employer Frames and the Union Menace in the Late Nineteenth Century." *Social Problems* 46 (3): 313-331.

Jasper, James M. 1997. *The Art of Moral Protest: Culture, Biography, and Creativity in Social Movements*. Chicago: University of Chicago Press.

Jasper, James M., and Jane D. Poulsen. 1993. "Fighting Back: Vulnerabilities, Blunders, and Countermobilization by Targets in Three Animal Rights Campaigns." *Sociological Forum* 8: 639-657.

Jenkins, J. Craig. 1995. "Social Movements, Political Representation, and the State: An Agenda and Comparative Framework." Pp. 14-38 in *The Politics of Social Protest*, J. Craig Jenkins, ed. Minneapolis: University of Minnesota Press.

Jenkins, J. Craig, and Charles Perrow. 1977. "Insurgency of the Powerless: Farm Workers Movements, 1946-1972." *American Sociological Review* 42: 249-268.

Johnston, Hank. 2002. "Verification and Proof in Frame and Discourse Analysis. Pp. 62-91 in *Methods of Social Movement Research*, Bert Klandermans and Suzanne Staggenborg, eds. Minneapolis: University of Minnesota Press.

Johnston, Hank, and Bert Klandermans. 1995. *Social Movements and Culture*. Minneapolis: University of Minnesota Press.

Keen, Mike Forrest. 1999. *Stalking the Sociological Imagination: J. Edgar Hoover's FBI Surveillance of American Sociology*. Westport, CT: Greenwood Press.

Kubal, Timothy. 1998. "The Presentation of Political Self: Cultural Resonance and the Construction of Collective Action Frames." *Sociological Quarterly* 39 (4): 539-554.

Kurzman, Charles. 1996. "Structural Opportunity and Perceived Opportunity in Social Movement Theory: The Iranian Revolution of 1979." *American Sociological Review* 61: 153-170.

Laraña, Enrique, Hank Johnston, and Joseph Gusfield. 1994. *New Social Movements: From Ideology to Identity*. Philadelphia: Temple University Press.

Leab, Daniel, ed. 1991. "Communist Activity in the Entertainment Industry: FBI Surveillance Files on Hollywood, 1942-1958." University Publications of America. Microfilm Collection.

McAdam, Douglas. 1982. *Political Process and the Development of the Black Insurgency, 1930-1970*. Chicago: University of Chicago Press.

————. 1994. "Culture and Social Movements." Pp. 36-57 in *New Social Movements: From Ideology to Identity*, Enrique Laraña, Hank Johnston, and Joseph Gusfield, eds. Philadelphia, PA: Temple University Press.

————. 1996a. "Conceptual Origins, Current Problems, Future Directions." Pp. 23-40 in *Comparative Perspectives on Social Movements: Political Opportunities, Mobilizing Structures, and Cultural Framings*, Doug McAdam, John D. McCarthy, and Mayer N. Zald, eds. New York: Cambridge University Press.

————. 1996b. "The Framing Function of Movement Tactics: Strategic Dramaturgy in the American Civil Rights Movement." Pp. 338-355 in *Comparative Perspectives on Social Movements: Political Opportunities, Mobilizing Structures, and Cultural Framings*, Doug McAdam, John D. McCarthy, and Mayer N. Zald, eds. New York: Cambridge University Press.

McAdam, Douglas, John D. McCarthy, and Mayer N. Zald, eds. 1996a. *Comparative Perspectives on Social Movements: Political Opportunities, Mobilizing Structures, and Cultural Framings*. New York: Cambridge University Press.

————. 1996b. "Introduction: Opportunities, Mobilizing Structures, and Framing Processes—Toward a Synthetic, Comparative, Perspective on Social Movements." Pp. 1-22 in *Comparative Perspectives on Social Movements: Political Opportunities, Mobilizing Structures, and Cultural Framings*, Doug McAdam, John D. McCarthy, and Mayer N. Zald, eds. New York: Cambridge University Press.

McAdam, Doug, and David Snow, eds. 1997. *Social Movements*. Los Angeles: Roxbury.

McCarthy, John, Jackie Smith, and Mayer Zald. 1996. "Accessing Public, Media, Electoral, and Governmental Agenda." Pp. 291-311 in *Comparative Perspectives on Social Movements: Political Opportunities, Mobilizing Structures, and Cultural Framings,* Doug McAdam, John D. McCarthy, and Mayer N. Zald, eds. New York: Cambridge University Press.

McCarthy, John, and Mark Wolfson. 1992. "Consensus Movements, Conflict Movements, and the Cooptation of Civic and State Infrastructures." Pp. 273-297 in *Frontiers in Social Movement Theory,* Aldon Morris and Carol McClurg Mueller, eds. New Haven, CT: Yale University Press.

Meyer, David, and Suzanne Staggenborg. 1996. "Movements, Countermovements, and the Structure of Political Opportunity." *American Journal of Sociology* 101: 1628-1660.

Mooney, Patrick, and Scott Hunt. 1996. "A Repertoire of Interpretations: Master Frames and Ideological Continuity in U.S. Agrarian Mobilization." *Sociological Quarterly* 37 (1): 177-197.

Morris, Aldon. 1984. *The Origins of the Civil Rights Movement: Black Communities Organizing for Change*. New York: Free Press.

Murray, Robert K. 1964. *Red Scare: A Study in National Hysteria, 1919-1920*. Minneapolis: University of Minnesota Press.

Naremore, James. 1991. "The Trial: The FBI vs. Orson Welles." *Film Comment* 27: 22-27.

Navasky, Victor. 1980. *Naming Names*. New York: Viking Press.

Noakes, John. 1994. "'A New Breed of Detective': The Rise of the FBI Special Agent." Pp. 25-42 in *Studies in Law, Politics, and Society*, Austin Sarat and Susan Silbey, eds., vol. 14. Greenwich, CT: JAI Press.

———. 1998. "Bankers and Common Men in Bedford Falls: How the FBI Determined That *It's a Wonderful Life* Was a Subversive Movie." *Film History* 10: 311-319.

Oberschall, Anthony. 1996. "Opportunities and Framing in the Eastern European Revolts of 1989." Pp. 93-121 in *Comparative Perspectives on Social Movements: Political Opportunities, Mobilizing Structures, and Cultural Framings,* Doug McAdam, John D. McCarthy, and Mayer N. Zald, eds. New York: Cambridge University Press.

O'Reilly, Kenneth. 1983. *Hoover and the Un-Americans*. Philadelphia: Temple University Press.

———. 1989. *Racial Matters: The FBI's Secret File on Black Americans, 1960-1972*. New York: The Free Press.

Orloff, Ann Shola, and Theda Skocpol. 1985. "Why Not Equal Protection? Explaining the Politics of Public Social Spending in Britain, 1900-1911, and the United States, 1880s-1920." *American Sociological Review* 49: 726-750.

Polletta, Francesca. 1997. "Culture and Its Discontents: Recent Theorizing on the Cultural Dimensions of Protest." *Sociological Inquiry* 676: 431-450.

Potter, Claire Bond. 1998. *War on Crime: Bandits, G-Men, and the Politics of Mass Culture*. New Brunswick, NJ: Rutgers University Press.

Powers, Richard Gid. 1987. *Secrecy and Power*. New York: The Free Press.

———. 1995. *Not without Honor*. New York: The Free Press.

Preston, William, Jr. 1963. *Aliens and Dissenters: Federal Suppression of Radicals, 1903-1933*. Cambridge, MA: Harvard University Press.

Robins, Natalie. 1992. *Alien Ink: The FBI's War on Freedom of Expression*. New York: William Morrow.

Ross, Lillian. 1948. "Come In, Lassie." *New Yorker* February 21, 1948, 32-52.

Roy, William, and Rachel Parker-Gwin. 1999. "How Many Logics of Collective Action?" *Theory and Society* 28: 203-237.

Ryan, Charlotte. 1991. *Prime Time Activism*. Boston: South End Press.

Scharr, John H. 1984. "Legitimacy in the Modern State." Pp. 104-133 in *Legitimacy and the Modern State*, William Connelly, ed. New York: New York University Press.

Schatz, Thomas. 1997. *History of the American Cinema*, Vol. 6, *1940-1949*. New York:

Charles Scribner's Sons.

Schrecker, Ellen. 1998. *Many Are the Crimes*. Boston: Little, Brown.

Sewell, William. 1992. "A Theory of Structure: Duality, Agency, and Transformation." *American Journal of Sociology* 98: 1-29.

Skocpol, Theda. 1979. *States and Social Revolutions: A Comparative Analysis of France, Russia, and China*. Princeton, NJ: Princeton University Press.

Snow, David, and Robert Benford. 1992. "Master Frames and Cycles of Protest." Pp. 133-155 in *Frontiers in Social Movement Theory*, Aldon Morris and Carol McClurg Mueller, eds. New Haven, CT: Yale University Press.

Snow, David, E. Burke Rochford, Jr., Steven Worden, and Robert Benford. 1986. "Frame Alignment Processes, Micromobilization, and Movement Participation," *American Sociological Review* 51 (4): 464-481.

Staggenborg, Suzanne. 1991. *The Pro-Choice Movement*. New York: Oxford University Press.

Swart, William J. 1995. "The League of Nations and the Irish Question: Master Frames, Cycles of Protest, and 'Master Frame Alignment.'" *Sociological Quarterly* 36 (3): 465-481.

Swidler, Ann. 1995. "Cultural Power and Social Movements." Pp. 25-41 in *Social Movements and Culture*, Hank Johnston and Bert Klandermans, eds. Minneapolis: University of Minnesota Press.

Tarrow, Sidney. 1994. *Power in Movement*. New York: Cambridge University Press.

Taylor, Verta. 1989. "Social Movement Continuity: The Women's Movement in Abeyance." *American Sociological Review* 54 (5): 761-775.

Theoharis, Athan, and John Stuart Cox. 1988. *The Boss: J. Edgar Hoover and the Great American Inquisition*. Philadelphia: Temple University Press.

Zald, Mayer. 1996. "Culture, Ideology, and Strategic Framing." Pp. 261-274 in *Comparative Perspectives on Social Movements: Political Opportunities, Mobilizing Structures, and Cultural Framings*, Doug McAdam, John D. McCarthy, and Mayer N. Zald, eds. New York: Cambridge University Press.

Zdravomyslova, Elena. 1996. "Opportunities and Framing in the Transition to Democracy: The Case of Russia." Pp. 122-140 in *Comparative Perspectives on Social Movements: Political Opportunities, Mobilizing Structures, and Cultural Framings*, Doug McAdam, John D. McCarthy, and Mayer N. Zald, eds. New York: Cambridge University Press.

Zuo, Jiping, and Robert Benford. 1995. "Mobilization Processes and the 1989 Chinese Democracy Movement." *Sociological Quarterly* 36 (1): 131-156.

Chapter 6

MOBILIZING THE WHITE MARCH: MEDIA FRAMES AS ALTERNATIVES TO MOVEMENT ORGANIZATIONS

Stefaan Walgrave and Jan Manssens

The White March of Sunday, October 20, 1996, was by far the largest demonstration in Belgian history. An estimated 300,000 participants—3 percent of Belgium's population—took to the streets. The march followed the discovery in mid-August 1996 of the bodies of four girls who had been abducted and murdered by a criminal named Marc Dutroux. When Dutroux was arrested, two more girls were found alive and set free. Soon it became clear that the police and the judiciary had made major errors in pursuing Dutroux. As details of the case became known, grief turned into criticism and protest against the judicial apparatus and the government. On Monday, October 14, 1996, the highest Belgian court decided that the examining magistrate, Jean-Marc Connerotte, a national hero since he arrested Dutroux and liberated the two girls, was no longer allowed to investigate the case because he had shown too much sympathy for the victims. An immediate and unprecedented protest explosion followed: in three days almost 500,000 people participated in riots, sit-ins, and strikes all over the country (Walgrave and Rihoux 1997). By week's end the nature of the protests changed. Out of respect for the young victims, the furious protests were replaced by quiet and dignified collective action—so-called "serene demonstrations." The White March itself was organized by the parents of the Dutroux's victims and represented the culmination of the "serene" demonstration style. Participants were mostly families with children carrying white flowers and balloons. No slogans or banners were present, only 300,000 silent participants. After the White March, interest in these protests decreased as rapidly as it began. Three months later, newly founded, local "white committees" were able to mobilize only about a hundred small local white marches throughout the country.

In this chapter, we ask how it was possible that so many people took to the streets in the White March. We are led to this question because the White March had no preexisting movement organizations, no mobilizing apparatus, and no support from the traditional mobilizing actors such as unions, political parties, professional associations, youth movements, or new social movements (Walgrave and Rihoux 1998). Our hypothesis is that framing activities of the Belgian mass media successfully and almost completely took over the functions normally performed by movement organizations. There is a long tradition in social movement analysis that recognizes the role of the mass media in shaping issue discourses and how the public may view a movement, but rarely does one find cases where the mass media play a central role in getting the protesters into the streets. To explore this hypothesis and to empirically test its accuracy we focus on the first months of the Dutroux case, from mid-August 1996 until the end of October 1996, ten days after the White March.

FRAMING AND PRECONDITIONS OF MOBILIZATION

Why do people demonstrate? Why do citizens commit themselves to a social movement? Why do they sign petitions? To mobilize large numbers of participants, there are several preconditions that have to be met and steps that have to be taken. Dominant social movement theory, influenced by the resource mobilization approach, emphasizes especially resources and organizations as necessary preconditions for mobilization (McAdam, McCarthy, and Zald 1996). The constructionist approach, in contrast, stresses the framing of social and political problems around which movements mobilize. Constructionist scholars consider framing to be at least as important as organization and resources (Snow and Benford 1988). The way that people perceive a problem is a central factor in their participation in protest events. If we take this line of argument farther, we could hypothesize that framing by itself—if it is especially compelling and resonant—could explain protest mobilization even when organizational structures are absent or very weak. In such a case, people would actively seek opportunities to display their discontent, anger, or grief. They would be disposed to take advantage of a wide variety of mobilization occasions and would be less reliant on organizational structures, resources, and networks to activate their participation. Moreover, people would tend to directly contact family, friends, and acquaintances and encourage participation. It is our belief that in these ways the Belgian White March shows the strength of media framing. The media succeeded in creating an extremely resonant mobilization frame that brought people onto the streets in the absence of traditional mobilizing agencies.

In order to get people into the streets, participants must not only be convinced of the rightness of the cause but also be encouraged to take action. Klandermans has coined the terms *consensus mobilization* and *action mobilization* to account for this crucial distinction (Klandermans 1984; Klandermans and Oegema 1987). Within the framing theory too, Snow and Benford (1988) capture the difference between ideas and action with their concepts of *diagnostic framing, prognostic framing,* and *motivational framing.* Diagnostic framing refers to the question, "What is the problem here?" Prognostic framing answers the question, "What must *be done?*" Finally, motivational framing provides an answer to "How can I act to accomplish what must be done?" For successful mobilization, all three questions must be answered. People need a definition of the situation; they have to get an idea of what is at stake and why this situation is unjust (Gamson 1992). Second, they need some clues for possible solutions to the problem. Third, they need a personal action perspective; they must come to see what they can do to support the proposed solutions. In sum, a mobilizing frame is needed to define a situation as unjust and to indicate that it can be changed through collective action (McAdam 1982: 52). Even if a movement's ideas are widely shared, mobilization for action is not automatically achieved. It is plausible that movements with large constituencies or large mobilization potentials will be unable to get people into the street if they do not accomplish motivational framing (Klandermans and Oegema 1987: 519), whereas movements with relatively little public appeal can mobilize relatively large protests with the right strategic framing. It is indeed common that a huge gap exists between the conviction that a certain situation is unjust (the diagnostic frame) and the opinion that collective action is warranted (the prognostic and the motivational frames). Klandermans and Oegema (1987: 529) state that only 5 percent of those respondents who agree with the objectives of a protest actually participate.

Successful collective action frames must take those barriers to participation down and persuade the public to put their ideas into action. In cost-benefit terms, getting persuaded does not cost anything, but participation costs time and money—and may involve the risk of violence. The type of action and its place and time also partly determine the cost of participation (Klandermans 1984: 588). On the other hand, the benefits of collective action are the values that derive from the possible outcomes and chances of success (or the efficiency perception [Oberschall 1980]). These are linked with the anticipated attendance (how many people will participate), the expectation that one's own participation will benefit the action, and the perceived chance that the action will be successful if many people participate (Klandermans 1984: 585). However, because mobilization depends on the weighing of the *perceived* costs and benefits (Klandermans 1984: 584-585), the mobilizing organization is confronted with somewhat different framing tasks. Mobilization for action requires motivational framing strategies that convince the potential participants that *their* presence at a protest can help dispel the problem.

In sum, mobilization can be thought of as a kind of elimination competition in which potential participants may drop out at different stages in the decision-making process, stages that are not necessarily sequential (Klandermans and Oegema 1987; Oegema and Klandermans 1994). The sequence goes something like this: (1) Not everyone agrees on the issue as the basis for action. (2) Not everyone who agrees is convinced to actively participate. (3) Not everyone who is convinced to participate weighs the costs and benefits positively and is thus motivated. (4) Not everyone who agrees, is persuaded, and is motivated to participate actually does so because of practical reasons (illness, bad weather, no time, etc.). A mobilizing agency wants to keep the dropout rate as low as possible by working on all factors. This enumeration clearly indicates that successful mobilization is more than increasing the motivation to participate by influencing the perception of costs and benefits. It is also a matter of eliminating practical barriers of participation and persuading and activating the potential grassroots support.

But how do mobilizing agencies promote the rightness of their cause and reduce barriers to participation? The answer is straightforward: they fine-tune their frames and manipulate them to be as persuasive and compelling as possible to the targeted constituency. Snow, Rochford, Worden, and Benford (1986) state that mobilization is facilitated when a movement organization's ideas are framed so that they align with the discourse of the potential constituency. When there is congruency between what a movement organization publicly claims and the opinions of the public, mobilization is likely. When congruency is weak, movement organizations can try to reframe the message in such a way as to align it with prevailing opinions or interpretative frameworks. Mobilization efforts aimed at activating and tuning into these sometimes hidden and implicit frames have greater likelihood of success. Properly aligned frames turn objective facts into meaningful ones that encourage collective action. According to Snow and his colleagues (1986), frame alignment between a movement organization's ideas and the broader population's occurs in four ways: (1) in cases of close affinity it suffices to emphasize similarities (frame bridging); (2) when the organization's frame is suitable, it can be elaborated and reinforced (frame amplification); (3) when the affinity is not immediately clear, frames of the potential participants can be broadened so that the organization's proposed collective action is included (frame extension); and (4) in cases where there is little affinity, a change in the frames of the potential participants is needed (frame transformation). The distinctions among these four modes of frame manipulation are not absolute, nor is it always possible to discern or empirically gauge their separate influences. Yet, it is obvious that frame bridging is easiest to accomplish since it is just a matter of fine-tuning an existing frame. Frame transformation is the most difficult task since it requires the changing of the ideas of potential participants. Frame amplification and frame extension are located somewhere in the middle. Hypothetically, for each of the three basic framing functions—diagnostic, prognostic, and motivational—bridging, amplification, extension, and transformation can occur.

THE ROLE OF MASS MEDIA IN MOBILIZATION

Kielbowicz and Scherer (1986: 72) claim that "the modern mass media have become central to the life and death of social movements." In modern societies, the media are an arena in which societal groups and ideologies compete for the definition and construction of social reality (Gurevitch and Levy 1985). Something exists *because* it appeared in the media. Media attention is crucial for the germination, growth, trajectory, and ultimate fate of just about all social movements. Most movements do not dispose of their own media and consequently they "must reach their constituency in part through some form of public discourse" (Gamson and Wolsfeld 1993: 116). Consequently, social movements are engaged in a "struggle for cultural supremacy" between themselves and other collective actors, including the state, countermovements, *and* the media (Tarrow 1998). For social movements this struggle consists of two separate battles: a fight for media access, and a fight for the definition and framing of the covered issue. In both battles, social movements are most of the time not fighting on even terms but are confronted with strong opponents making opposing claims.

In terms of the access struggle, institutional sources and political authorities have the advantage of being strong news sources (White 1950; Galtung and Ruge 1965; Shoemaker 1991). Social movements develop all kinds of media strategies to bypass the media's *selection* bias (Oliver and Maney 2000; McCarthy et al. 1998; Smith et al. 2001; McPhail and Schweingruber 1998), but that cannot compensate for the media's fascination for institutional and more professionalized newsmakers. Once a social movement and/or its issue have successfully passed the news gates, the framing becomes the issue. To what extent has the frame and the interpretation of the movement been taken over by the media and how favorable is the journalistic *description* bias (McCarthy et al. 1998; Smith et al. 2001)? The news media's account of protest is inevitably distorted. In some cases, the media rely on the familiar "protest paradigm" that trivializes and marginalizes social movement activities (Gitlin 1980). In contrast, a resonating media frame, aligning the media's with the movement's interpretation, can boost mobilization, while deliberate or unintentional opposite framing hinders mobilization (Cooper 2002; Gamson and Modigliani 1989; Gamson and Wolsfeld 1993). Since movements do not control access or the frames that the media use, they cannot rely on the media for mobilization. All this shows that, in a normal situation, mass media cannot be considered as a movement's ally or fellow traveler. The media have their own agenda, and they must be considered as political actors in their own right, engaged just like other political actors in a fight to control the construction of social meaning (Tarrow 1998). To put it in terms of this contribution, media are not suitable for motivational framing; they do not play the role of mobilizing agency.

Although there is a sizable social-scientific literature that examines the movement-media relationship (Gamson 1992; Gamson and Wolsfeld 1993; Gitlin 1980; Hansen 1993; Kielbowicz and Scherer 1986; Molotch 1979; Sampedro 1997; Schmitt-Beck 1990; Van Zoonen 1992; Wolsfeld 1984), the actual mobilization function of the mass media is indeed not central to the major theories of collective action, let alone in most empirical research on social movements. The media are considered as a validation for social movements (we exist), they can hold together the movement's members by reassuring them that the movement is doing its job (Smith 1999), they can broaden the range of the conflict (Gamson and Wolsfeld 1993), and they can facilitate the recruitment of new members or supporters (Schmitt-Beck 1990). The political opportunity structure approach (Eisinger 1973; Tarrow 1996) considers the mass media as filters, facilitators, or even barriers to collective action rather than as real actors that play strategic roles. Although it is generally accepted that the mass media are a means for the geographical diffusion of protest (McAdam and Rucht 1993; Tarrow 1991), the direct impact of the media on mobilization is inferquently considered (Koopmans 1995).

Moreover, in those studies where the mobilizing influence of the media is considered, it is not thought of very highly (Gamson 1992; Klandermans and Goslinga 1996; McQuail 1993: 381; Snow, Zurcher, and Ekland-Olson 1980). Klandermans and Oegema, for example, state that "the mass media are not very effective in convincing and activating people," and that mobilization for a concrete action could be better done via mailings, organizations, or friendship networks (1987: 520). Their study stresses the role of organization and/or informal networks in mobilization, and the direct influence of the media is indirectly minimized. Several researchers have pointed out that the media are especially ineffective mobilization channels for high-cost/high-risk activism (Briet, Klandermans, and Kroon 1987; McAdam 1986). Also, the media's role is questioned in low threshold actions because, as mentioned above, social movement organizations do not easily gain access to the mass media and cannot control the news coverage of their actions (Klandermans 1997).

In sum, mainstream mobilization theory suggests that the mass media are possible channels for diagnostic and prognostic framing because they are privileged providers of information and reference frames (Gamson and Meyer 1996; McQuail 1993), but that they fall short for motivational framing. The media are better in telling people what the problem is (diagnostic framing) and, possibly, what can be done (prognostic framing) than in persuading people to roll up their sleeves themselves and actively try to pursue a desirable solution (motivational framing). Klandermans (1997) states that the media are less important for persuasive communication (motivational framing) but certainly can play a role in creating a favorable mobilization climate (diagnostic and prognostic framing) although the actual creation of the collective action frame takes place in informal or formal groups. To put it another way, the mass media best function as (reactive) transmitters but not as (proactive) mobilizing actors. However, our analysis of Belgian newspapers on the White March suggests that this conclusion is not altogether correct. The central claim of this chapter is that the media *did* act as a mobilizing agency and *did* engage in large-scale motivational framing. Precisely the absence of partisan movement organizations gave the media the opportunity to celebrate the claims of the victim's parents and to champion their diagnostic, prognostic, *and* motivational framing of the events.

METHODOLOGY

Our empirical material consists of the news coverage of the Dutroux case in the five most important Belgian newspapers, *De Standaard, De Morgen, Het Laatste Nieuws, Gazet van Antwerpen,* and *Het Nieuwsblad.*[1] These newspapers are representative of the Belgian print media in terms of ideology, readership, and market share. Together they represent 75 percent of the 983,000 Flemish Belgian newspapers sold daily.

For the period from August 16 (the liberation of two girls) until October 31, 1996, each newspaper copy (sixty-six copies per newspaper, a total of 329 copies)[2] was scrutinized and encoded on the basis of a questionnaire. The questionnaire consisted of both quantitative (amount of attention for the Dutroux case) and qualitative items (type and content of the news coverage: words used, references to certain events or actors, etc.). For the quantitative approach the entire newspaper was reviewed. For qualitative measures, only articles on the Dutroux case on the front page were analyzed, or, when there was no article on the front page (or only a very short one), the first, long article that appeared was analyzed. We also encoded captions of Dutroux-case pictures, and the titles, subtitles, in-between-titles, and short introductory summaries of all the Dutroux articles, letters to the editor, and editorial comments. Finally, the editorials were also screened. We estimate that about 10 to 20 percent of the actual Dutroux news coverage was analyzed for its content.

The fortnight before the breaking of the Dutroux case, August 1-15, 1996, was taken as a reference period in order to test the hypothesis that the news coverage on the Dutroux case was out of the ordinary. The same titles were analyzed with a similar encoding scheme (n = 60). Since there was no mention of Dutroux during this period, we reviewed each newspaper to decide which news item was covered most and then proceeded with an identical qualitative and quantitative analysis of its news coverage.

AMPLIFICATION: THE DUTROUX CASE IN BLINDING SPOTLIGHT

For framing to directly cause mobilization, the public issue, grievance, or claim must first be salient in public opinion—simply put, people must care. Even the most resonant framing cannot cause mass mobilization if the public's attention is directed elsewhere. According to the classic agenda-setting theory in media studies, the public's issue priorities are simply determined by the quantity of media attention for the issue. That is why we focus first on the sheer amount of Dutroux-case news, the number and size of the news stories.

Belgian media coverage of the Dutroux case was enormous. Although comparable data of exceptional news event facts are lacking, we know of no other news item that attracted Belgian media attention for such a considerable time and to such an extent.[3] Table 6.1 provides some figures to support our claim. It combines eleven quantitative parameters for the five newspapers analyzed: (1) the average number of pages on the Dutroux case (per newspaper copy); (2) the average number of pictures on the case; (3) the average number of letters to the editor; (4) the Dutroux case's share of coverage in relation to total news coverage;[4] (5) the share of pictures in relation to the total number of pictures; (6) the share of letters compared to the total amount of letters; (7) the extent to which the lead story deals with the case;[5] (8) the extent to which the editorial is about the case; (9) the extent to which the Dutroux case is the newspaper's main item; (10) the extent to which the captivating title (the title in the largest type—not always on the front page) is on the Dutroux case; and (11) the share of pictures on the Dutroux case on the first page.

The data speak for themselves: all parameters point to a true Dutroux mania from mid-August to the end of October. This holds for all newspapers, both the quality dailies and the more popular press. Although table 6.1 indicates some differences between the newspapers—*De Standaard* especially—all papers focused on the Dutroux case for months. Therefore, in the discussion that follows, we will not refer to distinctions between the different newspapers but only to the totals. The fact that the newspapers bombarded their readers with Dutroux news cannot be overlooked. On average, one-third of all the national and international news coverage was on the Dutroux case. The same is true for the share of pictures. All this lasted for the period ranging between August 16 and October 31, or sixty-six daily editions for each newspaper. The parameters that take into account the importance of the news, and not just the space devoted to it, are even more impressive. In about six editions out of ten, the editorial and the lead story were devoted to the Dutroux case, the largest amount of space was given to the case, and the largest title was about the case.[6] The figures for the semitabloid *Het Laatste Nieuws* are even more than spectacular: on average, more than fourteen pictures per day on the case. The impact of these pictures and images cannot be underestimated: "There has been a general shift in society's regime of significance, from words to images, from the discursive to the figural" (Lash cited in Szaz 1994).

The extraordinary amount of news coverage is also clear from a comparison between this period and the reference period before the outburst of the Dutroux case. For every newspaper during this period, we identified the most extensively covered item.[7] For each of these items, which on the average was the most important news for only one day, we established the share of coverage, the number of pictures, editorials, and so forth. Although it was the middle of the summer, a dead season for news and not a representative period, the differences are striking. For all parameters, news coverage of the Dutroux case scores higher than the most important daily news items during the reference period. The most important news during the reference period had an average of 1.16 pages, versus 2.78 for the Dutroux case. An average of 16 percent of news coverage was given the most important reference-period items, compared to 33 percent for the Dutroux case; 2.63 pictures were printed on those items, compared to 7.95 pictures for the Dutroux case. The main news was discussed in 30 percent of reference-period editorials, for the Dutroux case, 59 percent.

Table 6.1 Quantitative Attention for the Dutroux Case in the Belgian Newspapers from August 16 to October 1, 1996 (n = 329)

	De Morgen	De Standaard	Het Nieuws- blad	Het Laatste Nieuws	Gazet van Antwerpen	Average
Average number of pages	3.09	1.77	2.77	3.71	2.65	2.80
Average number of pictures	6.56	2.55	7.73	14.35	8.60	7.95
Average number of readers' letters	2.41	1.91	4.02	4.76	5.12	3.64
Share news coverage (%)	28	23	38	40	35	33
Share pictures (%)	26	18	36	41	37	32
Share readers' letters (%)	40	36	55	54	48	46
Share editorials (%)	64	47	59	62	62	59
Share lead stories (%)	50	58	68	71	60	61
Share main items (%)	70	42	61	71	51	59
Share captivating title (%)	50	77	62	85	54	66
Share page one pictures (%)	46	36	68	68	55	55

Visual and layout data also indicate the amplification of the Dutroux case: in 67 percent of the 329 newspapers the normal layout was changed (see figure 6.1). In 65 percent of the newspapers, we found a special header on top of the page (for instance, a row of pictures of the victims). In thirty-one cases no advertisements were found on the first page, although that is not unusual. Extremely big titles were found in twenty-six cases, and in one case, a headline filled the complete page. In total, fourteen supplements on the case were found. A special layout of the first page was found twelve times. In twenty-eight newspapers a series of photographs on the case was found (for instance, a series of photos showing the victims growing up), and in eight newspapers a complete picture page was devoted to the case. One newspaper published black borders of mourning around the victims' pictures. If attention of readership is an important but often scarce commodity in protest events (Hilgartner and Bosk 1988), then it was assured for the Dutroux case.

DIAGNOSTIC FRAMING: THE GAP BETWEEN THE POPULATION AND THE INSTITUTIONS AS THE MASTER FRAME

The full study period of two and a half months can be divided into six periods. The first runs from Dutroux's arrest and the liberation of two victims, Sabine and Laeti-tia. It includes the recovery of the bodies of two other victims, Julie and Melissa, and ends with their funeral (August 16-26, nine newspaper days). The second includes the search, recovery of the bodies, and funeral of two more of his victims, An and Eefje (August 27 to September 12, fourteen newspaper days). The third is a period of national grief and revelation concerning these dramatic events (September 12-26, thirteen newspaper days). Next is Dutroux's lawyer's charges against the examining magistrate, Jean-Marc Connerotte, then the public's uproar, followed by the first protest marches (September 27 to October 8, ten newspaper days). The fifth period is the period of the White March. It begins with charges against Connerotte, includes his dismissal from the case and rising popular anger, and ends with the White March (October 9-21, eleven newspaper days). Finally, there is the period after the White March (October 22-31, nine newspaper days).

Central to the news coverage on the Dutroux case, especially in the period leading to the White March, is the articulation of a diagnostic master frame based on what we call "gap discourse." A broad interpretative schema based on the media's elaboration of a gap between the population and the government, the citizen and the system, the population and its institutions, acted as the master frame within which all events were interpreted. Concerning the Dutroux case, a typical issue culture did not develop wherein the media, the state, and social movements struggled among each other so that their definition of the issue prevailed (Gamson 1992). Rather, based on the newspapers we examined, they seemed to have agreed rapidly on a common interpretation. All other frames were implicitly or explicitly linked to this master

Figure 6.1 Changed layout in *De Morgen*'s front page, August 19, 1996: Marc Dutroux with the headline "The Face of Evil"

frame. Gap discourse pointed out how state institutions, the judicial apparatus, and politicians were at odds with the feelings of the population. Words such as "ivory tower," "caste," "other-worldliness," and "arrogance" were legion. The following segment from *Het Nieuwsblad* (October 18, 1996) nicely describes the gap discourse:

> Both the magistrates and the politicians seem to overlook the signals [from the population]. Their secret meeting places have become cocoons of inbreeding and cross-fertilization that radiate other-worldliness. In receptions, commission meetings, and informal meetings the "vox populi" is spoken of scornfully: the grumbling population that needs a release once a year but then relapses into a lethargy that can be politically exploited. Is this true? Some complacent inhabitants of "the system" or "the establishment" don't seem to understand that the protest is fundamentally against them and no longer against people like Dutroux or Nihoul [Dutroux's accomplice].

Elements of the gap master frame can be found in a quarter of all newspapers and reached a climax in the period around the White March: it was to be found in 50 percent of all analyzed newspapers and its frequency per newspaper copy increased.[8] From the very beginning of the case, however, the newspapers stressed the gap between the population and the institutions.

This image of the gap shows great similarity with the well-known expression of the "divide" between the citizens and the politicians in Belgium. Since the so-called Black Sunday elections of November 24, 1991, when the extreme right Vlaams Blok scored an electoral breakthrough, journalists, politicians, and social scientists have been pointing out that Belgian politics has lost contact with the population, that there is an intolerable distance, an estrangement, between the citizens and the politicians. Thus, gap discourse was not unknown and found especially fertile soil in the Dutroux case. As the master frame that guided interpretation of the Dutroux case, it connected with familiar themes in Belgian politics and as such it nicely exemplifies the process of frame bridging.

The day after Connerotte's dismissal, the front page of *Gazet van Antwerpen* symbolized this gap discourse: underneath an immense title, "Gap Still Wider," two pictures are literally divided by a tear; on one side a smiling judge draped in ermine, on the other side a furious mass of people (see figure 6.2). In a mere four paragraphs of text the gap between the population and the judicial apparatus is mentioned four times. The imagery used by the newspapers is highly symbolic. They represent what Szaz has called *icons* (1994: 62-63). Icons are particularly powerful since their production "speeds up the issue-creation process and makes that process take quite spectacular form." The use of icons is a powerful element in the frame amplification process. Szaz adds that because of icons, "attitude formation takes place without much need for detail in the cognitive component." The images used abundantly by the media were vehicles fueled by the popular gap discourse. They boosted emotions even more and strengthened the master frame.

The mass media not only reported on the estrangement between population and its institutions—the diagnostic master frame—but also definitely took sides. They disregarded common objectivity rules and plainly sided with the furious masses and the bereaved parents. The vocabulary used clearly indicates this: words such as "mine," "we," "our," and "I" indicate that journalists put aside their role as objective observers. A recurrent phrasing was the "for our children" mantra. On the average,

17 percent of all analyzed newspapers contained this kind of identification discourse. The period just before the White March had 32 percent. Again, the front page of *Gazet van Antwerpen* is revealing. On October 19, 1996, it carried a picture of a White March poster with the title: "*We* are the new citizens. *We* ask questions" (italics added). Elsewhere we found: "The feelings of powerlessness have abounded in your letters since the sad news on An and Eefje. All *our* values seem to have shattered to pieces—what should *we* believe in, who should *we* trust, what should *we* do?" (*Het Laatste Nieuws*, September 6, 1996, italics added).

Newspapers also suspended their objectivity by describing feelings of grief, powerlessness, and anger as universally shared sentiments. They frequently used words like "all," "everyone," "each," "everywhere," "the whole population," "the whole country," "the nation," "the citizens," and "the Belgians" to stress the generality of feelings. *Het Laatste Nieuws* (August 21, 1996, italics added) wrote: "The outcry over what happened to Sabine and Laetitia, the grief for Julie and Melissa and the fear for An and Eefje, are feelings *we're all sharing* these days and they *unite us* in a remarkable way." On An and Eefje's funeral it wrote: "A sad *nation* says goodbye Eefje, the two murdered girls we've *all* got to know so well" (*Het Laatste Nieuws* September 7, 1996, italics added). These words were found in almost half the newspapers (49 percent); again a peak was reached in the period of the White March, when 83 percent of the newspapers used them (an average of 3.01 times per newspaper). The use of such words may not be exceptional in journalistic writing,

Figure 6.2 The gap discourse in speech and print: the front page of *Gazet van Antwerpen,* October 15, 1996

but their extensive use during the Dutroux case was: during the reference period, just 22 percent of the newspapers used similar words in their coverage of the most important daily news items. The newspaper's identification with the population and the universalization of the public's feelings are elements of the diagnostic frame, yet they connect with prognostic and motivational framing. If all citizens are equally touched by grief and anger, it must be considered as normal that all citizens are encouraged to take the streets to express these feelings.

Gap discourse constituted the diagnostic master frame in the newspapers' interpretations of the Dutroux case, but other framing elements were connected with it. We speak of frame bridging or frame extension, when ideas and values that have many affinities are explicitly linked or when existing cultural frameworks are presented in such a way that they are relevant to the collective action situation. In the coverage of the Dutroux case, both these processes occurred, for example, when disappearances of other children that had nothing to do with the Dutroux case were invoked or when unrelated Belgian political affairs were linked with the Dutroux discourse, when the possible involvement of senior officials in child pornography was tied to it. The message was clear: the Dutroux case was not a separate issue, but rather the tip of the iceberg. Kielbowicz and Scherer (1986: 81) write: "The mass media are in a powerful position to synthesize seemingly fragmented and unconnected situations and create what appear to be widespread phenomena. . . . [They] strive to convert stories about particular cases into examples of a general situation." This occurred in the Dutroux case in three ways.

First, when the girls were found, reporters stormed newspaper archives in search of other unsolved disappearances. Almost daily, some newspaper had a new story about an unsolved case from days long gone that was implicitly, but quite often also explicitly, linked with the Dutroux case. Some newspapers seemed to consider it a point of honor to keep their sinister list as complete as possible. Child disappearance seemed a common thing in Belgium: 31 percent of all 329 editions wrote about other disappearances. For example, *Het Laatste Nieuws* (September 17, 1996) accused Michel Nihoul, Dutroux's accomplice, of kidnapping seventeen girls.

Second, for some years, Belgium had been engulfed by high-level scandals. Thirty percent of the newspapers mentioned these affairs in their coverage of the Dutroux case. For example, *Het Nieuwsblad* (October 18, 1996) wrote, "[The public outcry] is not only fed by the Dutroux case, but also by an accumulation of resentment and suspicion because of many unsolved cases of fraud, bribery, and murder, and because political immorality and judiciary failings are left unpunished." A related element is the extent to which the alleged involvement of "senior officials" in the case is mentioned: 15 percent of the newspapers speculated about it. On October 11, 1996, *De Morgen*'s front page heralded, "Neufchâteau [District] Discovers VIP's Network of Child Pornography," and for those who still doubted the involvement of senior officials, the editorial added: "And yes, what had been assumed seems to be correct: Bourlet and Connerotte have discovered a network of child pornography that has been operating for decades and in which senior officials participate." This highly suggestive writing is in line with the notorious canon of a conspiracy of silence in Belgium's higher circles. Connerotte's dismissal especially caused cover-up speculations: "Examining magistrate Connerotte has to leave because he knows too much" was frequently heard. It is no surprise that in the period before the White March, 30 percent of the newspapers mentioned involvement of senior officials.

Third, the mass media linked the Dutroux case with a political-structural frame that was widely held in Belgium. *Het Laatste Nieuws* (September 7, 1996) summarized this nicely in one headline: "No Coincidence Anymore." Not only was Marc Dutroux found guilty but so too were the judicial apparatus and the political system that supported it. From a case of criminal perversion, the case turned into a matter of structural responsibility: "The people are good, but the system is corrupt" (*De Morgen,* October 17, 1996). In the public media (TV and newspapers) this political-structural frame was used from the beginning, in part because the victims' parents had emphasized it (Walgrave and Rihoux 1998). As early as August 21, a *Het Laatste Nieuws* editorial began to push Dutroux into the background by stressing the "mistakes" and the "wrong elements" "in our country" that have caused the death of the girls—clearly a case of frame extension. The repeated failings of the judiciary system and the police were especially brought to the readers' attention in 62 percent of the analyzed newspapers. "Still More Mistakes," blared *Het Laatste Nieuws*'s headline on August 21, right after the affair broke. During the entire study period, failures were mentioned, but they decreased slightly from the beginning of the case to after the White March (78 percent to 52 percent).

A second indicator of the political-structural frame was the high number of references to the so-called Law Lejeune, which states that prisoners with good conduct can be released well before the end of their sentence. Dutroux had been in prison for sexual offenses, but was set free on the basis of this law. Immediately after his arrest, *Het Laatste Nieuws* (August 21, 1996) wrote: "Law Lejeune Creates Criminals." In total, the law was mentioned in 19 percent of the newspapers, with a major difference between the early and the last period. In the "Julie and Melissa" period, the Law Lejeune was premier topic of discussion (64 percent); after the White March it had become a minor theme (5 percent). Both indicators show how during the period of study the media attention shifted away from the specific juridical subjects.

The reverse happened regarding references to political appointments. Most magistrates in Belgium were politically appointed and were supported by a major party. As a consequence the judicial system was politicized and every party got its share of judicial nominations and promotions. On the average, 20 percent of the newspapers mentioned this theme; but especially just before and after the White March these references peaked (30 percent and 60 percent, respectively). Depoliticization of the judiciary became the most important problem to be solved: "It is typically Belgian that the depoliticization will start at the bottom, while meanwhile the proverb and also [the reality of political] affairs teach us that the fish starts rotting at the head" (*Het Nieuwsblad,* October 9, 1996). Over the period of study, a gradual shift away from the judiciary in favor of politics can be noted. The next quote is a perfect example: "The failing of the judiciary system is inevitable because it is inherent to the system due to its politicization" (*De Morgen*, October 5, 1996). The relatively high number of references to other structural themes—sanctions for the responsible (12 percent), the possibility that the culprits will be protected (22 percent) or that those politically responsible will escape punishment (23 percent)—indicates that the political-structural frame was pushed to the fore.

The politicization of the murders manifested itself also in the words chosen by the journalists. The percentage of newspapers articles in that mentioned the words "politicians" and "policy maker" was 34 percent, along with the occurrence of "the structures," "the institutions," or "the system" (25 percent); "politics" (32 percent); "the minister" or "the government" (51 percent); "the parliament" or "a member of parliament" (25 percent); and "the citizen(s)" (22 percent). Without exception, the frequency of each of these political-institutional words rose and, in most cases, peaked in the period of the White March: politicians or policy makers were mentioned in 54 percent of the newspapers in the White March period; the structures, the institutions, or the system scored 33 percent; politics 43 percent; the minister or government 48 percent; a member of parliament 30 percent; and citizens 61 percent. Especially "the citizen(s)" appeared in full glory in the period of the White March, while before that the term had been almost completely absent. The Dutroux case was formulated in the traditional political-institutional vocabulary and became a political story rather than a human-interest story, especially in the period of the White March.

This politicization of the murders and their structural diagnostic framing was a crucial precondition for the prognostic and motivational framing leading to the White March. Only when social problems can be blamed on something or someone (politics, the system), and only when the causes of the problem (politicization of the judiciary, Law Lejeune, corruption) are displayed does collective action make sense. Also, most collective action needs some kind of external goal, a *prognosis* about what should be aimed for, and it was the structural diagnostic frame that provided the White March with a target. Within the structural diagnostic frame used by the newspapers, the seeds of prognostic and motivational framing were already present.

In sum, the media used frame bridging and frame extension to draw upon cultural frameworks widespread among the population in its diagnosis and prognosis of the Dutroux case. The media took advantage of the already low legitimacy of the institutions and elaborated the idea of the gap between the people and their institutions into a diagnostic master frame. The symbol of the gap and gap discourse became iconic devices that forcefully presented the master frame.

THE CLIMAX TOWARD THE WHITE MARCH
AND MOTIVATIONAL FRAMING BY THE MASS MEDIA

The key to the White March's success is the extent that the media was able to link the diagnostic and prognostic framing with a motivational frame that specified what the *public itself* must do. In terms of the decision to participate, motivational framing decreases the perceived costs and increases the perceived benefits.

The first step in examining this question is to see whether the media paid more attention to the Dutroux case in the period of the White March than before. The implicit assumption is that the diagnosis, prognosis, and motivation are interrelated and that a kind of overflow effect of diagnostic and prognostic framing as it related to the Dutroux case impelled people to protest in the White March. In other words, when an issue and its diagnostic frame are emphasized heavily in the media, it is possible that there is a complementary mobilizing effect.[9] Figure 6.3, which presents the most important quantitative parameters by periods, shows that quantitative attention to the Dutroux case was higher in the period of the White March.

All parameters are almost parallel: in the period just before the White March the attention for the Dutroux case exploded. For some parameters the peak occurred at the beginning of the Dutroux case. The most lead stories (91 percent) and most pictures (54 percent) were published then, and the largest share of the coverage was devoted to the case (53 percent) at that time. Gradually less attention was paid to the case in the An and Eefje period, the aftermath period, and the beginning of the dismissal period. Attention soared again just before the White March and remained as high as in the first period. Just before the White March many lead stories appeared (87 percent) as well as a large share of pictures (43 percent). Almost half of the coverage was devoted to the case (45 percent). It is probably not coincidental that the parameters of the opinion coverage also peaked in the White March period. The number of editorials surpassed that of the first period (85 percent versus 78 percent). Also the number of readers' letters in the fifth period easily surpassed that of the first period (62 percent versus 45 percent).

There was more. Although three quantitative parameters were higher in total for the first period, the absolute day peaks of each of these parameters were situated in the period of the White March. The share of the Dutroux news (77 percent), the share of Dutroux pictures (82 percent), and the share of readers' letters on the case (100 percent), peaked around the White March. Furthermore, the whole White March period climaxed toward the White March. Every day more space was allocated to the case, every day more pictures, every day more readers' letters, and for several days only Dutroux editorials and Dutroux lead stories were published. Figure 6.4 clearly portrays the buildup to the White March, showing the relative share in the total news coverage per day.

The White March was not the only action in relation to the Dutroux case. From August onward, people started to demonstrate. At first these demonstrations were in honor of the victims, but gradually they turned into protests against the events. The quantitative pattern of these actions coincides with the pattern of media attention for the case.[10] Figure 6.5 shows both elements.

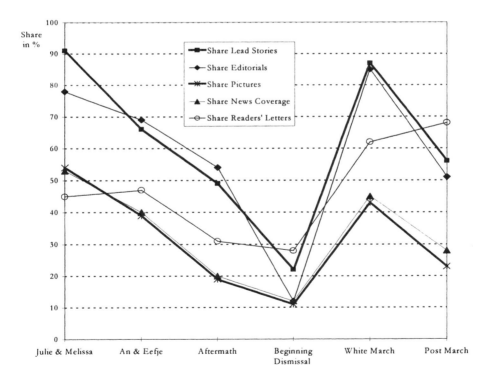

Figure 6.3 Quantitative attention for the Dutroux case throughout the six periods

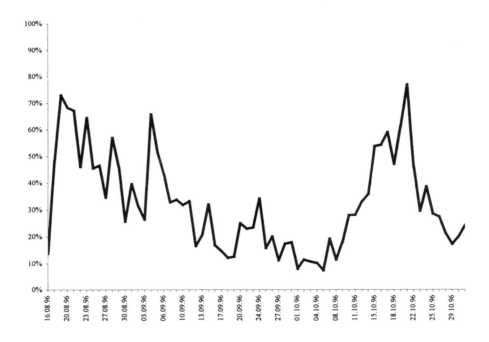

Figure 6.4 Share of Dutroux case in the total news coverage per day

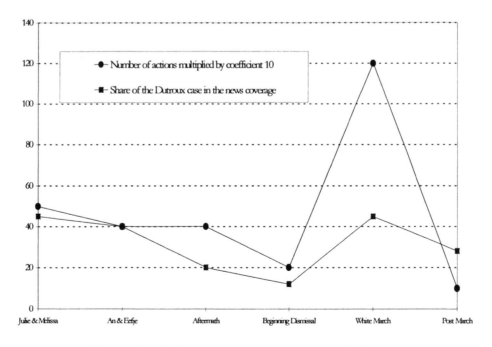

Figure 6.5 Media attention for the Dutroux case and number of collective actions

Of course, correlation between the number of actions and the size of the coverage does not by itself prove that the media created this mobilization wave. It is plausible that the events themselves—and not the media attention—may have motivated the people into the streets. Still, the parallels are strong and highly suggestive of the hypothesis that media attention made massive mobilization possible. The next step is to examine whether the media explicitly or implicitly supported participation in the march. Table 6.2 combines a number of indicators related to what was contained in the media coverage. For reasons of uniformity the table presents percentages, although the number of observations is small.[11]

We see three aspects of motivational framing. The first is the most straightforward: there must be widespread diffusion of information about the event—announcements and commentary. This happened in abundance. In more than four-fifths of the twenty-four newspapers, the White March was mentioned. In only five days the march was mentioned eighty-seven times by name—an average of more than twice per newspaper. We stress again that all the figures on the number of occurrences are from a sample of about 10 percent to 20 percent of the total text that was published in every newspaper without exception announced the march. On Saturday, October 19, the day before the march was to take place, fifty references were

Table 6.2 Action Mobilization for the White March in the Belgian Media, October 15-19, 1996 (n = 24)

	De Morgen	De Stan- daard	Het Nieuws- blad	Het Laatste Nieuws	Gazet van Antwerpen	Avg.
Share of references to the White March (%)	80	60	80	100	100	83
Avg number of references to White March	1.18	2.00	4.11	2.36	3.10	2.54
Share of references to Connerotte's dismissal	100	100	100	100	100	100
Avg number of references to Connerotte's dismissal	2.45	3.00	4.10	2.82	2.70	3.02
Share with forum for the parents (%)	20	40	40	60	25	38
Share with practical information about participation (%)	60	40	60	60	100	63
Share with reference to the expected turnout (%)	40	20	20	60	25	33
Share with reference to the expected results (%)	20	0	20	20	20	17
Share with references to the historic character of the White March (%)	0	0	20	40	25	17

counted, an average of ten references per newspaper. In short, every Belgian citizen knew about the march on the Dutroux case.

The second component in motivational framing relates to the rewards or benefits in deciding to participate in an action. What is the value of the possible outcome? What are its chances of success? What is the expected turnout for the protest or demonstration? In the White March, the value of the possible outcome is closely related to the diagnostic political-structural interpretation given to the drama of the girls. The media presented the White March as a logical reaction of the population to this drama: "The public outcry is understandable and justified" (*Het Nieuwsblad,* October 18, 1996). The value of the possible outcome was no more or no less than judicial and political reform.

One of six newspaper copies and three of the five Saturday editions speculated on the results of the White March by calling it a historic event. *Gazet van Antwerpen* (October 19, 1996) opened with the headline, "Sunday Historic White March in Brussels." The first paragraph portrayed participation favorably: "With white flags they'll march through Brussels tomorrow: white and blue collars, students, the self-employed, citizens. No one knows how many there'll be. It'll definitely be one of the most impressive manifestations ever held in this country. It's already referred to as a historic October Movement." *De Morgen* announced a day earlier: "It's a fact that the White March on Sunday will become a historic manifestation."

Exactly one-third of the newspapers reported on the presumed massive participation. Every newspaper, with the exception of *De Standaard*, told its readers at least once that many people were expected. Four of five newspapers announced this on the eve of the White March. Almost every day the expected turnout increased. The numbers of extra trains were mentioned, as was the fact that almost all coaches were booked for Sunday. In short, the benefits of participation were made clear: (1) there will be a huge number of participants (2) in a demonstration of historic proportions (3) that could initiate structural-political changes. Who would want to miss such an event? To a certain extent the White March is an example of Thomas's famous dictum that "when people define situations as real then they are real in their consequences." By calling the White March a historic event, expectations were made true.

The third component of a motivational frame relates to reducing the costs of participation. Szaz notes that "even if people have the motivation to act . . . their capacity to do so will be affected by a series of conditions" (1994: 86). There are costs of participating in a manifestation like the White March. These include, for example, money, time, uncertainty about the course of the demonstration, and chances of irregularities. Helping to overcome these barriers by framing the costs of participation favorably is essential. How did the media frame the perceived costs? First, general conditions minimized costs: the choice of the date (a free Sunday afternoon with the weather predicted to be 15° C, dry with sunny intervals), the action mode (a peaceful demonstration), and the place (in the central and accessible capital on a route from one railway station to another) had no effect on the objective costs (or practical hindrances) for participation. Although the subjective costs of participation differed individually, the media tried hard to portray them as minimal. For example, they could not resist stressing the special price of 200 BEF for a return train ticket, irrespective of the distance traveled. Since two-thirds of the newspapers provided their readership with practical information, the uncertainty about the further development of the march was largely taken away. On the Saturday preceding the White March, every newspaper mentioned the time of march's departure, its route, the price of a train ticket, and so on. And all this information was presented more than once to the reader.[12] The day before the march, *Gazet van Antwerpen* published a half-page map under the not-so-neutral title: "Cheap and Practical to the White March." The text stressed the ease of participation: the Antwerp-Brussels trip by train would take little more than half an hour, the march would start near the Gare du Nord (one of the main railway stations in Brussels), the march would always be straight ahead, and potential participants were kindly warned that the time of arrival could well be as late as 6:00 PM. The readers of *Het Laatste Nieuws* (October 16, 1996) were also presented with a practical map and were encouraged to go by train ("One only pays 200 BEF"). For those who preferred to come by car, all car parks were indicated on the map.

In the week preceding the march, media coverage of protests described vandalism, police charges, water cannons, and dozens of arrests. As such, participants in the White March might risk violence, injuries, panics, arrests, and the like. With the White March approaching, the attitude of the mass media changed. While in the beginning of the week they sympathized with the demonstrators' anger and forgave their violence, by the end of the week they were strongly disapproving of street violence. "Agitators tried to ruin the atmosphere of indignation . . . the same small group seized every opportunity to inflame the atmosphere" (*Gazet van Antwerpen,* October 19, 1996). *Het Laatste Nieuws* (October 18, 1996) reported that this was "not what the people wanted." Time and again it was stressed that the White March would be serene and dignified. "For the fifth day in a row massive actions were held. The demonstrations were usually peaceful and introduced the big Sunday demonstration" (*Gazet van Antwerpen,* October 19, 1996). Parents of the victims were given a forum in the newspapers to make clear their desire for a quiet demonstration. Editorialists concurred that the march "should be serene and dignified, quiet, and white" (*De Morgen,* October 19, 1996).

Experience with demonstrating is a crucial factor in the perceived costs of participation. People who had never before demonstrated no doubt experienced participation in the White March as a major step. We do not know the exact number of people who had never demonstrated before, but we do know that 60 percent of the participants in the local white marches—which occurred after the national White March—had demonstrated for the first time. A large number of these people participated in the White March (Walgrave and Rihoux 1997: 119). The costs for these people should not be underestimated despite the objective low costs. In any case, the cost was higher than simply signing one of the many petitions that circulated those days.[13]

The press not only provided people with information on the White March. Nor did they merely offer a favorable participation frame and an encouraging cost-benefit analysis to their readers. The media also played a major role in the actual mobilization of the participants, a fourth component of motivational framing. This was achieved implicitly by giving the girls' parents ample media attention and offering them free newspaper space to address the public. Parents' letters and appeals were printed in full. *Het Laatste Nieuws* (October 18, 1996) began publishing the diary of Paul Marchal, An's father—which would appear regularly—in which he mentions a "quiet march that will be dignified." "Parents Count on Serenity" was the front-page headline of *Gazet van Antwerpen* on the Saturday preceding the march. Four of five Saturday editions and 38 percent of the newspapers had something similar. Not only were the parents covered in the media, but also other authorities, for example, King Albert I himself: "King Asks to Keep Up the Fight" (*Gazet van Antwerpen,* October 19, 1996).

But the newspapers did even more. *Het Laatste Nieuws* and *Gazet van Antwerpen* supplemented their newspapers with mobilization posters for the White March and asked their readerships to display them. *Het Nieuwsblad* (October 19, 1996) considered this but decided on a simple announcement on the first page: "See You in Brussels on Sunday." *De Morgen* and *De Standaard* (October 19, 1996) published a large advertisement for "the march for the children"—it was not clear whether this was their own initiative or the parents'. *Het Laatste Nieuws* (October 16, 1996) placed its own advertisement on the front page with a free phone number for the public to announce their own "white action."

Taken as a whole, the White March discourse reveals the media's positive attitude and numerous unconcealed appeals to participate. There is no doubt that the media engaged in motivational framing for the White March until the public's actual activation. *Het Laatste Nieuws*'s headline on October 16, 1996, pleaded to "Make Brussels a White City on Sunday," and the front page was decorated with white balloons for four days before the march. Those not planning to go were made to feel guilty: *Gazet van Antwerpen* wrote on the Saturday preceding the White March that some "famous citizens used the 'yes-but' excuse for not going" and that "some politicians didn't dare to go." In short, every right-minded person had the solemn duty to demonstrate in Brussels. These appeals were not equally strong in all newspapers. The more popular press stood head and shoulders above the rest, while two quality papers, and especially *De Standaard,* were much more distanced in their coverage.

CONCLUSION: THE MEDIA MADE THE WHITE MARCH

When the parents of Dutroux's victims called for a demonstration in Brussels's streets, social movement watchers in Belgium were unanimous in their prediction: without movement organization backing, mass participation would be very difficult to achieve. The unexpected mobilization of 300,000 people—Belgium's largest demonstration ever—initiated our research into the machinery of its mobilization. Our hypothesis, which goes largely against current social movement theory, was that the mass media made the White March successful. Empirical materials point in that direction: the media not only gave massive coverage to the Dutroux case and to its political-structural interpretation but also helped define the White March's theme and remove obstacles to participation. The press not only engaged in diagnostic or prognostic framing—more "normal" functions for the media—but unmistakably undertook large-scale and unconcealed motivational framing efforts. The media openly played the role of fellow traveler alongside the parents of the victims and the discontented public. Usually social movements and protesting groups are covered by the media but have no control over the coverage. In contrast, the Belgian press presented themselves as actors and players in White March events with, as it seems, their own agenda and objectives. Indeed, turning the White March into a success seemed to be an implicit goal of several newspapers.

The most puzzling thing about the White March is that the media were engaged in diagnostic, prognostic, *and* motivational framing. Although we didn't survey White March participants and therefore cannot prove conclusively that the media mobilized the 300,000 demonstrators, there are three additional points of circumstantial evidence that support our argument about the media's active role. First, interviews with participants in the so-called Second White March that took place in Brussels more than a year later, after the media attention had diminished, show that a vast majority of the participants claimed that only the media informed them about the demonstration (Walgrave, Van Aelst, and Suetens 1998). Second, while it is not uncommon to find that most of the people didn't attend on their own but came as a part of a group, it is atypical to see that those networks primarily consisted of family and friends. The Second White March survey shows that the participants were mobilized through interpersonal networks, which suggests that media information is not processed by individuals in isolation but rather in a social context (see table 6.3). Third, earlier research shows that the participants in the Second White March and in the local white marches were very heterogeneous, suggesting that this was probably also the case at the White March (Walgrave and Rihoux 1997). This too is an indirect indication of the media's role. Kielbowicz and Scherer (1986: 85) write that movement participants who join after the press coverage have characteristics different from early joiners before media coverage. This suggests that media coverage has an influence on a movement's social composition. If the White March had been organized by social movement organizations and not by the media, participant profiles would have been less heterogeneous because the media reach a far larger population than the traditional mobilizing agencies.

DISCUSSION: THE MOBILIZING POWER OF MEDIA FRAMES

The fact that our hypothesis was not falsified by the empirical data raises three important questions regarding its generalizability. First, do the findings hold for other than written media? Second, what about the directionality of the relation between the citizen and the media? Third, where does the White March case lead us regarding social movement theory?

First, the Belgian electronic media seem to have acted less explicitly as action mobilizers and to have restricted themselves to diagnostic framing. To take one example, TV news reporters and anchors never dressed in white T-shirts or wore White March pins. However, quantitative attention given to the issue by both television channels was by no means less than the newspapers. Both the public broadcasting channel and the commercial channel twice devoted their entire evening news to the case (Verstraeten 1997: 90). Baeyens (1997) analyzed the coverage of the public broadcasting channel and the commercial channel during the first three weeks of the

Table 6.3 Comparison of the Second White March with Two Other Demonstrations[*]

	Second White March	Anti-Racist	Trade Union
% of participants mobilized exclusively through the media	70.0	6.7	0.5
% of participants mobilized by an organization	8.4	63.3	64.9
% of participants who came in the company of family	60.8	36.8	0.5

[*] Demonstrators in the Second White March (2/15/98; 30,000 participants, emotional theme), the Anti-Racist Hand-in-Hand Demonstration (3/22/98; 15,000 participants; postmaterialistic theme), and the Social Non-Profit Demonstration (3/26/98; 20,000 participants; trade-union theme).

controversy and concluded that they spent 50 percent and 63 percent, respectively, of their news time on the case. Although only the print media carried out all three kinds of strategic framing, it is possible that massive and intensive diagnostic framing might necessitate less motivational framing—as we discussed earlier. Klandermans (1984: 586) also claims that several motives can more or less compensate for one another—for example, a highly valued action outcome can take away the hindrances for participation. It seems that a good media mix with electronic media massively drawing attention to the issue and diagnostically framing it, combined with an openly mobilizing written press, can have an enormous impact. Although scientific discussion of written versus electronic media influence is still open (McQuail 1993: 330), our White March observations suggest directions for future research.

Second, regarding directionality, there has been a general discussion about the effects of the media on the audience, and vice versa, taking place for some time. Are the media capable of changing public opinion and public behavior or do they follow it? This is certainly a relevant question regarding our own research. According to McQuail, the greatest obstacles in pursuing these questions are methodological: "Most direct questions about the 'power of the media' either make no sense or cannot be answered" (1993: 381). This refers to the impossibility of isolating media effects from other possible effects outside of an experimental situation. Moreover, "the media are rarely likely to be the only necessary or sufficient cause of effect, and the relative contribution is extremely hard to assess" (McQuail 1993: 327). Our analysis suggests that a simple stimulus-response model (McQuail 1993: 330) is out of the question. It is better to speak of a dialectic between media and public, a mutual exchange. Even without the media's help, the Dutroux case struck a chord in the Belgian population, as evidenced by the hundreds of readers' letters published by the newspapers. Of course, the editors selected the letters, but more letters on the case were published than the readers' letters columns normally carried. Also the increasing circulation of the papers in the analyzed period indicates that the media and the population were on the same wavelength.[14] We tried to show the plausibility of our thesis, but causality cannot be proved. What we do know is that the media have activated all possible mobilization functions and that there were no other agencies, organizations, or social movements that mobilized for the White March (Walgrave and Rihoux 1997). The media are the only plausible explanation for the massive turnout.

The third question is how our findings can be reconciled with conventional social movement theory that doesn't think highly of the media's mobilizing abilities. The reason that social movement theory has been skeptical about the media's mobilizing capacity is twofold. First, people are mobilized through concrete networks and by organizations, not by abstract media messages that do not appeal as strongly as interpersonal communication. Second, although the media's role in framing processes is widely recognized, traditional mobilization theory states that media normally only engage in diagnostic framing, not in motivational framing. Yet our data suggest that the mass media, in specific circumstances can actually "co-produce" massive mobilizations. By large-scale, ubiquitous, and univocal framing of a specific issue, combining diagnostic, prognostic, and motivational framing, modern mass media seem to be capable of creating a very compelling and strong mobilization context able to compensate for the lack of organizational support and resources. To put it somewhat bluntly: in some circumstances, sheer framing suffices for mobilization.

What are those specific circumstances in which the media may engage in such extraordinary framing processes? Based on the case of the White March, we close by speculating about the contexts favorable for media mobilization.

1. The media only take an active role when there is clear and manifest disagreement between the people and the elites. This allows the media to present themselves as advocates for the public and to easily cash in on the widespread discontent. Our data show that this was very much so in the Dutroux case, where the preexisting and popular image of the gap between the public and their leaders served as the master frame.

2. The active role of the media is restricted to highly emotional and symbolic issues that create an atmosphere of consensus, emotion, and togetherness. At the heart of the White March lies the shock following the systematic kidnapping, abuse, and murder of young children by an exconvict living on welfare. Widespread discontent arose because these crimes remained unsolved due to repetitive failures of the judiciary and police system. There was so much emotional consensus that even King Albert took a public stance and assumed a role that would normally be considered beyond his position as impartial head of the nation. The media played these emotions to the fullest and identified with the public. Additionally, they portrayed the players in the drama in terms of victims versus perpetrators, good versus evil, and innocence versus perversion. The media abundantly used symbolic categories.

3. In the absence of a movement or a committed social organization, it is advantageous for the media to take an active role because it allows them to present themselves as sensitive and unpartisan watchdogs around a consensus issue. It is striking to see how the Belgian media so actively supported the White March when there was no movement behind it, but when a "white movement" began, their interest waned. The "white movement" was founded after the march and became strongly aware of the influence of the media (Walgrave and Rihoux 1997). Only six months after the White March, the white movement felt completely deserted by the media. By then the media had resumed a more normal coverage of the issue.

4. The media only take an active role when the issue is relatively simple. Gamson (1992) and Klandermans and Goslinga (1996) have shown that the media can do their part in consensus mobilization, but that their capacity decreases as an issue's complexity increases. Not only was the Dutroux case emotional and symbolic, but from the outset it was also straightforward and not too complex, making it easy for the media to report in full detail.

5. The media will only engage fully in peak mobilization when the controversy is politically impartial and can be considered as a valence issue. This allows them to act more autonomously and frees them from the obligation of remaining politically objective. In the beginning, when the public focus rested on the police and judicial system, the media did not treat the Dutroux case as a political matter. Moreover the sheer drama of the issue and the instant birth of an emotional consensus made political party recuperation nearly impossible. And even when the stress shifted to the politicization, *all* political parties were implicated. It was not before the issue became subject of a parliamentary investigatory commission (more than a year later), that it got into partisan debate. At that stage the media frenzy had ceased.

6. Only when the media environment is commercial and characterized by depoliticization and de-ideologization can the media create peak mobilizations. In a politically and ideologically divided media environment, frames are contradicted and confronted by other voices. Different media will try to impose their own frames, making it difficult to create an overarching master frame. In the past, when Belgian newspapers were the mouthpieces of political parties, they played a mobilizing role within their own territories by advocating a point of view (Johnstone, Slawski, and Bowman 1976: 114-116). The depoliticization of the Belgian media (Bilereyst and

Van Gompel 1997; De Bens 1997) made the openly active mobilizing approach to the Dutroux case possible. Moreover, all the newspapers reported more or less the same events and interpreted them more or less in the same way. De-ideologization and depoliticization—and thus commercialization—can lead to unanimity with politically enormous effects (see Noelle-Neumann 1984; Masuy 1997: 34).

7. The media are more likely to play an active role in what McQuail calls *disturbed times*. A general scandal atmosphere and a lack of confidence seem ideal. McQuail (1993: 332-333) suggests the mass media have a much greater impact in turbulent times than in normal circumstances: "It does seem that whenever the stability of society is disturbed, by crime, war, economic malaise or some 'moral panic,' the mass media are given some responsibility. . . . [But] we can only speculate about the reasons for such associations in time, but we cannot rule out the possibility that the media are actually more influential in certain ways at times of crisis or heightened awareness." The Belgian summer of 1996 was indeed a "disturbed time" when the nation seemed struck by moral panic (Hooghe 1998).

8. Finally, one can assume that the mobilizing impact of the media depends on the population's confidence in the media. Recent figures show that confidence in Belgian media, especially the written press, is considerably higher than in other European countries. Also, while other institutions in Belgium (parliament, government, political parties, and judiciary) lost the population's confidence during the Dutroux case, the media's trust level rose.[15]

This list is derived from the analysis of only one case and is not exhaustive of the preconditions for peak mobilization by the media. It is offered as a prototype to better understand when and how the conventional mobilization theory could be extended toward the mass media. While it is clear that such a set of preconditions will only seldom hold, it seems that the role of the Belgian media in the White March is not unique. In other West European countries, similar media patterns can be traced. Furedi (1997), for example, describes the role of the media in the antigun movement after the shootings in Dunblane, Scotland, in a similar way. The White March also indicates that the role of the media is temporary (see also Sampedro 1997). The media are unreliable allies: "Media coverage does produce an increase in expressions of concern about an issue, but . . . those expressions of concern fade just as quickly when coverage wanes" (Szaz 1994: 64). Like their readers, the media are easily bored and continually hunt for new facts (Downs 1972). Gamson and Meyer (1996: 288) note that "once media attention shifts to some other issue and the controversy has lost its salience, the open space closes again and would-be movement spokespersons no longer get their phone calls returned." The somewhat artificial unanimity in the Belgian press collapsed eventually, when in 1998 a media war burst loose between believers and disbelievers of files related to the Dutroux case.

This list of preconditions suggests that under very specific circumstances the media are able to mobilize for peak mobilizations, but that they are inappropriate for permanent and sustained mobilization. Inevitably the media will broaden their scope again once a dramatic event has faded and attention will be paid to other issues; political parties will jump onto topics that get huge public attention thus bringing it into the normal political process and making it partisan; emotions tend to fade quickly thus making the issue less salient; the ensuing search for those accountable (when there is someone to blame) soon becomes too complex and argumentative to explain straightforwardly and understand easily. These are all situations that go against the list of preconditions, making it highly improbable that the media are fit for permanent and sustained mobilization.

NOTES

1. About 60 percent of the Belgian population speaks Dutch. These newspapers all belong to the Flemish Press. The French Belgian press is omitted in this contribution. *Het Laatste Nieuws* is the top Belgian newspaper (on average 258,000 copies sold daily between October 1996 and September 1997). *Het Nieuwsblad* follows in second place (231,000 copies). *De Standaard* is the most intellectual newspaper (77,000 copies). *De Morgen* is the newspaper of the progressive intellectual (40,000 copies). *Gazet van Antwerpen* is a popular nationally distributed regional newspaper (125,000 copies).

2. One newspaper is missing, namely, *Gazet van Antwerpen* of October 18, 1996. Wherever necessary in the analysis, an average was taken of the three preceding and the three following days of *Gazet van Antwerpen.*

3. More or less comparable data on the Belgian French media are found in Lits (1993), on press coverage of King Baldwin's death in August 1993, but peak media attention only lasted a few days (Antoine 1993).

4. Total news coverage is defined as that section of the newspaper that might report on the Dutroux case, viz., national and international news, editorial comments, letters to the editor. Local news, economy, culture, television, classifieds, supplements, and large advertisements (minimum half a page) were not included.

5. A lead story is the newspaper's opening article, the main front-page article, usually in the top left or middle.

6. Even if the lead story was not on the Dutroux case, the first article on Dutroux was on the front page in 66 percent of the cases. In 87 percent of the total 329 newspapers, an article on the Dutroux case could be found on the front page.

7. We refer to, for instance, the deadly mudflow on a Spanish campsite (the main news item in 13 percent of the newspapers), a tax-dodging scandal (KB-Lux scandal—10 percent), money transport hold-ups (10 percent), a hormone mafia and the murder of a veterinarian (Van Noppen—7 percent); the EMU debate and the 3 percent norm (7 percent).

8. Figures on the frequency of certain items per newspaper copy are not shown in tables.

9. It could be that the stronger the diagnostic and prognostic framing, the less one needs motivational framing. Also it is possible that there is a media saturation threshold that, if exceeded by prognostic and diagnostic frames in terms of some quantative measure, the need for motivational framing is mitigated. These are hypotheses that future research might test.

10. The number of actions was determined by press coverage in the seventeen local editions of *Het Laatste Nieuws.*

11. For every newspaper, we examined the five daily editions in the week of October 14-20, 1996, starting with Tuesday, October 15, the day after Connerotte's dismissal. One newspaper was missing, *De Gazet van Antwerpen*, Friday, October 18.

12. Practical information about the march was not the only information provided in the period leading up to the White March. *De Standaard* (September 5) provided the reader with the addresses of the families of An and Eefje so that readers could send their condolences. *Het Laatste Nieuws* (August 22) provided a list of addresses "where in your neighborhood a mourning register can be signed."

13. On October 9, a petition demanding longer jail terms and less facilities for sexual delinquents, carrying the signature of 2.7 million people, was handed to the president of the Chamber of Representatives. It was by far the largest petition in Belgian history.

14. The sales figures of the newspapers were given to us under the condition that they would be treated discretely. As such we can only state in general terms that the circulation of the newspapers increased in the period of our research.

15. Comparative data on institutional trust are found in *Eurobarometer* 48.0, October-November 1998.

REFERENCES

Antoine, F. 1993. "Scores des unes: L'événement dans l'intra-médiatique." Pp. 141-155 in *Le roi est mort: Émotions et médias*, M. Lits, ed. Brussels: Vie Ouvrière.

Baeyens, N. 1997. *BRTN en VTM: Vergelijking van de nieuwsverslaggeving van de openbare en de commerciële omroep in verband met de zaak Dutroux.* Communicatiewetenschappen Leuven: KULeuven.

Biltereyst, D., and R. Van Gompel. 1997. "Crisis and Renewal of the Fourth Estate: On the Post-war Development of the Flemish Newspaper Press." *Communications: The European Journal of Communication Research* 22 (3): 275-300.

Briet, M., B. Klandermans, and F. Kroon. 1987. "How Women Become Involved in the Women's Movement." Pp. 44-63 in *The Women's Movement in the U.S. and Western Europe: Feminist Consciousness, Political Opportunity, and Public Opinion*, M. Katzenstein and C. Mueller, eds. Philadelphia: Temple University Press.

Cooper, A. H. 2002. "Media Framing and Social Movement Mobilization: German Peace Protest against INF Missiles, the Gulf War, and NATO Peace Enforcement in Bosnia." *European Journal of Political Research* 41: 37-80.

De Bens, E. 1997. *De Pers in België.* Tielt: Lannoo.

Downs, A. 1972. "Up and Down with Ecology: The Issue Attention Cycle." *Public Interest* 28: 38-50.

Eisinger, P. K. 1973. "The Conditions of Protest Behavior in American Cities." *American Political Science Review* 67 (1): 11-28.

Furedi, F. 1997. *Culture of Fear.* London: Cassell.

Galtung, J., and M. Ruge. 1965. "The Structure of Foreign News." *Journal of Peace Research* 2: 64-91.

Gamson, W. A. 1992. *Talking Politics.* New York: Cambridge University Press.

Gamson, W. A., and David S. Meyer. 1996. "Framing Political Opportunity." Pp. 275-290 in *Comparative Perspectives on Social Movements: Political Opportunities, Mobilizing Structures, and Cultural Framings*, Doug McAdam, John D. McCarthy, and Mayer N. Zald, eds. New York: Cambridge University Press.

Gamson, W. A., and A. Modigliani. 1989. "Media Discourse and Public Opinion on Nuclear Power: A Constructionist Approach," *American Journal of Sociology* 95 (1): 1-37.

Gamson, W. A., and G. Wolsfeld. 1993. "Movements and Media as Interacting Systems." *Annals of the American Academy of Political and Social Science* 528: 114-125.

Gitlin, T. 1980. *The Whole World Is Watching: Mass Media and the Making and Unmaking of the New Left.* Berkeley: University of California Press.

Gurevitch, M., and M. Levy. 1985. Introduction to *Mass Communication Review Yearbook 5.* Beverly Hills, CA: Sage.

Hansen, A. 1993. *The Mass Media and Environmental Issues.* London: Leicester University Press.

Hilgartner, S., and C. Bosk. 1988. "The Rise and Fall of Social Problems: A Public Arenas Model." *American Journal of Sociology* 94(1): 53-78.

Hooghe, M. 1998. "De 'witte mobilisatie' in België als moral crusade: De vervlechting van emotie en politiek." *Sociologische Gids* 45 (5): 289-309.

Johnstone, J. W. C., E. Slawski, and W. Bowman. 1976. *The News People: A Sociological Portrait of American Journalists and Their Work.* Urbana: University of Illinois Press.

Kielbowicz, R. B., and C. Scherer. 1986. "The Role of the Press in the Dynamics of Social Movements." Pp. 71-96 in *Research in Social Movements, Conflicts, and Change*, L. Kriesberg, ed. Greenwich, CT: JAI Press.

Klandermans, B. 1984. "Mobilization and Participation: Social-psychological Expansions of Resource Mobilization Theory." *American Sociological Review* 49: 583-600.

———. 1997. *The Social Psychology of Protest.* Oxford, UK: Blackwell.

Klandermans, B., and S. Goslinga. 1996. "Media Discourse, Movement Publicity, and the Generation of Collective Action Frames: Theoretical and Empirical Exercises in Meaning Construction." Pp. 312-337 in *Comparative Perspectives on Social Movements: Political Opportunities, Mobilizing Structures, and Cultural Framings*, Doug McAdam, John D.

McCarthy, and Mayer N. Zald, eds. New York: Cambridge University Press.

Klandermans, B., and D. Oegema. 1987. "Potentials, Networks, Motivations, and Barriers: Steps towards Participation in Social Movements." *American Sociological Review* 52: 519-531.

Koopmans, R. 1995. "The Dynamic of Protest Waves." Pp. 111-144 in *New Social Movements in Western Europe: A Comparative Analysis*, H. Kriesi, R. Koopmans, J. W. Duyvendak, and M. G. Giugni, eds. London: UCL Press.

Lits, M., ed. 1993. *Le roi est mort: Émotions et médias*. Brussels: Vie Ouvrière.

Masuy, C. 1997. "Une émotion populaire médiatisée : Laboratoire pour un autre journalisme." Pp. 25-40 in *La société indicible*, N. Burnay, P. Lannoy, and L. Panafit, eds. Brussels: Editions Luc Pire.

McAdam, D. 1982. *Political Process and the Development of Black Insurgency, 1930-1970*. Chicago: University of Chicago Press.

———. 1986. "Recruitment to High-Risk Activism: The Case of Freedom Summer." *American Journal of Sociology* 92: 64-90.

McAdam D., J. D. McCarthy, and M. N. Zald, eds. 1996. *Comparative Perspectives on Social Movements: Political Opportunities, Mobilizing Structures, and Cultural Framings*. New York: Cambridge University Press.

McAdam, D., and D. Rucht. 1993. "The Cross-National Diffusion of Movement Ideas." *Annals of the American Academy of Political and Social Science* 528: 56-74.

McCarthy, J. D., C. McPhail, J. D. Smith, and L. J. Crishock. 1998. "Electronic and Print Media Representations of Washington, D.C. Demonstration, 1982 and 1991: A Demography of Description Bias." In *Acts of Dissent: New Developments in the Study of Protest*, D. Rucht, R. Koopmans, and F. Neidhardt, eds. Berlin: Edition Sigma.

McPhail, C., and D. Schweingruber. 1998. "Unpacking Protest Events: A Description Bias Analysis of Media Records with Systematic Direct Observations of Collective Action—The 1995 March for Life in Washington, D.C." In *Acts of Dissent: New Developments in the Study of Protest*, D. Rucht, R. Koopmans, and F. Neidhardt, eds. Berlin: Edition Sigma.

McQuail, D. 1993. *Mass Communication Theory: An Introduction*. London: Sage.

Molotch, H. 1979. "Media and Movements." Pp. 71-93 in *The Dynamics of Social Movements*, M. Zald, and J. McCarthy, eds. Cambridge, MA: Winthrop.

Noelle-Neumann, E. 1984. *The Spiral of Silence: Our Social Skin*. Chicago: University of Chicago Press.

Oberschall, A. 1980. "Loosely Structured Collective Conflict: A Theory and an Application." Pp. 45-68 in *Research in Social Movements, Conflict, and Change*, Vol. 3, L. Kriesberg, ed. Greenwich, CT: JAI Press.

Oegema, D., and B. Klandermans. 1994. "Why Social Movement Sympathizers Don't Participate: Erosion and Nonconversion of Support." *American Sociological Review* 59: 703-722.

Oliver, P. E., and G. M. Maney. 2000. "Political Processes and Local Newspaper Coverage of Protest Events: From Selection Bias to Triadic Interactions." *American Journal of Sociology* 106(2): 463-505.

Sampedro, V. 1997. "The Media Politics of Social Protest." *Mobilization* 2: 185-205.

Schmitt-Beck, R. 1990. "Über die Bedeutung der Massenmedien für soziale Bewegungen." *Kölner Zeitschrift für Soziologie und Sozialpsychologie* 42(4): 642-662.

Shoemaker, P. G. 1991. *Communication Concepts 3: Gatekeeping*. Newbury Park, CA: Sage.

Smith, J., J. D. McCarthy, C. McPhail, and B. Augustyn. 2001. "From Protest to Agenda Building: Description Bias in Media Coverage of Protest Events in Washington, D.C." *Social Forces* 79(4): 1397-1424.

Smith, P. 1999. "Political Communication in the UK: A Study of Pressure Group Behaviour." *Politics* 19(1): 21-27.

Snow, D. A., and R. Benford. 1988. "Ideology, Frame Resonance, and Participant Mobilization." Pp. 197-217 in *International Social Movement Research: From Structure to Action*, Vol. 1. Greenwich, CT: JAI Press.

Snow, D. A., E. B. Rochford, Jr., S. K. Worden, and R. B. Benford. 1986. "Frame Alignment Processes, Micromobilization, and Movement Participation." *American Sociological Review* 51: 464-481.

Snow, D. A., L. Zurcher, and S. Ekland-Olson. 1980. "Social Networks and Social Movements: A Microstructural Approach to Differential Recruitment." *American Sociological Review* 45: 787-801.

Szaz, A. 1994. *EcoPopulism: Toxic Waste and the Movement for Environmental Justice.* Minneapolis: University of Minnesota Press.

Tarrow, S. 1991. *Struggle, Politics, and Reform: Collective Action, Social Movements, and Cycles of Protest.* Ithaca, NY: Cornell University Press.

———. 1996. "States and Opportunities: The Political Structuring of Social Movements." Pp. 41-61 in *Comparative Perspectives on Social Movements: Political Opportunities, Mobilizing Structures, and Cultural Framings,* Doug McAdam, John D. McCarthy, and Mayer N. Zald, eds. New York: Cambridge University Press.

———. 1998. *Power in Movement.* New York: Cambridge University Press.

Van Aelst, P., and S. Walgrave. 2001. "Who Is That (Wo)man on the Street? From the Normalization of the Protest to the Normalization of the Protesters." *European Journal of Political Research* 39: 461-486.

Van Zoonen, E. 1992. "The Women's Movement and the Media: Constructing a Public Identity." *International Journal of Communication* 7: 453-476.

Verstraeten, H. 1997. "De zaak-Dutroux: De media tussen publieke sfeer en markt." Pp. 77-94 in *Kritische Reflecties Omtrent de Zaak-Dutroux,* C. Eliaerts, ed. Brussels: Balans-VUBPres.

Walgrave, S., and B. Rihoux. 1997. *Van emotie tot politieke commotie: De Witte Mars, een jaar later.* Leuven: Van Halewyck.

———. 1998. "De Belgische witte golf: Voorbij de sociologische bewegingstheorie?" *Sociologische Gids* 45(5): 310-339.

Walgrave, S., P. Van Aelst, and M. Suetens. 1998. "Van witte beweging naar slachtofferbeweging." *Samenleving and Politiek* 5 (5): 35-41.

White, D. M. 1950. "The 'Gatekeeper': A Case Study in the Selection of News." *Journalism Quarterly* 27: 383-390.

Wolsfeld, G. 1984. "The Symbiosis of Press and Protest: An Exchange Analysis." *Journalism Quarterly* 61: 550-556.

Part III

Framing and Political Opportunities

Chapter 7

FRAMING, POLITICAL OPPORTUNITIES, AND EASTERN EUROPEAN MOBILIZATION

Padraic Kenney

When a half-dozen high-school and college students in the Freedom and Peace movement climbed onto the roof of a grocery store in Międzyrzecz, Poland, on September 2, 1987, and unfurled their banners protesting a nuclear waste dump planned nearby, they were scaling virgin peaks. For two hours that afternoon, they avoided arrest, threw leaflets from their perch, shouted slogans, and encouraged onlookers to participate in a march that coming Sunday.

By late 1987, such antics were not unusual in Poland and were not unheard of in other countries in Eastern Europe. Yet a successful protest in a provincial town of less than twenty thousand residents was something qualitatively different. This was far from the usual centers of opposition power. Międzyrzecz is not an important industrial town; a large percentage of the population was directly or indirectly employed by the military ("Najtrudniej" 1988). It was, from a political standpoint (even today the Pomeranian region votes more solidly postcommunist than any other part of Poland [Lubecki 2001]), an ideal place to store radioactive waste, much of which would come from a nuclear plant to be built in the area (Kossakowski 1988). The Freedom and Peace (Wolność i Pokój, or WiP—pronounced "veep") activists, who had come down from the city of Gorzów twenty-five miles to the north, could have expected to be ignored, or even denounced to the police.

When the six finally climbed down to await the police, the crowd refused to allow them to be arrested. In consternation—for they feared that the expected arrest might frighten the less savvy residents of Międzyrzecz—the protesters led an impromptu march to a nearby church, where Marek Rusakiewicz (twenty-three years old) made a brief speech thanking the crowd for its support. Then they escaped through the church, coming out a side entrance to allow the police to arrest them with as few onlookers as possible (Rusakiewicz 1997).

Four days later, three thousand to four thousand people marched through Międzyrzecz—a level of mobilization (relative to population) unmatched in Poland after the imposition of martial law in 1981. Soon the townspeople were performing acts of civil disobedience previously unthinkable. When the authorities cracked down after the march with detentions, beatings, and fines averaging one-and-a-half monthly wages, citizens responded with a protest fast in the church and one more march even more massive than that in September. The result was the first significant defeat of communist government policy in Poland by a group of citizens since the 1981 crackdown on Solidarity. The town council, meeting during the fast, unexpectedly voted against the dump; over the winter, Warsaw quietly shelved the idea (Wołyniec 1988).

The story of Międzyrzecz shows how a new generation of activists was essential to the revival of broad societal opposition, which by 1987 was virtually dormant outside of a few key cities. As important as Solidarity, the church, and the academic opposition were to many Poles, they had insufficient resources either to change communist practice or to reach ordinary citizens. "At this critical moment," wrote one local participant in the protests, "the boys from WiP from Gorzów helped us enormously. They started organizing pickets, which really emboldened people. . . . [Thanks to them] the issue took on momentum, and something in people began to crack" ("Najtrudniej" 1988). Rusakiewicz, the Gorzów group's informal leader, explains WiP's intentions: "To show people that they could be strong, that was our goal. We, as a small group, determined, very determined, would create an uproar" (Rusakiewicz 1997). This, says Kazimierz Sokołowski (then twenty-one), is what happened on September 2. "People saw that we are not afraid, [and] they stood up in our defense" (Sokołowski 1997). Rather than rejecting this scruffy band of students (most with jail terms behind them), the citizens of Międzyrzecz adopted their methods and won.

PERCEIVED OPPORTUNITIES AND THE LOGIC OF MOBILIZATION

That grassroots activism could reach even such a small, remote town at a moment when (and concerning an issue on which) there did not seem much chance that the regime would compromise, suggests that there are aspects to the fall of communism in Poland and across the region which have hitherto been neglected.

I argue that the literature on 1989 fails to appreciate the role social protest played in the early stages of that revolution. Specifically, the structural nature of the opportunities present in the region is overemphasized, and the extent to which opportunities were created or perceived is neglected. I will use a case study of one social movement, the Freedom and Peace Movement in Poland, to address this shortcoming. In his study of the Iranian revolution, Charles Kurzman (1996: 165) wonders if that case is an unusual example of "perceived opportunities affect[ing] the outcome of revolutionary protest independent of structural opportunities." The East European case shows that Kurzman's findings are not an exception to social movement theory; indeed, that the present example comes from within the largest revolutionary movement of recent decades suggests that perceived opportunities may be more central than has been previously recognized.

This chapter draws upon open-ended interviews conducted in 1996 and 1997 with participants in WiP and in many other Polish movements and subcultures that flourished between 1985 and 1988. These one- to two-hour interviews are part of a larger project (reaching nearly three hundred interviews in twelve countries) researching the role of social movements in the revolutions of 1989 (Kenney 2002). Most interviewees were chosen by following activist networks, using the recommendations of those already interviewed. Interviews did not follow a set of prepared questions or topics; they focused on activists' lives and movement histories. Interviews were supplemented by the leaflets and underground newspapers produced by WiP. My concern generally is with the place of social movements in late communism throughout Eastern Europe; WiP is only the most powerful example.

Studies of the revolutions in Eastern Europe have tended to focus on the moment of regime change in 1989. The burgeoning field of transition studies certainly pays attention to the changes occurring in 1989, including the role of social movements. However, insofar as "transitologists" are concerned with the acts and roundtables that facilitated nonviolent outcomes, they refer only to movements that participated in those talks: Solidarity in Poland, Charter 77 intellectuals in Czechoslovakia, and so forth. There has been no room in the transition literature for study of actors who were not already at the center of attention in 1989. Movements like WiP (absent from the Polish Round Table of February-April 1989) do not fit into the transitology model; their impact upon 1989 is thus left unexplored.

Specialists in the region tend to focus narrowly on the events of 1989. This is especially true of the German Democratic Republic's spontaneous revolution (Opp 1994; Philipsen 1993). It is also true for the cases of Czechoslovakia and Hungary, where opposition movements emerged slightly earlier (Wheaton and Kavan 1992; Glenn 2001; Tőkés 1996). While some studies in each case have looked at the development of opposition over a longer period of time (Torpey 1995; Otáhal 1994; Kenney 1999b), the lens generally focuses backward from the moment of revolution, often on negotiations between opposition intellectuals and the communists (Elster 1996; Tőkés 1996; Kennedy 1999; Kennedy and Porter 2000). The relationship between opposition movements and society, as a key factor in the road to those roundtables, is left largely unexamined.

Surprisingly, this is also the case for the literature on Poland, site of the most sustained opposition to communist rule in Europe. There is a great deal of research on the opposition up until 1981 (Bernhard 1993; Friszke 1994; Ost 1990; Kubik 1994; Laba 1991; Goodwyn 1991; Kenney 1999a; Flam 1996), and on the events of 1988-1989 (Tabako 1992; Raina 1999; Skórzyński 1995; Ekiert and Kubik 1999; Glenn 2001). There is no work which links these two periods, however; the years 1982-1987 between the imposition of martial law which crushed the Solidarity movement and the strikes which prompted negotiations to begin almost seven years later have remained insufficiently examined (Paczkowski 1999). This is not simply a historical lacuna; it rather decouples the building of oppositional social movements from regime collapse, leaving the connection between the two assumed.

A few studies have looked at WiP (Kennedy 1990; Lazarski 1990; Gliński 1996; Hicks 1996; Modzelewski 1996), focusing mostly on its concerns of peace and environmentalism and on its relationship to oppositional intellectual currents. Wylie (1999) places WiP within the context of the Cold War's end, as part of a transnational peace network bringing about détente from below. The literature on civil society in Central Europe (Weigle and Butter-field 1992; Tismaneanu 1990), meanwhile, has been open to consideration of movements like Freedom and Peace.

This chapter's purpose is to bring together social movement theory and an empirical study of one movement in late-communist Eastern Europe in order to better understand both the 1989 revolutions and the limits and possibilities of current trends in the social movement literature. To date, scholars who have employed the tools of social movement theory to study the revolutions of 1989 (Oberschall 1996) have relied on fragmentary data and insufficient knowledge of the region. We simply know too little about what kinds of movements emerged in Central Europe before 1989 and their origins, goals, and activities (Kenney 1999b).

A central problem in the study of the revolutions ending communism concerns how people are mobilized, in 1989 and before. Here, the literature is strangely silent. Chirot (1991: 21), for example, posits a two-stage process of revolution: first, the will of those in power is sapped; then massive popular discontent could come into the streets. This "hydraulic" model of opposition tells us little about mobilization and leaves no place for social movements. Oberschall (1996: 95) also emphasizes, "Lack of regime legitimacy is an opportunity for opponents." As a key explanation for the success of social protest, he proposes moral force: "The challengers acted with the moral conviction that they were in the right—huge crowds marched and demonstrated in squares and along avenues, making demands and supporting opposition leaders" (1996: 102). While this is highly imaginative, it strains credibility: the idea that bystanders were swayed by moral force rests purely on conjecture. It will be shown here, through the example of the Freedom and Peace movement, that new movements could offer something different: concrete, easily graspable issues around which mobilization was in fact quite probable. To do so, however, they would have to ignore the lack of real structural opportunities and frame unlikely situations as opportunities.

A useful expanation of mobilization in these regimes that looks at dissident networks has been advanced by Opp, Voss, and Gern (1995: chap. 7). Indeed, networks linking opposition groups, as well as those linking opposition groups and bystanders, are a key element in successful mobilization. But especially in a country like Poland, with a rich tradition of antiregime protest, it is still unclear why protest should burst beyond the boundaries of the relatively small opposition community and reach the wider public. Explanations of mobilization for the Czechoslovak case by Oberschall (1996: 116)—that "If the Germans had done it why not the Czechs and Slovaks?"—simply cannot suffice. After considering the nature of opportunities in late-communist Poland, therefore, this chapter will turn to the ways that Freedom and Peace framed those opportunities by examining the issues it raised.

INTRA-OPPOSITION POLITICAL OPPORTUNITIES

The political opportunities which give rise to social movements are generally considered to include one or more of the following: (1) a change for the better in the degree to which society can influence or participate in the political system; (2) a new instability in political alignments; (3) the presence of elites who are favorable toward change; (4) a decrease in the state's capacity for, or willingness to exert, repression. (Tarrow 1994; McAdam 1996). None of these factors, however, was clearly present in Poland before 1989. From the perspective of opposition activists and the wider public, there were no new opportunities for participation in or influence on the political system; political alignments did not appear unstable; reformist elites neither had the upper hand nor reached out to society; and repression did not decrease.

The argument for structural opportunities in the fall of communism follows this theory point by point: (1) Thanks to the policies of Mikhail Gorbachev, who was chosen general secretary of the Communist Party of the Soviet Union (CPSU) in March 1985, the Soviet state, and then East European states (some of which were previously so inclined, hampered only by the need for dogmatic unity within the communist bloc), became more open to participation in the political process by groups outside the communist party. (2-3) This also destabilized political alignments, allowing proreform elites to take a stronger (if not dominant) position in many East European regimes. (4) Finally, both because Gorbachev let East European leaders know that he would not back up their efforts to repress dissent, and because some leaders came to question the utility of such dissent, state repression declined. Those who once were beaten, jailed, or silenced now found they could demonstrate more freely and could reach a wider public with the ideas and demands which formed the discursive core of the events of 1989 (Ramet 1995; Brown 1991; Rothschild 1993; Völgyes 1990; Oberschall 1996; Tarrow 1991).

When, however, did Gorbachev make his intentions regarding Eastern Europe widely known? In the Polish case, this occurred no earlier than the summer of 1988, when the Soviet leader visited Poland and spoke openly about the need for experimentation (*Pieriestrojka* 1988). More commonly, the turning point is assumed to be Gorbachev's visit to Strasbourg and the Council of Europe in July 1989. To quote one such formulation: "The message to Eastern Europe [in the Strasbourg speech] was unmistakable and the consequences inevitable. From the summer of 1989 the peoples of Eastern Europe increasingly took to the streets. The communist parties, demoralized by the Soviet reforms, bereft of Soviet support and without any new ideas of their own simply crumpled under the impact" (Walker 1993: 217).

Before 1988, by contrast, the evidence that there were signals to which Polish opposition could respond is thin; only the relatively feeble "normalization" efforts of General Wojciech Jaruzelski's regime, such as a referendum on economic reform in November 1987 or an amnesty of political prisoners in September 1986, offer support to this narrative. But however such events may have seemed to outsiders, the Polish opposition was not prepared to give them much credit. Even the most realist Poles were deeply skeptical of Gorbachev's intentions as late as 1988 (Skórzyński 1995; Michnik, Tischner, and Żakowski 1998: 466-472). True, changes in Soviet policy toward Eastern Europe were evident as early as 1986; however, the liberalization of the Polish regime did not seem impressive from close up. The rhetoric of Polish communists in the mid-1980s was considered by some to echo that of high Stalinism thirty years earlier (Głowiński 1996, 1999); this was the regime Adam Michnik (1984: 25) called "communism with its teeth knocked out."

The traditional communist postinsurrection tactic of normalization—that is, defusing and diffusing popular dissatisfaction by offering material incentives for making peace with the regime and creating facade structures of national harmony while keeping a firm hand on the whip—had so far failed in Poland, in contrast to Czechoslovakia after the Prague Spring or Hungary after the national revolution of 1956 (Ekiert 1996; Helsinki Watch 1986; Łopiński, Moskit, and Wilk 1990). Yet the winter of 1984-1985 was a low point for underground Solidarity. The regime lacked the economic strength to normalize state-society relations as had the Czech and Hungarian regimes, but it still had isolated opposition, limiting it to relatively harmless, long-term strategies. Solidarity was becoming a legend, a closed chapter in Poland's long history of proud rebellions against dictatorships or repression. Popular response to that legend was increasingly ritualized, consisting of the wearing of pins and attendance at so-called Fatherland Masses, where participants sang forbidden songs and waved their fingers in the V sign, then went home to normal lives until the next Mass (Krzemiński 1989: 30-37). At best, Solidarity was stagnant, collecting dues and distributing literature to a committed but slowly eroding group of supporters. The underground press condemned the Jaruzelski regime in the harshest terms possible, but it also emphasized society's powerlessness against a state capable of such horrible acts. Debates over strategy and tactics appeared to have immobilized the underground (Ost 1990; Holzer and Leski 1990).

It was at this time, when Polish opposition was seriously threatened with extinction, that Freedom and Peace emerged, two and a half years before the confrontation in Międzyrzecz and well before more than a handful in Poland were ready to give credit to Gorbachev or regime reformers for liberalization. The example of WiP requires that, if the theory of political opportunities is to be applied at all in communist states, the parameters of opportunity must be expanded. Particularly in Poland, which came closer than any other to building the "parallel polis" (Havel 1985: 78-81) in which one could live as if in a free country, to limit one's search for appropriate opportunities to the state which the opposition tried to ignore is simply insufficient. The opportunity for movement emergence and flourishing was afforded not by any of the structural factors commonly cited but by three other factors: first, a crisis in the older opposition which prompted a search for new tactics (which would be borrowed from the opposition of an earlier generation); second, the experience of repression—a factor which depended in part on the way that repression was framed; and third, the movement's ability to frame a new set of issues in a fresh, unexpected challenge to the communist regime.

Freedom and Peace activists traced their roots back to the radical activism of 1980-1981 and beyond. The oldest among them had been active in the Student Solidarity Committee (SKS) in the years 1977-1980 (Budrewicz 1996). SKS was an ally of the first above-ground (that is, not covert) opposition movement in Poland, the Workers' Defense Committee (KOR), and learned its tactics of concrete action on behalf of the repressed, combined with a relentless publicizing of the movement's activities and membership (Zuzowski 1992; Bernhard 1993; Głębocki 1994; Lipski 1985).

A slightly younger cohort among the movement's founders had been active in the Independent Students' Association, formed in 1981, which was instrumental in a series of student strikes in several cities (Czaputowicz 1997; Rokita 1997; Niemczyk 1997). In the years 1982-1984, these students (many of whom identified strongly with a Catholic and nationalist program) were active in the militant underground's resistance to martial law, while maintaining loose ties to the "adult opposition," as some familiarly called Solidarity. Many were outed by arrest for printing or distribution of underground papers and thus could no longer work closely with still-covert colleagues.

Several crises in the winter of 1984-1985 forced consideration of new tactics. The most widely known event was the kidnapping and murder of Father Jerzy Popiełuszko by secret policemen in October 1984 ("Murder" 1985). An event that shocked the world, it also reinforced society's ritualized attitude toward opposition. Fr. Popiełuszko had been one of the leading practitioners of Fatherland Masses in his church in a middle-class neighborhood in the north of Warsaw. Though his sermons contained a call to action, they were also the most powerful expression of the new opposition ritual. His death was therefore interpreted the same way: he was a martyr whose death confirmed the futility of open opposition to the communist regime.

Even the unprecedented spectacle of the trial of the policemen connected with the murder did nothing to change this, for the communists simply gave notice in this way that they would handle problems within own their ranks (Krzemiński 1989: 35).

Popiełuszko's murder reaffirmed the state's power and the opposition's impotence ("Oświadczenie" 1984). It was followed that same winter by the spectacular arrest of three leading Solidarity figures, Władysław Frasyniuk, Bogdan Lis, and Adam Michnik, who were subjected to a Stalinist-style show trial in the spring (Michnik, Tischner, and Żakowski 1998: 461-463). An underground opposition, it seemed, was incapable of responding adequately to these violations of human rights. Thus, for a minority in the opposition, the Popiełuszko murder suggested a need for a radical break with current underground practice. In Wrocław, for example, Jerzy Żurko recalled 1984 as the year of covert murders (*rok skrytobójstw*) but also as the year he decided that the underground had no more to offer him and looked for an aboveground opposition (Żurko 1996). Out of this opposition crisis would come an opportunity for a new movement to emerge.

Some in the more established opposition saw the repressive measures of 1984-1985—the murders, fines, and imprisonments and the triumphant neo-Stalinist rhetoric of the regime, especially government spokesman Jerzy Urban—as nothing new, or perhaps as a sign of communist decrepitude. WiP activists, far too young to remember the brutal 1968 crackdown on students and born well after the Stalinist era of the early 1950s, could not see it that way.

Moreover, the regime's repression appeared to be targeted toward this new movement. At best, the signals about how the regime intended to treat opposition were mixed. A prominent opposition intellectual like historian Bronisław Geremek might enjoy freedom, and even be interviewed in the legal press, while WiP participants went on trial or sat in prison. Each issue of the movement's bulletin *Dezerter* (entitled *Serwis informacyjny Ruchu WiP* until mid-1987) highlighted dozens of beatings, fines, arrests, and sentences meted out to movement participants. Of course, one should keep in mind that what to Poles was repression would seem dramatic liberalization in other countries. The trend, however, *appeared* to be an increase in repression. And appearance, when considering political opportunity and mobilization, is what matters. Gamson and Meyer (1996: 283; see also Kurzman 1996) have pointed out that a political opportunity implies that activists *recognize* that opportunity. If they do not recognize it (rightly or wrongly), then it is unlikely that they will take advantage of it. Perceived opportunities will be of particular importance, I suggest, in a repressive regime. This can be so when a dominant opposition group (as Solidarity certainly was in Poland) decides the time has not come for renewed activism, leaving the door open for a new movement with adequate resources to act. The divisions or weaknesses within elites, familiar elements to scholars of political opportunity structures, are still there—except that the elites are comprised of leaders in an underground opposition, and the policy differences involve strategic interpretations of repression and/or choice of mobilizing issues.

That repression should furnish an opportunity for activism should not come as a surprise. Movements in opposition to the communist regimes emerged in the late 1960s and early 1970s, a period marked by labor camps and long prison sentences for many dissidents (Skilling 1981; Rubenstein 1980; Bernhard 1993). In Western democracies, repressive acts can provide a cause around which a movement can mobilize participants (Kriesi et al. 1995; Opp and Roehl 1990). In a repressive society, such as prerevolutionary Iran, Rasler (1996; see also Opp 1994) sketches a more complex dynamic in which repression alternates (or coexists) with regime concessions to encourage political protest. Similarities to pre-1989 Eastern Europe are strong. Of course, the mid-1980s in Poland were much less repressive than either the Brezhnev era in the Soviet bloc or the Shah's Iran. But the mixed signals were not dissimilar. The murder of a dissident priest, and show trials for opposition leaders, took place at the same time as limited amnesties of political prisoners. From the perspective of activists in Freedom and Peace and other new movements, again, repression was increasing, and it was time to act in response. Their goal, in fact, was to confront that repression and reframe it as ridiculous, outrageous, or not so frightening, and to communicate this attitude to the public. What is missing from Rasler's model is differentiation among opposition movements. While some movements may be chastened by repression or disoriented by concessions, others may perceive the same situation as an opportunity. This was the case with Freedom and Peace in Poland.

The catalyst to action was the arrest of Marek Adamkiewicz, a student who had been a member of SKS before 1980, for refusing the military oath. The authorities reacted with unexpected harshness, sentencing Adamkiewicz on December 8, 1984, to two and a half years in prison. Friends in Warsaw organized a weeklong protest fast in a church in nearby Podkowa Leśna in March 1985. Fasters sang "The Ballad of Marek Adamkiewicz," conveying their sense of a duty to act in the face of repression: "You knew him, after all, so why do you salute? / You drank beer with him, but you turned out a scoundrel / I, too, just sing and play / We're here together, and he is alone" ("Ballada" 1985). Meanwhile, Kraków students organized a similar fast to protest both Adamkiewicz's sentence and other examples of the regime's harder line against opposition activists. Twenty students signed WiP's founding declaration in Kraków on April 14, 1985; another fifteen from Warsaw and Wrocław added their signatures two weeks later (*International* 1988).

WiP activists felt that Gorbachev's peace overtures were simply pandering to the West, leaving Eastern movements and their concerns out in the cold and trampling human rights in the process. WiP's founding declaration, for example, had contained a protest of the war in Afghanistan. In a March 1987 open letter to American peace activist Joanne Landy, Piotr Niemczyk stated that despite Gorbachev's declarations, hundreds of dissidents (in particular those who objected to military service) still languished in jails and psychiatric hospitals, while the war in Afghanistan raged on. While applauding the idea of disarmament, he cautioned: "Only a sovereign society can be the guarantor of genuine disarmament and peace policy. An individual—even if, like the Secretary General of the CPSU, he possesses total power—can not be such a guarantor" (Niemczyk 1987; see also Rokita 1987).

Despite its supposed liberalization, the Polish regime tended to treat new movements more harshly than Solidarity itself. For example, in September 1986, after the government amnestied all political prisoners, two WiP participants, Jarosław Nakielski and Wojciech Jankowski, were left in prison. Against the advice of Solidarity leaders, a dozen or so WiP activists staged a sit-in in front of a downtown Warsaw department store on October 3. Before Western cameras, they linked arms and chanted for their colleagues' release. They carried slogans like "Refusal of military service is the right of every person" and "Freedom and Peace (and love) for everyone" on T-shirts, banners, and sandwich boards (Czaputowicz 1997; Kocięba 1996). Though all participants were detained and fined, Jankowski was released from prison the next day, and Nakielski two weeks later. Liberalization or benevolent neutrality (Mason 1992: 111-12) was won in this case by a movement action, and not the other way around.

Though WiP was irreproachably anticommunist, its attitude toward state power was remarkable. Due in part to a strong commitment to the practice of nonviolence (see below), WiP participants did not call the police "Gestapo" or even resist arrest. Years later, a secret police captain told Jankowski that WiP had been different from those groups which screamed at their jailers and threatened revenge (Jankowski 1997). It was still common for a demonstration to end with police beatings, and detentions were a matter of course until the end, but WiP participants generally reported more polite treatment and even cooperation or understanding from the police. At the same time, they also held the police accountable: in separate cases in 1986 and 1987, WiP activists won cases against the police for unlawful mistreatment (Rokita 1997; Michałek 1997).

Freedom and Peace thus responded to repression by advancing counter to the regime, moving not deeper into the underground but onto the surface. Like the activists in the Iranian Revolution, some in the Polish opposition saw that the door was closed, but felt that the opposition was powerful enough to open it (Kurzman 1996: 165). This belief was not shared by the entire opposition, however, as was clear when WiP staged its demonstration for the release of its colleagues in October 1986. The amnesty of political prisoners and other liberal actions on the part of the communists were, for much of the opposition, not an opportunity but a difficult challenge (Ost 1990: 160-165), as they threatened to take initiative away from clandestine organizations. Groups like WiP, already operating in the open, were better able to respond than the Solidarity leadership. They were a step ahead of the regime, not reacting to it. Because the opportunity was not obvious to all, however, framing it through careful selection and presentation of issues would be a crucial step.

FRAMING ISSUES IN A COMMUNIST STATE

Freedom and Peace developed a set of issues which functioned both as goals in themselves and as statements about the limitations of the communist system. They were well-chosen weapons. Each had the virtue of seeming to agree with basic tenets of doctrine or of law in the Polish People's Republic, yet was also a postulate to which the authorities could not easily agree without weakening their hold over society. To put this another way, each drove a wedge between the state and its ideology, forcing the regime either to admit that it had no ideological justification or to resort to sheer force to stay in power. Each was also fundamentally appealing to large social groups and was easy for the average citizen to comprehend.

The first new (or revived) issue was human rights, which had been central to the opposition of the late 1970s. Like its predecessor KOR, Freedom and Peace was born among students and intellectuals during a crisis period of heightened repression. WiP was not alone in trying to right the wrongs of the communist regime. One of its immediate predecessors was the Committee for the Protection of Legality (KOP), founded by a group of Kraków lawyers and underground politicians and activists in 1984. This was an explicit hearkening back to the oppositional methods of the Workers' Defense Committee; KOP hoped simply to document government repression and aid the regime's victims. Human rights work was the logical next step for those who had been condemning the martial-law regime and wanted to do more (Romaszewski 1984). WiP translated this advocacy work into a program for political action (Klich 1997; Rokita 1997; Huget 1996).

WiP's declarations adopted the language of legality and individual rights prevalent both in Eastern European dissident circles (such as Charter 77 in Czechoslovakia) and in Western groups like Amnesty International. Those arrested or sentenced for refusing military service were not, in WiP parlance, "political prisoners" but "prisoners of conscience." Indeed, WiP for a time produced and edited an Amnesty International Newsletter for Poland.

WiP's particular power among the younger generation was due to its focus on a second issue (which had spurred WiP's formation in 1985), the military's role in the Polish nation (Michta 1990). Even as Solidarity was forming in 1980, a handful of people, some close to Solidarity and in particular SKS, and others only distantly connected to Solidarity but with their roots in the Polish hippie culture of the 1970s, began to view opposition to the Polish army as a logical consequence of anticommunism, pacifism, or both. The problem was not the military itself—many prominent WiP participants felt that armed forces were necessary—but the military oath. Each soldier swore "to guard unshakably . . . the Polish People's Republic from the wiles of imperialism, to stand unbendingly in defense of peace, in brotherly alliance with the Soviet Army and other allied armies" (Śliwa 1992: 52; Michta 1990: 197-198). For each conscientious objector, refusal to serve or to take the oath was an individual decision and was generally not met with much opposition interest. Leszek Budrewicz, the architect of Wrocław's WiP circle, refused the oath in 1980, inspired in part by Roland Kruk, a Warsaw SKS colleague who had done the same a year earlier. At that time, both avoided any serious sanction (Budrewicz 1996).

After Adamkiewicz's jailing five years later, WiP's genius was to recognize that coordinated protest could force the state to reveal its hypocrisy: if the Jaruzelski regime really valued Poland's strength above all, as it constantly declared throughout the 1980s, then it could not object to young men who expressed their willingness to fight for Poland yet who desired a slightly different oath. The idea was in part to show other Poles to what absurd lengths the communist regime was willing to go and how empty its nationalist slogans really were. Participant Wacław Giermek made this point in an open letter at the time of his arrest: "If General W. Jaruzelski had sworn allegiance to allies in 1942, he would today have to be loyal to Ronald Reagan, President of the United States" (Giermek 1986).

Giermek (a Catholic) and Budrewicz (an atheist) were both influenced by the nonviolence or civil disobedience ideas propagated both within the church and out. As early as 1982, Father Ludwik Wiśniewski (a Dominican who had in the 1970s fostered the intellectual conservative opposition in Gdańsk) promoted an ethic of nonviolence in his church in Wrocław. Members of that church's academic ministry—and activists like Budrewicz who moved in the same intellectual circles—began to read Gandhi and Martin Luther King. Moving away from the violence and clandestine opposition of the early martial law years, they embraced peaceful methods and public stances as a key to breaking down societal fears (Giermek 1996; Budrewicz 1996).

The demand for alternative service followed precisely from this desire, as it allowed Freedom and Peace to draw a contrast between nonviolent opposition and the militarist regime. Refusal to serve, or to take a military oath, was made more palatable by being framed as a human rights problem. Polish law did theoretically allow for conscientious objector status, although this was almost never granted. Petitioners thus pointed to the Polish constitution's protection of the freedom of conscience and frequently based their request on religious grounds. They also emphasized their desire to work in health care or social work in place of military service (Krukowski 1997). The conscientious objector question did, however, risk offending those Poles who regarded military service as a national obligation or a test of manhood.

The first documented case of refusing military service altogether was that of Jankowski, a leading figure in the Alternative Society Movement (RSA), a Gdańsk-based anarchist group and a teacher of defense preparedness at a Gdańsk high school. Though his refusal came only in mid-1985, after WiP's founding, he had made his intentions plain since RSA emerged (in rejection of the religiosity and nationalism of Solidarity's birthplace) two years earlier (Waluszko 1992). Jankowski's search for support for his decision to abandon the underground—which caused a split in RSA—led him, ironically, to Father Wiśniewski, who pointed him in the direction, via Gdańsk conservatives, of WiP (Jankowski 1997). Jankowski remained a pacifist; he framed his resistance to military service, however, in terms both moral and national, using language calculated to make sense to an audience that might not share his convictions:

> The Naval Court stated that pacifist views are not compatible with my occupation, a teacher of defense preparedness, and that the special duty of inculcating the youth in my charge with the lofty ideals of love for one's Fatherland and its defense in the case of invasion or menace fell especially upon me as a teacher and pedagogue. So, first: there is a basic difference between defense preparedness and the science of killing, which is what military service is. . . . Indeed, I did not teach them to kill. I taught them how to save a person's life, health, and property from the weapons of mass destruction in modern arsenals. . . .
>   Second: the development of civilization means that today humanity is one family, linked by the common interest to live in peace and freedom. Violating human rights in one country or in a bloc is a threat to all the residents of our planet. . . . Freedom and peace are general human values, and the politics of militarizing entire societies, carried out in countries with compulsory military service, threatens those values. Compulsory military service is barbaric, in the full sense of that word. . . .
>   Defense of the Fatherland is but a pretext for actions which in reality aim to maintain the state's socialist status quo, the essence of which is the ruling of a privileged class over the overwhelming majority of society. The goal of the army and the militia in 1956, 1970, and 1981 was not defense of the fatherland. Nor did defense of the fatherland guide the tanks invading Czechoslovakia in 1968. They did not balk at murder, and the goal of their actions was, and is, one: to force slave's fetters upon people who fight for their rights. These fetters are all the more repulsive in that they are covered up with revolutionary, workers' slogans. (Jankowski 1986)

One year after WiP's first declarations (which included brief mention of environmental concerns), the Chernobyl explosion offered a third focus for the movement. Like the Popiełuszko murder, the catastrophe across the border in Soviet Ukraine raised troubling questions about the limitations of political-intellectual opposition and highlighted the need for new forms of opposition oriented toward tangible social issues. Like the military issue, the Chernobyl disaster was both an extremely personal concern (which also energized women's movements and peasant activists) and one on which the government (which at least promised to attend to the safety of its citizens) was largely defenseless. The general tenor of the opposition's response to Chernobyl, however, was passive: the accident, and its cover-up, were portrayed as further examples of the regime's perfidy and of the incompetence of communist states, to which there could be no response but disgust (Thompson 1988: 107; Helsinki Watch 1986).

WiP was the only movement in Poland to engage in public protest, in its very first demonstrations in Wrocław on May 2 and 9, 1986, and in Kraków on June 1. These protests were made to seem accessible to bystanders (after some trial and error) and framed the Chernobyl issue as one which would mobilize even those who, in the Polish context at least, were thought of as least likely to engage in protest: women, especially mothers. Both the Wrocław protests were staged during the afternoon rush hour, at one of the city's busiest intersections. The first one was silent: about twenty-five people sat on the ground, holding signs. About a thousand people watched, and some came to join the demonstrators. When the police detained only a few participants, the organizers planned another one for the following week. This time, most participants were women, many of whom led their small children by the hand or pushed them in strollers. The protesters carried signs demanding more information about the dangers to their health. They found at first that a march kept passersby at bay, so they eventually stopped marching, allowing a crowd to gather around them, and an intense discussion of Chernobyl ensued. The militia's reluctance to intervene—probably both because of the difficult position of the regime during the crisis and to avoid arresting women—made an impression on participants and observers alike. Participant Anna Gawlik, who marched with her infant daughter in a stroller, felt that she hadn't risked much—but that, of course, was precisely the point the march conveyed (A. Gawlik and Koczut 1996).

In Kraków, a group of women had been planning an ecological demonstration for Children's Day (June 1) for some time; the radioactive cloud gave the protest greater urgency, and brought WiP's involvement. The protest began with a noon Mass in the Marian church on Kraków's main square. Many of the women—the "mothers of Kraków," according to one banner—came holding dried flowers to symbolize the death of nature. As they left the church, Freedom and Peace banners greeted them. Singing nationalist, religious, and Solidarity songs, the group marched through Kraków's old town to the castle on Wawel Hill. Just as in Wrocław, the militia made no attempt to break up the demonstration.

The Chernobyl actions sparked further protest on other environmental issues, especially concerning Poland's nascent nuclear power industry. WiP's longest-lasting campaign opposed the building of Poland's first nuclear power plant at Żarnowiec, near Gdańsk, as well as plans for two other nuclear plants. These protests gathered speed after the Chernobyl explosion: an issue that had seemed rather distant to most Poles suddenly became very frightening, and participation in WiP demonstrations soared. Meanwhile, Wrocław activists conducted monthly marches to call for the closing of a metallurgical plant at Siechnice, which was poisoning the city's water supply. One can of course question whether so many people would have marched at Międzyrzecz in 1987 were it not for Chernobyl—but WiP was the only environmental group to attempt to mobilize that fear. By framing environmental opposition not as a matter for scientists but as a matter for families whose lives were threatened, Freedom and Peace found a peaceful way back onto the Polish streets, which had long been ceded to the police or to violent demonstrators.

WiP's framing of the delicate issue of national sovereignty—a mainstay demand of the older opposition—was the most innovative. In the person of Otto Schimek, the movement found a figure who simultaneously celebrated national martyrdom while destabilizing the idea of belligerence between nations. Schimek was an Austrian soldier during World War II who refused to participate in executions of Polish civilians. At the age of nineteen, he was himself executed and buried in the village of Machowa, near Tarnów. It was Leszek Budrewicz who proposed, at an early WiP gathering in the mountains, that participants visit Schimek's grave. The first trip in November 1985, for the forty-first anniversary of his death, ended with the detention of fourteen participants; six months later, some fifty marchers were detained as they attempted to mark Schimek's birthday. These twice-yearly pilgrimages were analogous to (and not in conflict with) the pilgrimages of Polish Catholics to holy shrines. If a movement as varied as Freedom and Peace had a spiritual center, it was the grave at Machowa (Budrewicz 1996; Czaputowicz 1997). When participants in the Wrocław WiP circle created a Peace Ministry at St. Dorothy's Church in 1988, they naturally christened it with Schimek's name.

Just like all other WiP weapons (if that word is not inappropriate), Schimek as a symbol put the communists in a difficult position. After all, he had refused to shoot Poles: was he not then a national hero, even if he were a soldier in an enemy army? The communists' problem was not that he was an Austrian, but that he had disobeyed his commander's orders. To honor Schimek implied that morality and human rights should take precedence over the rules of a regime—that nationalism must be rooted in respect for human rights and freedoms.

If these frames had any resonance—so that, for example, the citizens of Międzyrzecz knew whom to call in the summer of 1987—this was thanks to the movement's consistent use of the media. First, WiP published over a dozen national and local bulletins and journals. This was a tiny percentage of the underground periodicals in Poland (Helsinki Watch 1986), but a significant number for a new youth movement and more than any group except Solidarity itself. Second, WiP worked hard to get its story out to Western media. For example, in the Międzyrzecz protest, the "boys from Gorzów" included Barbara Hrybacz, whose role, as the one person from Gorzów's WiP with Warsaw contacts, was to get the story out to Western media. She stayed safely out of reach of police (Hrybacz 1997). Every protest, no matter how small, reached Warsaw and Radio Free Europe immediately. This was standard practice in Solidarity as well, but WiP was for a time the only opposition producing newsworthy events. Freedom and Peace events were often spectacular: participants (such as those in Międzyrzecz) climbed building scaffoldings (and sometimes chained themselves to scaffolding) to hang banners or scatter leaflets, or marched with their gently chiding slogan: "Come with us! They're not beating today!"

In every single campaign mentioned here, Freedom and Peace was successful. The military oath was changed in June 1988; one month later, the Polish parliament amended the law on universal military service. The Żarnowiec plant and the Siechnice plant were scrapped, and plans for other nuclear reactors were shelved, as was the radioactive waste dump at Międzyrzecz. All of these decisions were made, or at least begun, during communist rule and concerned issues which, with the possible exception of the Siechnice factory (whose closing Prime Minister Mieczysław Rakowski announced together with the closing of the historic Lenin Shipyard in Gdańsk), gained the government nothing for its retreat. No less a figure than Jerzy Urban—then government press spokesman and thus the author of much anti-WiP counter-propaganda—acknowledged in an interview that WiP itself (and not some internal liberalization of party or army) was responsible for its key victories (Urban 1997). No other movement, including Solidarity, could claim that the regime had given in on a specific issue. For the regime to even appear to give in to Solidarity and its demands for democratic elections or economic reform would have been unthinkable (until, of course, 1989 itself). It was even less likely that the communists would concede anything to a small band of students, except that this movement framed its protests in a way that the regime would find it difficult not to listen.

As an explanation for the reemergence of opposition and successful contestation of the communist regime, the role of Gorbachev (or, alternatively, of reform-minded communists in Warsaw)—indeed, any structural explanation—is clearly insufficient.

It is difficult to assert that, in Poland, would-be activists recognized and exploited Gorbachev's initiatives, testing the limits of what was possible. The success of the Freedom and Peace movement makes clear that its impact on civic mobilization before 1989 was quite independent from that of Gorbachev and the reformers, and was due primarily to WiP's framing strategies.

CONCLUSION

New movements like WiP rescued Polish society from the apathy and fear it had retreated to by 1985. Cultural or symbolic resistance, so effective during martial law, now threatened a re-atomization of society, and active opposition was becoming a part of legend. Fighting popular fear and apathy, breaking down isolation, Freedom and Peace reached people who had never before been involved, either because they were too young to have experienced free Solidarity or because the slogans of the political underground seemed empty to them. New movements like this could remobilize society, even in far corners like Międzyrzecz.

WiP could be said to have functioned as an usher, directing people back toward faith in a revived Solidarity as that movement began to reemerge in 1988. That the new movements and the Solidarity leadership did not share the same goals—a gulf evident to many activists during the strikes of 1988—was not important to Polish citizens: they came to see the new groups as harbingers of Solidarity. In June 1989, six WiP activists (including Marek Rusakiewicz of Gorzów, Jan Maria Rokita of Kraków, and Radosław Gawlik, who had led the Siechnice protests in Wrocław—as well as, outside WiP, Stanisław Bożek of Międzyrzecz) ran for parliament as Solidarity candidates and were easily elected. At that moment, however, the mobilized society which WiP and others had begun to create ebbed away, replaced by a more traditional relationship between democratic leaders and voters (R. Gawlik 1996; Rokita 1997; Rusakiewicz 1997; Budrewicz 1996). An understanding of the new movements in Poland reveals a rather different revolution imagined by the new activists, and hints at some of the frustrations which would be expressed in the post-communist era.

Other countries in the region saw movements like WiP emerge at the same time. A list of youthful, concrete, politically focused movements in the region would include Fidesz (the Federation of Young Democrats) in Hungary, the Independent Peace Association in Czechoslovakia, the Initiative for Peace and Human Rights in East Germany, and the Lion Society in L'viv, Ukraine. Existing in quite different conditions, these movements had varying roles in their countries' revolutions. Each is worthy of study by social movement scholars interested in the problem of frames and opportunities in 1989 (Kenney 2002).

Gorbachev, communist reformers, the faltering economy, the moral force of a senior opposition: without each of these factors, the revolution in Eastern Europe could not have happened; with all of them together, however, we still do not have enough information to understand the revolution. More precisely, we cannot regard these as creating the necessary conditions for new social movements to pose a powerful opposition to the communist state. In fact, it is doubtful that an opportunity of the sort described in the literature could even be relevant in a communist state. Bereft of ordinary politics, movement activists needed to create their own opportunity, in part by reframing the terms of political engagement. Let me conclude by summarizing how WiP's strategies contributed to the 1989 revolution.

The issues chosen, and their framing, weakened the state in ways Solidarity and the Church could not. Operating along the edge between legality and illegality, and between politics and social issues, WiP's campaigns destroyed the state's ideological pretensions and exposed both its hypocrisy and its weakness. Traditionally political movements, and Solidarity itself, opposed the state on issues where there could be no common ground: Poland's sovereignty and its relation with the Soviet Union, or the legality of martial law. They thus did not change popular attitudes toward the regime. New movements like WiP exposed the hypocrisy of the regime's professed love of peace, for example, or ridiculed the symbolism of communist anniversaries, or dispelled the illusion that in socialist Poland there was no ecological disaster. As people became aware of these problems *and* discovered ways to resolve (or at least address) them without the state's help, the state was irreversibly weakened.

This less aggressive, yet still confrontational, relationship (which would reach a new stage with the Orange Alternative movement in 1987-1988—in which, for example, participants dressed as elves gave flowers to policemen and waved merrily out the windows of police wagons) helped to lessen one of the gulfs that divided Polish society. The lighthearted, ironic, "velvet" nature of the new movements has often been commented upon; indeed, irony proved to be an effective, and easily accessible, antidote to fear. The style of the new activism, stressing nonviolence toward concrete and imaginable goals and affecting a satirical view of all trappings of power, was a product of some lessons learned from KOR, from Western activists, but most of all from new activists' encounters with the writings of anarchists and of Gandhi and King—and from a sense that tactics different from those of the first Solidarity era were necessary to battle the cold hand of normalization.

While few in Poland liked the regime by 1985, it certainly seemed both hermetic and very dangerous. WiP undermined this perception of the regime—even, arguably, for those who neither attended its demonstrations nor had ever heard of it—and exposed the holes in regime ideology. It also showed that while the regime would go to ridiculous lengths to protect itself, there were people who were not afraid to risk the consequences—and that the consequences were not that terrible, either. WiP's activism also demonstrated that change *was* possible: a polluting factory could be closed, or a repressive law could be changed. Each individual victory contributed to a growing reempowerment of society.

It is not easy to measure the extent to which the regime was prepared to give up on its ideology as a result of WiP's critique, nor the extent to which witnesses to WiP's actions felt somehow empowered by what they saw. The events at Międzyrzecz in September-October 1987 yield a clue, however. When thousands of citizens first protected "their" boys from arrest, then marched in the streets and supported a highly public protest fast, and when the government representatives in that town suddenly reversed a decision and opposed Warsaw, WiP's influence was immediate and evident. WiP helped to redirect Polish opposition tactics and attitudes toward concrete manifestations of communist power and the potential for change. By introducing powerful new mobilizing issues into political discourse, the movement drew new supporters into the opposition orbit and pluralized political discourse for a new generation of activists that still flourishes today. In so doing, it identified and attacked particularly vulnerable areas of the communist system, contributing in this way to the weakening of the system. To the extent that Solidarity leaders had become isolated from popular pressures and expectations by years in the underground and in Warsaw, groups like Freedom and Peace provided the essential link to the popular opposition expressed anew in 1989.

REFERENCES

"Ballada" 1985. "Ballada o Marku Adamkiewiczu." Ossolineum Library, Wrocław, Dział Dokumentacji Społecznej, Wolność Pokój collection (uncataloged); hereafter, Ossolineum collection.

Bernhard, Michael H. 1993. *The Origins of Democratization in Poland: Workers, Intellectuals, and Oppositional Politics, 1976-1980.* New York: Columbia University Press.

Brown, J. F. 1991. *Surge to Freedom: The End of Communist Rule in Eastern Europe.* Durham, NC: Duke University Press.

Budrewicz, Leszek. 1996. Interview by author, Wrocław, Poland, November 5, 1996.

Chirot, Daniel. 1991. "What Happened in Eastern Europe in 1989?" In *The Crisis of Leninism and the Decline of the Left: The Revolutions of 1989*, Daniel Chirot, ed. Seattle: University of Washington Press.

Czaputowicz, Jacek. 1997. Interview by author, Warsaw, Poland, January 31, 1997.

Ekiert, Grzegorz. 1996. *The State against Society: Political Crises and Their Aftermath in East Central Europe.* Princeton, NJ: Princeton University Press.

Ekiert, Grezigorz, and Jan Kubik. 1999. *Rebellious Civil Society: Popular Protest and Democratic Consolidation in Poland, 1989-1993.* Ann Arbor: University of Michigan Press.

Elster, Jon, ed. 1996. *The Roundtable Talks and the Breakdown of Communism.* Chicago: University of Chicago Press.

Flam, Helena. 1996. "Anxiety and the Successful Oppositional Construction of Social Reality: The Case of the KOR." *Mobilization* 1 (1): 103-121.

Friszke, Andrzej. 1994. *Opozycja polityczna w PRL, 1945-1980.* London: Aneks.

Gamson, William, and David S. Meyer. 1996. "Framing Political Opportunity." In *Comparative Perspectives on Social Movements: Political Opportunities, Mobilizing Structures, and Cultural Framings*, Doug McAdam, John D. McCarthy, and Mayer N. Zald, eds. New York: Cambridge University Press.

Gawlik, Anna, and Anna Koczut. 1996. Interview by author, Wrocław, Poland, December 9, 1996.

Gawlik, Radosław. 1996. Interview by author, Wrocław, Poland, November 25, 1996.

Geremek, Bronisław. 1990. *Rok 1989: Bronisław Geremek opowiada, Jacek Żakowski pyta.* Warsaw: Plejada.

Giermek, Wacław. 1986. Dlaczego odmówiłem złożenia przysięgi wojskowej? June. Ossolineum collection.

———. 1996. Interview by author, Wrocław, Poland, December 4, 1996.

Giugni, Marco G. 1998. "The Other Side of the Coin: Explaining Crossnational Similarities between Social Movements." *Mobilization* 3 (1): 89-105.

Głębocki, Henryk. 1994. *Studencki Komitet Solidarności w Krakowie, 1977-1980: Zarys działalności.* Warsaw: PiT.

Glenn, John K., III. 2001. *Framing Democracy: Civil Society and Civic Movements in Eastern Europe.* Stanford, CA: Stanford University Press.

Gliński, Piotr. 1996. *Polscy zieloni. Ruch spo eczny w okresie przemian.* Warsaw: IfiS PAN.

Głowiński, Michał. 1996. *Mowa w stanie oblężenia.* Warsaw: Open.

———. 1999. *Końcówka (czerwiec 1985–styczeń 1989).* Kraków: Wydawnictwo Literackie.

Goodwyn, Lawrence. 1991. *Breaking the Barrier: The Rise of Solidarity in Poland.* New York: Oxford University Press.

Havel, Václav. 1985. "The Power of the Powerless." In *The Power of the Powerless: Citizens against the State in Central-Eastern Europe*, John Keane, ed. Armonk, NY: M. E. Sharpe.

Helsinki Watch. 1986. *Reinventing Civil Society: Poland's Quiet Revolution, 1981-1986.* New York: Helsinki Watch.

Hicks, Barbara. 1996. *Environmental Politics in Poland: A Social Movement between Regime and Opposition.* New York: Columbia University Press.

Holzer, Jerzy, and Krzysztof Leski. 1990. *Solidarność w podziemiu.* Łódź: Wydawnictwo Łódzkie.

Hrybacz, Barbara. 1997. Interview by author, Warsaw, Poland, June 19, 1997.

Huget, Radosław. 1996. Interview by author, Kraków, Poland, December 11-12, 1996.

International. 1988. International Human Rights Conference/Międzynarodowa Konferencja Praw Człowieka, Cracow 25-28 August 1988.

Jankowski, Wojciech. 1986. Letter from Zwartowo prison. 13 August. Ossolineum collection.

———. 1997. Interview by author, Czarne k/Gładyszowa, Poland, June 29, 1997.

Kennedy, Michael. 1990. "The Constitution of Critical Intellectuals: Polish Physicians, Peace Activists, and Democratic Civil Society." *Studies in Comparative Communism* 23: 281-303.

———. 1999. "Contingencies and the Alternatives of 1989: Toward a Theory and Practice of Negotiating Revolution." *East European Politics and Societies.* 13: 293-302.

Kennedy, Michael, and Brian Porter, eds. 2000. *Negotiating Radical Change: Understanding and Extending the Lessons of the Polish Round Table.* Ann Arbor: Center for Russian and East European Studies, University of Michigan.

Kenney, Padraic. 1999a. "The Gender of Resistance in Communist Poland." *American Historical Review* 104: 399-425.

———. 1999b. "What Is the History of 1989? New Scholarship from East-Central Europe." *East European Politics and Societies* 13: 419-431.

———. 2002. *A Carnival of Revolution: Central Europe, 1989.* Princeton, NJ: Princeton University Press.

Klich, Bogdan. 1997. Interview by author, Kraków, Poland, January 15, 1997.

Kocięba, Paweł. 1996. Interview by author, Wrocław, Poland, December 16, 1996.

Kossakowski, Marek. 1988. "Leave the Bunkers to the Bats!" *Across Frontiers* 4 (2-3): 10-11, 48-49.

Kriesi, Hanspeter, Ruud Koopmans, Jan Willem Duyvendak, and Marco G. Giugni. 1995. *New Social Movements in Western Europe: A Comparative Analysis.* Minneapolis: University of Minnesota Press.

Krukowski, Marek. 1997. Interview by author, Wrocław, Poland, February 6, 1997.

Krzemiński, Ireneusz. 1989. *Czy Polska po Solidarności? Treści świadomo ści społecznej i postawy ludzi.* Warsaw: Instytut Socjologii UW.

Kubik, Jan. 1994. *The Power of Symbols against the Symbols of Power: The Rise of Solidarity and the Fall of State Socialism in Poland.* University Park: Pennsylvania State University Press.

Kurzman, Charles. 1996. "Structural Opportunities and Perceived Opportunities in Social-Movement Theory: Evidence from the Iranian Revolution of 1979." *American Sociological Review* 61: 153-170.

Laba, Roman. 1991. *The Roots of Solidarity: A Political Sociology of Poland's Working-Class Democratization.* Princeton, NJ: Princeton University Press.

Lazarski, Christopher. 1990. "The Polish Independent Peace Movement." Pp. 118-134 in *In Search of Civil Society: Independent Peace Movements in the Soviet Bloc,* Vladimir Tismaneanu, ed. New York: Routledge.

Lipski, Jan Jósef. 1985. *KOR: Workers' Defense Committee in Poland, 1976-1981.* Berkeley: University of California Press.

Łopiński, Maciej, Marcin Moskit, and Mariusz Wilk. 1990. *Konspira: Solidarity Underground,* Jane Cave, trans. and ed. Berkeley: University of California Press.

Lubecki, Jacek. 2001. "Worlds That Communism Built: Electoral Constituencies of 'Successor' Parties in Post-Communist Eastern Europe." Manuscript.

Mason, David S. 1992. *Revolution in East-Central Europe: The Rise and Fall of Communism and the Cold War.* Boulder, CO: Westview Press.

McAdam, Doug. 1996. "Conceptual Origins, Current Problems, Future Directions." Pp. 23-40 in *Comparative Perspectives on Social Movements: Political Opportunities, Mobilizing Structures, and Cultural Framings,* Doug McAdam, John D. McCarthy, and Mayer N. Zald, eds. New York: Cambridge University Press.

McAdam, Doug, and Dieter Rucht. 1993. "The Cross-National Diffusion of Movement Ideas." *Annals of the American Academy of Political and Social Science* 528: 56-74.

Michałek, Agata. 1997. Interview by author, Kraków, Poland, January 17, 1997.

Michnik, Adam. 1984. *Szanse polskiej demokracji.* London: Aneks.

Michnik, Adam, Józef Tischner, and Jacek Żakowski. 1998. *Między panem a plebanem.* Kraków: Znak.

Michta, Andrew A. 1990. *Red Eagle: The Army in Polish Politics, 1944-1988.* Stanford, CA: Hoover Institution Press.

Modzelewski, Wojciech. 1996. *Pacyfizm w Polsce.* Warsaw: Instytut Studiów Politycznych PAN.

"Murder." 1985. "The Murder of Father Popiełuszko." *Poland Watch* 7: 1-26.

"Najtrudniej." 1988. "'Najtrudniej było nam przekroczyć własną śmieszność . . .' o Międzyrzeczanach Międzyrzeczanki opowieść z taśmy spisana." *Pismo ruchu 'Wolność i Pokój'* (Szczecin) 4.

Niemczyk, Piotr. 1987. "List otwarty do Joanne Landy." *Biuletyn WiP*, 7-8.

———. 1997. Interview by author, Warsaw, Poland, February 2, 1997.

Oberschall, Anthony. 1996. "Opportunities and Framing in the Eastern European Revolts of 1989." Pp. 93-121 in *Comparative Perspectives on Social Movements: Political Opportunities, Mobilizing Structures, and Cultural Framings*, Doug McAdam, John D. McCarthy, and Mayer N. Zald, eds. New York: Cambridge University Press.

Opp, Karl-Dieter. 1994. "Repression and Revolutionary Action in 1989." *Rationality and Society* 6: 101-138.

Opp, Karl-Dieter, and Wolfgang Roehl. 1990. "Repression, Micromobilization, and Political Protest." *Social Forces* 69: 521-547.

Opp, Karl-Dieter, Peter Voss, and Christiane Gern. 1995. *Origins of a Spontaneous Revolution: East Germany, 1989.* Ann Arbor: University of Michigan Press.

Ost, David. 1990. *Solidarity and the Politics of Anti-Politics: Opposition and Reform in Poland since 1968.* Philadelphia: Temple University Press.

"Oświadczenie." 1984. "Oświadczenie TKK NSZZ 'S.'" *Tygodnik Mazowsze* 107, November 22.

Otáhal, Milan. 1994. *Opozice, moc, společnost 1969/1989.* Prague: Maxdorf.

Paczkowski, Andrzej. 1999. "Strikes and Revolts as the 'Polish Way' through Socialism." August Zaleski Lectures, Department of History, Harvard University.

Philipsen, Dirk. 1993. *We Were the People: Voices from East Germany's Revolutionary Autumn of 1989.* Durham, NC: Duke University Press.

Pieriestrojka. 1988. *Pieriestrojka i socjalistyczna odnowa wspólna przepustka w XXI wiek: Wizyta Michaiła Gorbaczowa w Polsce w dniach 11-14 lipca 1988 r.* Warsaw: Książka i Wiedza.

Raina, Peter. 1999. *Droga do Okrągłego Stołu: Zakulisowe rozmowy przygotowawcze.* Warsaw: Wydawnictwo von borowiecky.

Ramet, Sabrina. 1995. *Social Currents in Eastern Europe: The Sources and Consequences of the Great Transformation.* 2nd ed. Durham, NC: Duke University Press.

Rasler, Karen. 1996. "Concessions, Repression, and Political Protest in the Iranian Revolution." *American Sociological Review* 61: 132-152.

Rokita, Jan Maria. 1987. Wolność i Pokój, czyli jak zwiększy szanse pokoju w Europie. *Czas przyszły* 1: 16-25.

———. 1997. Interview by author, Kraków, Poland, May 26, 1997.

Romaszewski, Zbigniew. 1984. "Zamierzam działać jawnie: Rozmowa z Zbigniewem Romaszewskim." *Tygodnik Mazowsze* 102.

Rothschild, Joseph. 1993. *Return to Diversity: A Political History of East Central Europe since World War I.* 2nd ed. New York: Oxford University Press.

Rubenstein, Joshua. 1980. *Soviet Dissidents: Their Struggle for Human Rights.* Boston: Beacon Press.

Rusakiewicz, Marek. 1997. Interview by author, Gorzów, Poland, July 17, 1997.

Skilling, H. Gordon. 1981. *Charter 77 and Human Rights in Czechoslovakia.* London: Allen & Unwin.

Skórzyński, Jan. 1995. *Ugoda i Rewolucja: Władza i opozycja, 1985-1989.* Warsaw: Interpress.

Śliwa, Maciej. 1992. "Ruch 'Wolność i Pokój, 1985-1989." Praca magisterska, Uniwersytet Jagiellołski.

Sokołowski, Kazimierz. 1997. Interview by author, Gorzów, Poland, July 17, 1997.

Stokes, Gale. 1993. *The Walls Came Tumbling Down: The Collapse of Communism in Eastern Europe.* New York: Oxford University Press.

Tabako, Tomasz. 1992. *Strajk '88.* Warsaw: NOWa.

Tarrow, Sidney. 1991. "'Aiming at a Moving Target': Social Science and the Recent Rebellions in Eastern Europe." *PS: Political Science and Politics* 24: 1, 12-24.

———. 1994. *Power in Movement: Social Movements, Collective Action, and Politics.* New York: Cambridge University Press.

Thompson, Mark. 1988. "Lines of Latitude: People's Détente, East and West." Pp. 103-129 in *Something in the Wind: Politics after Chernobyl,* Louis Mackay and Mark Thompson, eds. London: Pluto Press.

Tismaneanu, Vladimir. 1990. "Unofficial Peace Activism in the Soviet Union and East-Central Europe." Pp. 1-53 in *In Search of Civil Society: Independent Peace Movements in the Soviet Bloc,* Vladimir Tismaneanu, ed. New York: Routledge.

———. 1993. *Reinventing Politics: Eastern Europe from Stalin to Havel.* New York: Free Press.

Tőkés, Rudolf L. 1996. *Hungary's Negotiated Revolution: Economic Reform, Social Change, and Political Succession.* New York: Cambridge University Press.

Torpey, John C. 1995. *Intellectuals, Socialism, and Dissent: The East German Opposition and Its Legacy.* Minneapolis: University of Minnesota Press.

Urban, Jerzy. 1997. Interview by author, Warsaw, Poland, July 17, 1997.

Völgyes, Iván. 1990. "By Way of a Conclusion: Controlled and Uncontrolled Change in Eastern Europe." Pp. 394-403 in *The Columbia History of Eastern Europe in the Twentieth Century,* Joseph Held, ed. New York: Columbia University Press.

Walker, Rachel. 1993. *Six Years That Shook the World: Perestroika, the Impossible Project.* Manchester, UK: Manchester University Press.

Waluszko, Janusz P. 1992. *RSA: Ruch Społeczeństwa Alternatywnego.* Sopot: Man-Gala Press.

Weigle, Marcia A., and Jim Butterfield. 1992. "Civil Society in Reforming Communist Regimes: The Logic of Emergence." *Comparative Politics* 25: 1-23.

Wheaton, Bernard, and Zdenek Kavan. 1992. *The Velvet Revolution: Czechoslovakia, 1988-1991.* Boulder, CO: Westview Press.

Wołyniec, Andrzej. 1988. "Atomy znowu straszą!!!" *Poznań Ekoforum: Nieregularnik ekologiczny Ruchu 'Wolność i Pokój* 1.

Wylie, Gillian. 1999. "Social Movements and International Change: The Case of 'Détente from Below.'" *International Journal of Peace Studies* 4: 61-82.

Żurko, Jerzy. 1996. Interview by author, Wrocław, Poland, November 23, 1996.

Zuzowski, Robert. 1992. *Political Dissent and Opposition in Poland: The Workers' Defense Committee KOR.* Westport, CT: Praeger.

Chapter 8

POLITICAL OPPORTUNITIES AND FRAMING PUERTO RICAN IDENTITY IN NEW YORK CITY

Cathy Schneider

On May 18, 1993, a fracas broke out at the Lower East Side Community Board between the Puerto Rican chairman, an appointee of the local Puerto Rican councilman, and the leaders of progressive community organizations concerned with housing, AIDS, and the arts, some of whom were also Puerto Rican. During the shouting match the chairman of the council and his allies accused his opponents of presiding over the deterioration of the Lower East Side, acting like "befogged apparatchiks," and bringing a population of predators into the neighborhood.

Across the Williamsburg Bridge in Brooklyn, Puerto Rican activists were planning an illegal occupation of the new public housing projects to protest preferential treatment for Hasidic Jews. Puerto Rican leaders of several housing-, AIDS-, and arts-related community groups met with the local Puerto Rican councilman, who promised his support of their struggle for equal access to low-income housing.

Meanwhile, in Mott Haven, in the South Bronx, activists were organizing to prevent the local machine boss from nominating another one of his cronies for city council, following the recent indictment of his last associate. Housing organizations and AIDS activists aligned themselves on opposing sides.

These three contrasting stories of local community activism raise significant questions about the relationship between local political opportunity structures, social movement strategies, and collective identity formation. First, why did local activists working in three low-income, predominantly Puerto Rican neighborhoods engage in such widely varying political strategies? Second, what accounts for the very different political coalitions formed to support or to oppose activism in these three neighborhoods? Third, why did local Puerto Rican residents respond to the activists in such divergent ways? And last, what accounts for the different political agendas associated with Puerto Rican identity in these three neighborhoods?

FRAMING AND POLITICAL STRUCTURE

Recent work on the relationship among opportunities, alliance structures, and framing sheds some light on the origins of these differences (Snow et al. 1986; Snow and Benford 1992; Taylor 1989; Tarrow 1994; Ellingson 1995; Diani 1996). The concept of framing, in particular, provides a useful link between macro-level concepts such as political opportunity structures, micro-level mobilization processes, and the long-term evolution of political and ethnic identities.[1]

While social scientists have long recognized that political institutions shape political culture and ethnic identities (Katznelson and Zolberg 1986; Morris and Mueller 1992; Marx 1995: 163), there has been little attention to the processes that reproduce or transform such identities. Ira Katznelson, for instance, argues that American workers identify with ethnicity and British workers with class, due to differences in the "organization of the state: that of a federal versus a unitary state" (Katznelson 1985: 273)." He argues:

> If we explore the effects that these differences had on the content of working-class organization located where workers lived, we shall be able to make more persuasive connections between the characteristics of these states and their activities and divergent patterns of working-class formation. (1985: 272)

The link between the structure of the state and the strategies and identities of local groups needs further specification, however. First, there needs to be more attention to local institutional variation and local political opportunity structures. Movements do not respond simply to changes in the central government but also to changes in the local environment in which they operate. Second, we need further study of intermediary processes, in particular those that explain how shifts in opportunity enter into the strategic calculations of individuals and/or organizations. As Ruud Koopmans puts it:

> By neglecting the mechanisms that connect structure and action, these structuralist versions of the POS [political opportunity structure] model prevent us from seeing that a specific structuralist setting may have a variety of concrete consequences, which sometimes may point in opposed directions. (1995: 15)

A focus on "frames," the cognitive constructs activists use to interpret grievances and events, links political opportunity structures to both social movement strategies and collective identity formation. As David Snow and colleagues argue, grievances are subject to interpretation, and differences in interpretation affect which "lines of action come to be defined as more or less risky, morally imperative despite risks, or instrumentally pointless" (Snow et al. 1986: 465). "To make participation more attractive," concurs Verta Taylor, "organizations must elaborate alternative cultural frameworks to provide security and meaning for those who reject the established order and remain in the group" (1989: 769). Social movement organizers must "frame the world in which they are acting" (Snow et al. 1986: 465).

Injustice frames, for instance, encourage collective action by challenging people's tendency to explain their situation as a function of individual rather than situational factors (McAdam 1982). "Revolutionary culture," Carol Smith observes, "is the product of politics." It is through the conscious strategies of political entrepreneurs that "communities, real or imagined . . . become active agents" of change (Smith 1990: 271). In Pinochet's Chile, for example, economic grievances could not explain the willingness of some impoverished residents, but not others, to risk their lives in protest against an authoritarian regime. The capacity of some poor urban neighborhoods, and not others, to mobilize mass political resistance lay in the political heritage of decades of work in the popular culture by the Marxist parties, which had convinced residents that solidaristic collective action could defeat the most powerful regime (Schneider 1995).

But organizers do not simply pick collective action frames from the air. Successful frames must link an organization's "goals to the predispositions of their target public . . . and set a strategic course between [the movement's] cultural setting, its political opponents and the militants and ordinary citizens whose support it needs" (Tarrow 1994: 123). The viability of a particular movement frame, then, is determined by the external context in which the movement acts. "Structural opportunities for action," as Ann Swidler argues, "determine which among competing ideologies survive in the long run" (1986: 273).

There are three main determinants of a successful frame. First, political opportunity structures such as the distribution of political power and access, the availability of elite allies, and the opportunity to form coalitions, all affect the success of different mobilizing messages (Tarrow 1994; Diani 1996). In the 1960s, for instance, Southern blacks framed their campaign around civil rights because the most vulnerable aspect of the political opportunity structure, and thus the earliest terrain of the movement, was the courts (Tarrow 1994: 129). In South Africa in the 1980s, in contrast, blacks responded to the state's use of racial categories with a Black Consciousness frame. "Exclusion defines and unifies who are subordinated and invites pressures for inclusion: identity formation and opportunity structures are connected" (Marx 1995: 159).

The second factor that determines the viability of a particular movement frame is the relationship between a movement and its competitors. As Stephen Ellingson observes, movement fields are populated by multiple organizations in systems of alliances and rivalries. "Social movements construct the identities of protagonists, antagonists, and audiences within a movement's field. . . . One of the common modes of differentiation is for speakers to structure their discourse around various sets of poles that condense what the debate is about and what can be discussed and what problems can be addressed" (Ellingson 1995: 105-106). Ethnic groups, for instance, may distinguish themselves from their rivals by asserting a distinct and morally superior categorical identity, thereby sharpening the contrast between the movement's constituents and members of competing groups. As Charles Tilly argues: "Social movements create or activate paired unequal categories. The 'we' of social movements comprises a whole category of unjustly treated persons or organizations. The 'they' consists of others whose action or inaction allegedly causes the condition activists are protesting. . . . Social movements involve the construction and enforcement of unequal paired categories" (1997: 128-130).

Third, cultural constructs and identities forged by previous social movements "enter the political culture . . . [and] serve as symbols mobilized by future movement entrepreneurs" (Tarrow 1994). As David Meyer and Nancy Whittier observe, "Collective identities constructed during periods of peak mobilization endure even as lective identities constructed during periods of peak mobilization endure even as protest dies down. One-time participants continue to . . . make personal and political decisions in light of this identity" (1994: 181). Choices made by one generation of movement organizers change the course for future movenet organizers by altering the cultures and identities of participating groups.

In this article, I examine three decades of Puerto Rican organizing in three New York City neighborhoods. The frames of these three generations of Puerto Rican activists were determined by the local political opportunity structure, in particular (1) the distribution of political power among competing ethnic groups, (2) the opportunity to form political coalitions, and (3) the divergent trajectories and frames of previous social movements. These frames, in turn, determined the ability of organizers to respond to new issues: influencing, in particular, activists' selection of targets, their choice of alliance partners, and their use of specific strategies, tactics, and discourse.

In each neighborhood, then, Puerto Rican activists in the late sixties and early seventies responded to local political opportunities by framing Puerto Rican identity in ways that helped build political coalitions and target opponents. These identities, as framed by movement activists, entered into the political culture of the neighborhood, shaping in particular the political orientation of community-based organizations (CBOs). When future activists tried to organize in these neighborhoods, the political orientations of these CBOs were already an important part of the political landscape, and one which helped determine the viability of newer social movement frames.

METHODOLOGY

The methodology for this study is qualitative comparative analysis (Ragin 1987; Ragin and Becker 1992). I compare three social movements, in three decades, operating in three New York City neighborhoods with large Puerto Rican populations (see tables 8.1-8.3). Data on the AIDS movement was gathered from three years of ethnographic research (1993-1996), including participation in community organizations (in particular needle exchanges, drug recovery groups, and housing organizations), interviews with political activists and organizational leaders, and focus groups with clients of needle exchanges and Narcotics Anonymous groups. Data on the Young Lords and on the housing movement were gathered through oral histories and interviews with former movement leaders, current neighborhood organizers, and other neighborhood residents. Publicly available demographic, public health, police, and other data, as well as historical accounts of previous local organizing efforts, were also collected. Data on frames were assembled from campaign literature, interviews, focus groups, and informal participant observation.

PUERTO RICAN SOCIAL MOVEMENTS IN NEW YORK CITY

Puerto Ricans, who arrived in New York neighborhoods in large numbers after World War II, brought with them a history of political participation and affiliation. While political participation on the island had always been very high and Puerto Ricans were accustomed to grassroots organizing, the island's repressive colonial heritage had also taught Puerto Ricans the high risk of political action and the rewards of political patronage.

Table 8.1 Racial and Ethnic Makeup of Neighborhoods

Neighborhood	% Puerto Rican	% Latino	% African American	% Nonwhite Latino
Mott Haven	50.2	65.4	31.7	2.0
Lower East Side	32.2	45.4	11.1	19.7
Williamsburg	45.2	68.9	13.9	14.1

Source: Hanson-Sanchez 1995.

Table 8.2 Poverty and Unemployment Rates of Neighborhoods

Neighborhood	Unemployment %	Puerto Rican Unemployment %	Poverty %	Latino Poverty %	Latino per capita Income
Mott Haven	19.3	20.4	52.0	54.1	$14,939
Lower East Side	10.1	16.6	34.7	44.0	$17,967
Williamsburg	15.5	16.8	43.0	46.0	$18,142

Source: Hanson-Sanchez 1995.

Table 8.3 Community Health Indicators per 100,000 by Neighborhoods

Neighborhood	Cumulative AIDS Rates 1992	Hospital Substance Abuse 1992	Homicide Rate 1992	Homicide 1993	Infant Mortality Rate
New York City	580.5	6.3	26.6	NA	10.3
Mott Haven	943.0	14.1	76.3	70	12.0
Lower East Side	1,304.5	6.9	11.6	6	8.1
Williamsburg	591.1	9.1	32.8	22	13.0

Source: New York City Health Atlas 1994.

The political system Puerto Ricans encountered in New York City also rewarded political acquiescence. The city's federated political structure restricted political competition to local districts, where competition for jobs and resources was fierce. Political machines, which distributed spoils based on votes and ethnicity, exerted significant power (Katznelson 1981; Shefter 1986). Puerto Ricans adapted in disparate forms to this system. Some Puerto Ricans endorsed local power brokers that promised jobs and resources to their community. Others, including those who had participated in independence struggles on the island, joined radical Cuban exiles and/or American communist and socialist parties and labor unions, and often boy-cotted the electoral arena. Still others declined to participate in mainland politics. The extremely low voting rate of New York Puerto Ricans (contrasted with ex-tremely high turnout on the island) made those machines that could guarantee the turnout of organized sectors very powerful.

In the 1960s a group of young radical Puerto Rican activists, called the Young Lords, attempted to challenge these machines and their control over the distribution of power and resources. The Lords was founded by a mix of college students, most of whom were members of the Pedro Albizpo Campos society, and barrio youth, many of whom were active in local street gangs. They modeled their movement after the Black Panthers, Latin American guerilla movements, and a politicized street gang in Chicago, from whom they took their name.

Although the Lords were most active in East Harlem (*el Barrio*), their home base, they organized chapters in most of the Puerto Rican neighborhoods in the city. They adapted to each neighborhood by framing their struggles in ways that resonated with the local terrain. In Williamsburg, for instance, Hasidic Jews and Puerto Ricans competed for political power. The Young Lords framed their competition with Hasi-dic Jews as an anticolonial struggle and forged a link between local Puerto Ricans and liberation movements in Puerto Rico, Cuba, and other Latin American countries. In contrast, in Mott Haven, where Puerto Ricans were also the majority (with African Americans constituting about 30 percent of the population, approximately twice that of the Hasidim in Williamsburg), the Young Lords challenged a political machine controlled by a Puerto Rican boss. Here the Lords used an antisystem frame, focus-ing on the conflict between the people (particularly people of color) and the state. This frame glorified the "outlaw" and depicted politicians and political parties as corrupt and untrustworthy. By using this frame, the Lords built alliances with local street gangs, drug dealers, drug users, and prison inmates.

On the Lower East Side, where Puerto Ricans made up a significant minority, the Young Lords formed alliances with preexisting socialist, communist, and labor organizations. They also worked with local Puerto Rican artists and poets to create organizations that challenged more conventional forms of cultural expression. They thus helped expand what had been a class-based socialist frame into a broader coun-tercultural frame. This new frame embraced local artists, bohemians, and gays as well as traditional blue-collar workers. The victory of this multiethnic coalition in the city council elections of 1978 opened a space for right-wing Puerto Rican activists to link ethnic identity to conservative family values and to cement alliances with de-posed real estate developers, co-op owners, and tenant associations in public housing projects.

The Young Lords' efforts to mobilize Puerto Rican residents in the early seven-ties determined how future movement activists, first those in the housing movement and later those in the AIDS movement, framed their local campaigns as well. For those in the AIDS movement, in particular, framing was critical. Since AIDS activ-ists in inner-city neighborhoods worked with intravenous drug users (intravenous drug use is the major form of HIV transmission in inner city neighborhoods, infect-ing not only drug users but also their spouses, lovers, lovers' lovers, and children), AIDS activists needed to frame drug abuse in ways that resonated with the frame of previous neighborhood movements. In Mott Haven, for instance, AIDS activists de-picted drug users as antisystem revolutionary actors. In Williamsburg, drug users were defined as victims of colonialism and oppression. In the Lower East Side,

AIDS activists won support from local community-based organizations by defining drug users as victims of class oppression in need of unions and organization, on the one hand, and members of the counterculture who were engaged in an alternate life-style, on the other. Conservative Puerto Rican politicians, in contrast, won support in the Lower East Side housing projects by labeling drug users as criminals and preda-tors and blaming AIDS activists for the deterioration of the neighborhood's "quality of life."

In each neighborhood, then, the frame used by previous movement activists helped decide the frame of later movements and their ability to win allies and avoid community opposition.

MOTT HAVEN: THE DEVELOPMENT OF AN ANTISYSTEM FRAME

Mott Haven is located in the southernmost tip of the South Bronx. Originally popu-lated by Germans and Jews, and later Irish and Italians, in the 1950s Mott Haven became predominantly Puerto Rican and black. It also became one of the poorest communities in the country.

The Bronx boss, Ramon Velez, began his ascent in the 1960s, when his multi-service center received several million dollars in city funds for methadone treatment programs. Velez expanded these clinics, and later received money for tuberculosis testing and prenatal and postnatal care. Through such services, he controlled access to over five thousand patronage jobs, including subcontractors and auxiliary services. This gave him a cadre of people to delegate for political events, campaigns, and elec-tions. "When Latinos were not considered worth pursuing," noted one former Bronx organizer, "he was pursued by national politicians of both parties. In the Bronx he could produce votes."

In 1969 the Young Lords challenged the machine, using an antisystem frame, which had proved effective in East Harlem. "We adopted the most militant ap-proach—direct confrontation," explained a former Lord. "We needed health care, so we took over a hospital. We worked according to a four-year plan. In four years we'll be free, in jail, or dead."

On July 14, 1970, for instance, the Young Lords occupied Lincoln Hospital by driving a truck up the emergency ramp. For twenty-four hours they occupied the hospital, demanding a new hospital, a raise in the minimum wage of health care workers, and worker control. In October 1970 they again occupied the local hospital, this time to demand free drug-treatment programs and alternatives to methadone maintenance, Velez's cash cow. They also opened the hospital cafeteria to local drug users as part of a "Feed the People" campaign. A former Young Lord explained, "We believed substance abusers should be agents in their own recovery. We invited everyone who was into drugs to eat free in the hospital cafeteria."

The Lords also opened chapters in several prisons, including Attica. Prison in-mates, like drug users, were, as enemies of the system, treated as allies of the revolu-tion. A Young Lord pamphlet phrased it this way:

> The first segment of our people that will join, work with and support the revolution is the lumpen, the street people: Prostitutes, junkies, two bit pushers, hustlers, wel-fare mothers. . . . The people come into the revolution because they have nothing to lose. . . . We're here because we are trying to take the power of the State and put it back in the hands of the people. (*P'alante* 1970: 79-81)

During this period the Lords also grew close to several Episcopal priests. Several churches in the Bronx had become influenced by the theology of liberation. Of these, "the Episcopal church," noted the former Lord, "was the most receptive, since they needed us. They were the least influential in this community and were looking to make headway." With church support, the Lords began clothing drives, liberation schools, and welfare rights and tenant organizations.

But this radical coalition of activists in hospitals, drug clinics, and the local church was unable to pose a viable alternative. By 1973 the Lords had fallen apart and their network of radical activists sunk into abeyance. Some found sanctuary in local churches where they had previously organized. Others found work in the various citywide organizations, while still others became addicted to heroin.

In the same year, Velez secured a seat on the city council (which he held until his antipoverty and community organizations came under city and state investigations in 1977). Later, he exercised his power privately, beginning with a successful maneuver to get his cohorts on the board of directors of the new Lincoln Hospital. He also opened a multiservice center that received large city contracts and subcontracted services from other agencies and businesses connected to the machine, allowing him and his cronies to "load their pocketbooks and enrich their bank accounts," claimed one local activist. As the machine grew, noted the head of the local needle exchange, it "undermined real movements from coming out in the Bronx."

In the years that followed, deindustrialization, housing abandonment, arson, and out-migration destroyed the remaining activist networks. The founder of a major South Bronx housing development recalled, "In the 1970s everyone who could leave did. They wrote off the community entirely."

By 1990 the neighborhood was saturated with drugs and open air drug markets. Drug dealers controlled the streets and public parks. The activist organizations that remained in the neighborhood were weak and secluded. Even the housing organizations created by local block associations in the late seventies (to save buildings destroyed by housing abandonment or arson) were overly dependent on private and public sources of finance.

It was in 1992 when a strategic alliance between drug dealers, drug users, Puerto Rican activists, and a local church facilitated AIDS outreach efforts in the area. As one AIDS activist explains, "In terms of community organizing I had to create a structure, there was no basis for it." Instead of relying on support from local CBOs, this activist, influenced by the antisystem frame of the Young Lords, created a new organization with the help of local drug dealers. "The drug war," she argued, "is a civil war, a class war, a war of color. Many institutional providers have become gendarmes in this war." From this point of view, working with local politicians or social service agencies would hinder organizing efforts in the community.

> There is not one family here not implicated in the drug scene. If organizers are gunning them [drug dealers], they are not going to start a mass movement. How can we turn a blind eye to the fact that these kids come from our community? Do we really want to keep incarcerating our children? We are pulling out our very innards. . . . Instead of looking at what goes on in a negative way, I flipped it around and looked in it for solutions. I started working with these folk [the drug dealers]—getting them involved in the community. Federal policy tries to screw us and turn us into Gestapo. But if I had not worked with drug dealers, I could not have created a clinic that saves lives and creates such goodwill.

In 1992 she opened an underground needle exchange with the help of a local drug gang that organized drug users by passing out information and stood guard at street exchange locations. Later the exchange found a home in a church where the Young Lords had organized in the early seventies. Its priest explained the church's work through the same antisystem frame. "I look at drugs as a symptom," he told a *Newsday* reporter. "In an area with 60 percent unemployment, he [the local drug dealer] had 200 people on his payroll" (Mandel 1993: 6).

This frame allowed the church to act as a bridge between AIDS activists, drug dealers, and drug users, and the community. The church quickly became the center of local political activism, housing a local theater group that presented dramas on HIV and other social issues; a Chilean *peña* (coffeehouse featuring political folk music); a peer education program for women affected by HIV; an environmental group fighting a proposed incinerator; and an antiviolence program, in addition to the local needle exchange. Even the local drug dealer participated in these activities. "When the church was closed he would come here for some peace," explained the priest. "He would help with the soup kitchen" (Mandel 1993: 6).

In 1992, however, the gang leader was shot by another gang member and buried at the church he had served. Shortly after, the diocese removed the priest and despite weeks of parishioner protest, the priest and his supporters were unable to win the support of established social service agencies or politicians. The new church leadership asked the community organizations to leave the church. The needle exchange program moved to a more isolated area, diminishing its impact. In the months that followed, police arrested the remaining members of the local drug gang.

In Mott Haven, then, political corruption discouraged activists from forming alliances with politicians and social service agencies. Indeed, for most activists, local politicians were the problem, not the solution. As one activist observed, "We're hired by the Department of Welfare to be poor. They need poor people to work the system, to keep the bureaucrats in office. People say you believe in conspiracies but look what's happening—a lot of people working to keep unemployment rates up here." Even the drug users that participated in the needle exchange echoed this sentiment of cynicism and distrust, during the focus group I conducted: "Everyone sells out here." "Everyone is after the dollar." "AIDS is just another form of genocide."

Rather than work with local politicians or social service agencies, AIDS activists sought alliances with drug dealers, drug users, gang members, and prison inmates. An antisystem frame cemented these alliances. As the leader of a human rights group trying to organize young gang leaders argued:

> Velez is a politician like any politician. They are all part of the same machine. Drug dealers here are seen as heroes, they are independent and don't have to answer to the man. They are the ultimate rebels, they cross over every line they tell us not to cross.

A local gang member concurs: "society puts a lot of effort to get things the way they are. When you try to change that you're an outlaw."

WILLIAMSBURG: ETHNIC RIVALRY AND THE ANTICOLONIAL FRAME

In Williamsburg the conflict between the politically powerful Hasidic Jews and the large, politically weak Puerto Rican community encouraged Puerto Rican leaders to

frame local campaigns for equal representation and a larger share of community resources in terms of national and international anticolonial and independence struggles, particularly those in Puerto Rico and Latin America. As one activist explained,
"In Williamsburg you have a colonial situation. It's a white-run community. The
schools are a major source of jobs, power, and reinforcement of white power. The
Latino community doesn't get proper political representation. Oppression organizes
and motivates."

Williamsburg is among the oldest communities in Brooklyn. Originally a
wealthy German suburb, it became home to thousands of poor and working-class
Jews when the Williamsburg Bridge opened in 1903. By 1917 the neighborhood's
blocks ranked among the most densely populated in the city. In the following years,
the area became a central manufacturing area, attracting Italians, Hasidic Jews, and
Puerto Ricans. When industry left the city, thousands of Williamsburg's residents
were left without jobs.

In the sixties Williamsburg became the center of the heroin trade in Brooklyn.
Just as drugs became widespread, several pastors, influenced by liberation theology
and later by the Young Lords, began neighborhood organizing in areas controlled by
the street gangs. The first wave of protests in Williamsburg came out of this intersection of church and street activism.

In 1968 the citywide school strike by the teacher's union prompted a student uprising at Eastern District High School (in Williamsburg), forcing the resignation of a
school principal. Young Puerto Rican activists, supported by radical clergy and
VISTA volunteers and influenced by the Young Lords, led the movement. As a
leader of this movement recalled, "The Lords revived a sense of pride and identity in
Puerto Rican culture. Much of what is happening currently can be traced back to the
school struggles. Community activists' contacts were made then. It turned out to be
an investment in our future—this community networking."

In the seventies, a local church group and a group of VISTA volunteers joined
efforts to save the neighborhood from being destroyed by housing abandonment and
arson. Out of these efforts, Los Sures housing organization was formed. Its board
included most of the leaders of the 1968 school strike. One member recalled, "A lot
of what they got money for, the network of organizations and people, had been involved a long time—a hallmark of struggles from the people's community school
board."

Luis Olmedo, the first chairman of Los Sures, also organized strikes against
preferential treatment of the Hasidim in the public housing projects. "From 1964 to
1978 there were legal racial quotas in public housing—75 percent went to the Hasidim, 25 percent to nonwhites," explained a local legal aid lawyer who worked with
Olmedo. This allowed Olmedo to frame the housing movement as an anticolonial
campaign to defeat the Hasidim. Olmedo drew a link between the situation of the
island of Puerto Rico, struggling for independence, and Puerto Ricans in Williamsburg struggling for equal rights to public housing. "Olmedo was a nationalist," notes
another local activist, and as such "able to take advantage. The nationalists supported
anyone who supported independence." When he ran for council in 1973, "he swept."

By this time the Young Lords had dissolved, and the Puerto Rican Socialist
party (PSP, formerly the Pro-Independence Movement and the Puerto Rican equiva-
lent of the Communist party) began to play a key role in Williamsburg. It was the
PSP that continued much of the organizing work around housing in the seventies.
For the PSP, Puerto Rican independence and socialism were inextricably linked. The
PSP frame contained a mixture of Third World nationalist and socialist themes

which linked the situation of Puerto Ricans in New York to that of liberation movements in Puerto Rico and Latin America and to the island of Cuba. Only in Williamsburg did this frame resonate with the concerns of Puerto Rican New Yorkers. As one activist noted, "This is the only neighborhood where working-class people supported the Puerto Rican independence movement, although their efforts were focused on the Hasidic community [instead of the U.S. government]." The success of this frame encouraged PSP militants and *independentistas* from other neighborhoods to center their organizing efforts in Willliamsburg.

In 1986 a fourth wave of political activism began during a period of scandals involving the administration of Mayor Ed Koch, which opened new opportunities for political action. Again, local Puerto Rican activists mobilized residents against Hasidic control of public housing, school boards, and the local area policy board (an institution established to distribute antipoverty money) using an anticolonial frame. "The Area Policy Board was divided so that the Hasidim would get control," noted a long time local organizer. "People started talking to me about that. I said fine. We want all the seats. We're going to lay the groundwork here so that this community can win." In the next election, the Puerto Ricans won all of the seats.

Later that year the Puerto Rican community led a successful boycott over a wall built to portion off one part of the Eastern School District for a Hasidic girls' program. Still later, Puerto Rican activists sued the city for discrimination in the awarding of public housing. They held "massive meetings with several hundred people. We kept building the movement," explained a leader of the struggle. "The Hasidim are very organized," argued another. "That has helped the Latinos coalesce—people come out in droves."

In 1989 the organization that led the struggle for control of the Area Policy Board led the fight for a new Latino congressional district. Two years later, a leader of this effort was herself elected to represent Williamsburg and other sections of the city in the U.S. Congress. Although she won overwhelming support in African American neighborhoods, in the Latino neighborhoods she competed with three other Latino candidates in the Democratic primary. In Williamsburg she focused her campaign against the only white challenger, the incumbent. "She played the nationalist card in Williamsburg, which was the only Latino neighborhood where she won the primary," commented one of her campaign organizers.

During the congressional campaign, the leader of the 1968 school strike, two years in recovery for heroin addiction, found office space at campaign headquarters for his AIDS organization "Musica against Drugs." The high rate of drug addiction in Williamsburg, he argued, was a result of Puerto Rico's colonial status and the low self-esteem of Puerto Ricans living in the United States. "Self-esteem can be built through culture and identity. There is a lot of pain and suffering in drug addiction that society doesn't pay any attention to. Using our culture as an essential tool for organizing facilitates it for us" (Maldonado 1993).

Musica and the director of a local drug rehabilitation program (also a former drug user) then joined efforts to create an AIDS network. Their emphasis on Puerto Rican identity and culture built on the legacy of previous struggles between the Puerto Rican and Hasidic communities. These struggles forged a strong network of political activists, social service agencies (directed by former activists and interlocking directorates), and local politicians. The strength of these networks helped AIDS activists connect drug users to a larger Latino community. In a focus group conducted with the clients of Musica against Drugs, one participant observed, "What makes this community great is that when there's a problem the community gets together as one to fight."

Yet it is rare that Puerto Rican activists work with other groups in the neighborhood. In 1992, Puerto Rican leaders organized a Latino/Hasidic march across the Brooklyn Bridge to protest the planned construction of an incinerator in the Brooklyn Navy Yard. Although the march successfully blocked the incinerator, such events have been unusual. More often, as one local activist commented:

> The division between the Hasidim and the Puerto Ricans diverted residents from real issues. Rather than protest the scarcity of low-income housing, they focus on the Hasidim, "they have, we don't." It is easier to see the Hasidim, easier to explain to people, but it is dangerous. People react, get very ugly. Puerto Ricans here find it difficult to work with other groups. They never link to African Americans, for instance.

The strength of the Puerto Rican activist network, bound together since the school board strike in 1968, has also discouraged younger activists from joining political activity. "Young people don't care about the Hasidim," said one local activist.

Last, the focus on Puerto Rican identity has allowed local politicians to "play the nationalist card." The community supports politicians that back the Puerto Rican community in its fight against the Hasidim. Yet there is little effort to organize residents against the privatization of social services, the cuts in basic health care and welfare, or the scarcity of or current assault on low-income housing. As one local leader insisted:

> Nationalism still mobilizes—300 people showed up at the last town hall meeting, but there was no follow-up. Everyone screamed fight, fight, fight. After that, nothing. There is a spirit to fight but there is no leadership. We're in disarray. The Lower East Side is proactive, we're reactive.

In Williamsburg, then, the power differential between the Hasidic and Puerto Rican communities allowed Young Lords and PSP organizers to frame local Puerto Rican concerns as part of a broader anticolonial struggle. This frame helped AIDS activists connect local drug users to a larger Latino community. The failure, however, of local activists to distinguish between the imperialism of the U.S. government and the political power of local Hasidic Jews (only slightly less poor than the Puerto Ricans) meant that the ethnic nationalist theme tended to dwarf the socialist, weakening the ability of Puerto Rican activists to address underlying social issues or to respond to Republican initiatives.

LOWER EAST SIDE: A MULTIETHNIC CLASS-BASED FRAME

The Lower East Side differs from both Williamsburg and Mott Haven. In Mott Haven local struggles were shaped by the opposition between the political machine and radical activists. In Williamsburg they centered on competition between Hasidic Jews and Puerto Ricans. In the Lower East Side, in contrast to both, the central conflict was between low-income residents and wealthy real estate developers. This was largely a consequence of the neighborhood's proximity to Wall Street (which makes it a potentially valuable source of real estate), on the one hand, and its history as an immigrant enclave (with a consequent concentration of tenements, public housing projects, and social service agencies), on the other. As Janet Abu-Lughod observed of the Lower East Side, "This is a neighborhood whose unity has been forged in contest. . . . Housing was the one issue that always galvanized Lower East Siders into action" (1994: 38, 110). It was a conflict that encouraged the use of a class-based socialist frame.

The Lower East Side is among the oldest and most diverse neighborhoods in New York City. First populated by poor European immigrants, particularly European Jews, and then after World War II by Southern blacks, it became home to thousands of Puerto Ricans. Later, immigrants arrived from Asia, the Dominican Republic, and Poland. In this immigrant neighborhood, no ethnic group commands a majority, and organizing efforts have always transcended ethnic lines.

At the turn of the century, socialist and communist activists led most organizing efforts and framed these efforts around class and class-based issues. They mobilized residents of different ethnic backgrounds to campaign for reasonable rents and living conditions. The most active labor unions also organized here and were responsible for the construction of the city's first public housing projects. Activists also established immigrant settlement houses. When Puerto Ricans began to arrive in large numbers, many joined the left-wing organizations or labor unions that were already organizing in the neighborhood. As one activist explained, "When I arrived here from Puerto Rico I lived with a cousin who was active with the Young Socialist party. Later I joined a housing organization that was similar to one I had participated in Puerto Rico. All of the progressive organizations in the Lower East Side were ethnically diverse."

Other Puerto Ricans, however, entered the political system through local power brokers that promised jobs and resources to community groups in return for votes. Many of these new participants became leaders of tenant associations in public housing projects and guaranteed conservative white politicians the support of newer Puerto Rican migrants. The politicians, in turn, gave the presidents of these tenant unions access to resources, including political patronage and sway with the local police. Tenant association presidents received funds to create tenant patrol organizations, ostensibly to control crime, but better known for their brutality and their corruption.

When the Young Lords began to organize in the 1960s, the political structure in the Lower East Side was considerably different from that of their home base in East Harlem or from that in Mott Haven or Williamsburg. First, Puerto Ricans were not a majority in the Lower East Side nor the most radical group in the neighborhood. Second, most radical Puerto Rican leaders were already members of multiethnic left-wing organizations. Third, several new groups, including artists, hippies, anarchists, and assorted street people, had begun to play an important role in the Lower East Side. Lastly, a politicized street gang had been organizing in the Lower East Side since 1965 and had already received funding for an arts center and economic planning studio. It was a branch of this group that helped form the Young Lords in East Harlem and that worked with, and sometimes merged with, the Young Lords in the Lower East Side.

Between 1969 and 1972, then, the Young Lords worked with local Puerto Rican activists, poets, artists, and theater people to create artistic institutions that emphasized Puerto Rican culture. Simultaneously they supported local struggles around housing, including efforts to integrate the monolithic Jewish co-ops on Grand Street. All of the organizations involved in these struggles were multiethnic and served as bridges, facilitating a multiethnic class-based frame with an increasingly countercultural tone.

In 1974 a coalition of housing advocates, social service agencies, gay rights activists, and liberal politicians successfully challenged the local city councilman, who had been aligned with the Grand Street co-ops and the community board. The progressive candidate who took over as councilwoman was also Jewish, crosscutting ethnic divisions. During the eighteen-year period she controlled the city council, real estate developers backed opposition candidates in local races with little success. In 1989, however, they threw their support behind a Puerto Rican council candidate with connections to the tenant associations that controlled the housing projects. The candidate, Antonio Pagan, framed his campaign around "traditional family values" of Puerto Rican residents, linking ethnicity to a conservative agenda. He blamed his white liberal opponent for filling the Lower East Side with social service operations and low-income housing and "presiding over the deterioration of the Lower East Side." As one of his staff members commented:

> The councilwoman who presided over the Lower East Side for eighteen years was very pro-services, anti-development. She wasn't interested in empowering communities. It was a pejorative attitude toward the Latino community. The largest employer was the social service industry, "you can't do it for yourself." The community had become such a dump, people were afraid to walk. Tompkins Square was full of kids from wealthy, dysfunctional families, self-styled anarchists. It was insulting, a glorification of poverty, demeaning to legitimate people struggling to break the cycle of poverty. The silent majority.

Pagan won by 121 votes, partly a consequence of the redrawing of the district, but also with strong support in the housing projects controlled by the tenant associations. In his 1993 reelection campaign, Pagan attacked two local needle exchanges, blaming the liberal white councilwoman for the proliferation of drug abuse and crime.

Local AIDS activists suddenly found themselves in the cross fire of a political skirmish not of their own making. Their very success in organizing active drug users and giving them a sense of community had made them a key target for a conservative, ethnic-based campaign. On the one hand, they had created a large support network that included most of the health care providers, CBOs, artistic organizations, and progressive politicians in the neighborhood. This network was held together by a group of longtime activists and a frame that challenged both dominant cultural attitudes and economic elites. Lower East Side AIDS activists were also the most successful at organizing and unionizing drug users. On the other hand, the community board accused them of legitimizing "drug use on the Lower East Side and . . . inviting a population of predators into our community" (Lee 1994: A1).

In 1991 the AIDS activists found backing from several activists who had been active in previous community struggles. These activists formed a new organization, CODA (Coalition for a District 2 Alternative), to pose a Puerto Rican alternative to the current councilman and his allies. In 1993, CODA backed two local Puerto Rican activists for Democratic district candidates. They campaigned in the housing projects, using a class-based frame, attacking Pagan for his work with real estate developers and linking the situation of the tenements with the public housing projects. The real estate developers, argued one of the candidates (now a city council candidate), "understand that they can't develop the tenements until they can eliminate the housing projects. That is why they are supporting legislation to privatize the projects. Once they do that we will all have to leave the neighborhood. Just because a politician is Puerto Rican does not mean he's on our side."

In 1995 CODA ran candidates for the local school board, contributing the highest voter turnout of any district in the city. CODA's candidates won half the new seats. Next, CODA organized a campaign to preserve public housing and mobilize against a federal bill that would lift the cap on rents in the projects. This allowed them to further link the concerns of residents of the housing projects to those of the tenements. The successful mobilization, targeted at the bill's sponsors, helped defeat the bill and culminated in the council candidacy and later victory of the district leader, a Puerto Rican woman (Margarita Lopez) who led the campaign, and funded her insurgent candidacy with five-dollar (city-matched) donations from residents in public housing and tenements.

CONCLUSION

In each neighborhood, then, the structure of opportunities at the local level, in particular the distribution of political power and access, the availability of elite allies, and the opportunity to form coalitions, affected the success of different mobilizing messages or frames. These frames, in turn, shaped the collective identity of neighborhood groups, determining the strategies, discourse, and coalition partners of later AIDS activists.

In Williamsburg, for instance, the political power of the Hasidim encouraged Puerto Rican activists to use an anticolonial frame. This frame linked local struggles around housing, AIDS, and drug abuse to the independence and anticolonial struggles of Puerto Rico and Latin America. Activists were able to mobilize the Puerto Rican community by stressing cultural pride and identity and by targeting the Hasidim as colonialists. This helped AIDS activists to win support from local Puerto Rican CBOs and to connect drug users to a larger Latino community, but made it difficult for them to fight against cuts to public housing, health care, and welfare alongside other ethnic groups.

In the South Bronx, where Puerto Rican activists challenged a machine controlled by a Puerto Rican boss, activists used an antisystem frame, attacking the political system itself and the political parties and politicians associated with the system. Their celebration of the "outlaw," and their tendency to engage in direct action, helped AIDS activists work with drug dealers, street gangs, and prison inmates, but made it difficult for them to win support from local CBOs and politicians.

In the Lower East Side, activists successfully used a socialist frame, mobilizing residents of tenements against real estate developers, while encouraging class solidarity. Later, in the sixties they began using art and poetry to challenge the dominant culture, adding a countercultural element to the more traditional socialist frame. This frame helped AIDS activists work with both local drug users and community organizations to develop an alternative to the "drug war" and to the more punitive aspects of drug policy. In the late eighties, however, opponents countermoblized by using a traditional family values frame, attacking liberal politicians and activists for promoting welfare over work and for bringing "a population of predators into the neighborhood." Activists countered with a campaign focused on equal housing and protecting residents from soaring rents, culminating in the victory of the CODA leader Margarita Lopez.

These differences suggest several possible hypotheses for future work. First, the impact of types of political structures on social movement frames and the impact of such frames on later movement activists might be investigated. Previous studies suggest that the structure of the political system (unitary or federal, proportional or majority rule) may influence social movement frames, with federal and majoritarian systems encouraging ethnic-based frames, and unitary and proportional systems encouraging class- or ideology-based frames (Katznelson 1985; Schneider 1995). This study suggests that differences in the structure of local political systems may also influence frames. Where political districts are divided between two competing ethnic groups, with one holding differential access and power, for instance, nationalist or anticolonial frames may enable subordinate groups to challenge the right of the more dominant group to maintain political power. In this way, the federal district of Williamsburg may be similar to a unitary system like South Africa.

Where the majority ethnic group holds political access power, in contrast, successful framing may depend on characteristics of both the government and the excluded groups. If the entire district is poor, and the government corrupt, an antisystem frame might allow movement entrepreneurs to unite a variety of excluded groups. Where districts are multiclass, with multiple bridge organizations among ethnic groups, then a class-based frame may be more successful. If the government is left-wing, excluded ethnic groups may link ethnicity to a conservative frame.

Second, future studies should examine the ways in which social movement frames alter collective identities and cultures, leaving a residue for future movement organizers. In Chile, for instance, social movement activists were most successful when they framed their struggles in ways that resonated with previous political organizing efforts (Schneider 1995). Similarly, in New York AIDS activists were most successful when they tapped into frames that had mobilized residents during previous neighborhood conflicts. As Tarrow observes, a focus on framing would allow us to shift the discussion of political culture and identity from one "oddly disembodied" to one embedded in and shaped by politics and political struggle (1994: 119).

NOTES

1. Peter Eisenger (1973), Sidney Tarrow (1983, 1989b, 1994, 1996a), and Doug McAdam (1982) have demonstrated the impact of dynamic political opportunity structures (such as shifts in ruling alignments, the opening of new channels of participation, changes in the availability or strategic posture of influential allies, and the emergence cleavages among elites) on the timing of collective action. Others (Kriesi 1996; Kriesi et al. 1992; Tarrow 1994, 1996a) have shown the impact of variation in political opportunity on the strategies pursued by similar movements in different countries, localities, or arenas. The relative strength and degree of centralization of the state, and the pattern of linkage between interest groups, political parties, and government, affect the form, strength, and discourse of social movements.

REFERENCES

Abu-Lughod, Janet. 1994. *From Urban Village to East Village: The Battle for New York's Lower East Side*. Cambridge, MA: Blackwell.
Bayer, Sherrie. 1984. "Puerto Rican Politics in New York City: The Post World War II Period." Pp. in *Puerto Rican Politics in Urban America*, James Jennings and Monte Rivera, eds. Westport, CT: Greenwood Press.

Berck, Judith. 1995. "Williamsburg(h)." Pp. 1263-1264 in *The Encyclopedia of New York City*, Kenneth T. Jackson, ed. New Haven, CT: Yale University Press.

Currie, Eliot. 1993. *Reckoning: Drugs, Cities, and the American Future*. Berkeley: University of California Press.

Diani, Mario. 1996. "Linking Mobilization Frames and Political Opportunities: Insights from Regional Populism in Italy." *American Sociological Review* 61: 1053-1069.

Drucker, Ernest. 1994. "Epidemic in the War Zone: AIDS and Community Survival in New York." Spring. New York: Centro de Estudios Puertorriqueños.

Eisenger, Peter K. 1973. "Conditions of Protest in American Cities." *American Political Science Review* 67: 11-28.

Ellingson, Stephen. 1995. "Understanding the Dialectic of Discourse and Collective Action: Public Debate and Rioting in Antebellum Cincinnati." *American Journal of Sociology* 101: 100-144.

Gamson, William A. 1992. *Talking Politics*. Cambridge: Cambridge University Press.

Gamson, William, and David Meyer. 1996. "Framing Political Opportunity." Pp. 275-290 in *Comparative Perspectives on Social Movements: Political Opportunities, Mobilizing Structures, and Cultural Framings*, Doug McAdam, John D. McCarthy, and Mayer N. Zald, eds. New York: Cambridge University Press.

Gonzalez, Evelyn. 1995. "Mott Haven." Pp. 776-777 in *The Encyclopedia of New York City*, Kenneth T. Jackson, ed. New Haven, CT: Yale University Press.

Gramsci, Antonio. 1957. *The Modern Prince*. New York: International Publishers.

Guinier, Lani. 1994. *Tyranny of the Majority: Fundamental Fairness in Representative Democracy*. New York: The Free Press.

Hanson-Sanchez, Christopher. 1990. *New York City Latin Neighborhoods Data Book*. New York: Institute of Puerto Rican Policy.

———. 1995. *Puerto Rican Specific Data, Institute of Puerto Rican Policy: Census through 1990*. New York: Microdata Supplies.

Hodges, Graham. 1995. "Lower East Side," Pp. 696-697 in *The Encyclopedia of New York City*, Kenneth T. Jackson, ed. New Haven, CT: Yale University Press.

Jennings, James, and Monte Rivera, eds. *Puerto Rican Politics in Urban America*. Westport, CT: Greenwood Press.

Johnston, Hank, and Bert Klandermans. 1995. "The Cultural Analysis of Social Movements." Pp. 3-24 in *Social Movements and Culture*, Hank Johnston and Bert Klandermans, eds. Minneapolis: University of Minnesota Press.

Johnston, Hank, Enrique Laraña, and Joseph Gusfield. 1994. "Identity, Grievances, and New Social Movements." Pp. 3-35 in *New Social Movements: From Ideology to Identity*, Enrique Laraña, Hank Johnston, and Joseph Gusfield, eds. Philadelphia: Temple University Press.

Katznelson, Ira. 1981. *City Trenches Urban Politics and the Patterning of Class in the United States*. Chicago: University of Chicago Press.

———. 1985. "Working-Class Formation and the State: Nineteenth-Century England in American Perspective." Pp. 255-284 in *Bringing the State Back In*, Peter Evans, Dietrich Rueschemeyer, and Theda Skocpol, eds. Cambridge: Cambridge University Press.

Katznelson, Ira, and Aristide R. Zolberg. ed. 1986 *Working-Class Formation: Nineteenth-Century Patterns in Western Europe and the United States*, Ira Katznelson and Aristide R. Zolberg eds. Princeton, NJ: Princeton University Press.

Knoke, David. 1990. *Political Networks: The Structural Perspective*. Cambridge: Cambridge University Press.

Koopmans, Ruud. 1995. *Democracy from Below: New Social Movements and the Political System in West Germany* Boulder, CO: Westview Press.

Kriesi, Hanspeter. 1996. "The Organizational Structure of New Social Movements in a Political Context." Pp. 152-184 in *Comparative Perspectives on Social Movements: Political Opportunities, Mobilizing Structures, and Cultural Framings*, Doug McAdam, John D. McCarthy, and Mayer N. Zald, eds. New York: Cambridge University Press.

Kriesi, Hanspeter, Ruud Koopmans, Jan Willem Duyvendak, and Marco G. Giugni. "New Social Movements and Political Opportunities in Western Europe." *European Journal of*

Political Research 22: 219-244.

Lee, Felicia R. 1994. "Needle Exchange Programs Are Shown to Slow HIV Rates." *New York Times,* November 26, A1.

Lusane, Clarence. 1991. *Pipe Dream Blues: Racism and the War on Drugs.* Boston: South End Press.

Maldonado, Manuel. 1993. Personal interview by author.

Mandel, Jonathan. 1993. "Steady Survivor: St. Ann's is a Beacon to Neighbors." *Newsday:* 6

Marx, Anthony W. 1995. "Contested Citizenship: The Dynamics of Racial Identity and Social Movements." *International Review of Social History* 40 (Supplement 3): 159-183.

Massey, Douglas S., and Nancy A. Denton. 1993. *American Apartheid: Segregation and the Making of the Underclass.* Cambridge, MA: Harvard University Press.

McAdam, Doug. 1982. *Political Processes and the Development of Black Insurgency, 1930-1970.* Chicago: University of Chicago Press.

————. 1983. "Tactical Innovation and the Pace of Insurgency." *American Sociological Review* 48: 735-754.

————. 1994. "Culture and Social Movements." Pp. 36-57 in *New Social Movements: From Ideology to Identity,* Enrique Laraña, Hank Johnston, and Joseph R. Gusfield, eds. Philadelphia: Temple University Press.

————. 1996. "Conceptual Origins, Current Problems, Future Directions." Pp. 23-40 in *Comparative Perspectives on Social Movements: Political Opportunities, Mobilizing Structures, and Cultural Framings,* Doug McAdam, John D. McCarthy, and Mayer N. Zald, eds. New York: Cambridge University Press.

Meyer, David, and Nancy Whittier. 1994. "Social Movement Spillover." *Social Problems* 41: 277-298.

Morris, Aldon D. 1984. *The Origins of the Civil Rights Movement: Black Communities Organizing for Change.* New York: Free Press.

Morris, Aldon D., and Carol McClurg Mueller. 1992. *Frontiers in Social Movement Theory.* New Haven, CT: Yale University Press.

New York City Community Health Atlas 1994. 1994. New York: United Hospital Fund.

Office of Technology Assessment. 1995. "The Effectiveness of AIDS Prevention Efforts." Washington, DC: Office of Technology Assessment, Congress of the United States.

P'alante. 1969-1971. Newspaper published by the Young Lords Party.

Portes, Alejandro, and Julia Sensenbrunner. 1993. "Embeddedness and Immigration: Notes on the Social Determinants of Economic Action." *American Journal of Sociology* 98: 1320-1350.

Portes, Alejandro, and John Walton. 1976. *Urban Latin America: The Political Condition from Above and Below.* Austin: University of Texas Press.

Portes, Alejandro, and Min Zhou. 1993. "The New Second Generation: Segmented Assimilation and Its Variants." *Annals of the American Academy of Political and Social Science* 530: 74-91.

Putnam, Robert. 1993. *Making Democracy Work: Civic Traditions in Modern Italy.* Princeton, NJ: Princeton University Press.

Ragin, Charles C. 1987. *The Comparative Method: Moving beyond Qualitative and Quantitative Strategies.* Berkeley: University of California Press.

Ragin, Charles C., and Howard S. Becker. 1992. *What Is a Case? Exploring the Foundations of Social Inquiry.* Cambridge: Cambridge University Press.

Reed, Adolph, Jr. 1995. "Demobilization in the New Black Political Regime: Ideological Capitulation and Radical Failure in the Postsegregation Era." Pp. 182-208 in *The Bubbling Cauldron: Race, Ethnicity, and the Urban Crisis,* Michael Peter Smith and Joe R. Feagin, eds. Minneapolis: University of Minnesota Press.

Schneider, Cathy. 1995. *Shantytown Protest in Pinochet's Chile.* Philadelphia: Temple University Press.

Shefter, Martin. 1986. "Trade Unions and Political Machines: The Organization and Disorganization of the American Working Class in the Late Nineteenth Century." Pp. 197-276 in *Working-Class Formation: Nineteenth-Century Patterns in Western Europe and the*

United States, Ira Katznelson and Aristide R. Zolberg, eds. Princeton, NJ: Princeton University Press.

Smith, Carol, ed. 1990. *Guatemalan Indians and the State.* Austin: University of Texas Press.

Smith, Michael Peter, and Joe R. Feagin, eds. 1995. *The Bubbling Cauldron: Race, Ethnicity, and the Urban Crisis.* Minneapolis: University of Minnesota Press.

Snow, David A., and Robert Benford. 1992. "Master Frames and Cycles of Protest." Pp. 133-155 in *Frontiers in Social Movement Theory,* Aldon Morris and Carol McClurg Mueller, eds. New Haven, CT: Yale University Press.

Snow, David A., E. Burke Rochford, Jr., Steven K. Worden, and Robert D. Benford. 1986. "Frame Alignment Processes, Micromobilization, and Movement Participation." *American Sociological Review* 51: 464-481.

Snyder-Grenier, Ellen Marie. 1995. "East New York." P. 357 in *The Encyclopedia of New York City,* Kenneth T. Jackson, ed. New Haven, CT: Yale University Press.

Swidler, Ann. 1986. "Culture in Action: Symbols and Strategies." *American Sociological Review* 51: 273-286.

Tarrow, Sidney. 1983. *Struggling to Reform: Social Movements and Policy Change during Cycles of Protest.* Western Societies Program Occasional Paper No. 15. Ithaca, NY: New York Center for International Studies, Cornell University.

———. 1989a. *Democracy and Disorder: Protest and Politics in Italy, 1965-1975.* New York: Oxford University Press.

———. 1989b. *Struggle, Politics, and Reform: Collective Action, Social Movements, and Cycles of Protest.* Western Societies Program Occasional Paper No. 21. Ithaca, NY: Cornell University.

———. 1994. *Power in Movement: Social Movements, Collective Action, and Politics.* New York: Cambridge University Press.

———. 1996a. "States and Opportunities: The Political Structuring of Social Movements." Pp. 41-61 in *Comparative Perspectives on Social Movements: Political Opportunities, Mobilizing Structures, and Cultural Framings,* Doug McAdam, John D. McCarthy, and Mayer N. Zald, eds. New York: Cambridge University Press.

———. 1996b. "Making Social Science Work across Space and Time: A Critical Reflection on Robert Putnam's *Making Democracy Work.*" *American Political Science Review* 90: 389-397.

Taylor, Verta. 1989. "Social Movement Continuity: The Women's Movement in Abeyance." *American Sociological Review* 54 (5): 761-775.

Tilly, Charles. 1978. *From Mobilization to Revolution.* Reading, MA: Addison-Wesley.

———. 1993. "Contentious Repertoires in Great Britain, 1758-1834." *Social Science History* 17: 2.

———. 1995. *Citizenship, Identity, and Social History.* Cambridge: Cambridge University Press.

———. 1997. *Durable Inequality.* Berkeley: University of California Press.

Torres, Andres. 1995. *Between Melting Pot and Mosaic: African Americans and Puerto Ricans in the New York Political Economy.* Philadelphia: Temple University Press.

Wallace, R. 1987. "A Synergism of Plagues: 'Planned Shrinkage,' Contagious Housing Destruction, and AIDS in the Bronx." *Environmental Research* 47: 1-33.

———. 1990. "Urban Desertification, Public Health, and Public Order: 'Planned Shrinkage,' Violent Death, Substance Abuse, and AIDS in the Bronx. *Social Science and Medicine* 31: 801-813.

Zald, Mayer N. 1996. "Culture, Ideology, and Strategic Framing." Pp. 261-274 in *Comparative Perspectives on Social Movements: Political Opportunities, Mobilizing Structures, and Cultural Framings,* Doug McAdam, John D. McCarthy, and Mayer N. Zald, eds. New York: Cambridge University Press.

Part IV

Refining the Perspective

Chapter 9

WHAT A GOOD IDEA!
IDEOLOGIES AND FRAMES
IN SOCIAL MOVEMENT RESEARCH

Pamela E. Oliver and Hank Johnston

The study of social movements has always had one foot in social psychology and the other in political sociology, although at times these two sides have seemed to be at war with each other. In the 1950s and 1960s, social psychology dominated, and collective behavior theorists saw social movements as long-lasting panics or crowds. In the 1970s, proponents of resource mobilization criticized collective behavior theory and stressed the importance of political and organizational factors. In the 1980s, social psychologists criticized resource mobilization and political process theories for treating social movements only in organizational and political terms and neglecting the problems of social construction. Snow, Rochford, Worden, and Benford's 1986 article on "frame alignment processes" was central in the social psychological turn and is widely credited with "bringing ideas back in."[1] Framing theory has provided a way to link ideas and social construction of ideas with organizational and political process factors.

Not surprisingly, frame theory has itself been criticized. Benford's "insider's critique" (1997) lists several shortcomings in the way the concept is applied in research studies and asserts that the term has become a cliché (p. 415). "Framing" is often inserted uncritically wherever there is a movement-related idea being defined or debated. It has been pointed out that the concept of frame does not do justice to the ideational complexity of a social movement (Munson 1999) and that it tends to reduce the richness of culture to recruitment strategies (Jasper 1997: 76). Steinberg (1998) criticizes frame theory as too static and stresses the contextual and recursive qualities of frames.

None of these critiques has identified what we consider to be two central problems in frame theory: its failure to address the relation between frames and the much older, more political concept of ideology, and the concomitant tendency of many researchers to use "frame" uncritically as a synonym for "ideology." Snow and Benford (1988) are often given credit for insights adopted from the older literature on the functions of and constraints on social movement ideologies and renamed as framing tasks and constraints on frames. Their article clearly credits this older literature and specifically says that they are drawing on the older literature to develop insights about framing processes. In this and their subsequent articles, they use the terms *frame* and *ideology* distinctly and explicitly cite older works. Nevertheless, they neither provide justification for abandoning the term "ideology" and substituting "frame" in this context nor explain the relation between frames and ideologies. Subsequent scholars have tended to cite the Snow and Benford article and its framing language as the original work in the area, and to use the terms "frame" and "ideology" interchangeably. This leads to muddled frame theory, diverts attention from a serious examination of ideology and its social construction, and avoids questioning relation between frames and ideologies.

Frames and framing processes are powerful concepts. Frame theory's insight into how movement activists construct their self-presentations so as to draw support from others is an important process. This line of theorizing has been extraordinarily productive of new research and new understandings of social movements. In seeking to back up and revisit a particular turn in framing theory, we should not be understood as trying to discount the value of a whole line of work. Nevertheless, the power of frame theory is lost if "frame" is made to do the work of other concepts. Ideology is of central importance in understanding social movements and other political formations, and it is trivialized when it is seen only as a frame. We need both concepts, and we need to understand the relation between them.

This is seen most starkly in movements for and against legal abortion. As Luker (1984) argues, these movements are rooted in deeply held ideologies and understandings of the meaning and purpose of a woman's life, as well as in the professional ideologies of physicians. Strong antiabortion beliefs were in the 1960s rooted in Catholic doctrine, which links sexuality to procreation, condemns artificial birth control, and condemns killing a fetus even to save the life of the mother (two deaths are morally superior to one murder); people who live according to these doctrines build lives in which pregnancies can be accommodated. As the abortion struggles evolved, conservative Protestants also adopted antiabortion ideologies that do not necessarily contain all the elements of the coherent Catholic worldview, but strong antiabortion sentiment remains deeply rooted in religious traditions and religious worldviews. Those with strong antiabortion ideologies reject abortion even for the "strict constructionist" reason of saving the mother from the immediate risk of death, although laws permitting such abortions do not outrage their moral sense. Initial impetus for abortion reform was rooted in physicians' desire to clarify the "broad constructionist" views of the medical necessity for abortion, which would include severe deformity of the fetus and threats to the mother's life and well-being such as the physical strains of excessive pregnancies or illnesses, psychological distress, and financial hardship. For physicians, the issue was the right to practice medicine in good conscience, unconstrained by others' religiously motivated intrusions. Physicians were not supporting "abortion on demand," but rather the ideology of themselves as the proper arbiters of medical necessity. As the women's movement energized and joined the abortion debate, feminists developed an ideology stressing women's autonomy and need to control their own bodies. As Luker argues, women in the labor force saw pregnancy as capable of disrupting a person's life, valued sex for enjoyment and intimacy, and wanted to choose when to have children so that they could devote proper attention to them.

Simply renaming these three ideological strands as frames (e.g., religious, medical necessity, women's need) would add nothing to the analysis and would, in fact, risk obscuring the complexity of the belief systems. But this does not mean that frames are unimportant or irrelevant in these debates. Rather, the frame concepts are most powerful precisely if they are sharply distinguished from ideology. The ways in which actors have self-consciously positioned the issue over time is very different from what one would think from a simple extrapolation of the underlying ideologies. Several examples illustrate this. First, Luker argues that the 1972 *Roe v. Wade* Supreme Court decision essentially framed abortion as a church-state issue: those who filed friend of the court briefs against abortion reform were all religious organizations, while those who filed briefs for abortion reform represented a broad spectrum of professional and secular organizations. The decision was constructed in the context of a recent decision that had overturned laws against the sale of contraceptives as representing an unwarranted intrusion of the state and particular religious beliefs into the personal lives of people. Beliefs about abortion were seen (framed) as religious beliefs. Second, the self-naming of each movement in the politics of the 1970s is a framing turn. From antiabortion and pro-abortion, the sides renamed themselves as pro-life and pro-choice as the pro-life movement sought to position itself in a secular space to reach out to people who did not necessarily share their religious views, and the pro-choice movement repositioned itself to emphasize its defense of contraception and personal responsibility, with abortion as a necessary backup to failed contraception. Third, both sides have adopted the civil rights master frame. The pro-life movement stresses the right of the fetus to life, while the pro-choice movement stresses the right of the woman to control a fundamental aspect of her life. If we think of frames as synonymous with ideologies, we will lack the analytic tools, even the very language, for talking about this fascinating instance of the same frame being tied to diametrically opposed ideologies. If we keep the concepts clearly differentiated, we have some vocabulary and tools for talking about how people present their issues in a public space, and we avoid the danger of simply extrapolating ideologies from their public presentations.

We suggest that the turn toward framing and away from ideology was largely due to the legacy of pejorative theories of ideology that laced the social movement writings in the early 1970s. A second agenda of this chapter is to revisit this pejorative legacy and call for a rehabilitated, nonpejorative understanding of ideology in the study of social movements. There is a huge literature on ideology to which this chapter cannot do justice. Our goal is to revisit the debates that were abandoned in the 1970s and suggest directions in which a rehabilitated theory of movement ideology should move.

The plan of this chapter is as follows. First we summarize the history of the frame concept and its roots in linguistics and cognitive psychology; then we review the history of the ideology concept and its roots in the study of politics. We then discuss the advantages of keeping these concepts separate and explore the important issues that are highlighted by considering the relations between frames and ideologies. We suggest that frame alignment theory correctly captures some of the important particulars of U.S. political culture in the 1990s, but is misleading for other problems, especially for movements in other times and other places.

A FRAME IS A FRAME IS A FRAME

The frame concept is rooted in the study of communicative interaction. Gregory Bateson introduced the notion of a frame as a metacommunicative device that sets parameters for "what is going on" ([1954] 1972). He showed that interaction always involves interpretative frameworks by which participants define how others' actions and words should be understood. Twenty years later, frame analysis was introduced to sociological research by Erving Goffman. In *Frame Analysis* (1972) and *Forms of Talk* (1981) Goffman explored types and levels of framing activities. In *Forms of Talk*, Goffman discussed the several layers of framing in interaction, and shifted his focus to linguistic analysis of conversational conventions that mark the application and changes in interpretative frames. Researchers building on Goffman's work have developed an extensive body of empirical knowledge about how speech occurs, how cultural knowledge is used, and how these interplay with interactional intentions and constraints; but this body of knowledge has not been utilized by social movement approaches to framing.

Within the linguistic tradition, there is divergence between those who treat a frame (or its synonyms, script and schema) as a relatively fixed template and those who treat it as malleable and emergent. Work in anthropological linguistics views frames as fully formed cognitive structures that constitute part of the cultural tool kit of everyday life. Frames are an aspect of cultural knowledge, stored in memory, that permit social actors to move in and out of different experiences as if they were not completely new. Frames are used to explain speech acts, rituals, and commonly occurring behaviors in other cultures (Hymes 1974; Frake 1964). The assumption is that the elements of frames can be elicited through ethnographic interview and reconstituted into a working schema or algorithm. This approach has also been adopted by researchers in artificial intelligence to explain speech behavior in everyday situations such as joking, gossiping, doing business, lecturing, shooting the bull, and so on (Schank and Ableson 1977; Minsky 1974, cited in Tannen 1993).

The other way to view a frame is as an inherently malleable and emergent mental construct. In Bartlett's terms, it is an "active developing structure" (1932) shaped in action and interaction as additional elements are added to existing structures based on new, incoming data. Frames are the instruments by which we infer "what is going on," with the caveat that they are under constant revision based on new occurrences and unexpected actions by others. Many ethnographic linguists stress the malleability of frames by asserting that the proper unit of analysis is an interactional event or activity. Frake, for example, points out that people are "doing something all the time" and that these activities, not "mental structures," are the proper units of analysis. Gumperz (1982) adds that when people speak, they do things with their words within culturally typical speech situations. Frake offers a poignant metaphor for the fluid and interactive view of frames: Rather than providing a few fixed cognitive maps to be unrolled and referenced to make sense of situations, culture gives people "a set of principles for mapmaking and navigation, resulting in a whole chart case of rough, improvised, continually revised sketch maps" (1977: 6-7).

Imported into the study of social movements, frames have been treated as both fixed and emergent. Early insights into framing focused almost wholly on the interactive level of analysis. In *Encounters with Unjust Authority* (1982), Gamson, Fireman, and Rytina created artificial focus groups of strangers who gradually were made aware that they were being manipulated into giving false statements on camera that could be used deceitfully in a civil lawsuit. This research focused on the emergence of a frame, of a shared understanding of "what's going on" that they labeled an "injustice frame," and how collective recognition of this frame was essential for rebellion against authority. A few years later, Snow and his colleagues. (1986) discussed the improvised and processual quality of sketch-map frames by elaborating frame alignment processes.

Subsequent elaborations of the framing perspective moved to a more fixed conception of collective action frames, even though the most influential scholars of framing have consistently stressed emergent and processual aspects of framing tasks. This paradoxical effect has occurred for two reasons. First, the concept of *frame resonance* (Snow et al. 1986) gave individual cognitive schemata an organizational dimension by making their generation a strategic task of social movement organizations (SMOs), namely, to link the movement's frame to existing beliefs and values. By "strategically framing" movement positions in accord with dominant values and folk beliefs, the SMO elicits greater participation. While strategic framing is a process, the emphasis is on the content. When a collective action frame is recast as something that leaders must articulate to better "market the movement," the interactive negotiation of "what's going on here" takes a back seat to a one-way, top-down process. The sketch maps are drawn up by the leaders to be passed on to the grass roots. Simultaneously, the cultural beliefs of the targets of these efforts are also viewed as relatively fixed, with framers merely putting the right "spin" on their issue to tap into these fixed preconceptions. It would be foolish to deny the importance of these processes in the United States in the 1990s, but few scholars with a sense of history would want to say that this is all there is to idea making in social movements.

The second source of fixity in framing theory is the growing use of the master frame concept. Master frames are linked to cycles of protest, and they work at the most general level of analysis to "turn the heads" of movement participants and movement entrepreneurs to see issues a certain way. Movement participants draw upon master frames to portray their perceived injustice in ways that fit the tenor of the times and thus parallel other movements. Snow and Benford (1992) cite as one example the psychosalvational master frame which TM, est, Scientology, Silva Mind Control, and other groups drew upon in the 1970s. Another example is the "rights frame" which was defined by the Southern civil rights movement, picked up by other racial/ethnic movements and the women's movement, and diffused to gay rights, animal rights, abortion rights, fetal rights, and student rights. Master frames are general assemblages of concepts that are often new and ascendant, but relatively unelaborated compared to established ideologies. They are often articulated by early-riser movements and then used by late-comer movements (Swart 1995; Carroll and Ratner 1996; see also Williams 1995 for "rhetorical models" which are utilized rather than master frames).

We draw four conclusions regarding frame analysis as it is currently practiced. First, frames are individual cognitive structures, located "within the black box of mental life," that orient and guide interpretation of individual experience. Frames "enable individuals to locate, perceive, identify and label occurrences" (Snow et al. 1986: 464) and "selectively punctuate and encode objects, situations, events, experiences and sequences of actions within one's present and past environment" (Snow and Benford 1992: 137). They are complex interpretative schemata—not just isolated ideas—which are relevant at different levels of experience. Second, frames become important in analyzing collective action insofar as they are shared by enough individuals to channel individual behaviors into patterned social ones. This presumes an ideal-typical formulation of a frame that rises above both idiosyncratic differences between participants and the contention, negotiation, and emergence that characterizes discursive behavior about the frames. This aggregated notion freezes the buzzing and swirling confusion of individual cognitive processing at a point in time, enabling comparisons at other points of time. Third, this snapshot of a frame is a methodological artifice that, in the best of worlds, enables an inventory of what cognitive orientations are shared by individual participants. Ideally, there would be some representations of the concepts and their interrelations to show how thinking within the frame occurs, but with very few exceptions (Gerhards and Rucht 1992; Johnston 1995) this kind of plotting is not found in the social movement literature.

Fourth, it is important to distinguish between these "snapshots," which represent the structure of cognitive frames, and framing processes which capture the contested and socially constructed quality of frames as they are molded in interaction. Frames are mental structures or schemata. Framing is a behavior by which people make sense of both daily life and the grievances that confront them. Frame theory, therefore, embraces both cognitive structures whose contents can be elicited, inferred, and plotted in a rough approximation of the algorithms by which people come to decisions about how to act and what to say, and the interactive processes of talk, persuasion, arguing, contestation, interpersonal influence, subtle rhetorical posturing, and outright marketing that modify—indeed, continually modify—the contents of interpretative frames. Applied to social movement studies, we can see instances of framing at the SMO level and, if we looked closely, we would see them in interaction at the membership level.

THE PEJORATIVE LEGACY OF IDEOLOGY

Ideology arose in a revolutionary era from politics and the study of politics. From the beginning, it carried evaluative and politicized connotations. The word *ideology* was coined in 1796 by the French writer A. L. C. Destutt de Tracy for his own "science of ideas" (influenced by John Locke), which emphasized verification of knowledge to create a program for democratic, rational, and scientific society (Cranston 1994; Rudé 1980). The word first took on a pejorative connotation in 1803 when the "ideologues" were suppressed by Napoleon Bonaparte. Marx and Engels adopted the pejorative meaning when they called ideology the class-motivated deceptions of the bourgeoisie, which they contrasted with the scientifically correct understandings of a class-conscious proletariat. Opponents of Marx soon countered by labeling Marxism itself as a distorting ideology, which they contrasted with objective theories of liberal democracy and the market.

Despite this pejorative tradition, there are also examples of ideology's nonpejorative—and even positive—usage, especially in twentieth-century political science. As Gerring (1997) documents in his extensive review, "ideology" has taken on a diversity of meanings, which are often directly opposed to each other. In the nonpejorative sense, some political scientists use the term to distinguish people with coherent and well-structured rational belief systems from those with inconsistent or illogical belief systems (Converse 1964). Others use it to refer to any belief system, regardless of its internal consistency (see Nelson 1977 for a discussion of these issues). Additionally, political scientists and many sociologists use "ideology" to refer to the belief system of any social movement. Among those who use the pejorative meaning of the term, there is a split between those who associate "ideology" with the defense of privilege and those who associate it with challenges to the system (Weberman 1997). Despite these evaluative and political debates, there is a common thread of shared meaning in the nonpejorative senses of "ideology" which is captured by no other term. Gerring (1997) concludes, "Ideology, at the very least, refers to a set of ideas—elements that are bound together, that belong to one another in a non-random fashion."

Scholars in the collective behavior tradition drew on these meanings when they wrote about ideology, and their works suffered from failing to sort out the pejorative and nonpejorative usages in their discussions. Nevertheless, the core of their work provides a solid basis for investigating ideology in its nonpejorative sense as the system of meaning undergirding a social movement. Heberle, in his 1951 text *Social Movements: An Introduction to Political Sociology*, defines the ideology of a movement in "a broad, nontechnical sense" as "the entire complex of ideas, theories, doctrines, values and strategic and tactical principles that is characteristic of the movement" (pp. 23-24). The second edition of Turner and Killian's *Collective Behavior* has a very similar conception: "Ideologies are prescriptions or maps that tell the individual how to look at events and people, and they provide a simplifying perspective through which the observer can make sense of otherwise overwhelmingly complex phenomena and find definiteness in otherwise vague and uncertain impressions. Ideologies tell the observer how to distinguish figure from ground" (1972: 270). Wilson's *Introduction to Social Movements* (1973) defines ideology as "a set of beliefs about the social world and how it operates, containing statements about the rightness of certain social arrangements and what action would be undertaken in the light of those statements." He continues: "An ideology is both a cognitive map of sets of expectations and a scale of values in which standards and imperatives are proclaimed. Ideology thus serves both as a clue to understanding and as a guide to action, developing in the mind of its adherents an image of the process by which desired changes can best be achieved" (Wilson 1973: 91-92).

Both Wilson and Turner and Killian take a functionalist approach to ideology, stressing what it does for a social movement in terms of providing an account of reality and justifying and motivating action. Wilson develops the very useful trichotomy of the structural elements of ideology which Snow and Benford adopted: diagnosis (how things got to be how they are), prognosis (which should be done and what the consequences will be), and rationale (who should do it and why). Turner and Killian emphasize ideology as a product of active social construction processes by which people understand their circumstances and their possible courses of action. Both discussions mostly emphasize the continuity between movement ideologies and other forms of meaning making, and each has passages suggesting that movements' opponents may be no more logical and just as ideological as the movements themselves. Turner and Killian stress that movement and antimovement ideologies develop dialectically. They argue, for example, that racist ideology developed in response to challenges to racial stratification and that the ideology of divine right of kings developed in response to challenges to monarchy.

At the same time, pejorative connotations make their way into all these presentations. Heberle approvingly cites Mannheim's definition of ideology as the inconsistent and illogical distortions of the ruling class, as contrasted with the challenger's rational and coherent Utopia (Heberle 1951: 28). Turner and Killian say ideologies "provide a simplifying perspective" (1972: 270), and Wilson says they "create highly simplified images of social process" (1973: 99). In context, these statements may refer to the cognitive process by which attention is directed to some elements at the expense of others; and all three authors recognize that some ideologies, particularly radical ones, are highly elaborated. However, these same contexts have other cues suggesting that this simplification is inappropriate or irrational, especially their citations of Smelser. Smelser (1962) did not use the term "ideology," but he made simplification and illogic central to movement belief systems. His notion of a generalized belief represents a cognitive "short-circuit" that leaves out complex and multideterminant steps between general principle and specific change. Turner and Killian cite Smelser and endorse his claim that movement ideologies include hostile elements, arguing that "villain and conspiracy themes are universal" and that "the visible effects of their [villains'] evil intent are supplemented by imaginary activities" (1972: 272). They do, however, suggest that this reasoning parallels that of the social control agents. Wilson also summarizes Smelser, but his text neither clearly endorses nor clearly critiques Smelser's arguments.

Despite their failure to overcome pejorative connotations, the works of Wilson and Turner and Killian point to a social constructionist view of ideology that has been missing from recent scholarship. The concept of ideology focuses on ideas, on their systematic relations to each other, and on their implications for social and political action based on value commitments. A tentative definition (based heavily on Wilson's) would capture this core meaning: a system of meaning that couples assertions and theories about the nature of social life with values and norms relevant to promoting or resisting social change. The "values" element refers to moral, ethical, or solidaristic commitments to some groups or social conditions as right or wrong, good or bad, moral or immoral, important or unimportant. The "norms" element refers to standards for behavior, especially behaviors relevant to promoting or resisting social change. The reference to "assertions and theories about the nature of social life" encompasses both simple descriptive claims (e.g., men have more power than women) and elaborate theories (including social science theories as well as religious or political belief systems) about how society works, and everything in between.

To study ideology, then, is to focus on systems of ideas which couple understandings of how the world works with ethical, moral, and normative principles that guide personal and collective action. We can ask how these ideas came to be, what the internal structure of the idea system is, whether the ideology accounts adequately for the phenomena it purports to explain, how the ideologies are distributed across populations, and what the variations are among proponents of a common ideology (see Gerring 1997 and Nelson 1977 for further elaboration of these points and others). Significantly, we suggest that an ideology links a theory about society with a cluster of values about what is right and wrong as well as norms about what to do. We use the term "theory" in a broad sense to refer to systems or sets of beliefs that explain how social arrangements came to be and how they might be changed or strengthened. These theories are linked to core values and norms in an ideological system. Value components animate the theory, and go a long way toward translating individual grievances into collective ones. If groups have the same values but different social theories, we would tend to think of them as different branches of the same social movement, such as the religious and secular branches of the civil rights movement. The socialist movement always contained groups advancing diverse and competing social theories which were nevertheless unified by their positive valuation of the lower strata of society and opposition to capitalism. By the same token, groups with similar social theories may be in opposing movements. There are both pro- and anticapitalist ideologues who share the assumption of rational individualism and a theory about how a capitalist market economy works, but disagree about whether to support or oppose capitalism and about whether they attach greater value to the entrepreneur or the worker. Similarly, groups may have similar norms for action (e.g., an ethic of self-sacrifice, advocacy of disruptive protest, or legislative lobbying) around widely different or even opposite values.

As part of the pejorative legacy of ideology it is often argued that movement activists are resistant to evidence or arguments that challenge their beliefs (Turner and Killian 1972: 249; Wilson 1973: 108-124). But distinguishing an ideology's value commitments from its theory may clarify some of these processes. Because an ideology links theory, norms, and values in one interconnected system, what may seem to outsiders to be an unreasonable attachment to a belief or norm can frequently be understood as a defense of core values by defending the whole belief system in which they are embedded. Conversely, what may seem to outsiders to be vacillation in belief or abandonment of prior beliefs may be seen by activists as a realistic reappraisal of their theory of society or their strategies as they seek better ways to pursue their core values. Distinguishing core values of an ideology from its norms and theory, and tracing the interrelations among them, may be helpful strategies for understanding how people construct and reconstruct their ideologies.

Emphasizing the theory component in ideology points to an element of ideation often neglected in the study of social movements: thinking. People think a lot in social movements, along with the related activities of reasoning, judging arguments, evaluating evidence, testing predictions, recognizing connections, and developing new knowledge. There is a continuity in the theorizing of ideologues and the theorizing of those who study ideologues. Heberle argues, "The ideologies of social movements stand to each other in a twofold relationship: first, as the integrating creeds and immaterial weapons of social groups in conflict with one another. . . . But there is a second kind of relationship between ideologies; that is the relationship between ideas in the realm of intellectual endeavor" (1951: 29-30). It is essential to appreciate the intellectual aspects of ideology (what Heberle calls the debate of ideas over the centuries) as well as their function in motivating action. The theories in ideologies can be understood as part of intellectual history and subjected to the same standards of logic and evidence as any other theories (Nelson 1977). Social networks, especially among small groups of intellectuals, are central in creating new theories and new ideologies. Rochon (1998: 22-25) calls these networks "critical communities," loci of ideological production. He distinguishes this ideological production from movement activities, particularly framing, which promote the ideas to a wider public. In this view, framing does not create ideological change, but can be a way of recruiting people into a context within which ideology can change.

There is a long history in ideological studies of questioning the origin of ideas and their fit with "reality" or "material interests." Snow and Benford (1988) point to these issues when they say frames need "experiential commensurability," but their awkward neologism elides the complexities of this issue. Materialism and the constraints on beliefs were treated with much more subtlety and greater constructionist insight by Turner and Killian, Wilson, and others upon whom they drew. Scholars in the Marxian tradition, such as Rudé (1980), have also developed social constructionist perspectives on ideology which link material constraints to social processes.

FRAME AND IDEOLOGY ARE NOT SYNONYMS

Frames and ideologies are related concepts, of course, and overlap somewhat in their empirical referents, but each points to different dimensions of social construction. Very roughly, framing points to process, while ideology points to content.

The concept of *frame* points to the cognitive process wherein people bring to bear background knowledge to interpret an event or circumstance and to locate it in a larger system of meaning. Framing processes are the ways actors invoke one frame or set of meanings rather than another when they communicate a message, thereby indicating how the message is to be understood. In everyday interaction, framing is often done tacitly by subtle linguistic and extralinguistic cues. Applied to social movement studies, framing processes mostly refer to the intentional activity of movement entrepreneurs at the organizational level (see Tarrow 1998: 108-112). The frame concept calls attention to the ways in which movement propaganda reflects both the frames of the writers and their perceptions of their targets. The malleable conception of a frame calls attention to everyday interactional processes in a movement organization and between movement participants and outsiders. The fixed conception of a frame has its greatest power when one frame is contrasted with another, when the question is how and why a person invokes one frame rather than another in a particular context. Clearly the concepts of frames and framing processes point to matters that the older ideology concept dealt with only obliquely, and for this reason they are important contributions to the understanding of social movements.

But there are other ideational processes that are obscured when authors try to make the concept of frame do the work of ideology. *Ideology* focuses attention on the content of whole systems of beliefs, on their multiple dimensions, and on how ideas are related to each other. Ideologies as sets of ideas can be abstracted from the thought processes of any particular individual. They can be elicited through interviews with movement participants, or written in books, articles, and pamphlets by movement intellectuals, or declaimed from platforms by leaders. The concept of ideology leads to questions about the origins of those ideas, their interrelations and consistency with each other and with other systems of ideas in the larger society, and the processes whereby people reconstruct their ideas as they encounter new ideas and accumulate experiences. It leads to questions about how the elaborated systems of intellectuals are related to folk ideologies of ordinary people (see Rudé 1980 on derived ideologies) and how these ideas are related to material circumstances. The concept of ideology leads us into the large literature that has used the concept and addressed these questions, offering a very wide variety of answers.

One can ask ideology questions while using the word "frame," but to do this you have to rework the meaning of frame away from its origin as a mental structure that orients interpretation and make it more like a thin ideology. Consider institutional racism. Frame theory can point to the need to have background knowledge to understand the concept, and to the fact that people who don't have this background may assume that the "racism" component refers to personal prejudice. It could help us study the alternative ways a particular racially charged incident was framed or understood. For its part, ideology would lead us to a theory of institutional racism, and to its diagnosis, prognosis, and rationale. Thinking of the ideology of institutional racism would lead to understanding where these ideas came from and to asking whether the theory of society seems correct according to some external standard and what its value and normative components are. But what happens when we make "ideology" and "frame" synonymous? We no longer have a vocabulary for distinguishing between the complex set of ideas and its invocation in a particular instance. Calling the diagnosis, prognosis, and rationale separate "framing tasks" or trying to distinguish among them obscures their fundamental unity as dimensions of the same coherent system of ideas.

Frame concepts have made great contributions to our understanding of social movements, but sometimes research in a framing perspective would be more illuminating if ideology instead of frames were invoked, when the data seem clearly to point to ideological issues. Benford (1993) develops the concept of frame disputes and distinguishes types of disputes (diagnostic, prognostic, and resonance), seeking to identify the predictors of each. But the axis along which most of the disputes in his data turned was the ongoing battle among moderates, liberals, and leftist radicals, and the disputes were more unified by their ideological underpinnings in competing social theories than distinguished by their emphasis on diagnosis, prognosis, or resonance. In framing terms, Carroll and Ratner's 1996 study of the correlation of cross-movement activism with master frames in different Vancouver SMOs seems quite different from Benford's. Their coding of interviewees' views of "injustice and domination" identified three master frames: political-economy/injustice, liberal, and identity.[2] Those giving the political-economy/injustice frame had the most cross-movement activism, while those giving the identity frame had the least. But in ideology terms, Benford's and Caroll and Ratner's studies seem very similar, with the same three strands appearing in both. Frame theory cannot explain why the frame disputes occurred nor why these master frames led to different patterns of activism. But interrogation of the ideologies of the liberals and the political-economy/injustice radicals could well explain the results of both studies, showing how the liberals view issues one at a time, while the political economy/injustice radicals link different specific issues in an overarching critique of society—and demonstrating that the same ideological conflicts occur in both Vancouver and Austin.

MARKETING AND RESONATING VERSUS EDUCATION AND THINKING

When framing processes are seen as distinct from although related to ideology, frame theory makes real contributions to social movements theory. But as a substitute for ideology, frames are woefully incomplete: they offer too shallow a conception of what is involved in developing ideologies and a one-dimensional view of how others adopt them. Ideologies are complex and deeply held. People learn them or are socialized into them. While a framing effort may successfully persuade someone that a particular issue can be explained by an ideology, framing processes do not persuade people to adopt whole new ideologies. At best, they may initiate the journey.

Frame alignment concepts and theories of ideology suggest very different accounts of the creation of ideas by movement intellectuals and the transmission of ideas to new recruits. It is recognized that intellectuals or "idea specialists" in social movements play different roles from the mass of other participants. In frame alignment, people's belief systems are taken largely as givens, and movement intellectuals perform the marketing task of packaging their issue so that it will be accepted by others. Three of the four "frame alignment" processes (Snow et al. 1986) involve taking others' ideologies as largely given and either bridging movement ideas to a new group, amplifying existing beliefs, or extending one's own interpretations to address others' concerns. The movement activists are never thought to change their actual thinking—just the way they package their thinking to make it more appealing to someone else.[3]

Significantly, this marketing approach to movement mobilization arises precisely when marketing processes have come to dominate social movements in the Untied States. Activists all over the country spend their time trying to figure out how to sell their ideas in advertisements and grant proposals. Frame alignment captures the reality of important empirical processes in the contemporary era. The New Left movements of the late 1960s made Daniel Bell seem premature when he proclaimed the end of ideology in 1960, but an emphasis on ideology does seem largely invisible in U.S. social movements after the 1980s. But ideology and ideological thinking are not really dead, not even in the United States. People still have ideologies, and ideologies still underlie action. What seems out of fashion right now is overt public discussion in terms of ideology, that is, in terms of theories of society coupled with explicit discussion of values and norms. The most visible ideologues as we write are those advocating unfettered markets and religiously governed sexual mores, but even their ideologies are rarely discussed as coherent systems. This feature of current U.S. politics should not blind us to the overt importance of ideology and ideological thinking in other historical eras, and in other parts of the world, nor to the continuing covert importance in our own society of ideology.

Although ideologies vary in their complexity and consistency, to use the concept is to evoke the image of people as thinkers. They are not just resonating with a frame, not just reacting to quick impressions while holding a TV remote, and not even interpreting cues in social interaction. When people are thinking ideologically, they are explicitly concerned with a theory of society, values, and norms and with creating a comprehensive and consistent understanding of the world. Not everyone thinks this way, and no one thinks this way all the time. But some people do some of the time, especially in social movements.

Ideologies cannot just be "resonated with," they have to be learned. Systematic ideologies are often developed by educated group members, usually in intellectual dialogue with prior ideas, ideologies, and cultural values (see Rochon 1998, chap. 3). "The masses" come to adopt systematic ideologies through processes of education and socialization. As Portes (1971), Wood and Hughes (1984), and others have argued, systematic ideologies are not something individuals create for themselves or fall into from accidents of daily life, but are rather belief systems that people are educated or socialized into. These processes take time and involve social structures and social networks. Sometimes, when people seek to inculcate ideologies, they create classes or study groups. Other times, people are informally socialized into an ideology through personal contact with activists and ideologues. Ideological and valuational conversion may be slow and unnoticed because there is no strong commitment to legitimating systems of meaning. Ideologies are complex systems of thought that cannot be communicated accurately in stock phrases or sound bites. A stock phrase can invoke intimations of an ideology for those who only know its bare outlines, or it can invoke the richness of the ideology for those who know it well. Persuading other people to take on an ideology is an education or socialization process: it takes time, involves repeated contact between the educator/socializer and the learner, and requires substantial effort on both their parts. These processes are reinforced by social group membership and networks in which other people share the same meanings and learn new ideas together.

What Snow and his colleagues call "frame transformation" is really "ideological transformation," either transmitting an ideology to a new believer or reconstructimg an existing one. Frame theory has inadequate conceptual tools for describing this process of ideological change. Snow himself has written elsewhere (Snow and Phillips 1980; Snow and Oliver 1994) about the socialization processes involved in conversion, when an individual adopts a new ideology. Conversion involves a reconstruction of a meaning system in the context of intense encounters with socializers and a heightened emotionality. Once conversion occurs, elements of the new ideology can function as frames, but the concept of ideology better describes the whole new system of meaning and points to the social processes of adopting it.

Less has been written about the processes that occur when a group of committed activists reconstructs their ideology. This is a weakness in extant theories of ideology, but frame concepts do not contribute much understanding. Detailed accounts of these processes reveal periods of intense interaction and discussion as people talk over new ideas or their experiences in practice and self-consciously develop new ideas, often writing them so that they can have an existence apart from their author (see Rochon's 1998 discussion of the philosophes). While outsiders might not agree with the ideologues' conclusions, it is obvious to observers that people reconstructing ideologies are doing active intellectual work, pulling out the logical consequences of ideas, weighing evidence, and discussing how these ideas might be received by others. For example, it can correctly be said that Brazilian antidam activists in the 1980s shifted from a land-struggle frame to an ecology frame, but calling it a frame shift implies that it was a relatively superficial problem of renaming. In fact, detailed case study materials revealed a long process of self-conscious discussion, debate, and political education before the shift could be accomplished (Rothman and Oliver 2002). People had to reconstruct their entire theory of society, holding on to some core values while molding new ones, and all the time dealing with the changing political context which weakened old alliances and created the possibility of new ones. The process took a lot of time and involved the creation of new intellectual products. The activists themselves changed their ideology, they did not just superficially repackage themselves to a new market.

Similarly, Johnston (1991) identifies frame alignments that occurred in the resurgence of Catalonian national opposition as formerly conservative Catholic ethnic Catalans became increasingly militant and adopted Marxist orientations and leftist militants and non-Catalan immigrants adopted nationalism. While new opportunities and options were opened by general Marxist and Catalan nationalist frames, these openings led to ideological syntheses at a deeper level of learning and change in personal beliefs. This "intellectual work" and not the frames provided a basis for concerted action by formerly disparate groups. The following quote from a Catalan activist, a member of the Socialist Movement of Catalonia (MSC), is a clear example of the thinking, reasoning, studying, and intellectual debate that went into Catalan left-nationalist ideology:

> For example, let's take Carlos. I would say that he made me into a Marxist and I made him into a nationalist. . . . We went out at night in Barcelona for hours, me trying to convince him that they should contact our party and accept political pluralism . . . and him, evidently resisting because of what then was very important for these young men, Castroism and the Cuban revolution. They were absolutely fascinated, bewitched, by Fidel Castro. Us, for us older ones, we took him with what we Catalanists say, *grànuls salís* [grains of salt]. So of course the Marxist history of Catalonia came to me through these kids. They showed an extraordinary intellectual inquisitiveness, and you don't know what they did to get a hold of those books.

Debates between friends, personal influence, arguing points of logic and fact, struggles to get hold of prohibited texts—these are not the activities of movement marketers or spin doctors. We have here an poignant example of the differences between a frame as an orientating principle and an ideology as a system of ideas arrived at through education, socialization, and debate.

MASTER FRAMES AND IDEOLOGIES

At a superficial level, ideologies and master frames may seem to be equivalent. Both are broad configurations of ideas within which more specific ideas are included. However, we believe that theorizing will be improved if they are clearly distinguished. Master frames were introduced to explain the clustering of social movements during cycles of protest (Snow and Benford 1992). Examples include the psychosalvational master frame (p. 139), the nuclear freeze master frame (p. 143), and the civil rights master frame (p. 145). Snow and Benford (1992: 139-140) distinguish "elaborated" versus "restricted" frames, following Basil Bernstein's well-known distinction between restricted and elaborated linguistic codes. The civil rights frame was highly elaborated, meaning that components of civil rights thought (equal opportunities, comparable worth, voting, and office holding) were general and inclusive and could be used by other aggrieved groups. Even broader is the nationalism master frame, which can be seen across epochs, regions, and cultures. Intellectuals of specific national movements elaborate ideologies within this frame drawing upon history, culture, and political context; typical actions are glorification of the past, exaltation of the language, drawing boundaries with other national groups, political contention based on national identity, and transcendence or coming to terms with class divisions. (At the lowest or most restricted level of generalization, Snow and Benford cite the nuclear freeze frame that shaped the U.S. peace movement in the 1980s, but this frame seems so restricted as to not really warrant the modifier "master.")

There is another kind of very broad frame that is not always associated with movement clustering and whose generality is so great the label "master frame" does not capture its utility. We refer to generic framing processes that can be applied across different cultural and political contexts and to a variety of movements. The most important examples are injustice frames (Gamson, Fireman, and Rytina 1982), mobilizing frames (Ryan 1991), oppositional frames (Coy and Woehrle 1996), and antisystemic frames, revitalization frames, and inclusion frames (Diani 1996). These function at a high level of abstraction to organize the specific content of collective action. We concur with Benford (1997: 414) that these activities hold potential for theoretical advance because of their generality.

Ideologies also occur at different levels of generality and can support more specific articulations of theory and value nested within more general ones. Dalton (1994), for example, demonstrates how environmentalist ideology embraces both conservationist and ecologist variants and how each shapes the horizon of action and opportunities available to different SMOs. Moreover, within ecologist ideology, there are variants such as "deep ecology," whose ideological treatises accentuate some values, prognoses, and theories while discounting others. Similarly the umbrella of feminist ideology has included the three broad tendencies of liberal, socialist, and radical or separatist feminism, each with a long history of ideological elaboration and specification, as well as more specific variants—many of which are highly theorized and articulated, including eco-feminism and lesbian feminism—and the subtleties of women-of-color feminism and womanism (which explicitly distance themselves from feminism).

With various levels of generality for both frames and ideologies, there is a temptation to treat ideologies as master frames because both inform the interpretation of many specific instances, and ideologies often function as frames. However, it is not appropriate to simply rename ideology as a master frame, such as recasting feminism as a "feminist frame" (Benford 1997: 420). A better conception, we believe, treats a master frame as markedly different from an ideology, as much closer to the original meaning of a frame. In this conception, a master frame lacks the elaborate social theory and normative and value systems that characterize a full-blown ideology, but instead is a signifier that points to a general category of socially recognized instances. In this sense, the "rights frame" is not an ideology but an angle or perspective on a problem. The rights master frame surely gave women a new perspective on work situations where they were paid less than men for the same work. This frame pointed many women in the direction of feminist ideology, but one can apply the rights frame without having a feminist ideology. Rather, the "rights" frame echoes themes from deep in U.S. political culture and has been invoked across the last two centuries in a wide variety of ideologically disparate movements including, as we argued above, both the pro- and anti-abortion movements.

A good example of the distinction between ideology and master frame can be seen in Johnston and Aarelaid's 2000 study of the Estonian national opposition. They identified a "pure Estonian nationality" master frame that was anchored in experiences and beliefs about the period of independence between 1918 and 1940, but did not include the specific political ideologies of the period. Essential orientations about the value of the language and the people were present, as was a strong affirmation of the nation embodied in a refusal to compromise with Soviet "occupiers." The frame guided actions of small groups of artists, intellectuals, and activists during fifty years that Estonia was part of the Soviet Union. These groups theorized their resistance with different assessments of the situation, tactics, and justifications for action that drew upon Estonian nationalism and Western models of human rights, democracy, and basic freedoms in different ways. The frame guided resistance and opposition, which was shared among different groups but was distinct from the ideological orientations of each.

PUTTING IT TOGETHER: CONCLUSIONS AND SUGGESTIONS

Frame and ideology are both useful concepts for students of social movements, as are grievance, interest, and culture. We are not calling for the abandonment of framing theory, nor claiming that framing processes are unimportant. We recognize that ideologies often function as frames and that not all frames are ideologies. Rather, we are saying that ideologies are worthy of study in their own right and that studying ideologies as ideologies involves different questions and different kinds of research than studying them as frames.

We are critical of the move that has appropriated the older theorizing about ideologies and recast it in framing language. The language of frames is perhaps the best way to explain our central point. To frame an ideology as a frame is to seek to understand how a particular ideology is invoked as relevant in a particular context and how, once invoked, it shapes the interpretation of words and the connections between words. It is to say that ideology is fundamentally a backdrop to an instance of interpersonal communication. The ideology is taken as fixed, and attention is focused on how it constrains understanding of a particular event or utterance. Frames can be understood as malleable, but this version of frame theory focuses on how meanings are negotiated in interpersonal contexts. To frame an ideology as a frame is to say that the social-psychological issues are paramount. By contrast, to frame an ideology as an ideology is to call attention to the ideas on their own terms, to the structure of beliefs about society (its social theory), and to its ethical, moral, and political content, its values and norms. It is to understand the origin and logic of those beliefs and potentially to be prepared to assess that belief system against one's own meaning system. Ideologies are socially constructed, and their social construction involves framing processes, but trying to reduce ideology construction to a series of framing processes at the interactive level or frame alignment at the organizational level loses its social and political content. Unlike frame theory, ideology theory has always grappled with the relation between people's material conditions or material experiences and their ideologies. Theorists of ideology have suggested that class or other material interests might underlie belief systems. It is they who are prepared to discuss the political implications of belief systems. In short, to frame an ideology as an ideology is to say that the political issues are paramount.

At the same time, there are latent political implications in frame theory, and latent social psychological implications in ideology theory. Exclusive emphasis on frames can suggest that politics are unimportant or can be reduced to simple difference of opinion. To imply that politics are unimportant and that everybody's ideas are structurally equivalent to everyone else's is a political choice. Those who criticized rational action theory for its narrow and ultimately wrong social psychology were right—that is not how people actually think—but at least rational action theory contained the political concept of interest. Pure social constructionism carried to its logical extreme lacks an explicit political model. Its latent political model will be worthy of the same critiques that led to the rejection in 1970 of the excessive psychologizing in collective behavior theory. (It should be noted that there are variants of ideology theory that fall to this same criticism.) Social movement frame theory has avoided the danger of complete depoliticization by its intellectual alliance with political opportunity theory and its models of how frames appeal to constituencies, access resources, or take advantage of political opportunities, although this very turn has led to the most mechanistic and superficial images of frame alignment processes.

The social-psychological implications of ideology theory are rather more diverse, as there is no single theory of ideology, and the different theories have radically different images of how people create and respond to ideologies. Nevertheless, a latent social psychology emerges from a focus on ideologies as systems of ideas. People are viewed as developing belief systems from a combination of reflecting on and interpreting their own experiences and learning ideas and idea systems from others. They are thinkers and interpreters. There is always a concern with where the ideas are coming from; they are never just taken as givens. Most ideology theories embody a social model of the production of ideologies, in which it is recognized that relatively few intellectuals or "idea specialists" create elaborate ideological systems. Intellectuals have learned ideas from others, and they build their ideas in dialogue with previous ideas, as well as with their own experiences. Ideas can be abstracted or alienated from the people who originally thought them. The relation between the intellectuals and nonintellectuals is a matter for explicit inquiry. There is generally a recognition that popular beliefs differ from those of the intellectuals. There is usually some kind of teaching model, an explanation for how intellectuals communicate with others, as well as a general recognition that those "taught" do not necessarily absorb the ideology intact from the teacher. In short, the fundamental assumptions about the nature of people are generally similar between ideology and social-constructionist social psychology. The difference would be that the social structure in which they are embedded is more directly considered as part of the theory.

Frame theory has stimulated a wide variety of research because it points to important processes in social movements. Framing concepts have been enormously valuable and productive and should not be abandoned. But no concept can serve all purposes, and the eclipse of ideology by frame theory has been a mistake. Ideology was abandoned because of its pejorative baggage, and this baggage needs to be stripped away if we are to have a vigorous and useful concept. Understanding ideology as a system of meaning that couples assertions and theories about the nature of social life with values and norms relevant to promoting or resisting social change opens the door to a serious investigation of ideologies and the social construction of ideologies. As we reopen the study of ideology and explicitly theorize the interrelations between ideologies and frames and framing processes, we will have a sounder body of ideational theory that is better able to speak to the ways in which ideas influence politics and political action.

NOTES

1. Another source was the resurgence of cultural studies and their application to social movement analysis (see Johnston and Klandermans 1995). It is an important trend embracing various perspectives and foci, but will not be reviewed here as it is tangential to our central argument.

2. Moreover, it is questionable whether factors that are used to code interviews are indeed interpretative "frames, schemata, or scripts." Are elements of a cognitive frame properly represented by recasting them as categories of similar responses to interviews or survey questions?

3. The fourth process, frame transformation, involves changing people's ideas, but the discussion largely focuses on what it feels like to undergo such a transformation, not on how the movement activists accomplish it. Their examples of frame transformation come from religious movements, in which the transformation involves reinterpreting one's personal biography, not reinterpreting the structure of society.

REFERENCES

Ableson, Robert P. 1981. "The Psychological Status of the Script Concept." *American Psychologist* 36: 715-729.

Bartlett, F. C. 1932. *Remembering.* Cambridge: Cambridge University Press.

Bateson, Gregory. [1954] 1972. *Steps to an Ecology of Mind.* New York: Ballentine.

Bell, Daniel. 1960. *The End of Ideology: On the Exhaustion of Political Ideas in the Fifties.* Glencoe, IL: The Free Press.

Benford, Robert. 1993. "Frame Disputes within the Nuclear Disarmament Movement." *Social Forces* 71: 677-701

———. 1997. "An Insider's Critique of the Social Movement Framing Perspective." *Sociological Inquiry* 67: 409-430.

Capek, Stella. 1993. "The Environmental Justice Frame: A Conceptual Discussion and Application." *Social Problems* 40: 5-24.

Carroll, William K., and R. S. Ratner. 1996. "Master Framing and Cross-Movement Networking in Contemporary Social Movements." *Sociological Quarterly* 37: 601-625.

Converse, Philip E. 1964. "The Nature of Belief Systems in Mass Publics." Pp. 206-261 in *Ideology and Discontent,* David Apter, ed., New York: The Free Press.

Coy, Patrick G., and Lynne M. Woehrle. 1996. "Constructing Identity and Oppositional Knowledge: The Framing Perspective of Peace Organizations during the Persian Gulf War." *Sociological Spectrum* 16: 287-327.

Cranston, Maurice W. 1994. *The Romantic Movement.* Cambridge, MA: Blackwell.

Dalton, Russell J. 1994. *The Green Rainbow.* New Haven, CT: Yale University Press.

Diani, Mario. 1996. "Linking Mobilization Frames and Political Opportunities: Insights from Regional Populism in Italy." *American Sociological Review* 61: 1053-1069.

Frake, Charles O. 1964. "How to Ask for a Drink in Subanum." *American Anthropologist* 66: 127-132.

———. 1977. "Plying Frames Can Be Dangerous." *Quarterly Newsletter of the Institute for Comparative Human Development* 1: 1-7.

Gamson, William A. 1992. "The Social Psychology of Collective Action." Pp. 53-76 in *Frontiers in Social Movement Theory,* Aldon D. Morris and Carol McClurg Mueller, eds. New Haven, CT: Yale University Press.

———. 1996. *Talking Politics.* New York: Cambridge University Press.

Gamson, William A., Bruce Fireman, and Steven Rytina. 1982. *Encounters with Unjust Authority.* Homewood IL: Dorsey Press.

Gerhards, Jurgen, and Dieter Rucht. 1992. "Mesomobiliztaion: Organizing and Framing in Two Protest Campaigns in West Germany." *American Journal of Sociology* 98: 578-584.

Gerring, John. 1997. "Ideology: A Definitional Analysis." *Political Research Quarterly* 50: 957-994.

Goffman, Erving. 1972. *Frame Analysis*. New York: Harper and Row.

————. 1981. *Forms of Talk*. Philadelphia: University of Pennsylvania Press.

Gumperz, John J. 1982. *Discourse Strategies*. Cambridge: Cambridge University Press.

Gumperz, John, and Dell Hymes. 1972. *Directions in Sociolinguistics*. New York: Holt, Rinehart, and Winston.

Heberle, Rudolf. 1951. *Social Movements: An Introduction to Political Sociology*. New York: Appleton-Century-Crofts.

Hymes, Dell. 1974. "Social Anthropology, Sociolinguistics, and the Ethnography of Speaking." In *Foundations in Sociolinguistics,* Dell Hymes, ed. Philadelphia: University of Pennsylvania Press.

Jasper, James M. 1997. *The Art of Moral Protest*. Chicago: University of Chicago Press.

Johnston, Hank. 1991. *Tales of Nationalism: Catalonia 1939-1979*. New Brunswick, NJ: Rutgers University Press.

————. 1995. "A Methodology for Frame Analysis: From Discourse to Cognitive Schemata." Pp. 217-246 in *Social Movements and Culture*, Hank Johnston and Bert Klandermans, eds. Minneapolis: University of Minnesota Press.

Johnston, Hank, and Aili Aarelaid Tart. 2000. "Generations, Microcohorts, and Long-Term Mobilization: The Estonian National Movement, 1940-1991." *Sociological Perspectives* 43: 671-698.

Johnston, Hank, and Bert Klandermans, eds. 1995. *Social Movements and Culture*. Minneapolis: University of Minnesota Press.

Luker, Kristin. 1984. *Abortion and the Politics of Motherhood*. Berkeley: University of California Press.

Marullo, Sam, Ron Pagnucco, and Jackie Smith. 1996. "Frame Changes and Social Movement Contraction: U.S. Peace Movement Framing of the Cold War." *Sociological Inquiry* 66: 1-28.

Munson, Ziad. 1999. "Ideological Production of the Christian Right: The Case of the Christian Coalition." Manuscript, Department of Sociology, Harvard University.

Nelson, John S. 1977. "The Ideological Connection: or, Smuggling in the Goods" *Theory and Society* 4: 421-448, 573-590.

Pichardo, Nelson, Heather Sullivan-Catlin, and Glenn Deane. 1998. "Is the Political Personal: Everyday Behaviors as Forms of Environmental Movement Participation." *Mobilization* 3: 185-205.

Portes, Alejandro. 1971. "Political Primitivism, Differential Socialization, and Lower-Class Radicalism." *American Sociological Review* 36: 820-835.

Rochon, Thomas R. 1998. *Culture Moves*. Princeton, NJ: Princeton University Press.

Rothman, Franklin Daniel, and Pamela Oliver. 2002. "From Local to Global: The Antidam Movement in Southern Brazil, 1979-1992." Pp. 115-132 in *Globalization and Resistance: Transnational Dimension of Social Movements,* Jackie Smith and Hank Johnston, eds. Lanham, MD: Rowman & Littlefield.

Ryan, Charlotte. 1991. *Prime Time Activism*. Boston: South End.

Rudé, George F. E. 1980. *Ideology and Popular Protest*. New York: Pantheon Books.

Schank, Roger C., and Robert P. Ableson. 1977. *Scripts, Plans, Goals, and Understanding*. Hillsdale, NJ: Lawrence Erlbaum Associates.

Smelser, Neil J. 1962. *Theory of Collective Behavior*. New York: The Free Press.

Snow, David A., and Robert D. Benford. 1988. "Ideology, Frame Resonance, and Participant Mobilization." Pp. 197-218 in *International Social Movement Research: From Structure to Action*, Bert Klandermans, Hanspeter Kriesi, and Sidney Tarrow, eds. Greenwich, CT: JAI Press.

————. 1992. "Master Frames and Cycles of Protest." Pp. 133-155 in *Frontiers in Social Movement Theory,* Aldon D. Morris and Carol McClurg Mueller, eds.. New Haven, CT: Yale University Press.

Snow, David A., and Pamela E. Oliver. 1994. "Social Movements and Collective Behavior: Social Psychological Dimensions and Considerations." In *Sociological Perspectives on Social Psychology*, Karen Cook, Gary Fine, and James House, eds. Needham Heights, MA: Allyn and Bacon.

Snow, David A., and C. L. Phillips. 1980. "The Lofland-Stark Conversion Model: A Critical Reassessment." *Social Problems* 27 (4): 430-447.

Snow, David A., E. Burke Rochford, Jr., Steven K. Worden, and Robert D. Benford. 1986. "Frame Alignment Processes, Micromobilization, and Movement Participation." *American Sociological Review* 51: 464-481.

Steinberg, Marc. 1998. "Tilting the Frame: Considerations of Collective Action Framing from a Discursive Turn." *Theory and Society* 27: 845-872.

Swart, William J. 1995. "The League of Nations and the Irish Question: Master Frames, Cycles of Protest, and Master Frame Alignment." *Sociological Quarterly* 36: 465-481.

Tannen, Deborah. 1993. "What's in a Frame?" Pp. 14-56 in *Framing in Discourse*, Deborah Tannen, ed. New York: Oxford University Press.

Tarrow, Sidney. 1998. *Power in Movement: Social Movements and Contentious Politics.* 2nd ed. New York: Cambridge University Press.

Turner, Ralph. 1996. "The Moral Issue in Collective Behavior and Collective Action." *Mobilization* 1: 1-16.

Turner, Ralph H., and Lewis M. Killian. 1972. *Collective Behavior.* 2nd ed. Englewood Cliffs, NJ: Prentice-Hall.

Weberman, David. 1997. "Liberal Democracy, Autonomy, and Ideology Critique." *Social Theory and Practice* 23: 205-233.

Williams, Rhys. 1995. "Constructing the Public Good: Social Movements and Cultural Resources." *Social Problems* 42: 124-144.

Wilson, John. 1973. *Introduction to Social Movements.* New York: Basic Books.

Wood, M., and M. Hughes. 1984. "The Moral Basis of Moral Reform: Status Discontent vs. Culture and Socialization as Explanations of Anti-Pornography Social Movement Adherence." *American Sociological Review* 49: 86-99.

Chapter 10

CLARIFYING THE RELATIONSHIP BETWEEN FRAMING AND IDEOLOGY

David A. Snow and Robert D. Benford

During the decade of the 1990s, the evolving framing perspective on social movements has found its way into an increasing amount of conceptual and empirical scholarship. There has been an almost meteoric acceleration in the number of articles, chapters, and papers invoking the frame concept or referring to framing processes in some fashion or another (Benford and Snow 2000). Presumably one reason for this escalating use of the framing perspective is that it helps fill a conceptual void and provides analytic purchase on understanding the interpretive work engaged in by movement actors and others within the movement field of action. Yet, as with any perspective, and particularly evolving ones, there are various glosses, untidy linkages, and misunderstandings that reveal themselves in both the application of the perspective and in its critical assessment. So it is not surprising that various issues with and questions about the movement framing perspective have been raised (e.g., Benford 1997; Fisher 1997; Hart 1996; Jasper 1997), issues and questions that one critic cleverly suggested constitute "cracks in the frame" (Steinberg 1998: 847). Oliver and Johnston's chapter in this volume contributes to this line of critique by zeroing in on one of the "cracks": the glossing of ideology and its relationship to frames. Their basic concern, as they state in no uncertain terms, is the "failure" of frame theory "to address the relation between frames and the much older, more political concept of ideology, and the concomitant tendency of many researchers to use 'frame' uncritically as a synonym for 'ideology.'"

We agree with the core contention that the relationship between frames and ideology has been glossed over, and so we would like to take this opportunity to sketch our understanding of that relationship. Before doing so, we want to clarify a number of misunderstandings and misrepresentations that appear throughout Oliver and Johnston's chapter.

MISUNDERSTANDINGS AND MISREPRESENTATIONS

The first misunderstanding, which can also be construed as a misrepresentation, flows from Oliver and Johnson's orienting contention regarding "the tendency of many researchers to use 'frame' uncritically as a synonym for 'ideology.'" Referring to us, they charge that we "neither provide justification for abandoning the term 'ideology,' and substituting 'frame.'" This was news to us, since we never recommended in any of our writings that the term *ideology* should be jettisoned or replaced by the term *frame*. In fact, we began our 1986 article by incorporating ideology into our conceptualization of frame alignment: "By frame alignment, we refer to the linkage of individual and SMO interpretive orientations, such that some set of individual interests, values and beliefs and SMO activities, goals, and ideology are congruent and complementary" (Snow et al. 1986: 464). In subsequent works (Snow and Benford 1988, 1992), we not only refer to ideology, but also draw on the discourses on ideology of Geertz (1973), Gramsci (1971), and Rudé (1980).

Although we do not elaborate the implied relationship between ideology and framing processes and frames in any of these works, and thus stand guilty of glossing over that relationship, that is not the same as calling for the abandonment of the concept of ideology. If there are other scholars who have made such a call, we are not familiar with their work and Oliver and Johnston do not reference them. It appears that they are guilty of creating a red herring by making an unsubstantiated inference. Had they asked, we would have been happy to inform them that we agree that frames and ideology are not the same thing and that neither concept should be discarded or subsumed under the other.

The second misunderstanding flows from the authors' decision, whether unwitting or intentional, to frame the critique in terms of the noun "frame" rather than the verb "framing" and thereby to accent, the constructed product over framing as a set of dynamic, negotiated, and often contested processes. Although they acknowledge the latter, their critique is clearly anchored in the former, thus misrepresenting what we regard as the cornerstone of the framing perspective. As we emphasized in the introduction to the 1988 article, our primary interest was in moving beyond the "description of movement ideology" (Snow and Benford 1988: 197) and the corollary tendency to "treat meanings or ideas as given, as if there is an isomorphic relationship between the nature of any particular set of conditions or events and the meanings attached to them" (198), to the analytical tasks of examining the "production of meaning"—in other words, the "signifying work" we referred to as "framing" (198). Our focus in that article, was not, as Oliver and Johnston suggest, to "rename" the ideology literature in frame analytic terms; rather we sought to specify the relationship between belief systems and framing activities—for example, how various characteristics of belief systems constrain the production of meaning and thus can affect the mobilizing potency of framings. Our focus on the core framing tasks was not simply a case of pouring Wilson's (1973) older wine into new wineskins. Instead, we sought to bring some dynamism to a rather static conceptualization of ideology. Granted, we refer to Wilson's three components of ideology as "core framing tasks." But we then show how these three component elements are socially constructed via various articulative, punctuating, and attributional processes (which we elaborated in 1992). In short, our objective was to attempt to specify the interactive processes by which frames are socially constructed, sustained, contested, and altered, the phenomenological and infrastructural constraints on those processes, and the consequences of these processes for aspects of mobilization. But most of this, which we regard as the heart of the framing perspective, is given short shrift by Oliver and Johnston.

The third misunderstanding is the authors' location of the essence of frames in cognition. As they note repeatedly, "frames are individual cognitive structures," "mental structures or schemata," that point to "a cognitive process wherein people bring to bear background knowledge to interpret an event or circumstance and to locate it in a larger system of meaning." Certainly collective action frames are, in part, cognitive entities that aid interpretation and social action, but their essence, sociologically, resides in situated social interaction, that is, in the interpretive discussions and debates that social movement actors engage in among each other and in the framing contests that occur between movement actors and other parties within the movement field of action, such as countermovements, adversaries, and even the media. Collective action frames are, to borrow on the language of Bakhtin and his circle, "dialogical" phenomena; their essence resides "not within us, but between us" (Medvedev and Bakhtin 1978: 8; Todorov 1984). And it is this understanding of frames as the products of the interindividual, interactional, and contested process of framing that is glossed over by Oliver and Johnston.

The fourth misunderstanding is the authors' failure to grasp that frames and framing are embedded within social constructionist processes that involve thinking and reasoning by the parties involved. This misunderstanding, which follows understandably on the heels of the chapter's focus on frames rather than on framing processes and the mislocation of the essence of frames in cognition rather than in dialogical interaction, surfaces in various questionable comments throughout their article. One such comment contends that work on ideology is evocative of a social constructionist view that "has been missing from recent scholarship." If the reference is to the framing scholarship, which we presume is the case given the focus of the chapter, we wonder how such a statement could be made unless the authors have misapprehended both the framing perspective on social movements and the broader constructionist perspective in which it is located. Such a statement also raises questions about the authors' understanding of how the concept of ideology has been used in the earlier social movement literature. That scholars such as Heberle (1951), Turner and Killian (1957), and Wilson (1973) invoke and define the concept is clear, but how it is used analytically is more ambiguous. Our reading of this earlier literature is that it treated ideology in a highly descriptive and relatively static and nondynamic fashion. Moreover, how it comes into existence and is appropriated by movement actors has been taken as given. Additionally, ideology has rarely been used as an important variable or determinant of the kinds of processes and outcomes that movement analysts have sought to explain. Rather, it has more commonly been invoked and described as an aspect of a movement and then left to linger in the background as analysis of some other movement process or conundrum proceeds. If this assessment of the use of ideology in much of the earlier movement literature is correct, where, we wonder, is the social constructionist influence? It may be asserted or implied, but it is neither analyzed nor demonstrated.

Equally curious is the authors' contention that ideology not only is predicated on thinking and reasoning, but that it "points to an element of ideation often neglected in the study of social movements: thinking." This strikes us as most puzzling in two ways. First, does it imply that thinking and reasoning are not salient aspects of framing processes? If that is the implication, then it is empirically unfounded, as any first-hand, up-close examination of movement encounters and meetings suggest. And second, it injects into ideology a degree of cognitive dynamism and interactional give-and-take that seems strikingly discordant with some conceptions of ideology, such as those that emphasize distortion, mystification, and illusion, as embodied in such corollary concepts as "false consciousness" (Marx and Engels 1989) and "hegemony" (Gramsci 1971).

A sixth misunderstanding of frames and the framing perspective is reflected in the authors' designation of the perspective as a social-psychological one, and ideology as basically a political-sociological designation. We would argue that such categorization is not so neat, since both frames and ideology have social-psychological and political dimensions to them. In fact, we have emphasized elsewhere that framing involves the "politics of signification" and that movements function as, among other things, framing agents that "are deeply embroiled, along with the media and the state in what (has been) referred to as the 'politics of signification'" (Snow and Benford 1988: 198). If so, then what is the rationale for associating framing solely with social psychology and thereby neglecting its links to politics and particularly the often contested character of framing processes?

Perhaps it is because of the foregoing misunderstandings and misrepresentations that Oliver and Johnston suggest that frame alignment processes correctly captures some of the important particulars of U.S. political culture in the 1990s, but is misleading for other problems, especially for movements in other times and places. On what grounds and in terms of what evidence are such assertions made? Were social problems and grievances so transparent in earlier periods of history and in other cultures that no interpretive work was required? Did political and economic disruptions or breakdowns not have interpretative debates and conflicts of the kind conceptualized by the framing perspective? If so, then apparently we have different historical and sociological understandings of the range of movements and revolutions that preceded the 1990s, including those that occurred in the 1960s, 1970s, and 1980s.

This takes us to a final issue that obfuscates Oliver and Johnston's conception of and claims for ideology. We refer to the ambiguous character of the concept of ideology and Oliver and Johnston's failure to come to grips with it. They correctly note that discussion of ideology has been characterized by a "tangle of pejorative connotations and contradictory definitions" since it was first employed the French philosopher Destutt de Tracy at the end of the eighteenth century, ranging from a general and more neutral conception, as reflected in the writing of Geertz (1973), Seliger (1976), and Gouldner (1976), to a more critical conception wherein ideology is seen as functioning to sustain existing class structures and relations of domination, as reflected in the writings of Marx and Engels (1989), Mannheim (1985), and Thompson (1984). But they invite us to accept the analytic utility of their definition—"a system of meaning that couples assertions and theories about the nature of social life with values and norms relevant to promoting or resisting social change"—without reconciling it with various contradictory and problematic aspects of the above tangle of definitions, such as the above-mentioned claims of distortion and mystification that attend the more critical conceptualizations. As well, they dance around some of the problematic features of their own conceptualization. For example, their conceptualization seems to assume, as do most treatments of ideology, a degree of coherence and integration among the elements of ideology (e.g., values and beliefs) that is not in accord with research on values and beliefs (Rokeach 1973; Williams 1970). The fact is that individuals acknowledge a host of values and beliefs that are often contradictory and rarely cohere in an integrated, systematic fashion. As Williams found in his examination of values in American society, there is neither "a neatly unified 'ethos' or an irresistible 'strain toward consistency'" (1970: 451).

Insofar as values and beliefs constitute salient components of ideology, such observations suggest that perhaps their presumed integration with respect to any particular ideology should be problematized, such that they can range on a continuum from being tightly coupled to loosely coupled. Such a conceptualization not only is consistent with the frequent observation that movements on different sides of the political spectrum can find sustenance in the same broader cultural ideology but also calls for an alternative concept that encompasses emergent sets of ideas and values that function either as innovative amplifications and extensions of existing ideologies or as antidotes to them. Obviously, we think the concept of collective action frames helps to fill this conceptual void. This, of course, begs the question of our understanding of the relationship between ideology and framing.

LINKING IDEOLOGY AND FRAMES

Because of limited space, we briefly sketch our view of the relationships and distinctions between the framing and ideology. First, we view *ideology as a cultural resource* for framing activity. Specifically, we contend that the framing process involves, among other things, the articulation and accenting or amplification of elements of existing beliefs and values, most of which are associated with existing ideologies. Hence, it is arguable and empirically demonstrable that collective action frames are typically comprised, at least in part, of strands of one or more ideologies. If so, then collective action frames are rooted, in varying degrees, in extant ideologies, but are neither determined by nor isomorphic with them. Instead, from a framing perspective, ideologies constitute cultural resources that can be tapped and exploited for the purpose of constructing collective action frames and thus function simultaneously to facilitate and constrain framing processes (Benford and Snow 2000; Snow and Benford 1988). Following Swidler (1986), we are arguing that if culture is best conceived as a "bag of tools," then clearly ideologies function in this fashion in relation to collective action frames. As well, extant ideologies, or aspects of them, can function as points of contention to which collective action frames are developed and proffered as antidotes or emergent counterideologies.

A second aspect of our view of the relationship between ideology and framing is that framing may also function as *remedial ideological work*. By that we mean that framing provides a conceptual handle for thinking about and analyzing the not-infrequent remedial, reconstitutive work that is required when members of any ideological or thought community encounter glaring disjunctions between their beliefs and experiences or events in the world. It was this very dilemma that was the basis for Berger's analysis of the remedial "ideological work" that rural communards in upstate California engaged in so as to "maintain some semblance of consistency, coherence, and continuity" between their beliefs and actions when circumstances rendered them contradictory (1981: 22). Such remedial discourse or ideological work is likely to be precipitated or called forth by a number of disjunctive occurrences, such as (a) when beliefs and events in the word are discordant, (b) when beliefs and behavior or outcomes contradict each other, and (c) when the existence of competing or conflicting beliefs within a group threatens its coherence and increases the prospect of schism or factionalization. What is called for in each of these situations is a reframing, or "keying" in Goffman's words (1974), of the tear or rip in the ideology, a stitching together of the disjunctions.

A third aspect of the ideology-framing relationship that warrants mention is that *framing mutes the vulnerability of ideology to reification.* As we have noted, the language of framing directs attention to the processes through which interpretive orientations develop, evolve, and change and thereby triggers warning signals about the prospects of reifying existing ideologies or the products of framing activity, such as emergent ideologies and master frames. The tendency to reify movement ideologies or mobilizing beliefs and ideas, as well as master frames, has been particularly prominent in the social movement literature. The concept of framing functions as an antidote to that tendency because framing is a social activity and accomplishment.

A final aspect is that *framing, in contrast to ideology, is an empirically observable activity.* It is one of the things that we have repeatedly observed social movement actors doing over and over again during the course of their conversations and debates in the context of movement meetings and activities. Framing is empirically observable, as we emphasized earlier, because neither frames nor framing processes are purely or merely mentalistic or cognitive entities. Instead, they are rooted in and constituted by group-based social interaction, which is readily available for first-hand observation, examination, and analysis. That too few movement scholars have made actual framing activity the focus of empirical inquiry is no reason to gloss over this characteristic interactive, constructionist feature of framing.

SUMMARY

Based on the foregoing observations and arguments, it should be clear that we agree with Oliver and Johnston (1) that "frames" and "ideology" are not different words for the same thing but are, in fact, different entities; (2) that both concepts should therefore be retained; (3) that frames and ideology thus merit studying in their own right; and (4) that the relationship between frames and ideology needs to be understood as well. Where we differ, it seems, is in our respective conceptualizations of ideology and of the relationship between ideology and framing. As well, we have argued that Oliver and Johnston have misunderstood or misrepresented aspects of our work on frames and framing processes and have ignored issues within the voluminous literature on ideology that, in the absence of further elaboration and clarification, undermine the utility of their take on ideology and its relationship to social movements and related processes. These concerns and unresolved issues notwithstanding, Oliver and Johnston's chapter has functioned usefully to focus attention on an important and neglected issue in the study of social movements.

REFERENCES

Benford, Robert D. 1997. "An Insider's Critique of the Social Movement Framing Perspective." *Sociological Inquiry* 67: 409-430.

Benford, Robert D., and David A. Snow. 2000. "Framing Processes and Social Movements: An Overview and Assessment." *Annual Review of Sociology* 26: 611-639.

Berger, Bennett M. 1981. *The Survival of the Counterculture: Ideological Work and Everyday*

Life among Rural Communards. Berkeley: University of California Press.

Fisher, Kimberly. 1997. "Locating Frames in the Discursive Universe." *Sociological Research Online* 2 (3), available at http://www.socresonline.org.uk/socresonline/2/3/4.html.

Geertz, Clifford. 1973. "Ideology as a Cultural System." Pp. 193-233 in *The Interpretation of Cultures*. New York: Basic Books.

Goffman, Erving. 1974. *Frame Analysis*. New York: Harper Colophon.

Gouldner, Alvin W. 1976. *The Dialectic of Ideology and Technology: The Origins, Grammar, and Future of Ideology*. New York: Seabury Press.

Gramsci, Antonio. 1971. *Selections from the Prison Notebooks*, Q. Hoare and G. N. Smith, eds. New York: International Publishers.

Hart, Steven. 1996. "The Cultural Dimension of Social Movements: A Theoretical Assessment and Literature Review." *Sociology of Religion* 57: 87-100.

Heberle, Rudolf. 1951. *Social Movements: An Introduction to Political Sociology*. New York: Appleton-Century-Crofts.

Jasper, James M. 1997. *The Art of Moral Protest*. Chicago: University of Chicago Press.

Mannheim, Karl. 1985. *Ideology and Utopia*. San Diego: Harcourt Brace Jovanovich.

Marx, Karl, and Frederick Engels. 1989. *The German Ideology*. New York: Individual Publishers.

Medvedev, P. N., and Mikhail M. Bakhtin. 1978. *The Formal Method in Literary Scholarship: A Critical Introduction to Sociological Poetics*. Baltimore: Johns Hopkins University Press.

Rokeach, Milton. 1973. *The Nature of Human Values*. New York: The Free Press.

Rudé, George. 1980. *Ideology and Popular Protest*. New York: Knopf.

Seliger, M. 1976. *Ideology and Politics*. New York: The Free Press.

Snow, David A., and Robert D. Benford. 1988. "Ideology, Frame Resonance, and Participant Mobilization." *International Social Movement Research* 1: 197-217.

———. 1992. "Master Frames and Cycles of Protest." Pp. 133-155 in *Frontiers in Social Movement Theory*, Aldon D. Morris and Carol McClurg Mueller, eds. New Haven, CT: Yale University Press.

Snow, David A., R. Burke Rochford, Jr., Steven K. Worden, and Robert D. Benford. 1986. "Frame Alignment Processes, Micromobilization, and Movement Participation." *American Sociological Review* 51: 464-481.

Steinberg, Marc W. 1998. "Tilting the Frame: Considerations on Collective Framing from a Discursive Turn." *Theory and Society* 27: 845-872.

Swidler, Ann. 1986. "Culture in Action." *American Sociological Review* 51: 273-286.

Thompson, James B. 1984. *Studies in the Theory of Ideology*. Cambridge, UK: Polity Press.

Todorov, Tzvetan. 1984. *Mikhail Bakhtin: The Dialogic Principle*. Minneapolis: University of Minnesota Press.

Turner, Ralph H., and Lewis M. Killian. 1957. *Collective Behavior*. Englewood Cliffs, NJ: Prentice-Hall.

Williams, Robin M. 1970. *American Society: A Sociological Interpretation*. New York: Knopf.

Wilson, John. 1973. *Introduction to Social Movements*. New York: Basic Books.

Chapter 11

BREAKING THE FRAME

Hank Johnston and Pamela E. Oliver

The central point of chapter 9 is to call for a revitalization of the nonpejorative concept of ideology and more careful theorizing about the relation between ideology and frames. The chapter makes clear this should not be construed as a comprehensive critique of the framing perspective. David Snow and Rob Benford have given us useful concepts for the cultural analysis of social movements under the rubric of framing, as well as extensive contributions to the research and theory about mobilization processes. Their response to our chapter is helpful in clarifying the relation between ideology and frames. Nevertheless, a few comments in reply seem in order.

Our focus on the "turn" away from ideology in the 1986 article by Snow and his colleagues, and especially the 1988 Snow and Benford article, does not do justice to the full corpus of their work, either in those two essays or in the many other works they have published. But the turn is nevertheless there. They essentially say, "Ideology is important and has been neglected by resource mobilization scholars. Let's look at framing processes as a way of remedying this." Our chapter asserts that Snow and Benford provided no "justification for abandoning the term 'ideology' and substituting 'frame' *in this context.*" They recast this assertion as an accusation put forward by us that they were "calling for the abandonment of the concept of ideology," a charge they deny—quite correctly—but also a charge that we never made. It goes without saying that nobody ever *called* for abandoning the concept of ideology; but it equally goes without saying that Snow and Benford moved to focus solely on frames instead of ideology. Our colleagues appear to believe sincerely that the framing approach is the best way to study those elements of ideology that are most relevant to mobilization, and thus they dispute the claim that they "abandoned" ideology. We believe that what was abandoned by them—at least in those essays—and by those following them was the full *concept* of ideology. Ideology has a rich history of scholarship, research application, conceptual elaboration, debate, and refinement by which its theoretical and empirical utility were grappled with by a long line of scholars. The concept of ideology embraces issues that framing does not. Although Snow and Benford themselves have been careful in the ways they use these terms, we have found that many scholars since them have been less careful. It is common to encounter "frames" and "ideology" being merged or used synonymously, for example, referring to the "liberal frame" or the "feminist frame."

We focused on the noun (the frame) instead of the verb (framing) because the vast majority of research in the framing perspective has done that. Our discussion of two approaches in the framing perspective, frames as either "fixed templates" or "inherently malleable and emergent" recognizes the grammatical division of labor; but we stand by our judgment that "subsequent elaborations . . . moved to a more fixed conception of collective action frames." This is clear in the reports we have cited. It is also clear in the way framing processes have been incorporated into political process theory, for example in Tarrow's *Power and Movement* (1998).

This noun-verb distinction goes to the heart of several other of their criticisms, most of which are about framing, not ideology. In our judgment, it is the noun—an interpretative frame defined as a cognitive structure with specifiable content—that will move the framing perspective forward, not the verb, not descriptions of framing processes as ends in themselves. Of course, *all of social life is emergent, negotiated, and contextual*, and so too is the social construction of frames and ideology. Detailed descriptions of these emergent social processes can be useful, but to insist on the primacy of emergent processes above all is to trap social scientists in an interactionist bubble that limits all research to descriptions of process. To get outside that interactionist bubble and talk about how frames or ideologies relate to other features of social life, it is necessary to make the verbs of process into nouns of ideas. That is why, Snow and Benford's concerns notwithstanding, most people who invoke frame theory study *frames* and not *framing*. To put it another way, it is necessary to freeze the process in time to take soundings, artificially halting the variation of the variables to make measures. As we stated in our chapter, this is a methodological artifice; but as far as we know, it is the best way to systematically analyze what changes, how much, and how these changes might be related to other factors so as to suggest a causal relation. It advances theory by offering concrete examples of how frames change and testing what factors may influence these changes.

It is puzzling that Snow and Benford claim that we said *a social constructionist view* "has been missing from recent scholarship," an incorrect assertion which is obviously contradicted by the rest of our chapter. The sentence that they refer to clearly focuses on ideology (not framing) and processes of *thinking* ideologically—especially thinking about the material world, the ideas that describe it and make sense of it, and the values that are often the basis of action to change it. Obviously, thinking is one kind of social construction, but that paragraph in our chapter discusses not social constructionism in general, but the narrower realm of self-conscious intellectual activity as a corrective to the pejorative conceptions of ideology. We go on to say:

> People think a lot in social movements, along with the related activities of reasoning, judging arguments, evaluating evidence, testing predictions, recognizing connections, and developing new knowledge. There is a continuity in the theorizing of ideologues and the theorizing of those who study ideologues.

In Snow and Benford's comments they revisit this sentence, this time to defend the claim that people think about framing, and then to argue that framing injects a give-and-take into ideology that is missing from some of the past conceptions. We certainly agree that people can think about tactical framing and that some older conceptions of ideology are too static, but if they think that all intellectual processes are best understood as framing processes, we disagree with them.

They question our assertion that frame alignment concepts are more relevant to modern social movements than older ones. Of course, framing is a fundamental cognitive processes in *all* interaction. Applied to social movements, it is as much an element in Greenpeace as it was in seventeenth-century peasant *jacquaries* when an act of the king was defined as warranting rebellion rather than quiescence. But *frame alignment processes* are a specific element of framing and were discussed by Snow and Benford in part as an element of SMO tactical framing. Subsequent treatments have seized the frame alignment concept as akin to marketing a social movement, a move that is consistent with the bulk of the 1986 article. Greenpeace uses media consultants to maximize alignment of their membership campaigns with target populations; leaders of the 1719 "harvesters" uprising in Catalonia did not. George W. Bush had a stable of media consultants and specialists to align his presidential campaign with the states' voters; Abraham Lincoln did not.

Our rhetorical juxtaposition of politics/ideology *versus* social psychology/framing is obviously unfair at the extreme, but we used the rhetoric to point to the problems with unfettered social constructionism, specifically its lack of a model of social structure and its risk of staying trapped in an interactionist bubble, of being unable to evaluate the relationship of ideas to other social structures. Ideologies are complex systems of ideas that are systematically related and which describe and explain the social world. They embrace a theory of how social relations came to be and how they can be changed, and they stipulate core values and norms. Ideologies are social constructions, to be sure. But they are continually tested and refined on the anvil of the material world. Arguing that an ideological system is grounded in the material world is different than merely asserting that "experiential commensurability" is an aspect of framing. Discussions of the "politics of signification" do not address these concerns.

Snow and Benford's last comment on our chapter finally *breaks their own frame* and takes up the issue of ideology. We stand accused of not offering a watertight definition that reconciles the various ways the term has been used over the last two hundred years. To this we must plead guilty; we avoided those issues because of space limitations. They are correct in sketching some of the key problems with ideology as it has been understood, and correct that those problems must be revisited if the concept of ideology is to be revived. Where we part company is with their assertion that frames and framing (here they blur the noun and verb) will solve all these problems. Frame theory needs to continue to advance and is a valuable element of our theoretical repertoire, but the core issues about movement ideologies and their relations to material conditions and experiences that are at stake in those older problems and debates and definitions point to real issues that need to be grappled with on their own terms, not redefined out of existence in framing language.

The last section of the response, in which Snow and Benford sketch some of the relations between frames and ideology, is useful and suggestive, and we commend those ideas to careful consideration by students of social movements. However, we disagree with their last point, that framing as an activity is more observable than ideology, which they seem to assert can reside only deep in the psyche. We made precisely the opposite point, that ideologies can be written down and take on a life of their own, apart from the mind of any particular individual. In fact, both frames and framing on the one hand, and ideology on the other, can be observed in texts, public utterances, and interviews with leaders and activists; and both are in the same sense ultimately unobservable within an individual's mind.

Indeed, more rigorous empirical work along these lines is necessary to rejuvenate both a nonpejorative use of ideology and the framing perspective. While details are beyond the scope of these comments, there are new methodologies that hold promise to move both approaches forward (see Johnston 2002). For example, story grammar analysis (Franzosi 1998, 1999) is one way to move beyond qualitative descriptions and measure the strength of what is being said or written about. Story grammars represent the essence of what is meant in textual episodes and are often presented in the form of hierarchical semantic structures. The occurrences of specific structures can be quantified to yield measures of how often specific meanings occur. Shapiro and Markoff's (1998) innovative approach to computer-assisted textual processing combines the advantages of story grammar analysis with the number-crunching abilities of computers. These methodological innovations hold promise to move both ideological analysis and frame analysis out of their descriptive bias and to give both firmer empirical grounding on which comparisons can be made.

Separately and together, Snow, Benford, and their colleagues have written a great deal of important sociology, and we have not pretended to do justice to all of their work. Our emphasis on key points of disagreement with them, our stress on a particular "turn," and our concerns about the ways in which their work has been used by others could easily but quite incorrectly be read as an attack on them or their work. As we have repeatedly stressed in our previous chapter and in this reply, we are not calling for an abandonment of work on frame theory. Rather, we believe that it is time for a serious reappraisal of the relations between newer work on frame theory and the older issues and ideas surrounding the nonpejorative understanding of ideology. As their response amply demonstrates, they are well prepared to bring rich scholarly and intellectual resources to this reappraisal.

REFERENCES

Franzosi, Roberto. 1998. "Narrative Analysis: Why (and How) Sociologists Should Be Interested in Narrative." Pp. 517-554 in *The Annual Review of Sociology*, John Hagan, ed. Palo Alto, CA: Annual Reviews.

———. 1999. "The Return of the Actor: Interaction Networks among Social Actors during Periods of High Mobilization in Italy, 1919-1922." *Mobilization* 4: 131-149.

Johnston, Hank. 2002. "Verification and Proof in Frame and Discourse Analysis." Pp. 62-91 in *Methods of Social Movement Research,* Bert Klandermans and Suzanne Staggenborg, eds. Minneapolis: University of Minnesota Press.

Shapiro, Gilbert, and John Markoff. 1998. *Revolutionary Demands: A Content Analysis of the Cahiers de Doléances of 1789.* Stanford, CA: Stanford University Press.

Tarrow, Sidney. 1998. *Power in Movement: Social Movements and Contentious Politics.* 2nd ed. New York: Cambridge University Press.

Chapter 12

STRATEGIC IMPERATIVE, IDEOLOGY, AND FRAMES

David L. Westby

From early on, social movement theory has understood framing as a strategic process.[1] Although Gamson's and Snow's early conceptions of framing were firmly grounded in social-psychological and symbolic-interactionist traditions, as framing concepts became more popular in social movement analysis, researchers emphasized the strategic use of frames.[2] I think that this can best be understood as an "elective affinity" between strategic framing and the intellectual climate of the social movement field, which was dominated by resource mobilization theory (RM) roughly between 1975 and 1985.

RM and political process theorists recast the frame concept from its original interactionist function that *vertically* connected structure with the social-psychological level to one that *horizontally* connected political opportunity and collective action (e.g., McAdam, McCarthy, and Zald 1996: 2, passim). The comprehensive inventory of frame-aligning processes was just what RM needed: a concept that simultaneously met the critiques emanating from the emerging cultural turn but that also fit the rationality axiom of the theory. It was a natural fit with McCarthy and Zald's (1973) "modern trend," with professional movement entrepreneurs systematically mounting their mobilizations and engineering their campaigns. And for RM theorists, it provided a more or less rationally ordered framework for McAdam's (1982) "cognitive liberation." Importantly, Snow and his colleagues were not working in a vacuum. At virtually the same moment, Swidler (1986) suggested that actors used culture as a tool kit in constructing the movement's persuasive discourse. So strategic framing was established early as a taken-for-granted process (see, for example, Zald's chapter 11 in McAdam, McCarthy, and Zald 1996;

Gamson 1992). It is perhaps fair to say that framing provided RM with a discursive resource that other "softer" ways of bringing culture into movement studies lacked, reinforcing the strategic rationality attributed to movements by RM. So it is Hardly surprising that by 1996 the leaders of the RM and political process schools had assigned framing a primary place in movement theory (McAdam, McCarthy, and Zald 1996).

It is clear that most strategic framing must be based on society's cultural stock. As Zald puts it, movements "draw on the cultural stock for images of what is an injustice" (1996: 266), generating frames from "a diverse set of actors in relation to a variety of audiences within and outside of a movement" (261), as well as from what he calls its "broken" and "contradictory" nature (268). So if frames are tool kits drawn from the diverse and shifting cultural stock, including (potentially) both oppositional and nonoppositional elements (Tarrow 1998: 106-107), it follows that framing also tends to be both shifting, complex, and multiple. Indeed, a cursory review of movement-framing studies seems to confirm this. Framing is situated contextually as a process of adjustment that mediates changes in opportunity structure and collective action from one state to another (McAdam, McCarthy, and Zald 1996: 2; McAdam 1994). To cite a few more examples: framing shifts are crucial in media framing (Gamson and Modigliani 1989); in a local-to-global shift in the Brazilian environmental movement (Rothman and Oliver 2002); in globalizing movements (Smith, Chatfield, and Pagnucco 1997; Marullo, Pagnucco, and Smith 1996); in unifying a master frame from the ideological diversity of Francoist Catalonia (Johnston 1991); in reversing the direction of racial struggle in mid-nineteenth-century Cincinnati (Ellingson 1995); in analyzing the appropriation of mainstream ideology by the Chilean women's movement (Noonan 1997); over the course of the pro-choice movement (Evans 1997); in post-Soviet politics (Zdravomyslova 1996); and similarly in Eastern Europe after communism's collapse (Oberschall 1996).

Strategic framing, then, often tends to embrace a multiplicity of frames. This occurs in part because of its shifting nature: frame components may just accumulate. Clemens (1996) has shown how the U.S. labor movement grew by a process of "bricolage," or accretion, as it faced new obstacles and a changing configuration of work. Diverse social bases or sentiment pools can also make multiple framing a more or less permanent feature of a movement, as in the case of the U.S. women's movement showing very different faces to its middle-class and working-class constituents (Press and Cole 1992), or in the framing battles in MADD, Mothers against Drunk Driving (McCarthy 1994). Multiple framing can also have ideological sources, as in the historic split between pragmatists and pacifists in the peace movement (Wittner 1984; Benford 1993; Marullo, Pagnucco, and Smith 1996). Situations in which movements that include diverse social movement organizations facing distinct political opportunities may be another, as Diani shows in his analysis of the North Italian Leagues (1996).

It does indeed appear that framing processes reflect the changing and diverse character of the cultural stock, and that these conditions impose imperatives to which movements respond strategically.

IDEOLOGY AND FRAMING

Now framing may be strategic, but this cannot be the whole of it. Mere restatement of the cultural stock obviously leaves vacant framing's key function of attracting new adherents. There must be some quality of the movement in terms of which its strategizing makes sense. Although the treatments of this are generally scattered and amorphous, it seems reasonably clear that a movement's ideology is ordinarily implicated in how strategic framing gets done. Thus, we must first ask: What is meant by "ideology" in the context of framing?

Oliver and Johnston (chapter 9 in this volume) have provided a helpful discussion explicating the distinct usages of "ideology" and "frame" in movement theory. Ideologies, they maintain, link theory, norms, and values in an interconnected fashion (44) and focus on "the content of whole systems of belief, on their multiple dimensions, and on how ideas are related to each other." They are historical and relatively stable in nature and lead us in the direction of other theories of society and social change. They define movement boundaries in terms of their values and connections to movement identities. Frames, on the other hand, have none of these qualities, but are relatively shallow, situated specifically in arenas of contention, and compared to ideologies, which must be studied and learned, are assimilated relatively easily and quickly.

But how exactly does ideology shape and constrain framing? Oliver and Johnston focus on explaining the differences and leave it at that. Ideology is indeed different from framing, but this just sets the stage for raising the question of their relationship. The recent literature reveals a broadly consensual understanding of the function of ideology in framing. Zald, for example, defines ideology as "a set of beliefs that are used to justify or challenge a given sociopolitical order . . . and interpret the political world, . . . and that tend to be more complex and logical systems of beliefs than frames, though frames may be embedded in ideologies" (and ideology itself within the global category of culture [Zald 1996: 262]). Tarrow (1992) advances a similar scheme: for him the oddly archaic concept of "mentalities" along with political culture combine with frame to comprise a hierarchy of progressive inclusiveness or scale. Theoretical formulations such as these have parallels in movement-framing research. In his study of the first abolitionist campaign in late eighteenth-century England, d'Anjou argues that the movement leaders' ideologies were the resource for constructing the frames employed in the two central movement functions, "the mobilization of resources . . . and . . . challenges of authorities" (1996: 41-42). In their study of ideological discourse and segregationist ideology, Platt and Williams claim that "ideology is a cultural resource acting as a structural and structuring feature in organizing social movements" (1999: 10). They go on to distinguish "operative ideologies" (clearly described like frames) from a higher-order level of ideology, which they designate as formal and abstract (itself derivative of broader cultural worldviews). Snow and Benford also refer to ideology as a cultural resource in framing (chapter 10 in this volume). It appears that these representations of ideology in framing reflect a common, if loose, understanding: frames are symbolic constructions that in different ways are derivative of ideologies. If this is accepted, it may be asked: What aspects of ideology are particularly important for framing processes? I suggest that two in particular present at least intuitive claims for recognition.

One of these may well be the ideological diversity commonly present in a movement. Although a single movement ideology from which frames are derived sometimes seems implicit in the ideology/framing commentaries, a moment's reflection reveals the limitations of this: (1) movements frequently have internal schismatic struggles over ideology; (2) the various forms of collaboration in movements often engender contentious ideological variants; (3) there may be differences regarding the primacy of particular aspects of the ideology; and (4) the movement may march under an eclectic banner of more than a single distinct ideology. Examples include communism in coming to terms with nationalist sentiments, the varieties of peace ideology often present in peace movements, and the sharp ideological differences in the earlier feminist movement.

Despite an absence of systematic treatment in the literature, there is at least some reason to think that ideological diversity can be important in framing. Snow suggests a parallel between the master frame/collective action frame distinction and Basil Bernstein's theory of the elaborated and restricted linguistic codes located respectively in the English middle and working classes (Snow 1992). This has never been developed, and may be unworkable; but at least a few others, in encountering ideological diversity in their research, have suggested that it has important effects—although just what these might be remains unclear. On the one hand, for example, Johnston maintains that the Marxist, Christian, and conservative Catalonian nationalist ideologies present in the Catalonian anti-Franco movement resulted in an "ability to encompass a variety of different interpretations, and to incorporate new and unfamiliar events" (Johnston 1995: 240). On the other hand, Benford found that the three divergent ideological strains in the peace movement (as present in Austin, Texas) created framing difficulties in a situation where unified framing was thought to be a priority (Benford 1993). Findings on both sides of this fence have been reported by others (e.g., Mooney 1995; Noonan 1997). Whatever the particularities of these and other examples, they do seem to support the intuition that ideological diversity is an important condition of movement framing.

A second ideological factor has to do with the strength of movement actors' ideological commitment, something familiar to those in movements everywhere. It makes sense to speak of a movement's *ideological salience* to capture the varying preeminence of ideology, not only in framing but also in movement activities generally. With this term I designate a shared commitment and normative accord that prioritizes movement ideology over competing beliefs, commitments, or demands. One would suppose prima facie that the greater a movement's ideological salience, the more the movement would constrain the range or variability of framing.

I have been discussing ideology from the standpoint of the movement. Indeed, I will employ a relatively restricted sense of ideology as delineated by Oliver and Johnston, understood specifically as the dominant discourse of a movement. It is not to be identified with the cultural stock, which I comprehend as the entirety of the life-world. But neither is it intended as a denial of the presence of ideological aspects of the cultural stock—which would be absurd. I specify movement ideology as a relatively elaborated code or doctrine that is the charter or template defining the movement itself and which exists only in the identities of its adherents. This difference is exemplified in the distinction between the concrete sentiments and beliefs arising out of an exploitative labor system and the doctrinal and theoretical elaborations of Marxist ideology.

FRAME AS JOINT STRATEGIC AND IDEOLOGICAL DISCOURSE

I have described framing as discourse derived from (1) strategic imperatives created in the course of the shifting and complex historical flow of the cultural stock and (2) the domain of movement ideology, manifest in varying degrees of ideological diversity and salience. Framing is thereby formulated as a jointly constituted process, as discourse that conjoins the ideological and the strategic. This way of thinking about framing has not inspired much theoretical attention.

Instead, one finds mostly critiques of movements' instrumental rationality from the standpoint of their cultural reality. Polletta (1997) claims that the framing duality of strategic action and cultural or ideological orientations undermines frame analysis by encouraging a reduction of movements' cultural aspects to little more than just another factor to be strategically manipulated. The reality of movements, she argues, is that their cultural richness cannot be reduced to an instrumental rationality, but must be conceptualized, as "a broad semiotic template." Similarly, from the standpoint of discourse analysis, Steinberg (1998: 742) maintains that the epistemology of framing cannot reconcile the model of rational action on which strategic frame-aligning processes are grounded with the constructionist identity-creating, value-oriented, discourse-centered actor. He proposes that this contradiction can be transcended by introducing Bahktian principles of discourse analysis, and he supports this claim through his analysis of early nineteenth-century English cotton weavers and spinners (Steinberg 1995a, 1995b, 1999). Oliver and Johnston, somewhat ambiguously—in the context of their broader endorsement of framing as an important concept—come close to suggesting that strategic framing may be more or less limited to market-dominated times like our own. The work of Kriesi and his colleagues supplements these remonstrations with an empirical analysis of framing in the European new social movements of the 1980s under differing national conditions, arguing that it was comprehensible only in terms of its embedding in political power relations, thereby seeming to undermine its status as a type of agency (Kriesi et al. 1995).

Critiques such as these are certainly valuable. In my view, however, they short-circuit a logically prior task, namely, that of this article, clarifying the theoretical status of framing within movement theory. The argument I have made suggests that a potentially more fruitful starting point would be to acknowledge the virtual incorrigibility of the linkage of ideological and strategic discourses in framing. This could be formulated as a recognition that ideologies may limit the range of strategic discourse in framing, but also that strategic discourse in framing may deviate from and even challenge movement ideology. Moreover, if we attribute a good deal of autonomy to both ideology and strategic action, it also satisfies a loose criterion of agency. Movements may be thought of as having a structurally grounded interest in ideological maintenance while facing a shifting and complex—yet broadly obdurate—strategic imperative conditioned, sometimes even imposed, by the flow of events.

In other words, movements by definition share to at least some degree (1) a common set of meanings and (2) some sense of a problem that they want to do something about. The first of these will to some extent include ideological elements. The second constitutes a strategic imperative. Both are interpretations, but also incorrigible. Ideologies interpret the world in a relatively unified, complex, and historical mode; a strategic imperative mandates interpretations that are particular and situational. Movement framing designates persuasive discourse that in one way or another incorporates both.

I proceed, then, on the assumption that the ideology-strategic discourse relation is the generic structure of framing. Its empirical manifestations are of course variable, indeed extraordinarily so, and now become the objects of our interest. Mainly from the movement literature, I select movements that vary greatly in their scale, grievances, goals, and social loci, to the end of formulating a provisional inventory of how ideology and strategic discourse work together in framing practices. I present abbreviated descriptive accounts of these, being especially attentive to those aspects of the strategic imperative and movement ideology. I show that at least six distinct variants of this linkage can be identified: (1) simple derivation of strategic discourse from ideology; (2) strategic discourse suppressed by ideology; (3) strategic discourse remote from ideology; (4) the fusion of ideology and strategic discourse in action; (5) strategic framing beyond ideological boundaries; and (6) framing that strategically appropriates hegemonic ideology.[3]

Simple Derivation of Strategic Discourse from Ideology

A good deal of framing manifests itself in a simple derivative fashion. By this I mean that framing processes are both strategic responses to changing circumstances and clearly derived from movement ideology. Evans's study of the pro-choice movement (1997) provides an example. He analyzes framing shifts in the religious pro-choice movement over three periods: (1) 1967-1973, when it served as an abortion service, and the framing audience(s) were liberal Jews and Protestants who could provide local references; (2) 1973-1980, after the Catholic Church and the organizations it created focused on overturning *Roe v. Wade*; and (3) 1980-1992, during which (a) it shifted from the issue of a woman's right to make the decision to conditions bearing on her ability to make them wisely and responsibly and (b) it targeted evangelical groups which had recently entered the multiorganizational field (Evans 1997).

Evans's analysis is mostly about the boundaries among organizations in issue arenas, or multiorganizational fields, and how these influence the successive frames. Activating the already rights-oriented clergy appears to have been a relatively low-cost strategy. Our interest here falls on the fact that the leaders were able to reframe from period to period as the abortion situation shifted strategically, constructing a series of effective frames derivative from the framework of the feminist abstract code, the core ideological tenet of which was a woman's right to choose.

Simple derivative framing also appears in more diverse ideological contexts. D'Anjou's 1996 study of the first campaign against the slave trade in England shows how elite representatives of two distinct ideologies collaborated in the construction of a unified frame demanding the abolition of the slave trade in late eighteenth-century England. He argues that several cultural trends—and two in particular—had for some time been creating a more facilitative cultural environment for antislavery sentiments. The first of these included (1) the Quakers turn to a morality-grounded, explicitly antislavery position, followed by (2) a similar shift among dissenting religious groups like the Methodists, and (3) emergence of an antislavery voice within the church itself. The second trend was the growing importance of an antislavery position in secular thought, from Montesquieu and Locke to contemporary representatives of the Enlightenment (d'Anjou 1996: chap. 4). A set of facilitating events (the "episodic context" in d'Anjou's lexicon) provoked spontaneous parallel protests, followed soon by a joint mobilization opposing the trade. D'Anjou then shows how these very different worldviews became consolidated as movement ideology, mainly through the efforts of its most important social movement organization, the Abolition Committee (chap. 7).

Within the elements constitutive of the "interpretive package" (taken from Gamson and Modigliani 1989), d'Anjou presents the frame as a dual one. One line sought to establish slavery as morally and religiously unacceptable, a difficult reversal of Christian doctrine. Slavery was portrayed in a variety of venues, graphically and through texts. In particular, vivid descriptions of the horrific practices of the trade left their imprint on many. The second line rejected it on practical grounds: its costs and the increasing burden on the economy. The distinct moral and practical arguments were intended to reach different pools of potential supporters identified with well-known, publicly voiced abolitionist sentiments: on the one hand, church members and the religiously inclined, and on the other, practical politicians who would have to balance abolition of the trade against other matters, especially economic considerations. The strategy of opposing only the slave trade, and not demanding the actual abolition of slavery, narrowed the range of opposed interests (whose counterframing was ineffective) and yet, from a practical political standpoint would eventually result in de facto elimination of slavery.

The anti-slave trade frame was strategically multiple in its appeals to very different sentiment pools, and it was derived from very different ideological sources. Of course in the longer historical sweep, although secular modernizing liberals and the notables who led strongly bonded Protestant religious communities have generally found little affinity with one another, at certain moments they have converged politically, most importantly perhaps in the seventeenth and early eighteenth centuries in the rise of rational capitalism (Weber 1948, but see also Zaret 1989), and during the political formation of the English working class (Thompson 1966). The slave trade question may have been another. It might be argued that in each of these instances the particular concatenation of events conspired to facilitate an affinity of ideas centering on the presuppositional theme of the individual, facilitating a bracketing or suspension of other aspects of the ideologies.

Strategic Discourse Suppressed by Ideology

Situations of this type exhibit exceptionally high ideological salience, in which movement actors, unconditionally committed to movement ideology, construct movement frames with disregard to strategic considerations. In such situations the possibilities of alternative interpretations are overwhelmed or suppressed. Communism, in at least some of its national manifestations, and anarchism generally seem to be close approximations. The cell structure of the party, devised for especially hostile environments like the United States, was in these terms an organizational form intended to protect a small and weak movement from the corrupt interpretations that might accompany a strategic approach. As the U.S. labor movement expanded, the party rejected its increasingly adaptive framing, clinging to the doctrine that capitalism was undermining itself dialectically, a process that would inevitably bring into being a revolutionary situation. Whatever the material interests of party leaders may have been—toadying to Moscow and maintaining their organizational positions certainly among them—the consequence at the level of ideas was a rigid adherence to a doctrine that ironically was employed to exclude and even denounce strategic considerations as apostasy.[4]

Strategic Discourse Remote from Ideology

Another way that the reality of framing departs from the "derivation model" is to be found in situations where ideology is absent or not implicated in framing. The chain of events following the nuclear accident at the Three Mile Island nuclear installation near Harrisburg, Pennsylvania, in 1979 appears to have been one such instance. The accident quickly generated a series of shifts in the collective action frame that evidently occurred apart from much ideological influence.

Walsh (1988) characterizes the accident, in which radioactive material escaped into the atmosphere, as a "suddenly imposed grievance." Three Mile Island is a mostly rural area about twelve miles south of Harrisburg on the Susquehanna River where, according to Walsh, antinuclear energy sentiments had scarcely penetrated. A branch of a quite ideological antinuclear energy organization had been active in the Harrisburg area for some time, but the community-based organizations formed in the accident's wake rejected the organization's ideological positions, particularly radical environmental critiques linking environmental issues to nuclear weapons. This was so despite the fact that, living as they did virtually next door to the plant, they had been the ones most affected and comprised the bulk of those involved in the massive evacuation.

Walsh describes these entities as representing "two relatively distinct paths to activism, . . . localites and cosmopolitans." Unlike cosmopolitan activists, the localites "were pragmatic, geared almost exclusively to the restart and cleanup issues" (1998: 127). This pragmatism both reflected and responded to the community's pervasive conservatism, while significant oppositional sentiments or beliefs were virtually absent. Indeed, local *nonideological* factors centering on threats to the community were the salient ones. Over the course of about two years, frame shifts occurred in response to emerging events, particularly "vulnerabilities" generated by legal rulings, positions taken by politicians such as the governor, and proposals floated by the targets, and by tactical errors on the part of the movement's targets—the operating company and the Nuclear Regulatory Commission. Frame shifts were, in short, opportunity-driven, reactive rather than proactive, responsive mainly to events initiated by the targets.

Walsh's account shows that there may be conditions that persist throughout a mobilization that inhibit the emergence of guiding ideologies, and that strategic actions may be mounted not only independently but even in opposition to ideology. Indeed, situations such as this may be more frequent in the early phases of protest than is commonly thought.

The Fusion of Ideology and Strategic Discourse in Action

Quite different from the clear derivation of frames from ideologies are movements in which ideology spontaneously transcends its sociocultural constraints—including even the interests of some movement constituents—to become an autonomous force. In such situations, at least for a time, the distinction between ideology and strategic action is erased. On occasion these may be events with world-historical significance. Sewell describes the phase of the French Revolution commencing on August 4, 1789, as a time when "ideology broke loose from its social moorings," creating "a world where mental representations of power governed all actions, and where a network of signs completely dominated political life" (1985: 73).

Similarly, in the course of his analysis of the anti-Franco movement in Catalonia, Johnston (1991) describes one particularly critical event in this scenario, the Capuchin affair. After nearly a decade of mild liberalization during the 1960s, a formal constitution of a new democratic union of university students was introduced through the agency of an illegal assembly at a Capuchin monastery outside Barcelona. This occurred after years of gradually building a unified anti-Franco master frame out of formerly separate and conflicting communist, church, and nationalist sectors in Catalonia. When the police arrived to break up the meeting (in violation of the church's concordat with the Vatican), a massive reaction broke out involving participants, including some from among the elite, that set in motion extended waves of mobilization. The mobilization transcended all particularism: it was "without labels . . . did not have names . . . was simply anti-Francoist, a national affirmation, social affirmation, democratic affirmation" (Johnston 1991: 147). The event transformed the consciousness of many and very quickly became an engine for spreading the movement.

In such events there seems to occur a fusion in action of ideology and strategic discourse. It is close to the image of the irrational mob caricatured by LeBon and other crowd and early collective behavior theorists (and indeed, a model derived from the very events in Sewell's account). And it calls to mind accounts of comparable actions in

China, Russia, and elsewhere. Less cataclysmic versions of such spontaneity are common enough, particularly in the workplace, where a form of what Scott has called "hidden transcripts" may have been festering and spreading.[5] The accounts of Steinberg (1995a), Fantasia (1988), and Scott (1974) reveal the joint emergent character of oppositional ideologies and frames in such settings.

Although such fusions in action of ideology and strategic discourse are intrinsically short lived, their consequences—although unpredictable—may be consequential, even fateful. The French Revolution itself devolved for a time into interest-driven warring factions. The public escalation of the anti-Franco movement, on the other hand, evidently solidified a movement already en route to unity and contributed greatly to its growth and power.

Strategic Framing Beyond Ideological Boundaries

Another way in which joint ideology/strategic discourse shapes framing occurs when framing goes beyond ideological limits. Intuitively, this might seem more likely in less diverse ideological settings. A case in point is that of European socialism during the late nineteenth and early twentieth centuries, which Wuthnow describes in terms amenable to my argument.

Wuthnow (1989) analyzes socialism as one of three transformative European social movements (the others being the Reformation and the Enlightenment), demonstrating that they all developed creative levels of discourse in similar political and economic circumstances. Socialism of course considered itself to be a transnational movement, a core ideological understanding. He describes how the various European states presented socialists with more or less intractable conditions, forcing each national mobilization to adapt strategically to the particular set of enabling and constraining factors. The national movements ended up creating parties that both acted and theorized those actions along revisionist lines, and departed from orthodoxy in virtually heretical ways. LaSalle's capitulation to nationalism in authoritarian Prussia, Bebel's courting of the petit bourgeoisie and artisans in Saxony, and Jaures's republicanism and moral idealism in France (Wuthnow 1989: 481ff.) are cases in point. To these, others could easily be added, for example, the Swedish Social Democrats' early embrace of the Liberals and the politics of suffrage, and later—in power—their coalition with the conservative Farmer's party.

On what basis can it be claimed that these frames were outside of socialism's ideological boundaries? Was not socialism a relatively ideologically diverse movement? Well, in one sense there was plenty of diversity: socialism was at one level an intellectual battleground, and many of the disputes had to do precisely with the problems associated with different national settings. Whatever their differences, however, socialists were generally united in their identification of the proletariat as revolutionary agents and of existing states and parliamentary parties as agents of the bourgeoisie. Collaboration with authoritarian regimes and class enemies, and embracing ideologies of national unity, can hardly be reconciled with the idea of history as driven by class struggle and the inevitable demise of capitalism through violent overthrow. I think it is reasonable to say that, at least from the standpoint of the opportunities available in different national settings, socialism was not a particularly diverse or flexible ideology. Perhaps the best evidence of this is the fact that, even as social democratic parties were injecting themselves into the European polities, there remained purist sectors of the movement, which resisted strategic revisionist reframing for decades.

If socialism was not an ideologically diverse movement, why did its bearers frame beyond its core ideology? The most obvious factor was the political intractability of the conditions confronting the national movements, situations that clearly encouraged elevation of the strategic imperative to primacy. Wuthnow places considerable emphasis on the potent, politically realistic imperative that workers confirm the validity of their historic assignment with some concrete political achievements. But it may also have had something to do with the fact that the Internationales, the only significant supranational socialist organizations (and always arenas of rhetorical struggles), were unfit to exert organizational or financial control over either ideas or practice. Perhaps we could say that because of this situation, European socialist ideology facilitated framing beyond its ideology not because it was a diverse code, but for the structural combination of (1) being faced with a set of diverse and intractable opportunity situations, (2) having a strong ideological incentive to engage in practical political action, and (3) having an organizationally weak center.

The workings of these factors, to borrow from Althusser, seem to have eventuated in a strategic overdetermination of framing despite highly salient movement ideology. Wuthnow emphasizes that the influence of state actors in strong states like Bismarck's Prussia in effect preempted the movements' very credentializing capacities. The party leaders would of course then claim (i.e., frame) the compromises as important socialist advances (1990: 487ff.). In our terms this is tantamount to the movement ceding away the power of framing.

One final and important point may be drawn from this. Over the course of these decades and into the twentieth century, socialist ideology certainly became more diverse. An appealing explanation for this may be the recursive play of national framing (and, of course, practice) on socialist ideology, as the parties began to experience some success. To a considerable degree it seems fair to say that framing processes dominated by strategic considerations lead to ideological adaptation. This is close to a point made by Snow and Benford in their objections to Oliver and Johnston's characterization of ideology and framing, namely, that framing can be a kind of antidote to the reifying tendencies of ideologies (Snow and Benford, chapter 10 in this volume). In this fashion, the strategic imperative may keep movement theorists and leaders abreast of social change and even ordain significant ideological transformations. Such instances exhibit a partial autonomy of some strategic actions—actions which become change-initiating in their own right.

Framing That Strategically Appropriates Hegemonic Ideology

By "hegemonic ideology" I mean an ideology promoted by an elite, but shared by at least a sector of the nonelite, and also embedded in widespread cultural practices. While this definition does not make hegemonic ideology coterminous with the cultural stock, it does mean that to some extent it is certainly present there. Incorporation of hegemonic ideology in framing appears to be commonplace. Because its manifestations are quite dissimilar, I will describe what appears to be three distinct types.

The appropriation by the civil rights movement (and later by other movements) of liberal democratic rhetoric is sometimes cited as that movement's most important frame (McAdam 1988; Morris 1984). While it might be thought that appropriation of the hegemonic ideology in a democratic polity would come naturally for a group seeking access, it should be remembered that the movement was—at least during certain extended periods—accompanied by alternative frames on both its left and right. What is important here is the meaning of democratic-rights ideology to frame specific categories of rights (civil and voting rights) and to justify various forms of civil disobedience as appropriate tactics. Over the course of its many mobilizations, the movement displayed a wide range of collective action frames, from mainly civil and voting rights frames in the South to frames focusing on economic challenges when it attempted to move north. These occurred in conjunction with a rich tactical repertoire of civil disobedience and other actions.

The premise of this framing was that there was a contradiction between the abstract code and the extent of its reach (see McAdam 1994). Frame rhetoric and action remind us of the code and seek to elevate the sense of contradiction to the status of a causal lever to force change. Politicians, sheriffs, discriminating employers, and even "white racists" are not enemies to be overcome, but misguided citizens who need education and persuasion. The frame displays the ideology and its lived contradictions in collective actions that affirm rather than deny the basic legitimacy of the system. This framing tactic might be called the *exposure of contradiction*.

However, revealing contradiction by no means exhausts the forms of appropriation of hegemonic ideology. A description of two additional types will demonstrate this. I call the first of these *inversion of meaning* and discuss how it occurred in the Chilean women's movement as described by Noonan.

Noonan (1997) analyzes women's resistance to the Pinochet regime in Chile between 1973 and 1988. Claiming that both framing theory and political opportunity theory had generally been applied by researchers too narrowly, Noonan asserts that women had been at the forefront of protest in many parts of Hispanic America. She argues that Chilean women played a powerful political role, constructing a feminist and democratic master frame that shook the regime's foundations and was strongly implicated in ultimately bringing about democratic change.

Until about 1953 there had been a strong women's movement in Chile that focused on suffrage and related issues. The rise of Marxist ideology after the war, with its prioritizing of class over other social divisions, set the women's movement on a path of decline. Upon seizing power, the Pinochet regime set out to obliterate every vestige of the Chilean left, not just the communists, and this opened a modest window of opportunity for the women's movement, which had been in abeyance. Women built what Noonan calls a "maternal frame." This combined both a muted feminist ideology and non-ideological aspects of the cultural stock, which strongly reinforced traditional women's roles and was promoted by governments of both left and right. But during the Pinochet years there was also a buildup of a network of maternal institutions such as mother's centers, and these became a significant resource, both materially and ideologically. Noonan writes, "A body of ideological and material resources that reinforced traditional (i.e., maternal) roles for women were not only available, but promoted by state agencies and political parties" (1997: 257). Coupled with the destruction of the left in the early Pinochet years, this "maternal frame," Noonan argues, revitalized a feminism that could legitimize itself by keeping one foot in the maternal door. In effect, women appropriated state maternal ideology and opposed the state by promoting family values while simultaneously building a new democratically oriented feminism.

Beginning in 1978 this mobilization had become widespread enough to support what Noonan calls "an explosion of women's activism" (1997: 261), and with its spread to other sectors (e.g., the urban poor) it escalated into a movement cycle with "a return to democracy" master frame, incorporating demands for an expansion of women's rights, including political rights, and capped by massive demonstrations in 1983.

Clearly in Chile the emergence of a feminist frame, and ultimately a democracy frame, was no simple derivation. It involved the rise, fall, and interpenetration of different ideologies, along with the interplay of ideology and nonideological aspects of the cultural stock, in frame construction that can be understood only historically. This critically included an incorporation of important aspects of an oppositional ideology. But for this to work it was necessary that it somehow undergo an inversion of meaning. How might this occur?

One possibility is that inversion of meaning in framing is effected through hidden transcripts. As Scott (1990) describes them, hidden transcripts are expressions of grievances that draw upon public transcripts of authoritative discourse, often through accompanying actions, even dramatizations, to scornfully and ironically invert them and thereby expose them as hollow. He convincingly argues that they are mainly if not entirely generated under authoritarian conditions. Hidden transcripts do seem to have in common with frames the essential property of deploying ideas through actions intending to communicate with particular audiences. Framing that rests on an inverted understanding of hegemonic ideology, then, does not express the grievance in a straightforward unambiguous statement; this remains nested in the hidden transcripts. So while the frame may be an interpretation, in this case its very existence presupposes yet another level of interpretation. It appears akin to the ironic and satiric accounts enacted elsewhere, for example, by dissidents in prerevolutionary underground Eastern Europe.

A third type of appropriation of hegemonic ideology may be seen in the case of the revolt of the Chinese students in their occupation of Tiananmen Square in 1989. Student unrest began to grow in China during the 1980s. Some degree of relaxation of social control, along with an erosion of elite unity, tended to encourage continuing activity, although the fear of a crackdown was ever present. In early 1989 Gorbachev, at his peak as a reformer, paid a state visit, and about the same time the Asian Development Bank, courted by the Chinese government, held its first meeting there. These events created a large press presence. University students in Beijing, packed by the thousands into overcrowded housing, moved to openly defy the government.

Zuo and Benford (1995) analyzed the events, concentrating on framing. Here was a situation where protesters with little in the way of resources other than their bodies—and networks—faced a powerful state with a history of repression. The only factor over which the students had some control was the way they framed their actions. They recounted the many forms of injustice and corruption that not only they but also large numbers of ordinary citizens had encountered for years. They mounted nonviolent actions, such as hunger strikes. They presented these actions in terms of a frame that combined the two dominant Chinese ideologies—communism and nationalism—with Confucianism, a widely embedded set of beliefs and practices in the cultural stock loaded with ethical implications regarding authority and rule. According to Zuo and Benford, this resonated widely among the people. In this fashion the students covered all-important available bases at the level of ideology, leaving little space for the authorities' counterframing. For some time, authorities did attempt to counterframe, although ineffectively, and it became clear that the students were "drawing millions to [their] side" (Zuo and Benford 1995: 143). Framing here appears to have been an attempt—in the short term, a successful one—to capture the moral high ground through a comprehensive appropriation of diverse ideologies and construction of a collective action frame complex enough to resonate with sentiment pools well beyond student circles. The government eventually declared martial law and sent in the tanks.[6]

How does this case compare with the preceding ones? First of all, there does appear to an element of exposure of contradiction in the use of communist ideology. There may also be a touch of ideological inversion. According to Zuo and Benford's account, there seems little doubt that along with the frame's appeal to ordinary Chinese, its purpose was mainly protective, to create as strong a moral shield as possible. We might call this *moral cover.*

It is worthwhile to set these situations against the framing that appeared during the collapse of the Soviet Union, based on Zdravomyslova's (1996) account. The upheaval in the Soviet Union began during the Gorbachev reforms during the late 1980s and was driven by a number of organizations, the most prominent being the radically democratic Democratic Union (DU). The DU mounted an escalating civil disobedience, then later became a force in electoral politics. In Zdravomyslova's judgment, it was chiefly responsible for the shape of the first Russian government. She shows that the DU's early framing emphasized building collective identities through infrastructure development and provocative collective actions of civil disobedience calculated to engage the police. Virtually from the beginning, the DU's framing took a totally oppositional stance, declaring a position of "negative opposition," and at all times pronouncing the regime to be unreformable. Although there were plenty of police actions, the overall response to this testing of the government's will revealed it as unwilling to engage in really serious repression against the backdrop of continuing reform. Later, during the electoral phase, the DU coupled its oppositional stance with specific aspects of an ideological import, Western democratic ideology, particularly the idea of the law-based state and American anti-communism.

It appears that once the movement had gained a foothold following the beginnings of reform, it was able to establish and validate its "negative opposition" through its escalation of direct actions. Inverted regime public transcripts never figured in the frame: it incorporated only "negative opposition" in the first phase and imported elements of Western democratic ideology in the second. This was successful framing in an opportunity situation resulting from the fact that the hegemonic ideology had lost its hold.[7]

CONCLUSION

I have examined a diverse set of movements to explore the implications of a theory of framing based on an integration of its ideological and strategic aspects. It appears that while some framing clearly conforms to a model in which shifting strategic imperatives are framed easily and consistently in terms of movement ideology, there is also a substantial range of framing that transcends the confines of this model. Movement ideology may be so dominant that strategic considerations are rejected. At the other extreme, framing may proceed on a more or less purely strategic plane, dissociated from any ideology. Distinct from this, moments of spontaneous collective action may bring about a fusion of ideological and strategic elements of framing. In still other instances, strategic considerations may overflow ideological boundaries and even assume primacy in significantly affecting the historic course of the movement, including the substance of its ideology. In circumstances of greatly varying opportunity, movement actors may strategically appropriate elements of hegemonic ideologies.

We may now ask: Is it likely that these varying scenarios have different implications for the fate of movements? Although this question takes us beyond the confines of this chapter, it nevertheless mandates some brief—if speculative—remarks.

It may be that movements in which strategic considerations are suppressed by ideology are limited in their ability to understand and relate to their environment. One might suppose that this reduces a movement's adaptability and survival capacity. Indeed, observations of this sort are fairly commonplace. The inversion of this, a strategic orientation isolated from any significant ideological presence, and perhaps in particular one that is self-consciously anti-ideological, would for a different reason also seem unlikely to contribute to sustaining a movement. Consolidation or cooperation with other groups, or even movements, is without question greatly facilitated by sharing a common code. A consciousness linked to little more than a particular grievance and a particular frame would seem to afford relatively slight leverage for such developments. This might apply with special force abeyance periods, which appear to be important to movements because of their implications for long-term survival and perhaps effectiveness.[8]

These two types of framing have in common an "imbalance" of ideology and strategic orientation, both of which—if the above comments are granted any plausibility—have negative implications for the movement.

The obverse of this may be seen in a similarity shared by the next two types, the fusion of ideology and strategic discourse in action, and framing that overflows ideological boundaries. The former is a kind of short-circuiting of what might otherwise occur as a drawn-out framing battle. In some instances, for example, the Catalonian anti-Francoist movement, events of this type may achieve in an instant a higher level of mobilization—and perhaps potential political power—which in turn may recursively prompt shifts in movement goals and tactics, doubtless accompanied by a revamped framing. Framing dominated by strategic discourse beyond ideological boundaries, on the other hand, poses potential challenges to ideological purity and has important implications for the course and survival of the movement. Although different in other respects, it is in this regard akin to those situations in which ideology and strategic discourse are fused in action.

These observations speak to framing as the play of agency. Framing may bring agency to life, but from the standpoint of the movement, the form it assumes may well be a difference that makes a difference. When ideology and strategic discourse are fused in action, it is likely to increase mobilization. This is also true when strategic framing extends beyond ideological boundaries. On the other hand, when either ideology or strategic discourse overwhelm framing processes, the opposite effect seems more likely.

In this regard, consider the strategic appropriation of hegemonic ideology. Clearly this is a form of framing that may enhance a movement's chances in diverse circumstances. It also hints at relationships between regime types and the different forms of hegemonic appropriation. The regime contexts of the movements discussed here suggest the following: (1) democratic polities might facilitate framing featuring *exposure of contradictions,* (2) authoritarian regimes may encourage *inversion of meaning* appropriation, (3) totalitarian regimes may correlate with *moral political cover* appropriation, and (4) weak regimes might be more likely to give rise to *negative opposition framing.*

Very generally, the fact that such an array of framing types can be identified in these terms strongly suggests that taking framing processes for granted as more or less uniformly strategic and generally ideological is not only difficult to support but even an obstacle to theoretical development and should be seen as more complex and flexible—as I have suggested here. The fact that the ideology/strategic imperative coupling can be applied across major dimensions of movements—their size, national/transnational character, and age, to mention just a few—supports this proposition.

Although this inquiry is intended as exploratory, some mention of its limits is nevertheless warranted. Drawing case material opportunistically from the voluminous movement literature is only the most obvious of these. Beyond this, I have not attempted to discuss the inner technical features of ideology or the strategic imperative, a necessary task to further advance framing theory. Empirically, despite the inherent flux of movements and my own emphasis on the shifting nature of framing, I have—of necessity, I think—presented the types in essentially static fashion. Of course, movements in their historical reality need not cling to one or another form of framing, but may, and often do, slide or consciously shift from one to another.

In conclusion, it is worth noting that Zald has recently proposed a major—and contested—shift in the direction for movement studies (Zald 2000a, 2000b; for dissenting views, see Diani 2000 and Klandermans 2000), from the resource/contentious action model to "ideological structured behavior," which he defines as behavior "guided and shaped by ideological concerns" (2000a: 3). He maintains that this would better accommodate movement studies to the cultural turn, facilitate needed work on socialization within movements, and expand the range of movement study beyond what he considers to be a relatively narrow political domain. Such an enhancement of the status of ideology would clearly seem to support a continuing theorization of the ideology/strategic discourse framing bundle in movement studies.

NOTES

1. A systematic treatment or definition of "strategic" in the framing literature is to my knowledge nowhere to be found. My sense is that framing theorists and researchers think of strategic framing as discourse that responds to an action imperative and is intended to influence beliefs or feelings—and ultimately action—in relatively specific preconceived ways.

2. This is not to naively equate them. Gamson himself charged that the early framing theorists had "their feet planted in . . . a positivistic epistemology" while their heads were "in the clouds of a post-positivist constructionist world" (Gamson 1992: 69).

3. A cautionary note: This will be an attempt to formulate not anything like a comparative analysis of movement framing, which would surely be premature, but only a provisional typology based on a preliminary exploration of the variety of ways in which ideology and strategic discourse are joined in framing.

4. It may be noted in passing that elsewhere the stance of the party at least at certain times seems to have been quite different. In much of Europe, where conditions were different from the start, mobilizing was generally open. In agrarian China, in a climate even more hostile than the United States, the party, while adhering to the same basic doctrine, framed the political situation in military terms and did not temporize or squabble over the appearance of the revolutionary moment. This was certainly ironic, but from a political standpoint realistic as well, since China hardly qualified as a developing—and therefore progressive—capitalist society.

5. Although prefigured at least as early as the 1960s in E. P. Thompson's great work on the English working class (Thompson 1966), Scott's analysis of hidden transcripts (1990), even after more than a decade, has in my opinion unfortunately not been very broadly assimilated into movement studies.

6. Zhao's recent study (2001) is of course more comprehensive than any of the earlier analyses and may well be the definitive analysis of Tiananmen, but it presents nothing that would necessitate a modification of either Zuo and Benford's framing account or the argument advanced here.

7. These distinctions imply nothing about the possible mix of types in particular movements, at either a given moment or over the historical stretch. These are important matters that cannot be entered into here.

8. It seems that movements can survive indefinite periods of abeyance if two conditions are met: (1) the maintenance of some form of organization or network, and (2) the persistence of an ideology that supports a continuing identity with the movement and perhaps movement organization(s) and even particular individuals (see Rupp and Taylor 1987; Taylor and Whittier 1995; and Whittier 1995).

REFERENCES

Benford, Robert. 1993. "Frame Disputes within the Nuclear Disarmament Movement." *Social Forces* 71: 677-701.
———. 1997. "An Insider's Critique of the Social Movement Framing Perspective." *Social Inquiry* 67 (4): 409-430.
Clemens, Elisabeth S. 1996. "Organizational Form as Frame: Collective Identity and Political Strategy in the American Labor Movement." Pp. 205-226 in *Comparative Perspectives on Social Movements: Political Opportunities, Mobilizing Structures, and Cultural Framings*, Doug McAdam, John D. McCarthy, and Mayer N. Zald, eds. New York: Cambridge University Press.
d'Anjou, Leo. 1996. *Social Movements and Cultural Change*. New York: de Gruyter.
d'Anjou, Leo, and John Van Male. 1998. "Between Old and New: Social Movements and Cultural Change." *Mobilization* 3 (2): 207-226.
della Porta, Donatella, and Mario Diani. 1999. *Social Movements: An Introduction*. Malden, MA: Blackwell.
Diani, Mario. 1996. "Linking Frames and Political Opportunities: Insights from Regional Populism in Italy." *American Sociological Review* 61 (6): 1053-1069.
———. 2000. "Mobilization Forum: The Relational Deficit of Ideologically Structured Action." *Mobilization* 5 (1): 17-24.
Ellingson, Stephen J. 1995. "Understanding the Dialectic of Discourse and Collective Action: Public Debate and Rioting in Antebellum Cincinnati." *American Journal of Sociology* 101 (1): 100-144.
Evans, John H. 1997. "Multi-Organizational Fields and Social Movement Organization Frame Content: The Religious Pro-Choice Movement." *Sociological Inquiry* 67 (4): 451-469.
Fantasia, Rick. 1988. *Cultures of Solidarity, Consciousness, Action, and Contemporary American Workers*. Berkeley: University of California Press.
Ferree, Myra Marx. 1992. "The Political Context of Rationality: Rational Choice Theory and Resource Mobilization." Pp. 29-52 in *Frontiers in Social Movement Theory*, Aldon D. Morris and Carol McClurg Mueller, eds. New Haven, CT: Yale University Press.
Gamson, William. 1992. "The Social Psychology of Collective Action." Pp. 53-76 in *Frontiers in Social Movement Theory*, Aldon D. Morris and Carol McClurg Mueller, eds. New Haven, CT: Yale University Press.
Gamson, William, Bruce Fireman, and Steven Rytina. 1982. *Encounters with Unjust Authority*. Homewood, IL: Dorsey Press.
Gamson, William, and Andre Modigliani. 1989. "Media Discourse and Public Opinion on Nuclear Power." *American Journal of Sociology* 95: 1-38.
Goffman, Erving. 1974. *Frame Analysis*. Cambridge, MA: Harvard University Press.
Jasper, James, and Dorothy Nelkin. 1992. *The Animal Rights Crusade: The Growth of Moral Protest*. New York: The Free Press.
Johnston, Hank. 1991. *Tales of Nationalism*. New Brunswick, NJ: Rutgers University Press.
———. 1995. "A Methodology for Frame Analysis: From Discourse to Cognitive Schemata." Pp. 217-245 in *Social Movements and Culture*, Hank Johnston and Bert Klandermans, eds. Minneapolis: University of Minnesota Press.
———. 2002. "Verification and Proof in Frame and Discourse Analysis." Pp. 62-91 in *Methods of Social Movement Research*, Bert Klandermans and Suzanne Staggenborg, eds. Minneapolis: University of Minnesota Press.

Klandermans, Bert. 2000. "Mobilization Forum: Must We Redefine Social Movements as Ideologically Structured Action?" *Mobilization* 5 (1): 25-30.

Kriesi, Hanspeter, Ruud Koopmans, Jan Willem Duyvendak, and Marco G. Giugni. 1995. *New Social Movements in Western Europe.* Minneapolis: University of Minnesota Press.

Marullo, Sam, Ron Pagnucco, and Jackie Smith. 1996. "Frame Changes and Social Movement Contraction: U.S. Peace Movement Framing after the Cold War." *Sociological Inquiry* 66: 1-28.

McAdam, Doug. 1982. *Political Process and the Development of Black Insurgency, 1930-1970.* Chicago: University of Chicago Press.

———. 1988. *Freedom Summer.* New York: Oxford University Press.

———. 1994. "Culture in Social Movements." Pp. 36-57 in *New Social Movements: From Ideology to Identity*, Enrique Laraña, Hank Johnston, and Joseph Gusfield, eds. Philadelphia: Temple University Press.

McAdam, Doug, John D. McCarthy and Mayer N. Zald. 1996. *Comparative Perspectives on Social Movements: Political Opportunities, Mobilizing Structures, and Cultural Framings.* New York: Cambridge University Press.

McCarthy, John D. 1994. "Activists, Authorities, and Media Framing of Drunk Driving." Pp. 136-167 in *New Social Movements: From Ideology to Identity*, Enrique Laraña, Hank Johnston, and Joseph Gusfield, eds. Philadelphia: Temple University Press.

McCarthy, John D., and Mayer Zald. 1973. *The Trend of Social Movements in America: Professionalization and Resource Mobilization.* Morristown, NJ: General Learning Press.

Mooney, Patrick, with T. J. Majka. 1995. *Farmers' and Farmworker's Movements: Social Protest in American Agriculture.* New York: Twayne.

Morris, Aldon. 1984. *The Origins of the Civil Rights Movement: Black Communities Organizing for Change.* New York: The Free Press.

Noonan, Rita K. 1997. "Women against the State: Political Opportunities and Collective Action Frames in Chile's Transition to Democracy." Pp. 252-267 in *Social Movements: Readings on Their Emergence, Mobilization, and Dynamics*, Doug McAdam and David A. Snow, eds. Los Angeles: Roxbury Publishers.

Oberschall, Anthony. 1996. "Opportunities and Framing in the Eastern European Revolts of 1989." Pp. 93-121 in *Comparative Perspectives on Social Movements: Political Opportunities, Mobilizing Structures, and Cultural Framings*, Doug McAdam, John D. McCarthy, and Mayer N. Zald, eds. New York: Cambridge University Press.

Platt, Gerald, and Rhys Williams. 1999. "Ideological Discourse and Social Movements: A Sociolinguistic Analysis of Segregationist Ideology." Presentation at the annual meetings of the American Sociological Association in August at Chicago.

Polletta, Francesca. 1997. "Culture and Its Discontents: Recent Theorizing on the Cultural Dimensions of Protest." *Sociological Inquiry* 67 (4): 431-450.

Press, Andrea L., and Elizabeth R. Cole. 1992. "Pro-Choice Voices: Discourses of Abortion among Pro-Choice Women." *Perspectives on Social Problems* 4: 73-92.

Rothman, Franklin Daniel, and Pamela Oliver. 2002. "From Local to Global: The Antidam Movement in Southern Brazil, 1979-1992." Pp. 115-132 in *Globalization and Resistance: Transnational Dimension of Social Movements,* Jackie Smith and Hank Johnston, eds. Lanham, MD: Rowman & Littlefield.

Rupp, Leila J., and Verta Taylor. 1987. *Survival in the Doldrums: The American Women's Rights Movement, 1945 to the 1960s.* New York: Oxford University Press.

Scott, James. 1990. *Domination and the Arts of Resistance.* New Haven, CT: Yale University Press.

Scott, John Wallach. 1974. *The Glassworkers of Carnaux: French Craftsmen and Political Action in a Nineteenth-Century City.* Cambridge, MA: Harvard University Press.

Sewell, William H. 1985. "Ideologies and Social Revolutions: Reflections on the French Case." *Journal of Modern History* 57 (1): 57-85.

Smith, Jackie, Charles Chatfield, and Ron Pagnucco. 1997. *Transnational Social Movements and Global Politics: Solidarity beyond the State.* Syracuse, NY: Syracuse University Press.

Snow, David. 1992. "Master Frames and Cycles of Protest." Pp. 133-155 in *Frontiers of Social*

Movement Theory, Aldon S. Morris and Carol McClurg Mueller, eds. New Haven, CT: Yale University Press.

Snow, David, and Robert Benford. 1988. "Ideology, Frame Resonance, and Participant Mobilization." Pp. 197-217 in *From Structure to Action: Social Movement Participation across Cultures*, Bert Klandermans, Hanspeter Kriesi, and Sidney Tarrow, eds. Greenwich, CT: JAI Press.

Snow, David A., E. Burke Rochford, Jr., Steven W. Worden, and Robert D. Benford. 1986. "Frame Alignment Processes, Micromobilization, and Movement Participation." *American Sociological Review* 51: 464-481.

Steinberg, Marc. 1995a. "Repertoires of Discourse: The Case of the Spitalfields Silk Weavers and the Moral Economy of Conflict." In *Repertoires and Cycles of Collective Action*, Mark Traugott, ed. Durham, NC: Duke University Press.

———. 1995b. "The Talk and Backtalk of Collective Action: A Dialogic Analysis of Repertoires of Discourse among Nineteenth-Century English Cotton-Spinners." *American Journal of Sociology* 105 (3): 736-780.

———. 1998. "Tilting the Frame: Considerations on Collective Action Framing from a Discursive Turn." *Theory and Society* 27: 845-872.

———. 1999. *Fighting Words: Working-Class Formation, Collective Action, and Discourse in Early Nineteenth-Century England*. Ithaca, NY: Cornell University Press.

Swidler, Ann. 1986. "Culture in Action: Symbols and Strategies." *American Sociological Review* 51: 273-286.

Tarrow, Sidney. 1983. *Struggling to Reform: Social Movements and Policy Changes during Cycles of Protest*. Ithaca, NY: Cornell University Press.

———. 1992. "Mentalities, Political Cultures, and Collective Action Frames." Pp. 174-202 in *Frontiers in Social Movement Theory*, Aldon S. Morris and Carol McClurg Mueller, eds. New Haven, CT: Yale University Press.

———. 1998. *Power in Movement: Social Movements and Contentious Politics*. 2nd ed. New York: Cambridge University Press.

Taylor, Verta, and Nancy Whittier. 1995. "Analytical Approaches to Social Movement Culture: The Culture of the Women's Movement." Pp. 163-187 in *Social Movements and Culture*, Hank Johnston and Bert Klandermans, eds. Minneapolis: University of Minnesota Press.

Thompson, E. P. 1966. *The Making of the English Working Class*. New York: Vintage Books.

Tilly, Charles. 1978. *From Mobilization to Revolution*. New York: Random House.

Walsh, Ed. 1988. *Democracy in the Shadows*. New York: Greenwood Press.

Weber, Max. [1930] 1948. *The Protestant Ethic and the Spirit of Capitalism*, Talcott Parsons, trans. London: Allen and Unwin.

Whittier, Nancy. 1995. *Feminist Generations*. Philadelphia: Temple University Press.

Williams, Rhys, and Robert Benford. 1996. "Two Faces of Collective Action Frames." *Current Perspectives in Sociological Theory* 20: 200-220.

Wilson, John. 1973. *Introduction to Social Movements*. New York: Basic Books.

Wittner, Lawrence S. 1984. *Rebels against War: The American Peace Movement, 1933-1983*. Philadelphia: Temple University Press.

Wuthnow, Robert. 1989. *Communities of Discourse: Ideology and Social Structure in the Reformation, the Enlightenment, and European Socialism*. Cambridge, MA: Harvard University Press.

Zald, Meyer. 1996. "Culture, Ideology, and Strategic Framing." Pp. 261-274 in *Comparative Perspectives on Social Movements: Political Opportunities, Mobilizing Structures, and Cultural Framings*, Doug McAdam, John D. McCarthy, and Mayer N. Zald, eds. New York: Cambridge University Press.

———. 2000a. "Ideologically Structured Action: An Enlarged Agenda for Social Movement Analysis." *Mobilization* 5 (1): 1-16.

———. 2000b. "Mobilization Forum: New Paradigm? Nah! New Agenda? I Hope So." *Mobilization* 5 (1): 31-36.

Zaret, David. 1989. "Religion and the Rise of Liberal-Democratic Ideology in Seventeenth-

Century England." *American Sociological Review* 54 (1): 163-179.

Zdravomyslova, Elena. 1996. "Opportunities and Framing in the Transition to Democracy: The Case of Russia." Pp. 122-137 in *Comparative Perspectives on Social Movements: Political Opportunities, Mobilizing Structures, and Cultural Framings*, Doug McAdam, John D. McCarthy, and Mayer N. Zald, eds. New York: Cambridge University Press.

Zhao, Dingxin. 2001. *The Power of Tiananmen: State-Society Relations and the 1989 Beijing Student Movement.* Chicago: University of Chicago Press.

Zuo, Jiping, and Robert A. Benford. 1995. "Mobilization Processes and the 1989 Chinese Student Rebellion." *Sociological Quarterly* 36: 131-156.

Chapter 13

COMPARATIVE FRAME ANALYSIS

Hank Johnston

With the clarity of hindsight, we can look upon the notion of collective action frames and say that it was an idea whose time had come. When Gamson, Fireman, and Rytina applied the framing concept to collective rebellion in 1982, it reintroduced ideational and social-construction elements of mobilization to the field. Subsequent elaborations by David Snow, Rob Benford, Scott Hunt, and others rode on a wave of interest in cultural factors during the 1990s that shifted social movement theory away from an exclusive focus on structural and resource-based approaches. As a measure of this interest, Benford listed almost sixty movement-specific frames in his review and critique of framing studies (1997). By now, this number has surely doubled, perhaps tripled.

As interest in frame analysis burgeoned, scholars have expressed concern about several trends. Benford's own review lists several unproductive patterns. He identifies a preference for descriptive research rather than looking at frames causally. He also notes a tendency to reify frames and conceptualize them as "things" rather than processes—to consider frames as static rather than dynamic. Others have pointed out that frame research tends to confuse the concepts of frame and ideology (see Oliver and Johnston's chapter in this volume) or to focus on recruitment campaigns rather than participation (Jasper 1997) and on mobilization processes in Western liberal democracies rather than Third World movements (Noonan 1995).

This chapter takes seriously Benford's observations, and attempts to plot directions for framing research so as to avoid unproductive biases. It suggests an empirically grounded language with which researchers can discuss and test the causal influence of collective action frames. This language, representing a formal method for reproducing frames, their content, and relations, enables comparison of frames among different movements and/or at different points in time for the same movement. These kinds of comparisons are crucial for testing hypotheses and refining theory.

As Benford points out, most framing studies are descriptive. He has in mind those that look at a movement, its textual production (internal documents, public statements, press releases) and/or media treatments (coding of newspaper reports) to identify one or several collective action frames. Such a strategy is useful and important because it provides the empirical foundations for theory building, but causal influence and direction are typically only implied. While there exist numerous ways to do good frame analysis, at some point the social science of collective action frames requires studies that test the variable relationships between frame content and movement-related dependent variables such as protest events and levels, policy outcomes, media attention, and organizational development. By offering a language that enables temporal comparison of frame components, aspects of a frame can more easily be analyzed as independent variables—bringing the logic of social science into frame analysis (and reducing pure description, as interesting as that may be). A secondary benefit is that this language moves to the forefront what precisely we mean when we talk about frames, namely, cognitive schemata that shape behavior—not related concepts such as attitudes, beliefs, or ideologies.

Frames are mental constructs, not observable behaviors. This means that researchers are confronted by two problems inherent in any attempt to gauge the influence of ideational variables. The first problem goes to the heart of doing research about mental constructs, namely, operational measurement. If this research is to be convincing and relevant to other scholars, especially ones skeptical of the utility of cultural analysis and narrative data, the criteria for asserting the presence and influence of an ideational variable must be clear and convincing, fully disclosed, and consistently applied. Penetrating the mental life has always been a challenge to social science, but with the use of questionnaires and focus groups, or by inferring from documents and/or observed behavior, it has been possible to identify collective action frames, and in a general sense see their influence. In this chapter, I will show how the structure of mental frames can be reconstructed through close analysis of social movement texts. The goal is to present a method by which frame analysis might strengthen its case through empirical grounding in the texts on which they are based, thereby demonstrating the rationale of operational decisions made in the presentation of research findings.

The second problem is that definitions of ideational concepts tend to be inherently imprecise. In the task of describing social movement processes or isolating causative factors, the distinctions between beliefs, values, goals, attitudes, frames, ideologies, and discourses are frequently blurred. Cultural discourses often include frames, and some discourses can be characterized as the broadest kinds of frames. Ideologies often do the same things frames do—and are sometimes *called* frames. Discourses include goals, beliefs, attitudes, grievances, attributions of causes, and proposals for action. The next section reviews what we mean by "frames" and "framing," so that these concepts might be used clearly and consistently in research designs.

GOFFMAN AND COGNITIVE STRUCTURES

Erving Goffman's *Frame Analysis* (1972) focused on the cognitive organization of everyday life. He defined frames as mental constructs that organize perception and interpretation. From a cognitive perspective, frames are often described as problem-solving schemata, stored in memory, for the interpretative task of navigating everyday life and making sense of presenting situations. Abelson (1981: 717) describes frames as "structures that when activated reorganize comprehension of event-based situations. . . . In its strong sense [they involve] . . . expectations about the order as well as the occurrence of events." There is a huge body of literature in cognitive science and cognitive psychology about frame structure, which we will discuss in the next section, but for present purposes, frames are mental templates of appropriate behavior for common situations, acquired through socialization and experience and fine-tuned by the individual on the basis of what worked in the past and/or what others report as useful. Thus, they are *both* individual and social.

Elaboration of the framing perspective by Snow, Rochford, Worden, and Benford (1986) and Snow and Benford (1988, 1992) emphasized this social character of shared frames, and especially the organizational processes relevant to their creation, articulation, and extension. Similarly, Gamson (1988) has emphasized their social character by looking at framing processes as the intentional assembly of frame packages, both for media consumption and as a stage in consensus mobilization. I have previously (Johnston 1991) looked at frames as both the result of strategic planning and of cultural currents of international scope. In these studies, a collective action frame can be thought of as an aggregation of numerous individual interpretative schemata around an average, holding in abeyance idiosyncratic differences in order to approximate the fundamental structure of the mental construct. While Goffman never applied his frame analysis to social movements or protest, the social movement applications mentioned above are consistent with his definition of a frame as a social construct. Speaking in Goffman's lexicon, these basic social templates are *primary frameworks* (1974: 22-27), and their relevance to social movement culture is evident:

> Taken all together, the primary frameworks of a particular social group constitute a central element of its culture, especially insofar as understandings emerge concerning principal classes of schemata, the relations of these classes to one another, and the sum total of forces and agents that these interpretive designs acknowledge to be loose in the world. (1974: 27)

Goffman's brand of frame analysis is to explore how people know what is going on in social situations and how they behave based on their apperceptions. Most of his book is a discussion of social encounters that demonstrate basic patterns of frame change and frame breaking, of being in or out of a frame or being in the wrong frame—the point being that frames are cognitive attributes that are so basic and so taken for granted that we see them better when they are incorrectly applied or need reevaluation. The central premise of *Frame Analysis* is that we glance at nothing without applying primary frameworks (or basic everyday frames). Simply put, we could not negotiate daily encounters as culturally competent actors without them. Goffman describes how several primary frameworks are invoked in such an everyday activity as handing letters to a postman, chatting briefly, and getting into one's car to drive to work. The existence of primary frameworks can be demonstrated by the following narrative: "Javier entered the classroom and took a seat. The exam was passed out and brief instructions given by the professor. When done, he turned in the bluebook and left the room." Notice that the description refers to "the classroom," "the exam," "the professor," and "the bluebook" as if their existence was already known. The point is that their preknowledge is taken for granted because a primary framework, stored in memory, introduces all of them as part of the total schema—a final-exam primary framework—in which the classroom, the professor, and the exam booklet, plus numerous other items such as other students, pencils and erasures, the clock, the proctors, and so forth, are *mentally* present (see Tannen's 1993 example).

The point of this brief excursion into cognitive processing is that the "true location" of a frame is in the memory of the social actor. Although primary frames are social phenomena, they do not exist in the "collective mind" of a group—empirically no such thing exists. They are always individually held ideational structures stored in memory as experiential information and invoked by individual actors according to presenting situations. The social quality of primary frames lies in the fact that they may be shared widely and may coordinate and pattern individual behaviors so that they assume a social aspect. This means that although we are interested in primary frameworks because they shape collective behaviors, their structure and content will always mirror an individual cognitive schema.

There are three ways to replicate the social nature of a frame—three gates of empirical access—even though the reality of all cognitive frames, in the strictest sense, is an individually held mental structure.

The first is to examine social texts that are collectively produced and generally accepted as representing a group's position. These social texts would be, above all, movement documents, especially those offered by key movement organizations as position statements. The description of these frames is useful insofar as we accept the presumption that their content is widely shared by movement participants. This is the strategy that is presented in figure 13.1 in the next section.

The second research strategy is to rely on the narratives of activists and participants as gleaned from interviews, statements, and written texts such as diaries and memos. Here, the spoken and written words of movement participants comprise the raw data for reproducing a frame's content. This method presumes that by sampling movement documents and participant speech, we can approximate the content of the shared frame. This strategy (presented in figure 13.3 in the next section), uses frame content and structure reconstructed from the narratives of numerous respondents and offered as a general schema for a class of movement participants.

The third strategy is to reconstruct the content of a collective action frame from the narrative of one respondent. This narrative is chosen above all because it is representative of others—at least in its general contours—and because its detail and richness of description allow an elaborated specification of frame content. Although this strategy may incorporate some idiosyncratic features unique to the respondent, these are usually identifiable and should be held in abeyance. Its main advantage is that, if the narrative is chosen carefully, we can approximate the frame content of all movement participants from one representative text. This method demands clarity about the criteria for selection of the narrative because the generalizability of the analysis rests on it.

These three approaches all reconstruct individual cognitive schemata that we assume are shared among movement participants—that is, shared to a sufficiently broad extent that they channel individual behavior to impart a collective and social aspect. We know from research in cognitive psychology that there are two fundamental characteristics of schematic mental models: (1) they must be based on processes of memory retrieval by which details of experience are grouped under general categories, that is, they are organized hierarchically; and (2) their content depends on the presenting situation for which they guide interpretation. These two characteristics will help us to more accurately represent collective action frames.

The Hierarchical Organization of Frames

Although there are differences in specifics, most models of cognitive processing presume that experience is organized hierarchically. Higher-level categories subsume a multiplicity of detail and serve as points of access for retrieval from memory. Because so much of mental life is linguistic, researchers have focused on cognitive processes of speech. For example, Kintsch and Van Dijk (1978) examined how speakers produce grammatically correct texts. They have specified two levels at which spoken and written texts are organized: a microstructure that orders the specific ideas contained in the text, and a macrostructure, "where a list of macropropositions represents a kind of abstraction of the text" (Hormann 1986: 181). For the reader or hearer of a text, Kintsch and Van Dijk propose the use of cognitive schemata for interpretation. These represent cognitive templates—paralleling Goffman's primary frameworks—for how texts should be organized. As the "raw inputs" of microstructure are processed, they are checked with the schemata in order to assess their significance for the text as a whole. If there is a fit, they are taken as macropropositions and assigned a place in the macrostructure.

Another approach to the hierarchical organization of speech falls under the rubric of story grammars (Thorndyke 1977; Rumelhart 1975). Story grammars are normative schematic forms by which stories, tales, accounts, and histories are organized and remembered. Story grammar research builds upon Bartlett's (1932) theory of memory, which postulated that remembering is a process of accessing memory according to schemata. In other words, the process of recalling "how a story should go" (the schema) also guides the process of recall. Folktales and myths are particularly useful in this respect because of their long oral tradition and the feats of memory often required in their telling. According to Thorndyke (1977), simple stories are organized by deep structures that take a common form: first the setting (characters, location, and time are described), then the theme is told (one or several events are described, and the goals of the characters are specified), then plot—with substructures consisting of several episodes, and episodes being ordered according to subgoals, attempts, and outcomes.

The Content-Specific Nature of Interpretative Frames

In work in computer models of artificial intelligence, the relation between content and structure is a basic theme, exemplified by the treatment of cognitive processes by Schank and Ableson (1977: 10): "It does not take one very far to say that schemas are important: one must account for the content of schemas. . . . In other words, a knowledge structure theory must make commitment to a particular content schema."

Schank and Abelson hold that semantic and contextual features are directly related to the shape an interpretative schema takes (p. 9). Research on story grammars have shown that memory and language are inextricably bound (Norman and Rumelhart 1976). Most memory is episodic, organized around personal experiences or episodes, as opposed to "scholastic," organized around abstract semantic categories. In an episodic memory, for example, a trip is stored as a sequence of the conceptualizations describing what happened on the trip. Some conceptualizations will have been marked as salient and some will have been forgotten altogether.

A central cognitive procedure then is to recognize repeated or similar sequences. When an appropriate schema is present, it can be accessed for knowledge that is helpful in "filling in the blanks" in understanding. An economy measure used to access episodes is to store them by abstract categories rather than numerous details, allowing people to deal with a great deal of material in little time. They enable a quick processing of situations that otherwise would be handled less confidently. Accessing a certain schema brings up a wide array of subevents with which experience can be compared. For example, a typical script on file may be *restaurant*. It would include knowledge of entering, taking a table, ordering, appropriately consuming the food, paying, tipping, and exiting—all indexing a wide variety of even more micro-events representing different ways each of these could be accomplished. For our purposes, another schema might be *protest*, which provides access to events such as placard making, gathering, singing, chanting, marching, confrontation, solidarity, even after-protest socializing. The point to keep in mind is that the structure of a schema is contingent on the situation that it represents. Content and structure are fused in this cognitive process.

THE REPRESENTATION OF COGNITIVE STRUCTURES

My goal is to provide a language of presentation whereby frame analysis can be accomplished systematically and with greater empirical fealty. The grammar of this language is the hierarchically organized schema that organizes the content of the interpretative frame and specifies the relations among its different components. To date, few studies of collective action frames have reproduced in any detail the relationships among the different ideas that make up the frames, nor have their empirical referents been presented in a way that is open to close scrutiny by the community of scholars.

One exception is Gerhards and Rucht's (1992) study of anti-cruise missile and anti-International Monetary Fund (IMF) campaigns in Germany. The authors reproduce the frame structure of two master frames based on two leaflets distributed widely in the campaigns (see figure 13.1). There are several advantages in this strategy. First, because the flyers are presented, the critical reader can compare Gerhards and Rucht's summary interpretations with the texts themselves. Second, in a schematic diagram that presents the frame, the relation among the various concepts are demonstrated. These too can be compared with the texts. Third, the analysis is based on a plausible assumption that the flyers are representative of the campaign's master frames. These flyers were signed and supported by all groups supporting the campaigns and therefore were taken as valid indicators that those elements of the master frames were shared. Modified version of the anti-IMF master frame and the document on which it is based are presented in figures 13.1 and 13.2.

Gerhards and Rucht's approach to empirical verification of frame concepts is similar to the strategy that I have used in some of my own work (Johnston 1995: 2002). The difference is that I have suggested incorporating a formalized method of linking the different points in the schema to the texts on which it is based. To demonstrate this, I have added to Gerhards and Rucht's original figure reference to the lines in the anti-IMF flyer that support the frame components. This is a minor mechanical adjustment, reflecting the need to be assiduous about empirical verification in frame analysis; but it also holds the possibility for comparing frames from the same movement at different points in time. Being able to document how frame structure has changed and correlating these changes with, say, protest size, strategic adjustments in the movement, or variations in the political context, allow the analysis to make stronger proposals about causal linkages.

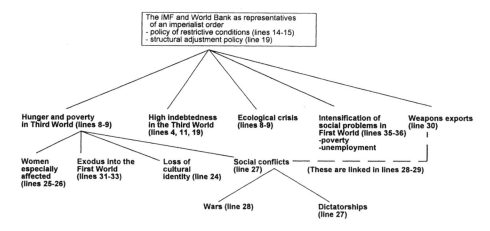

Figure 13.1 Master frame of the Anti-IMF campaign
Source: Gerhards and Rucht (1992). Used with permission of University of Chicago Press. Line numbers added.

These two examples parallel common research strategy for frame analysis: using a representative text as the basis of frame reconstruction. A slightly different approach to schematic representations of texts would be to order relevant categories hierarchically based not on one text but on a sample of texts. This requires that the same question or set of questions be asked of all respondents, or if using textual analysis, that a sufficiently large sample is available to identify subcategories within the frame. Rather than the lines of text being presented, the number of mentions or percentage of mentions relative to the total sample indicate measures of the frame's generality. This is represented in figure 13.3, which is based on my own research about how the Estonian nationalist movement spearheaded the opposition against Soviet rule in the 1980s and eventually won independence in 1991. Figure 13.3 represents the structure of one of the movement's master frames, the "pure Estonian master frame," a schema by which politics, culture, and social organization were interpreted under Soviet Estonia. The analysis was based on transcribed interviews with seventy-two respondents, of whom about half discussed this master frame.[1]

These are not the only strategies for systematic presentation of frame analysis. Other researchers have seen the need for formalized analytical methods and have responded in different ways. In a study of media framing and grassroots organizing, Ryan (1991) distills the essence of both media and movement frames. Her analysis systematically lists key frame elements in charts, each of which present four general themes: (1) the key issue in the frame; (2) responsibility/solution proposed in the frame—or its diagnosis and prognosis; (3) the symbols used, especially visual images, metaphors, historical examples, stereotypes, and catch phrases; and finally (4) the supporting arguments, especially in terms of historical roots of the grievance, consequences of the frame's success, and appeals and links to broader cultural values. Ryan's approach has been applied by Fuks (1998) in his analysis of frames in environmental conflict in Rio de Janeiro. Ryan presents selected examples of text from qualitative analysis. Fuks presents texts of a key publication. However, neither presentation links text and frame closely, as shown in figures 13.1 and 13.2. By failing to do so, the process by which the analysis moves from raw data to specification of

For the resolution of the debt crisis - for a just world economic order

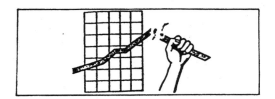

(1) For resolution on the debt crisis and for a just world economic order!

(2) In September 1988, the International Monetary Fund (IMF) and the

(3) World Bank will hold their yearly meeting in Berlin (West). These insti-

(4) tutions of the international financial system have a key responsibility in

(5) the indebtedness crisis of the 'third world,' which has been worsening

(6) since 1982. Through their rigorous conditions and their so-called struc-

(7) tural adjustment loans, the leading Western industrial countries are

(8) decisively responsible for the economic exploitation of the 'third world,'

(9) for the impoverishment of the people living there, and for the brutal

(10) destruction of their natural prerequisites for living.

(11) The present foreign debt of the 'third world' amounts to the gigantic,

(12) prohibitive 1,2 trillion US dollars. The interest and principal payment

(13) for these countries far exceed the influx of new capital generated.

(14) The debtor countries must expend a larger and larger share of their

(15) export income to pay them back. Less and less remains for meeting basic

(16) internal needs and making domestic investments.

(17) The causes for this situation are rooted above all in the existing world

(18) economic order which forces the countries in the 'third world' to play a

(19) subordinate role tailored to the needs of the Western industrial countries

(20) Through a policy of granting initially cheap loans, which changed the US

(21) high interest policy, the problem of indebtedness and unjust exchange

(22) relations was intensified. Each attempt to escape from underdevelopment,

(23) dependence, and misery is doomed to fail under these circumstances.

(24) The economic ruin of the 'third world' is linked with the dissolution of ex-

(25) isting social relations, the destruction of cultural identity and especially

(26) affects the women, who have to bear the greatest burden of the devastated

(27) living and production structures.

(28) Misery and want lead to societal disruptions. Dictatorship, regional conflicts,

(29) and wars are the consequences. In many 'third world' countries almost

(30) 2/3 of national budgets are to purchase weapons and arm the police. In the

(31) meantime, the first world weapons manufacturers earn money from this!

(32) More and more people are trying to escape this situation. The borders are

(33) closed to them here. As (economic) refugees they are repressed again and

(34) usually deported to face exploitation, torture, and death. The circle of

(35) impoverishment, underdevelopment, and militarization is closed again.

(36) Even the people here do not remain unscathed: unemployment, new

(37) poverty, and the cutback of social services are only other expressions

(38) of the same crisis which is driving the 'third world' into ruin. We must

(39) find the way out. The disastrous development has to be stopped. The

(40) prevailing debt management by the IMF, the World Bank, commercial

(41) banks, and Western governments with refinancing new loans and

(42) case by case treatment does not provide a solution; on the contrary, it

(43) strengthens the dependence and intensifies the crisis.

(44) There is no way out without writing off the debts. The burdens must be

(45) borne by those who are responsible for the situation. This requires, at

(46) the same time, a change in international relations and the balance of

(47) power. This is why the political and social movements who have to push

(48) their interests against the cartel of corporations, banks, the IMF,

(49) the World Bank, and elites need our solidarity.

(50) We support the demand of many countries in the 'third world' to layout

(51) the concrete conditions of debt write-off in the framework of an inter-

(52) national debt conference with the equal participation of all countries.

(53) The debt payment should be suspended until the negotiations are

(54) concluded. A debt write-off alone will not be able to solve the problems

(55) in the long run. As long as relations between the peoples of the world

(56) are regulated by the "free" world market and the principle of the largest

(57) possible profit determine political and economic behavior, then the

(58) chain of economic crises with their devastating effects will not be

(59) broken off.

(60) Resources and finances are tied up world-wide through military arma-,

(61) ment, both in the 'first world' and in the countries of the 'third world.'

(62) We demand concrete arms control and steps toward disarmament They

(63) must be linked with the goal of placing the resources thus freed up at

(64) the disposal of the countries in the 'third world' for their development.

(65) Disarmament and development must be directly connected.

(64) The establishment of a new, just world economic order is unavoidable.

To mark the yearly meeting of the IMF and the World Bank we are calling for a demonstration and rally on the 25th of September 1988 in Berlin (West)! 11:00, Joachimstaler Straße / corner of Kurfürstendamm SOLIDARITY WITH THE PEOPLES OF THE "THIRD WORLD"

Figure 13.2 Leaflet Protesting 1988 Meeting of IMF and World Bank

Source: Gerhards and Rucht (1992: 93-94). Used with permission of University of Chicago Press. Adapted for this chapter. Line numbers added.

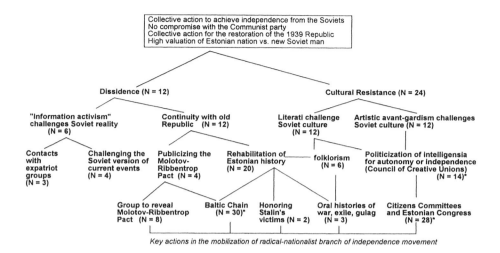

Figure 13.3 The pure-nationality master frame for the Estonian national opposition.
Note: * indicates popular actions that drew upon both dissidents and cultural resisters

frames is left implicit. The reader does not have the opportunity to verify the frame's fealty, by either specific reference to key texts or the proportion (relative to the total N) of the texts containing the items. In contrast, the use of systematic methods of presentation, such as schematic representations, standardizes frame analysis and increases confidence in interpretations. As imperfect as these schemata might be, they represent gains over more tacit approaches to the content and structure of frames.

TEXT AND EVIDENCE

Gerhards and Rucht's schema leads us to a second principle of frame analysis as applied to social movement research: there is no way to avoid the analysis of texts, whether the documents of movement organizations or the spoken discourse of activists, leaders, and protest participants. One might deduce the presence of a frame from behavior, but without textual evidence, such an exercise is mostly inference and speculation. Simply put, written and spoken words are the best evidence we have for frame content and structure. Early research on cognitive processing has shown that there is a fundamental relationship between the structures of mental life and the production of written or verbal discourse (Bartlett 1932; Kintsch and Van Dijk 1978; Thorndyke 1977; Rumelhart 1975; Buschke and Schaier 1979), and because social movement frames are cognitive structures, a window of access exists through the spoken words of participants and written texts of social movement organizations. If we are to research interpretative frames more rigorously, as I think we can, the most compelling data are to be found in how speech and text are structured.

In my judgment, the most convincing research about cultural elements of social movements stays close to the original empirical texts. For example, Daniels's analysis of white supremacist discourse (1997) examines 369 issues of white supremacist newsletters and publications.[2] She calls her method *compositional analysis*, referring to the arrangement of textual material and visual components in the text (in her case, cartoons) in a newsletter.[3] Another example is Marc Steinberg's analysis of class formation and protest repertoires in nineteenth-century Britain (1999). His study shows how what is written and talked about influences protest action, which in turn influences what is talked about again. One section of his study, in which he examines a petition in support of the Wages Protection Bill (pp. 114-117), also exemplifies close textual analysis of a representative document.[4]

Both these studies offer analyses that the reader can take with greater confidence because the texts are present. However, there was a tendency in the first wave of frame research references to treat the actual texts more casually. These early studies relied on samples of movement documents and/or transcribed ethnographic interviews with movement activists as primary data. For example, Capek (1993) used in-depth interviews plus movement documents to identify an environmental justice frame. Mooney and Hunt (1996) used secondary sources and interviews with current movement leaders to specify three master frames. Swart (1995) reviewed political pamphlets and other publications to identify the frames of the Irish Sinn Fein movement. In all these cases, the authors offer rich analyses of the movement's ideas and their relation to mobilization. Their research goals were to identify collective action frames and document their central role in movement development, or to identify basic framing processes, as in Benford's 1993 study. He used a huge database— 1,400 movement documents and 153 formal and informal interviews—to trace conflicts and debates over framing processes. Although these studies have helped set the foundations of framing theory, now—almost a decade later— theoretical advance demands a more rigorous approach to texts. If frame analysis is to take its texts seriously, it is worthwhile familiarize oneself with body of knowledge that focuses on how texts are produced.

INTENSIVE TEXTUAL ANALYSIS

For a long time, linguistic researchers were concerned with questions of language structure and grammar: namely, how people composed well-formed sentences. Some linguists realized that sentences were but the building blocks of larger textual units— stories, speeches, essays, letters, diaries, and interactional episodes—and that grammatical rules by themselves do not explain how sentences are put together into larger units, or *connected discourse.* Larger texts are shaped by the introduction and resolution of themes and by culturally prescribed rules about how this is accomplished. Cultural knowledge of appropriate forms of speech and writing is a crucial input. Also, interactional considerations—to whom one is talking and under what circumstances—affect the shape of what gets said and written. Also, other channels of information such as intonation or facial expression, or accompanying pictures in the case of documents, often indicate when different or shaded interpretations of texts are required.

The fundamental task of intensive textual analysis is the specification of all sources of meaning—all that is left implicit in a text, and all that is taken for granted in its interpretation. In natural speech, people process several channels of information such as intonation, gestures, posture, and so on. In written texts—including social movement documents and manifestos—interactional, organizational, and cultural constraints also may partly determine their shape and structure. To bring these factors to bear in the analysis, however, the researcher must be aware of the situations in which these texts are produced—sometimes a very tall order. Full textual analysis employs a wide variety of interactional, biographical, and behavioral data to verify and broaden interpretations of text. While the method is not perfect, it represents an advance over accepting all text at face value. Closer attention to the nuanced meanings in texts offers a more empirically grounded approach to the "black box" of mental life, to the structures of social experience that are resident therein, and therefore to the frames by which social experience is organized. Next, I review five principles of intensive textual analysis that I have drawn from various attempts to microanlayze spoken texts. [5]

1. The Context of Textual Production

It is a basic social-psychological principle that social influences shape individual behaviors, and this holds for the behaviors of textual production as well—both for speech and movement documents. Regarding conversations and other kinds of verbal interaction, a relevant concept comes from sociolinguistic research: the speech situation. A speech situation is a bounded episode of talk in which there are recognized rules for what should and should not be said. For the most part, these rules are understood, taken for granted, and rarely verbalized. They specify what can be said, how to say it, and what the appropriated responses are. These rules come from the general culture, subcultural relations, and organizational culture. Similar rules may also constrain written documents. For example, organizational culture specifies how an interdepartmental memo or an academic job description should be written. The tacit rules of speech oil the gears of communication and are usually not seen as problematic. This holds for most social research, too, including framing research—that the tacit rules of speech are taken for granted. But by doing so, one may run the risk of confusing form with content, for example, taking the sterile form of a contemporary office memo as evidence of the absence of personal relationships. For social movement analysis, misinterpretation may occur when the researcher enters movement subcultures—religious, youth, ethnic, or lifestyle—where expectations of appropriate speech may not fully understood. Briggs (1986) discusses several instances of cross-cultural interaction in which different definitions of the speech situation lead to outright misunderstanding between the interviewer and respondent.

2. Pragmatics

A slightly different aspect of context is what the speaker or writer is trying to accomplish in the text—the *pragmatic intent* behind the actual words. Intent can reflect political, economic, or social goals. That people do things with words, to use John Austin's phrase (1962), is a commonsense and everyday input to interpretation. A salesman's scripted speech can be understood in terms of the overarching goal of selling a product. The customer's awareness of this goal shapes his interpretation to what is going on. High awareness may mean that the sales pitch is interpreted with a grain of salt (cynicism); low awareness may mean it is naively accepted (gullibility). Wilson (1990) has shown how the vagueness of political speech can be analyzed from a pragmatic perspective. Similarly, in interview situations or archival research, misapprehension of pragmatic intent raises the possibility of invalid interpretations. On a practical level, the pragmatic intent is often revealed by looking at the overall structure of the text, especially toward the end when the goals of interaction often become more transparent. The same is true of conversational speech that superficially seems less goal-directed. All speech and writing embodies interactional goals that can often be ascertained by looking at the overall structure of the text in terms of its narrative direction—where it's moving.

3. Role Perspectives

What gets said or written is also influenced by social role. One speaks differently as a social scientist than as a father or a teacher. One writes differently in a diary than in a letter or an official document, partly because of changing speech situations, but also partly because changing one's role perspective changes assessments of what is important to say and what is not. Regarding the interpretation of speech and documents, there are two key points: first, that speech or writing is produced from within a role perspective; and second, those role perspectives may change in the course of textual production. Clearly, understanding textual production from the perspective of role requires that the analyst know something about the speaker or writer. Biographical data about the respondent is sometimes available elsewhere in the text (see principle 4 below). If not, it can be gathered from organizational sources and from other participants. In long interviews, this information may be widely distributed, with bits and pieces coming early on, but more likely than not, there is a good deal to be found later in the interview when the situation relaxes.

In my own research, I once observed alternation among no less than three role perspectives in the course of a long interview (see Johnston 1991: 179-194). At first, the respondent, who was an activist in the Socialist party, spoke from the role of a party functionary, his speech being peppered with the programmatic rhetoric of an election campaign. Later, speaking as a recent immigrant, he described ethnic discrimination and blended class and ethnicity. Finally he spoke as a husband and father and made several claims about social mobility and his hopes for his children's future that seemed to counter earlier statements of socialist ideology. At first, these different parts of the interview seemed contradictory and confusing to me, but by identifying changes in role perspective, I saw how he spoke from different roles in the process of becoming more relaxed in the interview. Role analysis puts fluctuations and inconsistencies of this sort in a different light. In this case, by seeing these role changes, information that may have been lost or misinterpreted provided important insight into the respondent's activist frame.

The other side of the coin is that not only does one's role perspective shape what gets said but so too do perceptions of the other interlocutor's role status. Prevailing patterns of class, gender, and/or ethnic stratification affect speech. It is a well-known sociolinguistic principle that if group affiliation is not known at the outset of an interchange, cues are picked up in the course of interaction that impart role identities (see e.g., Blom and Gumperz 1972). In the analysis of political and social movements, a speaker's role in a social movement organization (SMO) can shape what he or she says or writes—especially if there is conflict over strategy or policies.

4. Total Text

In the example of the socialist militant, complete interpretation was possible only by looking at the interview in its totality. This is a fundamental principle that embraces all of the previous points, in that it is sometimes necessary to refer to distant sections of a document to grasp fluctuations in speaker roles and definitions of the speech situation or to ascertain pragmatic intent. Indeed, it may be required to go to information gathered in other parts of the research process, for example, biographical data, or strategic policies for the movement to interpretation of a segment of text.

A more immediate justification for taking the text in its totality is that written and spoken texts are often full of unclear and vague references. Here information from distant sections is often necessary for clarification. The referents of pronouns, for example, may not be immediately clear. Vague or cryptic semantic choices (such as "these things," "that stuff," or "those guys") may require a distant search for what they refer to. Also, if the text being analyzed is a transcript of a meeting or a discussion among activists, factual material from outside the immediate text may be required to clarify information that is tacitly shared among the speakers. Without this information full interpretation by a third party is difficult and may produce incorrect coding.

5. Nonverbal Cues

The final principle refers to how nonverbal information can bend and change meanings significantly. These inputs to interpretation include inflection, tone, pitch, cadence, and the melodic contours of speech. In written documents, such channels obviously do not apply, although other channels can be used, such as accompanying pictures, cartoons, or page layout. Gumperz (1982) has shown that nonverbal cues often mark changes in role status and definitions of the speech situation, and that interlocutors share knowledge about what these nonverbal cues mean—such as when the interaction becomes more informal or intimate. Questions regarding participation, motivation, and beliefs, especially regarding recollection of past events, often create highly complex speech situations in which this kind of information may be crucial for complete and valid interpretations.

The rationale for these five principles of textual analysis is that through close attention to all sources of meaning, the analyst can more accurately reconstruct a frame schema that systematically shows the relationships between higher-level organizing concepts and details that fall under them. Close textual analysis helps achieve several important objectives in research:

- avoiding factual errors—by analyzing the text in its totality
- strengthening interpretation—by reference to nonverbal data, role changes, and changes in the respondent's definition of the speech situation
- providing insights into frame organization—by seeing what concepts the respondent discusses in different styles of speech—formal versus informal, for example (as indicated by nonverbal cues, role position, and word choice)

Obviously, specifying these data is highly labor intensive, and it would be impossible to scrutinize fifty interview transcripts with such intensity. The analyst must balance the utility of what is gained with the resources and time at one's disposal. If one representative interview serves as the basis of frame construction, attention to these five factors is necessary to avoid any misinterpretation (see the appendix, a textual analysis that serves as the basis of figure 4 in the next section, for an example of how these principles might be applied). Otherwise, intense analysis may be warranted if there is difficulty in making sense of an important interview segment, or if the analyst, using one's abilities as a culturally adept speaker-hearer, suspects something is being communicated beyond the words alone. When interviews are audio-recorded, full-narrative texts can be transcribed and nonverbal and intonational information can be referred to in these situations. Regardless of the intensity of the analysis, when frames are presented, representative texts on which they are based should be included in the presentation.

COMPARATIVE FRAME ANALYSIS

Taken together, close textual analysis and hierarchical schemata that organize a frame's content allow social movement researchers to engage the broader social science community with stronger empirical evidence of ideational and cultural influences. Once we have verifiable hierarchical structures, the next step is to compare them at different points in a movement's trajectory or to compare them among different movements to see how movement-related dependent variables (e.g., protest size, membership rolls, fundraising, or media coverage) correlate with changes in the ideational content of a frame.

One straightforward way to compare frames is to look at changes in their organization and content according to the principles in this chapter. Figure 13.4 presents collective action frame for participating in a protest in the final years of the Francoist regime in Spain and will be compared with another one at a later point in the movement's development. By the mid-1970s, the Spanish authoritarian state was unraveling. Franco died in 1975, and demonstrations in Barcelona—where the interview that is the basis of this schema was conducted—were increasing. Barcelona is located in the region of Catalonia, an ethnically and linguistically distinct region whose native language and political autonomy were subordinated by the central authoritarian state under Franco. These demonstrations were in favor of political change, democracy, and regional nationalism. The interview was chosen because the respondent was representative of a group of twenty others (out of a total N = 80) who were nationalists and anti-Francoists but not full-time, militant activists in the late 1970s. A verbatim transcription of the interview segment using the principles of intensive textual analysis is found in the appendix with the lines numbered on the right and the corresponding textual expansion of intended meanings on the right. The lines correspond to the numbers in the branches below in figure 13.4.

In figure 13.4, three higher levels in the schema are general categories that organize the six mid-level concepts, which in turn subsume seven lower-level concepts beneath them. Middle and lower levels are represented by statements from the actual text and corresponding line numbers. It should not come as a surprise that the three higher-level concepts correspond to well-known theoretical understandings of mobilization processes; namely, that people are drawn into protest participation via interpersonal networks (the left-hand branch—"participation with primary relations") and in order to send messages of dissent to governments where institutional channels are closed (the right branch—"send a message to the government"). The middle branch represents a calculation of risk in the participation decision. Fear of injury or arrest is balanced with social pressure to participate, a consideration that looks at the safety in numbers that may obtain, and a solidarity element ("others taking risk").

Figure 13.4 represents a collective action frame for Catalonian nationalist protest participation in 1976. As such, it is an approximation—a snapshot taken at a point in time (the protest demonstrations in February 1976) to represent the cognitive orientations of participants. Its utility rests on the assumptions that the respondent's words are representative and that they offer insight into the cognitive orientations of a multitude of

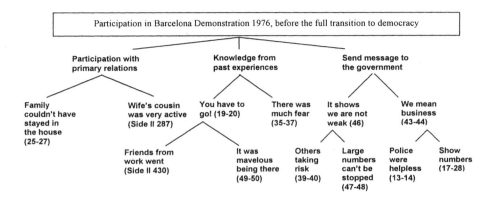

Figure 13.4 Frame schema for 1976 anti-Francoist protest demonstration

protesters. As long as these assumptions are made clear and the bases for making them explained, this kind of representation is an advance over purely descriptive accounts—which, by the way, must make similar assumptions—because it demonstrates the relationships between ideas and permits comparisons.

Figure 13.5 presents a collective action frame for a mass demonstration that occurred nineteen months later, on September 11, 1977. This frame was constructed by the same strategy of relying on a representative text from an interview with a participant. By 1977, the political context changed rapidly in the intervening period, and mobilization in Barcelona became white-hot in anticipation of *la ruptura democrática* (the outbreak of democracy). This demonstration combined several elements: elections for regional political autonomy for the Catalonian region were to be held shortly, Francoism was ending, and working-class parties were showing their support for regional political autonomy, and September 11 is the national holiday of Catalonia. The mobilization was huge —by some estimates, over one million attended.

By comparing the collective action frame for this mobilization (figure 13.5) with one from a year and a half earlier (figure 13.4), certain continuities and differences become clear. First, the importance of interpersonal networks remains constant in both mobilizations. Second, we see a fundamental shift in the calculation of the decision to participate, which reflects the changing political context. Participants were liberated from fear because of the commitment of the regime to reform. The consequence of this, our third point, is that the motivation for being there (which reflects internalization of the calls for mobilization by nascent political parties) changed radically. The key component no longer was to send a message to the government but rather to affirm celebratory and solidary statements prior to the outbreak of democratic competition. This motivation transcended partisan politics and augmented participation considerably. Figure 13.5 offers systematic evidence for interpretative elements that help explain the difference between twenty thousand participants in 1976 and one million in 1977.[6]

In sum, this brand of analysis is straightforward and systematic, and helps identify key aspects of mass participation in 1977 versus 1976. It allows comparison of two diagnoses of a protest situation, two prognoses of protest effect, and the motivations for taking part in two different protests. By careful selection of the protest events to be compared and careful construction of the interview questions used to produce the textual

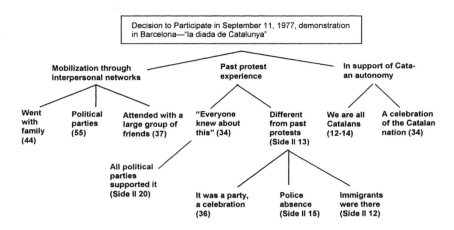

Figure 13.5 Frame schema for participation in mass demonstration, Barcelona, September 11, 1977

data, one can reconstruct and compare frame changes to suggest hypotheses at a more general theoretical level, such as the variable importance of mobilizing networks when motivational components of a frame strengthen. This synchronizes with McAdam, Tarrow, and Tilly's call for a focus on the mechanisms of protest mobilization rather than general laws (2001).

Finally, these procedures are not the only way to comparatively analyze frames and their influence on movement-related effects. Marullo, Pagnucco, and Smith's 1996 examination of frame changes and organizational contraction in the U.S. peace movement used a stratified sample based on listings in a national directory of grassroots peace organizations (N = 411). The leaders or staff members of these organizations filled out a questionnaire that contained nineteen items about the groups' goals, strategies, and values—ideational elements often contained in frames. Responses to these items yielded six higher-level factors about the peace movement, which were defined as organizational frames. Another comparative study (Carroll and Ratner 1996) examines changes in activism in several Vancouver SMOs as it relates to master frames. The authors used open-ended interviews, which were then coded using Ethnograph, a textual analysis program (Seidel, Kjolseth, and Seymour 1988), to produce numerical outputs that were used to identify three master frames. Computer analysis holds the promise for greater empirical rigor because, rather than relying on the researcher's selection of texts, huge quantities of textual data can be processed and converted to numerical outputs, which then can be statistically analyzed. Both Shapiro and Markoff (1998) and Franzosi (1998) use computer analysis of text to construct "semantic structures" or "story grammar" structures. These are different from the hierarchically organized frames discussed here, but in all cases, the basic research problem is similar: taking large quantities of text and accurately summarizing the meanings they carry order to produce a portrait of what is being talked about. This is the topic for another chapter in another book (see Johnston 2002: 78-82, for a detailed discussion of these methods applied to frame analysis), but it's enough to point out that computer methods can be applied straightforwardly to constructing frame structures of the kind discussed here.

CONCLUSION: A PRACTICAL EPISTEMOLOGY

Theorists of the framing perspective have mostly stressed framing *as a process* of interaction by which people construct understandings that are neither unanimously shared nor fixed—a view that, at first glance, seems to preclude seeing frames as snapshots of hierarchical mental schemata as I have done here. Readers will find that the chapter by Oliver and Johnston in this volume and the response by Snow and Benford that follows it contain a lively conversation that in part takes up the debate about frames as cognitive structures versus framing as a interactive process.

I do not see that these two perspectives are irreconcilable. Indeed, there are three good reasons that studies of frame *structures* as presented here can reinforce, inform, and test findings about framing *processes*. First, studies of movement framing processes almost always refer to frame snapshots. To repeat Snow and Benford's definition: frames are interpretative schemata that signify and condense "the world out there by selectively punctuating and encoding objects, situations, events, and experiences." (1992: 137). Implicit in just about every study of framing processes is the concept of a frame as a mental schema that is broadly shared among participants in its general contours.

Second, studies that are designed to examine the process of frame construction are also usually always—at least implicitly—concerned with how these processes shape mobilization; or to put it another way, even when researchers focus only on *descriptions* of framing processes, they often are legitimated by the background assumption that they ultimately will help to *explain something*: the success of a protest mobilization, the vicissitudes of a movement career, the expansion of a particular SMO or its failure. So, in the broader enterprise of the social science of protests and social movements, a case study of the *process* of how a movement organization arrives at, battles over, and variously interprets frames of participation usually always points to the next step of generalizing the observations to other cases of mobilization. This is a presumption that implies frame construction as an independent variable insofar as the cases of comparison are different from the original one. Although it is possible to compare only processes, it is unlikely that it can be done without treating the collective action frames themselves as variables, and to do this, one must take a measurement of their content and compare it with other frames (see chapter 2 in this volume).

Third, even in these cases where the dependent variable is not overtly stressed, studies of framing processes would benefit from visually comparing frame structures at different points in time. Mapping out the structure of frames as a movement develops enables the researcher to trace the framing process step by step. Here, rather than comparing frames of different mobilizations as we did in figure 13.5, a more narrow temporal window becomes the focus of analysis so that changes in the details of frames can be described. In doing so, we get a more fine-grained examination, closely tied to the original data, about the components of the meaning system that have changed and the ones that have not.

The approach described in these pages has a strong empirical and positivistic social-science focus. The idea that ideational factors such as frames are measurable and that they shape behavior in ways that can be analyzed by the logic of cause and effect falls well within the social-psychological approach to framing characterized by Gamson's research and more generally by Klandermans's approach to social movements in his *Social Psychology of Protest* (1997). Conversely, the brand of textual analysis presented here, and the call for comparative research designs it represents, contrasts sharply with the hermeneutic tradition of textual analysis (Ricoeur 1981; Gadamer 1976)—which never had a significant impact in political research and social movement analysis. A more recent development, one more relevant to mobilization processes, is culturally based discourse analysis that stresses how language is inherently conflictual, negotiated, and recursive. This is a perspective that emphasizes how meaning is never fixed or constant but rather is in continual flux, a presumption that on the surface challenges our method of comparing snapshots of mental schemata. It is a focus that has been given several different labels: rhetorical analysis (Billig 1992), dialogic analysis (Steinberg 1999; Sampson 1993), sociocultural discursive analysis (Potter, Edwards, and Wetherell 1993; Wertsch 1991; Potter and Wetherell 1988), rhetorical turn (Simon 1990). These (and related approaches such as Moscovici's social representations [1984, 1987]) all focus on the performative aspects of discourse and how they emerge in interaction, a view recently applied to frame analysis by Steinberg (1998).

Steinberg argues that frame analysis has not "problematized" discourse and text, but rather has taken it as a straightforward bearer of meaning, which he labels a "referential perspective on discourse." This is to be contrasted with an approach that recognizes the "semiotic dynamics" of discursive production as "collective and contested process of meaning production." Steinberg's basic point is that failure to emphasize the changeful and conflictual character of discourse is an empirical oversight that misleads theorizing about the role of framing in mobilization. Such a failure, he observes, (1) obscures the relation between ideology and frame (see chapters 9, 10, and 11 in this volume); (2) freezes frames as stable systems of meaning (as in Gerhards and Rucht's anti-IMF frame and the other schemata reproduced in this chapter) when there is no real evidence for how people use them to make sense of the world; and (3) diverts attention from the processes of individual cognition whereby broader cultural factors "circulating in the public sphere" are aligned with personal experience (Steinberg 1998: 849).

These observations tend to deny the utility of a cognitive-structural approach that reconstructs pictures of mental schemata. Although this negation appears to be fundamental, in practice I believe it can be resolved rather easily by recognizing that it is quite common that empirical observation in the social sciences involves a "closest-fit" trade-off between fine-grained measurement and costs of data gathering, constraints imposed by the research setting, and constraints derived form methodological strategies—survey research, for example—that are not perfect but offer adequate descriptions of the phenomenon under study. On the one hand, there is little doubt that discursive production can be productively thought of as processual, contested, and emergent. This applies to social science discourse, too, although I would argue that some analytical categories are more objective and less context-specific, evolving, and conflict-riven than others. On the other hand, there are theoretical questions—examining the causal influence of frame components, to take one example—that cannot be approached by staying within the bubble of social construction. This means that some research questions demand placing constraints on the "swirling, buzzing confusion" of social life—to apply William James's label. To move beyond descriptive reports, as Benford calls us to do, including reports portraying the conflictual nature of discourse, a methodological artifice is needed, namely, freezing the discursive process at a point in time to construct a representation of what is presumed to be the substance of mental life.

In his discussion of framing, Gamson recommends this, too, asserting that it is unwise to stress emergence on empirical grounds (1995: 89 n. 1). He points out that discourse and frames can become fully developed prior to mobilization or may become congealed as a result of some collective action. Justified either way, our strategy of taking empirical snapshots of frames does not deny that frames and discourse (or ideologies) are dynamic, emergent, and contested, nor does it negate that chronicling these processes is valuable. Rather "freezing the frame," so to speak, at various points in time is simply a *practical way* to demonstrate how frame content changes and that these changes may have independent influences on social movement development.

If we can agree on this, this chapter's ideas would seem compatible with *the practical methodology* of the rhetorical turn (if not its epistemology), namely, that a focus on the spoken and written texts of social movement participants is the best way to empirically ground discourse and frame analysis. There is an inextricable link between text and frames, and it is through intensive analysis of text that collective action frames are reconstructed. What kind of frame mobilizes more effectively? Or more specifically, do elaborated prognostic frames (or prognostic branches in a master schemata, to put it another way) get people into the streets more effectively than motivational aspects of a frame? These are important questions, and they have not been fully answered, or even explored, to date. While both kinds of research—explanatory and descriptive—are needed to advance our knowledge about mobilization processes, the methods presented in this chapter hold the promise of notching forward this goal in ways that are perhaps more generalizable to the broader community of social movement researchers in sociology, political science, and social psychology who continue to be interested in the *why* questions of mobilization—in addition to the *how* questions.

APPENDIX: TEXTUAL EXPANSION FOR FIGURE 13.4

Verbatim transcription	Textual expansion
1 R: [There were] two impressive demonstra- 2 tions in February '76. On the first and on 3 the eighth, when Franco had just recently 4 died. There was one on Sunday, it was one 5 day for amnesty and the other Sunday was 6 for autonomy. For the first time in Barce- 7 lona, seventy, eighty thousand people who 8 went into the streets, hounded by the police 9 still, and still . . . still beaten by the police, 10 and some were detained. But it was . . . all 11 of Barcelona was a battle during the entire 12 morning for two consecutive Sundays. 13 And the police could not do anything! 14 They ran around a lot and at times they'd 15 arrive at a spot in a police jeep and get 16 down and find some isolated people. 17 I: Did you go out? 18 R: Eh? Yes, yes, of course, evidently. In 19 these cases you have to go. H:hhhh. You 20 can't stop. 21 I: Why? 22 R: Because we thought it was a necessary 23 thing at that time. Come on! These mob- 24 ilizations . . . uh, come on! I couldn't 25 have stayed in the house. H:hhhh, evi- 26 dently. Nor could have any of my family 27 either. 28 I: But let us say five years earlier. Would 29 you have gone into the streets? 30 R: Well, it's that in the period of Franco the 31 things were much more serious. You had 32 to think twice. Then too, we went, but 33 with much fear. And the demonstrations 34 were small. There was one on May 1. It 35 was small thing, but with a lot of fear 36 and much caution. But these two demonstra- 37 tions they were the first ones in *which the* 38 people massively risked *going* out into the 39 streets, because . . . *they* thought . . . I think 40 it was decisive for the politics developing 41 later in *Catalonia* because the Spanish 42 *state* . . . well . . . the gentlemen in 43 Madrid saw that we were serious, that 44 it was not a minority, because to send 45 police to repress seventy, eighty thousand 46 people, well, you pay a high price because 47 there are many more who think that way. 48 And it was . . . Come on! . . . it was mar- 49 velous for us to be in the streets, *in Calle* 50 Aragon—you know it—*it was filled* from 51 one end to the other. . . .	The topic of these two demonstrations was introduced by the respondent, <u>suggesting his definition of the speech situation that the interviewer wants this kind of information.</u> (The group he belonged to organized these demonstrations. He participated with friends who were members.) **A change in tone, suggesting the drama of the encounter.** Repetition with **forceful tone, suggesting drama.** **Forceful tone again.** (Police inefficiency is a common theme in several other interviews.) **Pause, almost disbelief. Laugh.** He took for granted that his attendance was understood by his definition of interview's speech situation. <u>Understanding of participation assumed</u>: "You must be able to understand this." **Lower pitch. Laugh.** A break in narrative flow occurs when expectations are broken. ATTEMPT TO FILL IN BACKGROUND INFORMATION. **Slower, considered speech.** SPEAKING AS AUTHORITATIVE OBSERVER. The "we" refers either *to* family members, as in line 26 or "we Catalans" in lines 38 and 49. *(He is referring to May 1, 1974)* He refers again to the two demonstrations of 1976. HE WANTS TO TALK ABOUT THESE EVENTS. **Slower speech** marking a change in role and pragmatic focus. *He is speaking as an expert on the anti-Francoist opposition.* The "we" refers to all Catalans. HE IS OFFERING A POLITICAL ANALYSIS OF EVENTS. Shift to informal mode of speech. "Come on" spoken in **lower pitch, quickly.** ELICITING AN UNDERSTANDING OF WHAT IT WAS LIKE.

Key: <u>Underline</u>—*changing speech situation*
(parentheses)—information drawn from other sections of the text

CAPITAL LETTERS—pragmatic intent
Bold—nonverbal cues
Italics—changing speaker roles

NOTES

1. See Johnston and Aarelaid-Tart 2000 for a full methodological discussion. The frame schema is presented here for illustrative purposes of a method and is not contained in the published report. Number of mentions is presented in the figure rather than percentages.

2. This is a large sample size for a discourse study and is further amplified by the fact that the unit of analysis is the article, editorial, or cartoon within the publication rather than the publication itself.

3. Strictly speaking, Daniels's study is of white supremacist discourse, not frames. She reviews publications that were part of the collection of Klanwatch, a division of the Southern Poverty Law Center in Montgomery, Alabama. Compositional analysis is an important methodological innovation, which could also include the positioning of articles (front page versus inner pages), their clustering, and their distribution by article type.

4. The widespread support of the petition (20,000 signatures) for the bill imparts confidence that the patterns revealed by the close textual analysis are generalizable. Steinberg does not offer the close textual analysis that I will discuss in this section, but he does stress the broader political context in which texts are juxtaposed with others in discursive struggle. A key point in his analysis is that texts must be considered in their broader political and economic contexts—a key principle that we will return to shortly.

5. These five points represent a summary of several different approaches, but especially draw on Labov and Fanshel's classic analysis of a psychoanalytic interview (1977). For other examples, see Grimshaw's 1982 intensive study of a doctoral dissertation defense; Stubbs's 1983 general codification of analytic procedures; and Van Dijk's 1987 intensive analysis of racial conflict using these and other methods. A fuller discussion of these principles is found in Johnston 1995.

6. See Johnston 1991 for a full discussion. Figure 13.5 is not presented in the original research monograph but rather composed for the purpose of demonstrating comparative frame analysis. This brief presentation glosses over Catalonian politics and the Spanish democratic transition and is not offered as an empirical finding about this period. Rather, it is an example of a method only.

REFERENCES

Abelson, Robert P. 1981. "The Psychological Status of the Script Concept." *American Psychologist* 36: 715-729.

Austin, John L. 1962. *How to Do Things with Words.* London: Oxford University Press.

Bartlett, F. C. 1932. *Remembering.* Cambridge: Cambridge University Press.

Benford, Robert. 1993. "Frame Disputes within the Nuclear Disarmament Movement." *Social Forces* 71: 677-701.

———. 1997. "An Insider's Critique of the Social Movement Framing Perspective." *Sociological Inquiry* 67: 409-430.

Billig, Michael. 1992. *Talking of the Royal Family.* London: Routledge.

Blom, Jan-Peter, and John J. Gumperz. 1972. "Social Meaning in Linguistic Structures: Code-switching in Norway." In *Directions in Sociolinguistics,* John J. Gumperz and Dell Hymes, eds. New York: Holt, Rinehart, and Winston.

Briggs. Charles L. 1986. *Learning How to Ask.* New York: Cambridge University Press.

Buschke, H., and A. H. Schaier. 1979. "Memory Units, Ideas, and Propositioning in Semantic Remembering." *Journal of Verbal Learning and Verbal Behavior* 18: 549-563.

Capek, Stella. 1993. "The 'Environmental Justice' Frame: A Conceptual Discussion and an Application." *Social Problems* 40 (1): 5-24.

Carroll, William K., and Robert S. Ratner. 1996. "Master Framing and Cross-Movement Networking in Contemporary Social Movements." *Sociological Quarterly* 37: 601-625.

Daniels, Jessie. 1997. *White Lies: Race, Class, Gender, and Sexuality in White Supremacist Discourse.* New York: Routledge.

Franzosi, Roberto. 1998. "Narrative Analysis—Why (and How) Sociologists Should Be Interested in Narrative." Pp. 517-554 in *Annual Review of Sociology*, John Hagan, ed. Palo Alto, CA: Annual Reviews.

———. 1999. "The Return of the Actor: Interaction Networks among Social Actors during Periods of High Mobilization in Italy, 1919-1922." *Mobilization* 4: 131-149.

———. 2000. *From Words to Numbers: Narrative as Data.* Cambridge: Cambridge University Press.

Fuks, Mario. 1998. "Arenas of Public Action and Debate: Environmental Conflicts and the Emergence of the Environment as a Social Problem in Rio de Janeiro." Paper presented at the XIV World Congress of Sociology, July 26-August 1, Montreal, Quebec, Canada.

Gadamer, Hans Georg. 1976. *Philosophical Hermeneutics.* Berkeley: University of California Press.

Gamson, William A. 1988. "Political Discourse and Collective Action." Pp. 219-244 in *International Social Movement Research: From Structure to Action,* Bert Klandermans, Hanspeter Kriesi, and Sidney Tarrow, eds. Greenwich CT: JAI Press.

———. 1992. *Talking Politics.* New York: Cambridge University Press.

———. 1995. "Constructing Social Protest." Pp. 85-106 in *Social Movements and Culture,* Hank Johnston and Bert Klandermans, eds. Minneapolis: University of Minnesota Press.

Gamson, William A., Bruce Fireman, and Steven Rytina. 1982. *Encounters with Unjust Authority.* Homewood, IL: Dorsey Press.

Gerhards, Jurgen, and Dieter Rucht. 1992. "Mesomobilization: Organizing and Framing in Two Protest Campaigns in West Germany." *American Journal of Sociology* 98: 555-595.

Goffman, Erving. 1972. *Frame Analysis.* New York: Harper and Row.

Grimshaw, Allen D. 1982. "Comprehensive Discourse Analysis: An Instance of Professional Peer Interaction." *Language in Society* 11: 15-47.

Gumperz, John J. 1982. *Discourse Strategies.* Cambridge: Cambridge University Press.

Gumperz, John J., and Dell Hymes. 1972. *Directions in Sociolinguistics.* New York: Holt, Rinehart, and Winston.

Hormann, Hans. 1986. *Meaning and Context.* New York: Plenum.

Jasper, James M. 1997. *The Art of Moral Protest.* Chicago: University of Chicago Press.

Johnston, Hank. 1991. *Tales of Nationalism: Catalonia, 1939-1979.* New Brunswick, NJ: Rutgers University Press.

———. 1995. "A Methodology for Frame Analysis: From Discourse to Cognitive Schemata." Pp. 217-246 in *Social Movements and Culture,* Hank Johnston and Bert Klandermans, eds. Minneapolis: University of Minnesota Press.

———. 2002. "Verification and Proof in Frame and Discourse Analysis." Pp. 62-91 in *Methods of Social Movement Research,* Bert Klandermans and Suzanne Staggenborg, eds. Minneapolis: University of Minnesota Press.

Johnston, Hank, and Aili Aarelaid-Tart. 2000. "Generations, Microcohorts, and Long-Term Mobilization: The Estonian National Movement, 1940-1991." *Sociological Perspectives* 43 (4): 671-698.

Kintsch, W., and Teun A. Van Dijk. 1978. "Toward a Model of Text Comprehension and Production." *Psychological Review* 85: 363-394.

Klandermans, Bert. 1997. *The Social Psychology of Protest.* Oxford, UK: Blackwell.

Labov, William, and David Fanshel. 1977. *Therapeutic Discourse.* New York: Academic Press.

Marullo, Sam, Ron Pagnucco, and Jackie Smith. 1996. "Frame Changes and Social Movement Contraction: U.S. Peace Movement Framing of the Cold War." *Sociological Inquiry* 66: 1-28.

McAdam, Doug, Sidney Tarrow, and Charles Tilly. 2001. *The Dynamics of Contention.* New York: Cambridge University Press.

Mooney, Patrick H., and Scott A. Hunt. 1996. "A Repertoire of Interpretations: Master Frames and Ideological Continuity in U.S. Agrarian Mobilization." *Sociological Quarterly* 37: 177-197.

Moscovici, Serge. 1987. "Answers and Questions." *Journal for the Theory of Social Behaviour* 17: 513-529.

———. 1984. "The Phenomenon of Social Representations." In *Social Representations,*

Robert M. Farr and Serge Moscovici, eds. Cambridge: Cambridge University Press.

Noonan Rita K. 1995. "Women against the State: Political Opportunities and Collective Action Frames in Chile's Transition to Democracy." *Sociological Forum* 10: 81-111.

Palmquist, Michael, Kathleen M. Carley, and Thomas A Dale. 1997. "Applications of Computer-Aided Text Analysis: Analyzing Literary and Non-Literary Texts." Pp. 171-189 in *Analysis for the Social Sciences: Methods for Drawing Statistical Inferences from Tests and Transcript,* Carl Roberts, ed. Hillsdale, NJ: Lawrence Erlbaum Associates.

Popping, Roel. 1997. "Computer Programs for the Analysis of Texts and Transcripts." Pp. 209-221 in *Text Analysis for the Social Sciences: Methods for Drawing Statistical Inferences from Tests and Transcript,* Carl Roberts, ed. Hillsdale, NJ: Lawrence Erlbaum Associates.

Potter, J., D. Edwards, and M. Wetherell. 1993. "A Model of Discourse in Action." *American Behavioral Scientist* 36: 383-401.

Potter, J., and M. Wetherell. 1988. "Accomplishing Attitudes: Fact and Evaluation in Racist Discourse." *Text* 8: 51-68.

Ricoeur, Paul. 1981. *Hermeneutics and the Human Sciences: Essays on Language, Action, and Interpretation,* John B. Thompson ed. and trans. New York: Cambridge University Press.

Roberts, Carl. 1997a. "Semantic Text Analysis: On the Structure of Linguistic Ambiguity in Ordinary Discourse." Pp. 55-77 in *Text Analysis for the Social Sciences: Methods for Drawing Statistical Inferences from Texts and Transcripts,* Carl Roberts, ed. Hillsdale, NJ: Lawrence Erlbaum Associates.

———— ed. 1997b. *Text Analysis for the Social Sciences: Methods for Drawing Statistical Inferences from Texts and Transcripts.* Hillsdale, NJ: Lawrence Erlbaum Associates.

Rumelhart, David E. 1975. "Notes on a Schema for Stories." In *Representation and Understanding,* S. A. Bobrow and S. M. Collins, eds. New York: Academic Press.

Ryan, Charlotte. 1991. *Prime Time Activism.* Boston: South End Press.

Sacks, Harvey, Emmanuel Schegloff, and Gail Jefferson. 1974. "A Simplest Systematic for the Organization of Turn-Taking for Conversation." *Language* 50: 696-735.

Sampson, E. 1993. *Celebrating the Other.* Boulder, CO: Westview Press.

Schank, Roger C., and Robert P. Abelson. 1977. *Scripts, Plans, Goals, and Understanding.* Hillsdale, NJ: Lawrence Erlbaum Associates.

Seidel, John V., Rolf Kjolseth, and Elaine Seymour. 1988. *The Ethnograph: A User's Guide.* Corvallis, OR: Qualis Research Associates.

Shapiro, Gilbert, and John Markoff. 1998. *Revolutionary Demands: A Content Analysis of the Cahiers de Doléances of 1789.* Stanford, CA: Stanford University Press.

Simon, Herbert W. 1990. *The Rhetorical Turn: Invention and Persuasion in the Conduct of Inquiry.* Chicago: University of Chicago Press.

Snow, David A., and Robert D. Benford. 1988. "Ideology, Frame Resonance, and Participant Mobilization." Pp. 197-218 in *International Social Movement Research: From Structure to Action,* Bert Klandermans, Hanspeter Kriesi, and Sidney Tarrow, eds. Greenwich, CT: JAI Press.

————. 1992. "Master Frames and Cycles of Protest." Pp. 133-155 in *Frontiers in Social Movement Theory,* Aldon D. Morris and Carol McClurg Mueller, eds. New Haven, CT: Yale University Press.

Snow, David A., E. Burke Rochford, Jr., Steven K. Worden, and Robert D. Benford. 1986. "Frame Alignment Processes, Micromobilization, and Movement Participation." *American Sociological Review* 51 (4): 546-481.

Somers, Margaret. 1992. "Narrativity, Narrative Identity, and Social Action: Rethinking English Working-Class Formation." *Social Science History* 16: 591-630.

Steinberg, Marc. 1998. "Tilting the Frame: Considerations of Collective Action Framing from a Discursive Turn." *Theory and Society* 27: 845-872.

————. 1999. *Fighting Words.* Ithaca, NY: Cornell University Press.

Stubbs, Michael. 1983. *Discourse Analysis.* Chicago: University of Chicago Press.

Swanson, Guy E. 1976. "Review of Erving Goffman's Frame Analysis." *Annals of the American Academy of Political and Social Science* 420: 218-220.

Swart, William J. 1995. "The League of Nations and the Irish Question: Master Frames, Cycles of Protest, and 'Master Frame Alignment.'" *Sociological Quarterly* 36: 465-481.

Tannen, Deborah. 1993. "What's in a Frame?" Pp. 14-56 in *Framing in Discourse*, Deborah Tannen, ed. New York: Oxford University Press.

Thorndyke, P. W. 1977. "Cognitive Structures in Comprehension and Memory of Narrative Discourse." *Cognitive Psychology* 9: 77-110.

Van Dijk, Teun A. 1987. *Communicating Racism: Ethnic Prejudice in Thought and Talk.* Newbury Park, CA: Sage.

Wertsch, James V. 1991. *Voices of the Mind.* Cambridge, MA: Harvard University Press.

Wilson, John. 1990. *Politically Speaking: The Pragmatic Analysis of Political Language.* New York: Basil Blackwell.

INDEX

ABOUT THE CONTRIBUTORS

Robert D. Benford is professor and chair of sociology at Southern Illinois University, Carbondale. He has published on framing processes, narratives, collective identity, and other social constructionist issues associated with social movements in various journals, including the *American Sociological Review*, the *Annual Review of Sociology*, *Social Forces*, *Sociological Quarterly*, and the *Journal of Contemporary Ethnography*.

Jorge Cadena-Roa (Ph.D., University of Washington-Madison) is professor of sociology at Universidad Nacional Autónoma de México (UNAM). He is currently working on social movements and democratic consolidation in Mexico. Recent publications include "State Pacts, Elites, and Social Movements in Mexico's Transition to Democracy" in *States, Parties, and Social Movements* (2003) and (with P. Oliver and K. Strawn) "Emerging Trends in the Study of Protest and Social Movements" in *Political Sociology for the 21st Century* (2003).

Lyndi Hewitt is a Ph.D. candidate in the Department of Sociology at Vanderbilt University. Her research interests include social movements, feminist theory, and feminist methodology. She is currently working on a dissertation that will examine the relationships between feminist scholars and grassroots activists in transnational movements for women's rights.

Hank Johnston is editor of *Mobilization* and assistant professor of sociology at San Diego State University. He is the author of *Tales of Nationalism: Catalonia, 1939-1979*, as well as many research articles and chapters about social movement theory and about protest and resistance in repressive states. Also, he has coedited several collections of social movement research: *Social Movements and Culture*, *New Social Movements*, *Globalization and Resistance*, and *Repression and Mobilization*. Currently, he is researching protest repertoires in newly industrializing states.

Padraic Kenney is professor of history at the University of Colorado, Boulder. His work focuses on the social experience of politics in communist and postcommunist Central Europe, with particular emphasis on revolution and social movements. His books include *A Carnival of Revolution: Central Europe, 1989* (2002) and *Transnational Moments of Change: Europe 1945, 1968, 1989,* coedited with Gerd-Rainer Horn (2004). He is currently researching the experience of political prisoners across seven regimes in Poland in the twentieth century.

Jan Manssens is a graduate of the University of Antwerp, Belgium, and the Institut d'Etudes Politiques of Strasbourg, France. At Antwerp University he did research on various topics, including the impact of Pierre Rosanvallon's new social question on social movements and on mobilization theory. He now works for the strategy division of Belgium's new telecom operator.

Holly J. McCammon is professor of sociology at Vanderbilt University. She has published a number of articles on the U.S. women's suffrage movement. Currently, she is gathering data for a new study on women's attempts to win property ownership rights for married women in the nineteenth century and their efforts to win the right to sit on juries in the twentieth century, both in the United States.

John A. Noakes is an adjunct assistant professor of sociology and the associate director of the Center for Teaching and Learning at the University of Pennsylvania. His research focuses on the intersection of the state and political dissent, including the origins of the Federal Bureau of Investigation and how it determined which Hollywood movies were subversive in the 1940s. His research on this topic appeared in *Sociological Quarterly, Film History,* and *Ethnic and Racial Studies.* He is currently examining changes in the policing of protests in the United States since the 1999 WTO protests in Seattle.

Pamela E. Oliver is Conway-Bascom Professor of Sociology at the University of Wisconsin. Her current research interests are the interplay of protest, media coverage, and repression; the dynamics of policing and repression; and racial disparities in imprisonment. She is at work on a book about imprisonment disparities tentatively titled "Repressive Injustice." She is coauthor with Gerald Marwell of *The Critical Mass in Collective Action* and is past chair of the Political Sociology and Collective Behavior and Social Movements sections of the American Sociological Association.

Cathy Schneider is an associate professor in the School of International Service at American University in Washington, D.C. She holds a Ph.D. from Cornell University and is the author of *Shantytown Protest in Pinochet's Chile* as well as numerous articles on social movements, identity, and political violence in Latin America, the United States, and Europe. Most recently she coedited and wrote the introduction to a special issue of *NACLA Report on the Americas* on the theme of "COPS: Crime, Disorder, and Authoritarian Policing." She is currently working on a book on crime wars, racial intolerance, and boundary activation in Paris and New York.

David A. Snow is professor of sociology at the University of California, Irvine. He has conducted research on crowd dynamics; recruitment and conversion to religious movements; the emergence, the operation, and consequences of movements among the homeless in the United States; framing processes and outcomes; and collective identity. He has published extensively on these topics in a variety of edited volumes, and professional journals, including *American Sociological Review*, the *American Journal of Sociology*, *Annual Review of Sociology*, and *Social Problems*.

Stephen Valocchi is professor of sociology at Trinity College in Hartford, Connecticut. His current research examines the utility of queer theory for the socio-logical study of gender and sexuality. He is also completing an oral history project on progressive activism and activist identity formation in the Hartford region. His work on the gay liberation movement, the relationship of gay liberation to the Left, and on African American protest and the New Deal has appeared in *Social Problems*, *Mobilization*, *Sociological Perspectives*, and *Sociological Forum*.

Stefaan Walgrave is associate professor at the University of Antwerp, Belgium. He teaches political science and political communication. His research focuses on social movements and protest behavior, and on the interaction between mass media coverage and politics.

David L. Westby was professor of sociology at Pennsylvania State University until his retirement in 1991. He has worked in the areas of sociological theory and political sociology, particularly social movements. Among his publications are *The Growth of Sociological Theory: Human Nature, Knowledge, and Social Change* (1991) and *The Clouded Vision: The Student Movement in the United States in the 1960s* (1976). Most recently, he has been engaged in a historical study of the Swedish peace movement.